JAMES HOGG

Midsummer Night Dreams
and Related Poems

THE STIRLING / SOUTH CAROLINA RESEARCH EDITION OF
THE COLLECTED WORKS OF JAMES HOGG
GENERAL EDITORS – DOUGLAS S. MACK AND GILLIAN HUGHES

THE STIRLING / SOUTH CAROLINA RESEARCH EDITION OF
THE COLLECTED WORKS OF JAMES HOGG
GENERAL EDITORS – DOUGLAS S. MACK AND GILLIAN HUGHES

Volumes are numbered in the order of their publication in
the Stirling / South Carolina Research Edition

JAMES HOGG

Midsummer Night Dreams
and
Related Poems

Edited by the late Jill Rubenstein
and completed by
Gillian Hughes with Meiko O'Halloran

EDINBURGH UNIVERSITY PRESS
2008

© Edinburgh University Press, 2008

Edinburgh University Press
22 George Square
Edinburgh
EH8 9LF

Typeset in Manchester
Printed by CPI Antony Rowe, Chippenham, Wiltshire

ISBN 978 0 7486 2440 9

A CIP record for this book is available from the British Library

The Stirling / South Carolina Research Edition of

The Collected Works of James Hogg

The Aims of the Edition

James Hogg lived from 1770 till 1835. He was regarded by his con-
temporaries as one of the leading writers of the day, but the nature
of his fame was influenced by the fact that, as a young man, he had
been a self-educated shepherd. The third edition (1814) of his poem
The Queen's Wake contains an 'Advertisement' which begins as fol-
lows.

> *The Publisher having been favoured with letters from gentlemen in various
> parts of the United Kingdom respecting the Author of the Queen's Wake,
> and most of them expressing doubts of his being a Scotch Shepherd, he
> takes this opportunity of assuring the public, that* THE QUEEN'S WAKE *is*

really and truly the production of James Hogg, a common Shepherd, *bred among the mountains of Ettrick Forest, who went to service when only seven years of age; and since that period has never received any education whatever.*

The view of Hogg taken by his contemporaries is also reflected in the various early reviews of *The Private Memoirs and Confessions of a Justified Sinner*, which appeared anonymously in 1824. As Gillian Hughes has shown in the *Newsletter of the James Hogg Society* no. 1, many of these reviews identify Hogg as the author, and see the novel as presenting 'an incongruous mixture of the strongest powers with the strongest absurdities'. The Scotch Shepherd was regarded as a man of powerful and original talent, but it was felt that his lack of education caused his work to be marred by frequent failures in discretion, in expression, and in knowledge of the world. Worst of all was Hogg's lack of what was called 'delicacy', a failing which caused him to deal in his writings with subjects (such as prostitution) which were felt to be unsuitable for mention in polite literature. Hogg was regarded as a man of undoubted genius, but his genius was felt to be seriously flawed.

A posthumous collected edition of Hogg was published in the late 1830s. As was perhaps natural in the circumstances, the publishers (Blackie & Son of Glasgow) took pains to smooth away what they took to be the rough edges of Hogg's writing, and to remove his numerous 'indelicacies'. This process was taken even further in the 1860s, when the Rev. Thomas Thomson prepared a revised edition of Hogg's *Works* for publication by Blackie. These Blackie editions present a bland and lifeless version of Hogg's writings. It was in this version that Hogg was read by the Victorians. Unsurprisingly, he came to be regarded as a minor figure, of no great importance or interest.

The second half of the twentieth century has seen a substantial revival of Hogg's reputation; and he is now generally considered to be one of Scotland's major writers. This new reputation is based on a few works which have been republished in editions based on his original texts. Nevertheless, a number of Hogg's major works remain out of print. Indeed, some have been out of print for more than a century and a half, while others, still less fortunate, have never been published at all in their original, unbowdlerised condition.

Hogg is thus a major writer whose true stature was not recognised in his own lifetime because his social origins led to his being smothered in genteel condescension; and whose true stature has not been recognised since, because of a lack of adequate editions. The poet Douglas Dunn wrote of Hogg in the *Glasgow Herald* in September 1988: 'I can't help but think that in almost any other country of Europe a complete, modern edition of a comparable author would have been available long ago'. The Stirling / South Carolina Edition of James Hogg seeks to fill the gap identified by Douglas Dunn. When completed the edition will run to thirty-four volumes; and it will cover Hogg's prose, his poetry, and his plays.

General Editors' Acknowledgements

We record with gratitude the support given to the Stirling/South Carolina Research Edition of the Collected Works of James Hogg by the University of Stirling and by the University of South Carolina. Valuable grants or donations have also been received from the Carnegie Trust for the Universities of Scotland, from the Modern Humanities Research Association, from the Association for Scottish Literary Studies, and from the James Hogg Society. The work of the Edition could not have been carried on without the support of these bodies.

Gillian Hughes was general editor for the present volume, and the earlier stages of her work were facilitated by a major grant awarded by the Arts and Humanities Research Board. The text of the present volume was proof-read by Meiko O'Halloran.

Volume Editor's Acknowledgements

The late Jill Rubenstein recorded among her papers for this volume her gratitude to the Charles Phelps Taft Fund, the Research Council, and the Faculty Development Council of the University of Cincinnati for their generous support for her research on this volume. The W. Ormiston Roy Fellowship permitted her access to the extensive collection of Scottish literature at the Thomas Cooper Library of the University of South Carolina. She also expressed her appreciation of the kind and learned hospitality extended to her there by Professor Emeritus H. Ross Roy and by Patrick Scott, Professor of English and Director of Rare Books and Special Collections of the Thomas Cooper Library. The second part of the Introduction to the present volume, 'The Anthropology of Pilgrimage and *The Pilgrims of the Sun*' was previously published in *Studies in Hogg and his World*.

My own work on the present volume would have been impossible but for the financial as well as moral support of David Sweet. An honorary research fellowship at the University of Manchester has allowed me to access the resources of the John Rylands University Library of Manchester.

I would like to thank the following friends and colleagues for their help and advice: Ian Alexander, John Ballantyne, Val Bold, Robert Calder, Ian Campbell, Ian Duncan, Penny Fielding, Gillian Garside, Peter Garside, Richard Jackson, Douglas Mack, Robin MacLachlan, Karl Miller, Sally Moffitt, Murray Pittock, Tom Richardson, Maggie Scott, Deirdre Shepherd, David Shirt, and Rachel Sweet.

A special word of thanks must go to Meiko O'Halloran who, besides contributing an essay to the volume, read all the other component parts and made a number of valuable comments and suggestions. The support of Hogg's descendants has been essential for this volume, and I am grateful to Chris Gilkison, Liz and Alan Milne, and David Parr in particular. The Hogg Edition team at Edinburgh University Press have been generous with their time and trouble, particularly Claire Abel, Máiréad McElligott, Ian Davidson, and Catriona Murray.

Every scholarly edition owes a considerable debt to librarians and archivists and this one is no exception. I am grateful to the staff of the National Library of Scotland and of the Edinburgh Room of the Edinburgh Central Library in particular. I would also like particularly to thank Sheila Mackenzie, Virginia Murray, and Rachel Thomas, assistant curator of the John Murray Archive.

I wish to thank the following institutions for permission to cite manuscript materials in their care in the present volume: Alexander Turnbull Library, Wellington, New Zealand; The British Library; The John Murray Collection, London; and the National Library of Scotland.

Finally, I would like to record my gratitude to the original editor of this volume, the late Jill Rubenstein, and not only for her invitation to me to contribute an 'Essay on the Genesis of the Texts' to it. I am grateful to her memory for her friendship as well as for the scholarship she was always willing to share. She is greatly missed.

Gillian Hughes
Manchester

Note to the Reader

When the editor of the present volume, Professor Jill Rubenstein, died suddenly and unexpectedly in August 2002, her work on *Midsummer Night Dreams and Related Poems* was quite well advanced though still unfinished. It may be helpful to the reader to have a brief explanation of the way in which her work was completed for publication.

As the general editor for this volume, I had been closely involved in planning it from the beginning and was accordingly entrusted with the responsibility of gathering together what my friend and colleague, Jill Rubenstein, had left, and supplementing it where necessary. Jill had, at an early stage, invited me to contribute an 'Essay on the Genesis of the Texts' to the volume. After her death several noted scholars suggested that an additional essay on Hogg's otherworld journeys and their context would also be useful for an assessment of Hogg's achievement in *Midsummer Night Dreams and Related Poems*. Meiko O'Halloran was therefore invited to contribute an essay to the volume and she subsequently influenced the present organisation of material for it.

At the time of her death, Jill Rubenstein had carefully prepared and edited the text of *Midsummer Night Dreams and Related Poems* using the second volume of *The Poetical Works of James Hogg* of 1822 as the copy-text. Jill had also prepared draft editorial notes and a glossary: I have checked, updated, and supplemented these where necessary, but they are substantially her work. The 'Note on the Texts' had been less carefully detailed on paper: it now includes a larger input from me. I decided to include the two appendices to the volume in the light of my research on the genesis and publishing history of the work.

Among Jill Rubenstein's papers was a brief plan for her Introduction to *Midsummer Night Dreams and Related Poems*, indicating that the core of it was to be three surviving conference papers presented in the following order: '"Idiot Kings": "The Field of Waterloo" and the Ideology of Sacrifice'; 'The Anthropology of Pilgrimage and *The Pilgrims of the Sun*'; and 'Hogg and the Uses of Enchantment in *Midsummer Night Dreams*'. This was to be followed by an as yet unwritten final section on reception, and preceded by a brief introduction linking the four sections (of which only an initial draft had been written). The present Introduction conforms to this plan: I have written the final section on reception. Had Jill lived she would no doubt have led the reader gently and capably from the general context of the volume towards her first specific section on 'The Field of Waterloo': under existing circumstances it seemed sensible to provide the reader with a sense of the shape of the entire volume and its place in Hogg's writing career by preceding the Introduction with the 'Essay on the Genesis of the Texts'. This allows Jill Rubenstein's own introductory paragraph to appear substantially unchanged at the start of the Introduction itself, as a reminder of her characteristic voice.

Jill Rubenstein was one of the earliest and most enthusiastic supporters of the S/SC Edition, as a volume editor and as a member of the edition's Advisory Board. Fine scholarship, common sense, good humour, and plain speaking invariably characterised her contributions to the work of the edition. Her voice is much missed.

Gillian Hughes
August 2008

Contents

Midsummer Night Dreams and Related Poems

List of Illustrations

Essay on the Genesis of the Texts

Gillian Hughes

1. The Original Plan of *Midsummer Night Dreams*

Hogg's mood after the first publication of *The Queen's Wake* at the end of January 1813 was understandably euphoric. As Douglas Mack has indicated, this was 'a life-changing event' for Hogg, a dazzling success that converted him from a disgraced ex-shepherd and would-be literary man to a famous author.[1] The resulting confidence triggered an explosion of creativity over the following year or so, of apparently effortless and rapid writing in several different genres. An autumn visit to his friend Eliza Izett at Kinnaird House in 1813 sparked the rapid composition of his long narrative poem *Mador of the Moor*, in some ways a personal interpretation of and alternative to Scott's *The Lady of the Lake*. Hogg's tragedy *The Hunting of Badlewe* was written that summer and six copies printed for the literary advisors with whose help he hoped to become a successful dramatist for the London stage.[2] Just as Hogg's narrative poem rivalled Scott's his drama looked ultimately perhaps to Shakespeare, and another work, generated during the spring and summer of 1814, was given the Shakespearean title *Midsummer Night Dreams*. Midsummer day is 24 June, dedicated to John the Baptist, the herald of the coming Messiah and thus of a new age, and the preceding evening is one of the old world of superstition and magic power, just as All Saints' Day is preceded by the witcheries of Hallowe'en. Shakespeare's *A Midsummer Night's Dream* creates from this an enchanted night world which influences the daylight future of the waking world of Duke Theseus and his courtiers and of the city-state of Athens ruled by him.

Hogg's plan was to form a collection of visionary poems, in which a supernatural world also shapes a waking reality. He had experienced visionary states from time to time in his own life, it seems. Returning to Blackhouse as a young man in a state of chilled exhaustion, after a hard night labouring to find and free his sheep from the drifts of a snow-storm, he had seen a group of trees as 'over my head flourishing abroad over the whole sky', only returning to everyday perception after running against the ruined tower of Blackhouse:

So that after all they were trees that I saw and trees of no great magnitude neither but their appearance to my eyes it is impossible to describe. They flourished abroad not for miles but for hundreds of miles to the utmost verges of the visible heavens.[3]

At any rate, by 11 February 1814 Hogg had almost finished *Mador of the Moor*, writing to Eliza Izett, 'I am positively within a few lines of the end now',[4] and according to his 'Memoir of the Author's Life' he turned to the new project straight away:

> In the same year, and immediately on finishing the above poem, I conceived a plan for writing a volume of romantic poems, to be entitled "Midsummer Night Dreams," and am sorry to this day that a friendly advice prevented me from accomplishing my design, for of all other subjects, there were none that suited the turn of my thoughts so well.
>
> The first of these dreams that I wrote was "Connel of Dee," [...] and the second was "The Pilgrims of the Sun." (*Altrive Tales*, p. 35)

This second poem, Hogg later recalled, was written 'in about three weeks', and was offered to the Edinburgh publisher Archibald Constable on 25 July [1814] (*Letters*, I, 211, 187–88). 'Connel of Dee' (subsequently published from Hogg's manuscript in his prose fiction collection of *Winter Evening Tales*) alludes clearly to the proposed series title, with Connel at the start of the poem under 'cloudlets of June', and the author reflecting that 'It was but a night, and a midsummer night', defining Connel's adventure as 'his midsummer dream'.[5] Connel's discontent with the simple life of a shepherd leads to a visionary social promotion that comes with multiple threats of castration and death, and on awakening he is resigned to his lot, though the shadow of his dream prevents him from marrying thereafter. *The Pilgrims of the Sun* is its opposite, a vision of heaven rather than hell, ending in a fruitful marriage between the heroine and a fairy or angelic lover who bears some resemblance to the hero of the ballad 'Tam Lin', while also appearing to be a historical presentiment of James Hogg, the Ettrick minstrel and shepherd author.

David Groves initiated the current critical consensus that the two poems, one of a hellish and the other of a heavenly vision, complement each other well.[6] It seems likely that Hogg added a third poem, 'Superstition', to his collection during September or early October 1814, while staying at Elleray, John Wilson's house at Windermere in the Lake District. Groves argues that this poem was 'intended as a third and final part of *Midsummer Night Dreams*',[7] but it seems from Hogg's own note written for his collected poems of 1822 that the project had been temporarily abandoned without ever having been completed:

> THIS poem and the following two [*The Pilgrims of the Sun*, 'Connel of Dee', and 'Superstition'] were originally written with the intention of their forming part of a volume to be entitled MIDSUMMER NIGHT DREAMS; but having submitted it to the perusal of the late James Park, Esq. of Greenock, a friend in whose good taste and discernment I had the most perfect confidence, he chanced to think so highly of it that he persuaded me, against my own inclination, to publish it as a poem by itself, assuring me of its success. The approbation which the ballad of "Kilmeny" had received, probably influenced him in this opinion [...][8]

Hogg here describes the group of three poems as forming only 'part' of his intended *Midsummer Night Dreams* volume, his plans for the collection as a whole remaining fluid.

The visionary quality of 'Kilmeny' from *The Queen's Wake* is indeed continued forward to *The Pilgrims of the Sun*, and with a marked variation also into the dystopic imaginative world of 'Connel of Dee', while 'Superstition' links the visionary to Scottish history and to the traditional culture into which Hogg himself was born. In his edition of *The Queen's Wake* Douglas Mack has commented on the value Hogg (in marked contrast to Edinburgh's literary heirs of the Enlightenment) found in 'an old, pre-Enlightenment world-view' often dismissed as barbarous and superstitious. Here superstition accompanies true religion; both are the treasures of the visionary bard and his defences against a 'cold saturnine morn' that represents the disenchantment of the world.[9] Superstition is thus in spiritual terms, the 'Great ruler of the soul', a visionary queen to whom due homage is paid by the poet in this and the preceding poems of the partially-completed *Midsummer Night Dreams* collection.

Hogg's letter to Archibald Constable of 25 July [1814] signals his intention to postpone the planned publication of *Mador of the Moor* to his newly-written poem, and goes on to hint at a sequel should it be successful:

> I spoke to you some months ago about publishing a poem price 12/ about which I believe we were mostly agreed but on mature calculation I am resolved first to publish one not half so long price 7/6 this will be a less venture, and more

will buy it; and if it sell very rapidly I can the sooner add another the same length and price which will come to 15/ whereas were they both in one they would be thought dear at 12/ The title of this will be *The Pilgrims of the Sun* A poem in four parts by James Hogg &c.–It will not exceed ten sheets fine.[10]

Hogg's letter thus provides further evidence that the collection of *Midsummer Night Dreams* was still in the process of development in the summer of 1814. The final shape and the number and extent of the component parts of this abandoned collection are beyond our knowledge as they were almost certainly beyond Hogg's knowledge at the time. It was almost eight years before Hogg returned to the title and tried once again to form a collection of 'romantic poems' under the title of *Midsummer Night Dreams*, and the result in 1822, as we shall see, differs substantially from what would have been possible in the summer of 1814.

2. The Publication of *The Pilgrims of the Sun* and its Aftermath

Although he was understandably delighted with his longed-for success in *The Queen's Wake* and his Edinburgh standing as a celebrated author, the horizon was not entirely clear and cloudless for James Hogg in 1814. He was losing confidence in the financial stability of his publisher, George Goldie, and urgently needed to find another and more secure producer of his poetry. In the autumn of 1813 he had read *Mador of the Moor* aloud to Goldie as well as to John Grieve as his poem progressed and Goldie must have assumed that he would be its publisher.[11] Yet on 1 February 1814 Hogg offered the poem instead to Archibald Constable (*Letters*, I, 173–74), the leading Edinburgh publisher whose list included the poetry of Walter Scott and the successive issues of the *Edinburgh Review* and who had previously published Hogg's own volumes of *The Mountain Bard* (1807), *The Shepherd's Guide* (1807), and *The Forest Minstrel* (1810). As Hogg subsequently indicated in his 'Memoir' (*Altrive Tales*, p. 31), he then also made arrangements for Constable to publish a third edition of *The Queen's Wake* itself, and only reluctantly agreed (under pressure and after the printing had begun) to give this to Goldie as the original publisher of the work.

By the middle of 1814 Hogg was desperate to escape the clutches of George Goldie, who was by this time undoubtedly on the verge of bankruptcy. On 3 June 1814 he grumbled to Byron that 'I get but

shabby conditions from my booksellers here and these not very punc-
tually fulfilled' (*Letters*, I, 179), a complaint which was made more
specific in his subsequent letter of 30 July [1814]:

> I have an abominable shabby Book seller here who never
> keeps his word with me nor even lifts his bills when they
> become due they come back on me and distress me more
> than I had never seen them. G–d d–m him and them both I
> wish you could procure me some feasible conditions with
> yours (*Letters*, I, 192)

Eager to detach his work from Goldie's foundering business, Hogg
was making moves within a few days, on 25 and on 30 July, to at-
tempt to secure for his new poem either the leading London pub-
lisher John Murray or the leading Edinburgh publisher Archibald
Constable. (Murray's name, incidentally, had already appeared on
two of Hogg's title-pages, since he was Constable's London partner
for both *The Mountain Bard* and *The Shepherd's Guide*.) In view of his
debts, dating back to 1808 when he had been farming in Dumfries-
shire, Hogg naturally wanted his new poem published and paid for
as soon as possible. He was intending to be absent from Edinburgh
that autumn, on a visit to Elleray in the Lake District, where as the
guest of his friend John Wilson he would be able over several weeks
to hunt down contributions from the poets resident in the district for
a proposed poetical repository along the lines of the *Poetical Regis-
ter*.[12] It was natural that he should wish to see his book in production
before leaving Edinburgh and an agreement had been reached for
this by 14 August, though with the secondary publishing house of
Manners and Miller rather than with Archibald Constable. Accord-
ing to Hogg's subsequent account, Constable feared that Hogg was
writing too much and being over-ambitious and was accordingly less
than enthusiastic about *The Pilgrims of the Sun*:

> He received me with his usual kindness, and seemed to en-
> courage the plan; but, in the mean time, said he was busy,
> and that if I would call again on Saturday, he would have
> time to think of it, and give me an answer. With the solicitude
> of a poor author, I was punctual to my hour on Saturday, and
> found Mr. Constable sitting at his confined desk up stairs,
> and alone, which was a rare incident. He saluted me, held
> out his hand without lifting his eyes from the paper, and then,
> resuming his pen, continued writing. I read the backs of some
> of the books on his shelves, and then spoke of my new poem;
> but he would not deign to lift his eyes, or regard me. (*Altrive*

Tales, p. 36)

When Constable did speak he ironically congratulated Hogg as a great genius who, since the publication of *The Queen's Wake*, had written three new poems and would 'write Scott, and Byron, and every one of them, off the field' (p. 37). Declining to publish Hogg's poem himself, he nevertheless brought forward the firm of Manners and Miller as a potential publisher and it is surely a mark of Hogg's mistrust of Goldie and his sense of urgency that he agreed to this and handed over his manuscript without waiting for the outcome of his strategic appeal to John Murray through Lord Byron. The forthcoming issue of the *Edinburgh Review*, he was aware, would contain the glowing review of *The Queen's Wake* that would help to sell his new poem too.

Hogg clearly regretted a lost opportunity to increase the prestige of his poem when he found, almost as soon as the Edinburgh bargain had been concluded, that Byron's publisher, John Murray, was genuinely interested in it. Writing to Murray on 17 August, he explained, 'I got an offer from Constable and Manners & Millar which in my circumstances I did not think fit to refuse for *the first edition* of the small poem which I mentioned to his lordship as ready for the press and which is of course now in it' (*Letters*, I, 198). Indeed by mid-October Hogg had reclaimed *The Pilgrims of the Sun* from Robert Miller and offered it to Murray instead.

The firm of Manners and Miller was by no means equal in weight to that of John Murray of Albemarle Street in London, as a brief account written by Lockhart a few years subsequently amply demonstrates. The shop of this particular bookseller was a 'scene of elegant trifling' and Miller himself something of a ladies' man, 'the favourite bibliopole of almost all but the writers of books':

> Upon the leaves of these books [...] a groupe of the most elegant young ladies and gentlemen of the place may probably be seen feasting, or seeming to feast their eyes; while encomiums due to their beauties are mingled up in the same whisper with compliments still more interesting to beauties, no doubt, still more divine. In one corner, perhaps, some haughty blue-stocking, with a volume of Campbell's Specimens, or Dr Clarke's Scandinavia, or the last number of the Edinburgh Review, or Blackwood's Magazine in her hand, may be observed launching ever and anon a look of ineffable disdain upon the less intellectual occupation of her neighbours [...]. One sees, in a moment, that this is not a great

publishing shop; such weighty and laborious business would put to flight all the loves and graces that hover in the perfumed atmosphere of the place. A novel, or a volume of pathetic sermons, or pretty poems, might be tolerated, but that is the utmost.[13]

Within a remarkably short period indeed *The Pilgrims of the Sun* had been transferred from Robert Miller to John Murray, a very desirable change despite the fact that it caused some inevitable delay in the appearance of the poem.

While Hogg's bargain with Miller was concluded before he wrote to Byron on 14 August he must have made some changes to the poem after this date, perhaps in the course of production, since the closing lines refer to the death of Harriet, Duchess of Buccleuch on 24 August.[14] By the end of August, however, Hogg had left Edinburgh for the Lake District and on 1 September he was doing the honours of Yarrow to the Wordsworths en route. By mid-September while staying with John Wilson at Elleray Hogg heard that his old publisher, George Goldie, had become bankrupt. The sequestration of Goldie's publishing business temporarily halted sales of the third edition of *The Queen's Wake,* making publication of the new poem all the more urgent.[15]

Hogg returned to Edinburgh on 8 October (*Letters*, I, 205), and within a few days Miller was no longer the publisher of *The Pilgrims of the Sun*, as Hogg recounted in a letter to Lord Byron of 14 October:

I told you I had sold an edition of a new poem to Constable and Miller—on my return to town after an absence of 9 weeks, by which time it was to have been published, I found it in the same state in which I left it, and the m. s. taken out of the press and passing thro' all the notable *blues*. I went to the shop in a tremendous rage, threatened Miller with a prosecution, and took the M. S. out of his hands (*Letters*, I, 205)

Hogg had been absent from Edinburgh for only five weeks, the period of nine weeks probably referring instead to the interval between the making and breaking of his arrangement with Robert Miller. At the time he wrote to Byron Hogg was expecting to meet Murray in Edinburgh any day, for his letter continues, 'Murray is probably by this time in Edin. if so you shall hear from me in a few days', also expressing his fear that 'if Murray and I do not agree I am in a fine scrape'. Four days later Hogg wrote to Byron again to tell him that Murray had agreed to publish *The Pilgrims of the Sun*: 'I have had a very pleasant crack with Mr. Murray and we have sorted very well I hope we shall long do so' (*Letters*, I, 209). In other words within ten days of his return from the Lake District Hogg had ended his agreement with Robert Miller and made a new one with John Murray.

The account in Hogg's 'Memoir' misleadingly suggests a much longer time-scale for these events:

> Week passed after week, and no proofs arrived. I grew impatient, it having been stipulated that the work was to be published in two months, and wrote to Mr. Miller; but I received no answer. I then wrote to a friend to inquire the reason. He waited on Mr. Miller, he said, but received no satisfactory answer: "the truth of the matter," added he, "is this: Mr. Miller, I am privately informed, sent out your MS. among his blue-stockings for their verdict. They have condemned the poem as extravagant nonsense. Mr. Miller has rued his bargain, and will never publish the poem, unless he is sued at law." How far this information was correct I had no means of discovering; but it vexed me exceedingly, as I had mentioned the transaction to all my friends, and how much I was pleased at the connexion. However, I waited patiently for two months, the time when it ought to have been published, and then I wrote Mr. Miller a note, desiring him to put my work forthwith to the press, the time being now elapsed; or, otherwise, to return me the manuscript. Mr. Miller returned me the poem with a polite note, as if no bargain had existed, and I thought it beneath me ever to mention the circumstance again, either to him or Mr. Constable. [...]
>
> Some time after this Mr. Blackwood introduced me to Mr. John Murray, the London bookseller [...] (*Altrive Tales*, pp. 37–38)

Without questioning the fact that Miller's female literary advisors thought the poem extravagant and that the printing may consequently have been delayed, one wonders if Hogg was not unduly impatient with Miller knowing that Murray was due to visit Edinburgh at this time and might be persuaded to publish the poem instead. Hogg was, after all, reluctant elsewhere in his 'Memoir' to admit that he sometimes changed publisher partly for the advantage to be gained for his work.[16] It seems likely that in this case the transfer to Murray suited both Hogg and Miller.

Hogg was introduced to Murray by William Blackwood, who was then Murray's Edinburgh agent, between 14 and 18 October and he seems to have read a carefully selected portion of the poem to both publishers, obviously the opening section which most resembles 'Kilmeny', one of the most admired parts of *The Queen's Wake*. In the first canto of *The Pilgrims of the Sun* the pure maiden Mary Lee is visited by a mysterious stranger and accompanies him on an out-of-body journey initially through the air to view the Scottish landscape and then to other worlds, Hogg using a metre which he described as the music of his 'hill-harp'. Blackwood clearly had no idea at this time that the poem then embarked on a description of Heaven itself, and changed its metre in the second canto to echo the poetry of Milton. Writing to Murray subsequently on 11 December Blackwood was not sanguine about the success of the poem, adding, 'The portion which he read us appears to me [the] only part that is interesting. His Miltonic soaring into the empyreal heavens will not do'. Murray, ignorant of the full scope of the work, was clearly enthusiastic on the basis of what he had heard, and Blackwood later chided him gently for his rashness in making a bargain with Hogg without insisting that the whole manuscript should be submitted to him. 'Your quickness & rapidity' he wrote, 'which have enabled you to do so much and so well on many other occasions misled you here'.[17] Murray had been prepared to treat Hogg almost as if he were another Lord Byron so far as terms are concerned, offering him £500 for the copyright, greatly to Hogg's astonishment. Hogg was equally sanguine about the worth of his poem, however, since he preferred to take instead a payment of £80 for an edition of a thousand copies and the right to sell as many as he could dispose of at cost price (*Letters*, I, 211). He was to be paid £50 when the work was published, the balance to depend upon sales of the work. Murray was to be the chief publisher of *The Pilgrims of the Sun*, taking the majority of the copies of the edition.

The poem was printed by the firm that produced the thrice-weekly *Caledonian Mercury* newspaper, and by 26 October, little more than a week after Hogg's agreement with Murray, Hogg expected it to be published in three weeks' time and had received a proof of 'the first sheet of the third canto', indicating that the printers had gone as far as p. 64, and were about half-way through the volume. (Hogg's simultaneous complaint about 'dilatory printers' may, however, suggest that the work had been partly printed for Robert Miller previous to Hogg's agreement with Murray.) Two days later, writing to Byron, Hogg reported that the poem was 'now all through my hands save three sheets', which probably indicates that about half of the final part of the poem had then been typeset. At this point Hogg expected the printing to be finished during the following week and he sent Byron two alternative drafts of a dedication to the work, one addressed to himself and the other to Miss Milbanke, written on the assumption that Byron might have married her by the time the poem was published. In fact it was not until 25 November that William Blackwood notified John Murray, 'Hogg's Poem is finished and will be shipt for you next week'.[18] The poem that had taken only three weeks or so to write was ready for publication in little more than six weeks from the time of Hogg's agreement with John Murray.

On 30 November Blackwood, according to his usual practice, sent Murray an advance copy of the printed work by the mail a day or two before sending the bulk of his copies to London by sea, and he followed this up by sending printed sheets of six more copies by mail two days later. By this date the dedication had clearly been printed since Blackwood instructs Murray to tell his binders to 'attend to last sheet which is cut off from the Contents same as the boarded copy', an indication that the final sheet was composed of the last two leaves of the text of the volume and the prelims to it. Byron had failed to reply to Hogg's letter about the dedication, so it must have been Hogg who chose to dedicate the work to Byron himself, as an author he greatly admired and the man who had probably secured Murray as the work's publisher.[19]

Hogg was in high spirits, expecting publication of the issue of the *Edinburgh Review* containing Jeffrey's very favourable review of *The Queen's Wake* to coincide with the publication of *The Pilgrims of the Sun*. The *Edinburgh Review* was highly influential and also known to be exacting in its standards, and an endorsement of Hogg as an important poet there would be extremely favourable to sales of Hogg's poetry. As William Blackwood reported:

> The Author is in great spirits as he has just seen Jeffrey's Critique upon his poem which is most favourable—indeed according to his acc[t] very extravagant in the praise. [...] Hogg says there are 10 sheets of the Review printed and they expect to be out in 10 or 12 days.[20]

Blackwood shipped 200 copies of *The Pilgrims of the Sun* to London for Murray on Tuesday, 6 December, and another 400 copies two days later, announcing on 11 December that he intended to publish in Edinburgh on the following day.[21]

Hogg was understandably nervous about the reception of the work to appear next after his outstanding success with *The Queen's Wake* and had found it difficult to concentrate for some weeks past. He had told Eliza Izett on 26 October 'I am not doing much at present if you except gossiping for though I have no serious doubts about the success of the Pilgrims yet I feel a certain anxiety which prevents me from composing to any sense—my mind always reverting to that' (*Letters*, I, 212). On the day of publication things looked well. Hogg himself was clearly able to dispose of more copies than he had expected, for he was obliged to send a hasty note to Blackwood for a further twenty copies and had the impression from what he heard that 'the publick opinion of it is high'. Blackwood too a month after publication noted, 'The Pilgrims are moving off'.[22]

With the situation looking promising in Edinburgh for *The Pilgrims of the Sun* Hogg scanned the London newspapers each day for an announcement of Murray's publication of his poem in London, but looked in vain for over two weeks. Finally on 26 December he wrote in a tone of jocular exasperation to Murray himself for news:

> What the deuce have you made of my excellent poem that you are never publishing it while I am starving for want of money and cannot even afford a Christmas goose to my friends? I think I may say of you as the countryman said to his friend who asked him when his wife had her *accouchement* "Troth man said he she's aye gaun about yet I think she be gaun to keep this ane till hersel athegither" However I daresay that like the said wife you have your reasons for it but of all things a bookseller's reasons suit worse with a poet's board—
> (*Letters*, I, 223)

The truth was that when Murray at last read the entire poem he had impulsively bargained for in Edinburgh in August he was alarmed by what he felt was its extravagance, and consulted with various trusted literary advisors accordingly, rather as Robert Miller had done some months previously. Their opinion was much the same and Murray can only have been further alarmed by Blackwood's telling him in his letter of 11 December that Hogg's 'Miltonic soaring into the empyreal heavens will not do'. He seems to have over-reacted, fearing that he would lose prestige as a publisher if his name appeared on the title-page of the work, and delayed the publication while a new title-page was prepared in London. On this William Blackwood in Edinburgh features as the chief publisher of *The Pilgrims of the Sun*, which is only 'sold by J. Murray, London' (see the two illustrations).

While Hogg was waiting for an answer to his Christmas letter and continuing to inspect the London newspapers for the expected publication announcement he fell seriously ill as a result of the late hours and daily carousals of the Right and Wrong Club, and was confined to bed for more than three weeks. It was during this illness that at last his poem was advertised in London, in the *Morning Chronicle* for Friday, 13 January 1815. When Hogg saw the announcement four days later in Edinburgh he was in a state of 'high chagrin' and in a pencil note of 18 January written to Murray from his sick-bed told him, 'nothing could have displeased me more—Blackwood is the publisher (his name being first)—not you—this was not generous to a poor Shepherd I considered your name of greater importance to the success of the work than mine' (*Letters*, I, 230–31). A letter written three days later, after he had received Murray's explanation and excuses, was written in better humour with Murray's unaccountable lapse of judgement:

> I freely forgive you for if I had thought the same way I would have acted the same way. But I cannot help smiling at your London critics—they must read it over again I had the best advice in the three kingdoms of the poem men whose opinions, even given in a dream, I would not exchange for all the critics in England before I even proposed it for publication. I will risk my fame on it to all eternity (*Letters*, I, 233–34)

William Blackwood, though he did not share Hogg's high valuation of *The Pilgrims of the Sun*, also seems to have felt that Murray's reaction to the poem was exaggerated. He reported on 14 January, 'The Pilgrims are moving off, and really if you will go through it, you will find some very beautiful passages'. On [21 January] he was more forthright:

> I think you are fretting yourself a great deal more than there is the least necessity for with regard to poor Hogg's Pilgrims. It has many faults certainly, but on the other hand contains passages which should redeem it from utter damnation. [...] I am surprized as well as amused at the horrors in which you seem to be in about the ridicule & damnation that we must have been subjected to. I can assure you your fears are wholly groundless. My not saying any thing about the poem did not proceed fom my being *feeared* to tell you all that was said, but simply from my not being interested by it, and of course not a little disappointed with it. [...] The opinions with regard to the poem have been very various, but no one here has ever hinted or thought that it was in the smallest degree discreditable to us to have published it. His character

THE

Pilgrims of the Sun;

A POEM.

___

BY JAMES HOGG,

AUTHOR OF THE QUEEN'S WAKE, &c.

═══════════

A pupil in the many chambered school
Where Superstition weaves her airy dreams.
WORDSWORTH.

═══════════

LONDON:

PRINTED FOR JOHN MURRAY, 50, ALBEMARLE STREET:
AND WILLIAM BLACKWOOD, SOUTH BRIDGE STREET,
EDINBURGH.

___

1815.

Title-page to *The Pilgrims of the Sun*
(Edinburgh, 1814)

THE

Pilgrims of the Sun;

A POEM.

———

BY JAMES HOGG,

AUTHOR OF THE QUEEN'S WAKE, &c.

═══════

A Pupil in the many chambered school
Where Superstition weaves her airy dreams.
WORDSWORTH.

═══════

EDINBURGH:

PRINTED FOR WILLIAM BLACKWOOD, SOUTH BRIDGE
STREET;

AND SOLD BY J. MURRAY, LONDON.

———

1815.

Title-page to *The Pilgrims of the Sun*
(London 1815)

in the Edin Review is quite sufficient to prevent such a thing being ever thought of.[23]

The initial sale appears to have been reasonably promising. John Murray's record of the number of sales of his publications made to other London booksellers notes that on 13 January when the poem was published in London he shifted 177 copies, 'Subscribed at 5/2 sells 7/6', and by 10 April he had sold 381, not far off two-thirds of the 600 copies he had received from Blackwood. He wrote to Hogg of this and of the fourth edition of *The Queen's Wake*, 'They are, each, selling every day & I have no [*sic*] that they will both be out of print in two Months'. On 21 April, less than four months from first publication, he remitted Hogg the remaining thirty pounds of the promised payment stating that this would 'only anticipate by a few days the time when this sum would otherwise have become due'.[24]

The remaining copies of *The Pilgrims of the Sun*, however, seem to have lingered on the publishers' hands. William Blackwood guessed on 9 October 1815 that there might be about 400 of the edition of one thousand copies remaining, and Murray was still including the work in his advertising catalogues as late as May 1817.[25] Hogg himself later reported that 'the work sold heavily' (*Altrive Tales*, p. 39).

The initial critical response was also not altogether unfavourable, as Hogg explained in his 'Memoir':

> The poem came out, and was rather well received. I never met with any person, who really had read it, that did not like the piece; the reviewers praised it; and the Eclectic, in particular, gave it the highest commendation I ever saw bestowed on a work of genius. It was reprinted in two different towns in America, and ten thousand copies of it sold in that country. (*Altrive Tales*, p. 39)

While there is no surviving indication of how many copies were sold in America, Hogg's statement (though perhaps a little exaggerated) is otherwise supported by the digest of contemporary periodical reviews given in the Introduction to the present edition and by surviving copies of editions published by Moses Thomas in Philadelphia in 1815 and 1816 respectively.[26]

Hogg came to believe eventually, however, that the separate volume publication of *The Pilgrims of the Sun* had been a mistake. He declared in the version of his 'Memoir' prefacing *The Mountain Bard* of 1821 that '[a]mong other wild and visionary subjects, the Pilgrims of the Sun would have done very well, and might at least have been judged one of the best; but, as an entire poem by itself, it bears a trait of extravagance, and affords no relief from the story of a visionary existence'.[27] When the poem was included in his 1822 *Poetical Works* Hogg was at pains to minimise this effect as far as possible, emphasising that Mary Lee's journey should not be interpreted as a literal account of her adventures. 'The erratic pilgrimage' he asserted 'is given merely as a dream or vision of a person in a long trance', while the section which portrays 'the throne of the Almighty' in the centre of the sun 'must be viewed only as of a piece with the rest of the imaginary scenes exhibited in the work; infinitude and omnipresence being attributes too sacred and too boundless for admission into an enthusiast's dream'. A similarly defensive tone recurs in Hogg's note on the description of the comet in the poem, which he says 'has been copied into several miscellaneous works, and has been often loudly censured for its utter extravagance by such as knew not the nature of the work from which it was taken'.[28] Had it appeared, Hogg felt, along with the companion-piece 'Connel of Dee' it would have been more readily apprehended as a visionary dream, part of the collection named *Midsummer Night Dreams*.

These passages, however, date from 1821 and 1822. The evidence suggests that during the period between first publication and then Hogg would have been content to republish *The Pilgrims of the Sun* outside the *Midsummer Night Dreams* collection.

3. Projecting a Collected Edition of Hogg's Poetry

Very soon after the first publication of *The Pilgrims of the Sun* Hogg had begun to suggest to various publishers that he would like to achieve the status of a Wordsworth, Byron, Scott, or Southey in having his various poems brought out together as a collected edition. A two-volume edition was tentatively suggested to John Murray in Hogg's letter of 31 March 1815, and more seriously to Blackwood in the autumn of that year. Following the recent appearance of *The Minor Poems of Robert Southey* in a three-volume set costing eighteen shillings, Hogg declared to Blackwood on 6 October 1815, 'I am fully resolved to have an edition of all my poetry published this season in 3 vols post 8vo such as Southys; one of them original unpublished poetry'. With unsold copies of both *The Queen's Wake* and *The Pilgrims of the Sun* on hand neither Blackwood nor Murray would further such a project. Nevertheless Hogg mentioned it once more in a letter to Byron of 26 February [1816], asking him to 'stand my friend with Murray as you formerly did', and he made a renewed attempt to interest Murray himself on 1 March 1816. Hogg's plan for the collection is interesting in that he clearly had no idea at this date of resuscitating the abandoned *Midsummer Night Dreams* collection, but wished to group *The Pilgrims of the Sun* together with *The Mountain Bard*: 'I should publish in 3 vols The *Wake* to constitute the first. *The Mountain Bard* and the Pilgrims the second, and the third to consist of original poetry'. Hogg's new poem, *Mador of the Moor*, was clearly to feature largely in the volume of original poetry.[29]

Over the next few years Hogg continued at intervals to mention the desirability of a collected edition of his poetry to potential publishers. Indeed it seems clear that both the subscription edition of *The Queen's Wake* published by Blackwood and Murray in 1819 and the 1821 edition of *The Mountain Bard* published by Oliver & Boyd may well have been spin-offs from this larger publishing project. Writing to William Blackwood on 8 December 1816 Hogg regretted that 'you decline the 12mo. ed. of my poetry farther than the Queen's Wake'. To George Boyd of Oliver & Boyd on 5 February 1820 Hogg projected a seven-volume collected poems as follows:

> *The Mountain Bard* will make make one vol *Songs &c* a second.
> *The Pilgrims* and Mador of the Moor a third The Queen's Wake
> a fourth and the first mentioned works [*The Poetic Mirror* and
> *Dramatic Tales*] other three seven in all and every one of them
> may be sold seperately as well as in sets.[30]

Be that as it may, Hogg still envisages *The Pilgrims of the Sun* not as part of a volume of *Midsummer Night Dreams* but as making up a volume in combination with a separate and distinct work, by this time *Mador of the Moor* rather than *The Mountain Bard*.

Hogg's breach with William Blackwood in the autumn of 1821 over John Wilson's scathing review of the version of the 'Memoir' in the third edition of *The Mountain Bard* effectively threw Hogg once more into the orbit of the rival Edinburgh firm of Constable. Hogg became a contributor to the firm's *Edinburgh Magazine*, and tried to get the firm's stellar author, Sir Walter Scott, to persuade Robert Cadell as the managing partner to publish a four-volume *Poetical Works* for him. Writing to Scott on 10 December 1821 Hogg thought that the set should exclude *Dramatic Tales* and *The Mountain Bard*, adding 'I wish you would settle with Mr. Caddell about them He will grant you much better conditions than me [...]'. Scott clearly obliged, since Cadell's letter to Hogg of 2 February 1822 offering £150 for an edition of a thousand copies begins by stating, 'I have had a conversation with Sir Walter Scott on the subject of an edition of your prominent poetical productions—I think we can manage with the addition of the original poems alluded to in your letter of 15 Decr to make 4 vols foolscap size'.[31] Hogg replied, addressing Archibald Constable, on 8 February, asking for £200 instead of £150 and (feeling that this was likely to be granted) outlining arrangements for the production of the edition. 'I will make up each volume to the size of the Queen's Wake', he told the publisher, 'which must be the standard in size'. Hogg's careful consideration of the contents is shown in his instruction, 'be sure to take either the *fifth* or *sixth edition* of the Wake for sake of the late additions and also the *second edition* of the poetic Mirror'. He was naturally anxious that the most recently-revised versions of his poems should form the basis of the new edition.

Hogg's surviving correspondence with Robert Cadell is incomplete, but his letter of 6 March 1822 gives an outline of the contents of the collected edition of his poetry, reiterating 'the arrangement mentioned in my letter some months ago'. Although in the 1821 edition of *The Mountain Bard* Hogg had regretted the publication of *The Pilgrims of the Sun* outside the framework provided by the *Midsummer Night Dreams* collection, he is at this point still not thinking of reinstating it in the collected edition. In this letter Hogg is noticeably urgent that *The Pilgrims of the Sun* and *Mador of the Moor* should be published together in one of the volumes of the set.

> You have forgot the arrangement mentioned in my letter some months ago. *The Pilgrims of the Sun* and *Mador of the Moor* being to lye in one bed and form the 2^d volume The Poetic Mirror the third and a volume of Miscellaneous poems and a few of my best and most popular songs to form the *Fourth vol* all are alike ready the *Mirror* only will require a little adition [*sic*]. I am not sure if Mador and the pilgrims will lack any thing I should think not if they do I will add a few pages of curious notes. As I recieved yours of the 28th Feb. only this day I lose no time in answering it lest you should put *Mador* and *the Pilgrims* to press seperately and be obliged on account of the pages to print them over again. See about this without delay. put any of the two first you please Mador is the most perfect poem The pilgrims has been a greater favourite. Remember they two form *The Second vol*[32]

When Robert Cadell had informed Hogg on 16 February that he had given the printing to the firm of Walker and Greig (the printers of Hogg's *The Forest Minstrel* more than ten years previously) he had added a reassurance that 'the Queens Wake is the sixth edition'. Replying to this letter on 13 March he once more placated Hogg, emphasising 'that your wishes as to the arrangement of your Poems shall meet every attention, and Mador and the Pilgrims shall lye in the same lid as you wish'. Only the suggestion made by Hogg through the medium of his nephew, Robert Hogg, that the four volumes should be given to different printers and produced simultaneously was firmly refused as '*impossible*' since 'the uniformity of the volumes must be consulted'.[33]

Hogg's nephew, Robert Hogg, had recently completed a general degree course at the University of Edinburgh but then refused to go on for the further study that would prepare him for becoming a minister of the Church of Scotland. Hogg was anxious to secure some employment for him, even asking Blackwood on 27 October [1820] if he could do anything for this deserving young man. Robert Hogg was a useful literary assistant to his famous uncle, and when the Second Series of *The Jacobite Relics of Scotland*, published by Blackwood and printed by Oliver & Boyd, was in preparation during 1820, he had assisted by transcribing songs and ordering material for the work.[34] With the four-volume collected poems in mind Hogg was quick to recommend him to Archibald Constable:

> I have a nephew in town the best corrector of a press that ever [*sic*] born either in English, Greek, Latin, or German. I should like that he looked over the proofs for I never yet have got an edition without blunders, and most gross ones in my old language, such as "The Witch o' Fife" "The Gude Grey Catte" "Hymns of the fairies" &c. Robert is Master of all these matters and they are safe with him.[35]

In the absence of concrete evidence Robert Hogg's precise part in the formation and preparation of the four volumes of *The Poetical Works of James Hogg*, published by the Constable firm in mid-June 1822, is hard to determine. It is clear that Hogg expected to be able to delegate the mundane tasks of proof-reading to him and to be able to use him as a messenger in communicating with Robert Cadell in Edinburgh while he himself was at Altrive, forty miles away. It seems unlikely, however, that Hogg would have allowed his nephew to over-ride his own wishes on matters he saw as crucial, and his letter to Cadell of 6 March reveals that he did think that the arrangement of the poems in the collection was crucial. Cadell, as his letter of 13 March clearly demonstrates, recognised this and was quick to reassure Hogg that his wishes would be met.

Nevertheless, when the edition was published around 13 June 1822 *Mador of the Moor* appeared in the fourth volume (pp. 1–130), and *The Pilgrims of the Sun* was the first item in the second volume, the

contents page of which carried the heading 'Midsummer Night
Dreams'. At some point between 6 March and the printing of the
prelims to this volume Hogg had revived the series title he had cre-
ated for his visionary poems in 1814. Hogg's surviving correspond-
ence with Robert Cadell is incomplete and provides no information
about this change of heart, which may indeed have been communi-
cated by word of mouth during one of Hogg's visits to Edinburgh in
the spring and early summer of 1822. His letter to Cadell of 6 March
had promised, 'I will see you on the 1st or 2d of April. Farewell till
then but push on the printing'. A letter to William Blackwood of 11
April dated from Edinburgh suggests that he kept his word to be in
Edinburgh in the early part of April to work on the publication of
the collected edition of his poetry, particularly as the letter contains a
reproach that Hogg had 'been obliged to publish my poems without
"The Highlanders" my own favourite poem which I gave to you and
never could recover'.[36] Hogg arrived in town again on 7 May, in-
tending to stay for about a week, and on the day after his arrival
wrote home to his wife, 'I find the printing in a forward state and
hope I shall do well enough'.[37] The available evidence, then, sup-
ports the theory that Hogg maintained a personal involvement in
the production of *The Poetical Works of James Hogg*, despite the conven-
ience of having his nephew in Edinburgh. When Robert Hogg, some
years older and more experienced than he was in 1822, played a
major part in shaping the volume publications of *The Shepherd's Calen-
dar* and *A Queer Book* he was fulfilling the wishes of the publisher,
William Blackwood. In this case, however, Cadell was perfectly will-
ing to adopt Hogg's own arrangement for the volumes. The change
to *Midsummer Night Dreams* must surely have been initiated by Hogg.

During the year or two before the publication of his *Poetical Works*
Hogg seems to have re-engaged with the visionary and fantasic in
several contributions to Constable's *Edinburgh Magazine*, such as the
poems of 'The Mermaid' and 'The Powris of Moseke', and his deci-
sion to revive the idea of a *Midsummer Night Dreams* collection may
have been made when he considered these for inclusion in the 1822
collection. He may also have been influenced by David Laing's re-
view of the 1821 edition of *The Mountain Bard* in the *Edinburgh Monthly
Review* of June 1821. Laing disapproved of Hogg's prefatory 'Memoir',
and in conclusion advised him how his pen might be better employed:

> In one word, let us counsel him to abandon confessions and
> disclosures, and revert to an old project, that of filling up a
> volume with those delightful subjects which he contemplated
> for his MIDSUMMER'S NIGHT DREAMS.[38]

THE

POETICAL WORKS

OF

JAMES HOGG.

IN FOUR VOLUMES.

VOL. II.

EDINBURGH:

PRINTED FOR ARCH. CONSTABLE & CO. EDINBURGH ;

AND HURST, ROBINSON & CO. LONDON.

1822.

Title-page to the second volume of
The Poetical Works of James Hogg (1822)

CONTENTS OF VOLUME SECOND.

MIDSUMMER NIGHT DREAMS.

Contents Page to the second volume of
The Poetical Works of James Hogg (1822)

Careful examination of the four volumes that make up *The Poetical Works of James Hogg* emphasises Hogg's statement to Constable of 8 February that *The Queen's Wake* must be the standard of size for the volumes. Hogg's most successful narrative poem occupies the first volume of 381 pages, and the other three are a mixture of longer works with shorter poems added to make them of similar thickness. The second, or *Midsummer Night Dreams*, volume consisted of the poems Hogg had written for his visionary series in 1814 and a further seven items, together with some authorial notes. This raises the question of how many of the poems in the second volume are *Midsummer Night Dreams* poems and how many ought to be classed as makeweights added simply to bring the volume up to the required size.

The contents page merely lists the entire contents of the volume without distinction under the *Midsummer Night Dreams* heading, while the original paper spine-label gives the volume number and then the name of the lead poem, *The Pilgrims of the Sun.* Half-titles are supplied between the cantos of the lead poem, and at the start of every other item in the volume, including Hogg's notes. A brief comparison of this volume with the other three volumes of *Poetical Works* is suggestive. The paper spine-labels for the other three volumes also name the lead poem in each case. Half-titles are supplied between the Nights of *The Queen's Wake*, the individual cantos of *Mador of the Moor*, and the individual parodies of *The Poetic Mirror.* In the third volume there are half-titles reflecting the sub-headings of 'Miscellanies' and 'Songs', and in the fourth volume similarly for 'Sacred Melodies', 'Miscellaneous Poems', and 'Songs'. However, in this latter volume the narrative poems immediately following *Mador of the Moor* have no collective half-title as there is a half-title for each separate poem. That these are not part of *Mador of the Moor* is indicated merely by an increased space on the contents page between the entry for the Conclusion of *Mador* and the one for 'Lines to Sir Walter Scott, Bart.', the first of the following items. There is no such space between *The Pilgrims of the Sun* and the following poems in the second volume, and no other indication of groupings of the poems in the volume by means either of spacing or the use of headings (see illustration). *The Poetical Works of James Hogg* was carefully printed, and it seems reasonable to conclude that Hogg may well have intended the heading of *Midsummer Night Dreams* to refer to the entire contents of the volume.

4. *Midsummer Night Dreams* of 1822

Examination of the individual poems following *The Pilgrims of the Sun* in the *Midsummer Night Dreams* volume of the 1822 *Poetical Works of James Hogg* supports the argument that Hogg did not intend the collection to refer simply to those poems he had written for the abortive collection of 1814, namely *The Pilgrims of the Sun* itself, 'Connel of Dee' and (probably) 'Superstition'. There are a number of thematic and other links between these original core items and the other contents of the volume.

Three of them ('The Mermaid', 'Verses to the Comet of 1811', and 'The Powris of Moseke') had recently been printed in the *Edinburgh Magazine*, a periodical owned by the Constable firm that was also publishing *The Poetical Works of James Hogg*. Hogg's breach with William Blackwood in the autumn of 1821 had temporarily realigned Hogg as one of Constable's authors at this time, and this is naturally enough reflected in the collected edition of his poetry. Hogg's contributions to the *Edinburgh Magazine* were varied, a mixture of old pieces from *The Spy*, prose tales in the manner of John Wilson, Jacobite songs not included in his volumes of *The Jacobite Relics of Scotland*, and so forth.[39] They also indicate, however, a re-engagement with the visionary, romantic mode embodied in the abortive *Midsummer Night Dreams* collection of 1814, and have thematic links with it.

'The Mermaid. A Scottish Ballad' in the *Edinburgh Magazine* for May 1819 continues the theme of love between a human being and a spirit, and concludes with the Mermaid's lament for her dead lover, which contrasts his eventual resurrection at the end of time with the uncertainty of her own fate. It therefore suits well with both *The Pilgrims of the Sun* where Mary Lee finds happiness with her otherworldly lover in the form of Hugo, and with 'Connel of Dee' where a shepherd is haunted by fear of persecution from a visionary wife.

'Verses to the Comet of 1811' had been published under the title of 'Stanzas Addressed to a Comet' in the *Edinburgh Magazine* for July 1819, an instance of Hogg quietly recycling his earlier work (see 'Note on the Texts' for its previous publication history). It also has a clear thematic link with *The Pilgrims of the Sun*. Mary and Cela in their other-worldly voyaging had witnessed the death of a world and its transformation to a comet, a passage commented on by reviewers after publication of the first edition and picked up by Hogg for specific comment in his annotation to the poem in 1822 (see p. 150 in the present volume). The poet's fantasy in 'Verses to the Comet of 1811' about travelling with the comet through space has obvious links to this key passage, and would appear to account for Hogg's decison to resituate it within the *Midsummer Night Dreams* collection.

Hogg published 'The Powris of Moseke, Ane Rychte Plesant Ballaunt' in the *Edinburgh Magazine* for October 1821. Its humour, its emphasis on the grotesque, and its sheer wild exuberance make it a natural companion piece to 'Connel of Dee'. Shakespeare's *Midsummer Night's Dream* had famously described the 'lunatic, the lover, and the poet' as 'of imagination all compact' (v. 1. 7–8), and 'The Powris of Moseke' with its blind minstrel might be taken as a comic representation of the poet, just as 'Connel of Dee' is a comic representation of the lover. The quality and energy of the poem also form a very strong indication of Hogg's re-engagement with the visionary and fantastic during the period preceding the publication of *The Poetical Works of James Hogg*. In 'The Powris of Moseke', unlike Hogg's earlier visionary poems of 1814, the visionary is unambiguously delusional. The blind minstrel is misled partly by his own vanity as a musician and partly by his mischievous boy into misinterpreting the everyday world around him: it is quite clear to the reader that the fairy folk and the devil do not in fact appear when he plays. This is consonant with the way in which Hogg's notes to *The Pilgrims of the Sun* in the 1822 volume emphasise that Mary Lee's experiences are the visions of a person in a trance and not literal, historical events. Hogg's caution in writing of visionary experiences in the early 1820s perhaps results from the reception given to *The Pilgrims of the Sun* on first publication.

Hogg's use of pseudo-medieval Scots, what he termed in his letter to Archibald Constable of 8 February 1822 'my old language', was also of course a way of distancing the Regency author James Hogg from his visionary or supernatural subject-matter. Peter Garside has commented on its liberating effect for Hogg in relation to several ballads in *A Queer Book*.[40] In relating a supernatural tale in language that signalled pre-Reformation and pre-Enlightenment times Hogg was able to evade assumptions that as an uneducated farm-worker he had a literal belief in the fantastic events he recounted. 'The Powris of Moseke' had been written in Hogg's 'old language' and he also included a second 'old language' poem in the *Midsummer Night Dreams* volume of 1822, 'The Gyre Caryl'. This had previously appeared under the title of 'The Harper's Song' in *Mador of the Moor*, taking the form of an interlude created by an ancient minstrel to amuse the King of Scotland's hunting party. The theme of 'The Harper's Song' is almost identical to that of 'Superstition', the disenchantment of the world, in this case the departure of the fairies from Scotland with the birth of Grace. The composition of *Mador of the Moor* immediately preceded that of the poems written for a *Midsummer Night Dreams* collection in 1814 and Hogg must have realised in retrospect that 'The Harper's Song' was, among other things, a precursor of the visionary poems he wrote not long afterwards. He therefore removed it from *Mador of the Moor* in the fourth volume of his 1822 collection, and relocated it as a separate poem in the *Midsummer Night Dreams* volume. The removal of this poem is arguably an impoverishment of *Mador of the Moor*–Jim Barcus argues persuasively that it is of great thematic significance to the longer poem–but it certainly is a fine and fitting component of the *Midsummer Night Dreams* collection nevertheless.[41]

Hogg's inclusion of 'The Haunted Glen' in the *Midsummer Night Dreams* volume of his 1822 *Poetical Works* is a similar exercise in recontextualisation. In the abridged version of 1822, consisting only of the fairy scenes, the resemblance of the story to that of the ballad 'Tam Lin' is emphasised, both marking the boundary where the human and spirit worlds mix and mingle.[42] Lu, like Tam, is a human being who has been partly absorbed into the fairy world, from which he is again removed to common life through the love of a country girl. The haunted glen also perhaps invokes the wood outside Athens in which much of the action of Shakespeare's *A Midsummer Night's Dream* is laid.

The nature and extent of Hogg's revisions to suit 'The Field of Waterloo' for inclusion in *Midsummer Night Dreams* can only be guessed at, since except for a single fragment (see 'Appendix 1: MS Fragment of "The Field of Waterloo. A Poem"') Hogg's original version written in 1815 has not survived.[43] A comparison of this fragment with the 1822 version of the poem, however, indicates that Hogg undoubtedly revised his poem for publication in 1822 and that the revision included giving the poem a new sub-title, 'and Death-Bed Prayer of a Soldier'. This points up the visionary conclusion of the poem, where the dying soldier's request to God to become a spiritual guardian to his wife or lover and her baby after death has apparently been granted. The poem's narrator in the course of subsequent visits to their cottage in the Scottish Borders observes that the baby 'bent its eyes on air and smiled, | Stretching its arms with fervent mien, | As if to reach to something seen' (ll. 716–18). The domestic and wild animals there also seem to be aware of an invisible presence, and the poem's concluding lines express the narrator's sense of being, like the protagonists of many of the component poems of *Midsummer Night Dreams*, on a borderland between human existence and a visionary or spiritual world:

> Then chilling thoughts have on me pressed
> Of an unbodied heavenly guest,
> Sent there to roam the lonely wild,
> To guard the mother and the child;
> For to the death-bed prayer is given
> Free passage to the throne of Heaven! (ll. 723–28)

In the absence of Hogg's original manuscript it is impossible to tell whether this passage was present in the version of 'The Field of Waterloo' Hogg created in 1815 or whether, like the title, it was part of his reshaping of this earlier work for the *Midsummer Night Dreams* volume which it suits so well.

The final item in the second volume of *The Poetical Works of James Hogg* of 1822 is 'Verses Addressed to the Right Honourable Lady Anne Scott of Buccleuch'. Although recycled by Hogg on a number of occasions, in this context the poem aptly draws together a number of the threads running through the *Midsummer Night Dreams* volume. There is an obvious chronological thread running through the volume, from the composition of the core collection in 1814 to final publication in 1822, so that the final verses summarise a period of Hogg's life between the success of *The Queen's Wake* and his abandonment of long poems for prose fiction in the early 1820s.[44] The allusions in the poem to Harriet, Duchess of Buccleuch, and to her absence also chime with the ending of *The Pilgrims of the Sun* where Hogg laments the death of a benevolent local aristocrat and kind patron. (Most of the component poems of *Midsummer Night Dreams* are placed within Hogg's native district.) Finally the reference to the fairy world in the Shakespearean title is summarised in this last poem, with its yearning to view a supernatural world that now appears to have been lost. The exclamation 'Oh, can it ever be forgot, | What Scotland had, and now has not!' (ll. 149–50) might well be taken as the impetus behind *Midsummer Night Dreams*.

The integrity of the complete and extended *Midsummer Night Dreams* formed by Hogg in 1822 was apparently not appreciated by succeeding generations, perhaps because of the larger and more easily grasped context of a collected poetical works. The second volume of the five-volume *Poetical Works of the Ettrick Shepherd* published by the Glasgow firm of Blackie and Son between 1838 and 1840 prints a group of ten shorter narrative or meditative poems between the opening work, *The Pilgrims of the Sun*, and the ballad-imitations of *The Mountain Bard*. These include seven of the poems from *Midsummer Night*

Dreams of 1822, but also two poems of the late 1820s ('St Mary of the Lowes', and 'A Greek Pastoral'), as well as 'Superstition and Grace', a rewriting of 'The Gyre Caryl' for an Annual. These three additions mask the coherence of the others, and the title of *Midsummer Night Dreams* does not appear in this printing. In the poetry volume of the same firm's *The Works of the Ettrick Shepherd* of 1865, *The Pilgrims of the Sun* is grouped with Hogg's other poetry volumes of the 1810s, between *Mador of the Moor* and *The Poetic Mirror*, while five of the shorter poems of *Midsummer Night Dreams* form part of the section of 'Poetical Tales and Ballads', three more are classed as 'Poems Descriptive and Sentimental', and 'The Gyre Caryl' does not appear at all. Subsequent collections of Hogg's poetry were based, either directly or indirectly, on these Blackie editions. More recently two one-volume selections of Hogg's work, *Selected Poems* edited by Douglas Mack and *Selected Poems and Songs* edited by David Groves, have partially reinstated the *Midsummer Night Dreams* collection.[45]

In general Hogg's *Poetical Works* of 1822 has been greatly underrated and very little attention has so far been devoted to its structure and meaning, perhaps because Hogg subsequently published his epic poem *Queen Hynde*, a multitude of poems intended as periodical contributions, and of course many songs, before his death in November 1835. As a collected poetical works the 1822 edition is, therefore, obviously deficient. Nevertheless it has important things to say about the way Hogg in 1822 regarded his previous career as a poet, and in the completion and restoration of *Midsummer Night Dreams* it was the only embodiment of one of his major works before the publication of the present volume in the Stirling/South Carolina Edition.

Notes

1.   James Hogg, *The Queen's Wake*, ed. by Douglas S. Mack (S/SC, 2004), pp. lii–liii.
2.   For information about the composition of *Mador of the Moor* see Hogg's 'Memoir of the Author's Life', in *Altrive Tales*, pp. 34–35, and *Mador*, pp. xi–xv. Several of Hogg's letters written during the summer of 1813 refer to *The Hunting of Badlewe*—see, for instance, Hogg's letter to Bernard Barton of 14 May 1813 and notes in *Letters*, I, 139–42. The abbreviations used in this essay for works frequently referred to are the same as those in the 'Editorial Notes' of the present volume and are listed on pp. 177–78.
3.   See 'Storms' in *The Shepherd's Calendar*, ed. by Douglas S. Mack (S/SC, 1995), pp. 1–21 (p. 10).
4.   Hogg to Eliza Izett, 11 February 1814, in *Letters*, I, 176.
5.   'Country Dreams and Apparitions No. II Connel of Dee', in *Winter Evening Tales*, ed. by Ian Duncan (S/SC, 2002), pp. 410–25 (pp. 410, 423, 425).
6.   See David Groves, *James Hogg: The Growth of a Writer* (Edinburgh: Scottish Academic Press, 1988), pp. 62–65. His view has been supported subsequently

by Douglas Mack and Ian Duncan—see *Winter Evening Tales*, p. 582.

7. David Groves, *James Hogg: The Growth of a Writer*, p. 65.

8. See Hogg's 'Notes to The Pilgrims of the Sun' in the present volume (p. 148).

9. James Hogg, *The Queen's Wake*, ed. by Douglas S. Mack (S/SC, 2004), p. xlii. See also 'Superstition' (ll. 99, 234) in the present volume.

10. *Letters*, I, 187–88.

11. See George Goldie's letter to Bernard Barton of 28 October 1813, in NLS, MS 1002, fols 85–86. Hogg, he relates, 'at present [...] is engaged in a descriptive poem in the spenserian stanza [...] M\[r.] Grieve and I read it along with him a few nights ago, and we intend to do the same tonight with what he has written since, from which I anticipate another treat of no ordinary relish'.

12. Some of Hogg's invitations to various well-known contemporary poets to contribute to such a periodically-published volume are printed in *Letters*, I, 178–90, while the accompanying notes to these letters provide evidence of others. Hogg eventually abandoned the design and instead published a volume of parodies of Romantic poets, *The Poetic Mirror* (1816).

13. John Gibson Lockhart, *Peter's Letters to his Kinsfolk*, 3 vols (Edinburgh: William Blackwood; London: T. Cadell and W. Davies, 1819), II, 177–80.

14. See Gillian Hughes, 'Hogg's Poetic Responses to the Unexpected Death of his Patron', *SHW*, 12 (2001), 80–89 (pp. 82, 85–87).

15. For an account of Hogg's visit to the Lake District in the early autumn of 1814 see Gillian Hughes, *James Hogg: A Life* (Edinburgh: Edinburgh University Press, 2007), pp. 125–29. Hogg's letter to Robert Southey of [8 October–end November 1814], written after his return to Edinburgh (*Letters*, I, 203–04), grumbles about the copies of *The Queen's Wake* having been taken out of circulation as a result of Goldie's bankruptcy.

16. In his 'Memoir' (*Altrive Tales*, pp. 25–26) Hogg attributes his decision to transfer the printing of *The Spy* from James Robertson to the Aikman firm to his anxiety about the effect of his lunchtime drinking with Robertson's printers in the Cowgate. However, it seems likely that the desire to improve the production quality of his weekly paper was also an important factor—see *The Spy*, ed. by Gillian Hughes (S/SC, 2000), pp. xxiii–xxv.

17. Blackwood to Murray, 11 December 1814 and [21 January 1815], in the John Murray Archive: NLS, Acc. 12604/1113 and Acc. 12604/1114 respectively. Murray seems actually to have received 600 of the printed copies of *The Pilgrims of the Sun*—see note 21.

18. See Hogg's letters to Eliza Izett of 26 October 1814 and to Byron of 28 October 1814, in *Letters*, I, 211–12, and 215–17. See also Blackwood to Murray, 25 November 1814, in the John Murray Archive: NLS, Acc. 12604/1113.

19. See Blackwood to Murray, 30 November and 1 December 1814, in the John Murray Archive: NLS, Acc. 12604/1113. In his letter to John Murray of 26 December 1814 Hogg says that he has not heard from Lord Byron for 'these two months and more'—see *Letters*, I, 224.

20. See Blackwood to Murray, 1 December 1814, in the John Murray Archive: NLS, Acc. 12604/1113.

21. Blackwood to Murray, 11 December 1814, in the John Murray Archive: NLS, Acc. 12604/1113. Murray's Ledger 'A' records the receipt of 413 plus 171 copies of *The Pilgrims of the Sun*, confirming the figure of 600 as the number he took of the one thousand copies printed (John Murray Archive: NLS, MS 42,724, p. 1).

22. See Hogg's letters to Blackwood of [12 December 1814] and to Southey of 15

December 1814, in Hogg, *Letters*, I, 220–21, and Blackwood's to Murray of 14
January 1815, in the John Murray Archive: NLS, Acc. 12604/1114.

23. For Blackwood's comments on *The Pilgrims of the Sun* see his letters to Murray
of 11 December 1814 and 14 January and [21 January] 1815, in the John
Murray Archive: NLS, Acc. 12604/1113 and Acc. 12604/1114 respectively.
Douglas Mack, however, suggests that the cooling of Murray's enthusiasm
for Hogg's poem reflected colder relations obtaining at this time between
Hogg and the stellar authors Scott and Byron–see his 'Hogg, Byron, Scott,
and John Murray of Albemarle Street', *Studies in Scottish Literature*, 35–36
(2007), 307–25.

24. See the entry for 13 January 1815 in John Murray's 'Sales Book 1812–1817'
(John Murray Archive: NLS, MS 42,809, fol. 81), and his letters to Hogg of
10 and 21 April 1815, in NLS, MS 2245, fols 15–16 and 17–18 respectively.

25. See Blackwood's letter to Hogg of 6 October 1815 and notes, in Hogg, *Letters*,
I, 252–53. Among the bound volume of catalogues produced by the Murray
firm between 1774 and 1824 (John Murray Collection, London) is one
dated 'May, 1817' that includes *The Pilgrims of the Sun*.

26. See Stephanie Anderson-Currie, *Preliminary Census of Early Hogg Editions in
North American Libraries*, South Carolina Working Papers in Scottish Bibliog-
raphy 3 (Columbia: Department of English, University of South Carolina,
1993), p. 7.

27. James Hogg, 'Memoir of the Life of James Hogg', *Mountain Bard*, p. 218.

28. See Hogg's 'Notes to The Pilgrims of the Sun' in the present volume, pp. 148,
149, 150.

29. For Hogg's letters to John Murray of 31 March 1815, to William Blackwood
of 6 October 1815, to Lord Byron of 26 February [1816], and to John Murray
of 1 March 1816 see Hogg, *Letters*, I, 244–45, 252–53, 266, and 270–71 respec-
tively.

30. Hogg to Blackwood, 8 December 1816, in *Letters*, I, 285, and Hogg to George
Boyd, 5 February 1820, in *Letters*, II, 4.

31. Hogg to Scott, 10 December 1821, in *Letters*, II, 130, and Cadell to Hogg, 2
February 1822, in NLS, MS 2245, fols 74–75.

32. Hogg to Archibald Constable, 8 February 1822, in *Letters*, II, 136. This letter
should have been addressed to Cadell, but Hogg had misread the signature
on the letter from Cadell to which he was replying. See also Hogg's letter to
Cadell of 6 March 1822 in *Letters*, II, 150.

33. Cadell to Hogg, 16 February and 13 March 1822, in NLS, MS 2245, fols 76–
77 and 80–81 respectively.

34. Hogg to Blackwood, 27 October [1820], and to Constable, 8 February 1822,
in *Letters*, II, 55–56 and 136. Robert Hogg's involvement in the production
of the Second Series of *The Jacobite Relics of Scotland* is indicated in Hogg's
letters to Blackwood of 7, 16 and 27 October 1820 in *Letters*, II, 46, 51, and 55–
56. For a discussion of Robert Hogg's probable part in the production of
Hogg's surviving notebooks of songs for the two-volume collection see *The
Jacobite Relics of Scotland [First Series]*, ed. by Murray G. H. Pittock (S/SC,
2002), pp. xx–xxi, and *The Jacobite Relics of Scotland. Second Series*, ed. by Murray
G. H. Pittock (S/SC, 2003), pp. xi–xii. For further biographical information
about Robert Hogg see Gillian Hughes, 'The Ettrick Shepherd's Nephew',
SHW, 16 (2005), 20–35, and also *Letters*, III, 334–37.

35. Hogg to Constable, 8 February 1822, in *Letters*, II, 136.

36. There is an announcement of *Poetical Works* as 'This day are published' in
the *Edinburgh Evening Courant* of 13 June 1822. See also Hogg's letters to
Cadell of 6 March 1822 and to Blackwood of 11 April 1822 in *Letters*, II, 150–

51 and 159.

37. Hogg to Margaret Hogg, [8 May 1822], in *Letters*, II, 160–61.

38. See the *Edinburgh Monthly Review*, 5 (June 1821), 662–72 (p. 672). Hogg's anger on reading this review is expressed in letters to George Boyd of 27 June 1821 and to David Laing of 17 October 1822 (*Letters*, II, 94–95, 173).

39. For a list of Hogg's contributions to the *Edinburgh Magazine* see Douglas S. Mack, *Hogg's Prose: An Annotated Listing* (Stirling: The James Hogg Society, 1985), pp. 237–38, and Gillian Hughes, *Hogg's Verse and Drama: A Chronological Listing* (Stirling: The James Hogg Society, 1990), Items 164, 165, and 181–85. References for the previous appearances there of the three poems reprinted in the *Midsummer Night Dreams* volume of *Poetical Works* are as follows: 'The Mermaid. A Scottish Ballad', *Edinburgh Magazine*, 4 (May 1819), 400–01; 'Stanzas Addressed to a Comet', *Edinburgh Magazine*, 5 (July 1819), 30; 'The Powris of Moseke, Ane Rychte Plesant Ballaunt', *Edinburgh Magazine*, 9 (October 1821), 356–61.

40. Hogg to Archibald Constable, 8 February 1822 in *Letters*, II, 136. For Peter Garside's discussion of Hogg's 'old language' see *Queer Book*, pp. xv–xvi, where he remarks that the use of Hogg's 'ancient stile' creates 'a kind of "magic realism" not dissimilar to that now seen in postmodern fiction'.

41. Compare 'The Harper's Song' in *Mador*, pp. 23–27, with the equivalent place in the poem in *Poetical Works*, IV, 1–130 (pp. 28–29). The implications for the longer poem of Hogg's relocation of 'The Harper's Song' in the 1822 *Poetical Works* are discussed in James E. Barcus's Introduction to *Mador* (pp. xxxvii–xxxix), and in his 'Appendix 1: The Harper's Song', pp. 87–95.

42. See the entry for 'The Haunted Glen' in 'Note on the Texts' for a discussion of the abridgement for the 1822 *Poetical Works* of 'The Haunted Glen' in *Dramatic Tales*, 2 vols (Edinburgh: John Ballantyne; London: Longmans, 1817), II, 189–271.

43. For details of Hogg's composition of 'The Field of Waterloo' in 1815, and the reception it met with in Edinburgh shortly afterwards, see the entry for 'The Field of Waterloo' in the 'Note on the Texts' in the present volume.

44. Hogg's poem was originally published as the dedication to *The Brownie of Bodsbeck: And Other Tales* of 1818, and also served as the dedication to *Altrive Tales* of 1832. For further details see *Altrive Tales*, ed. by Gillian Hughes (S/SC, 2003), pp. 191–94.

45. See the second volume of *Poetical Works of the Ettrick Shepherd*, 5 vols (Glasgow: Blackie and Son, 1838–40), and *The Works of James Hogg: Poems and Life*, ed. by Thomas Thomson (Glasgow: Blackie and Son, 1865). Douglas Mack includes three poems from *Midsummer Night Dreams* ('Superstition', 'Verses Addressed to the Right Honourable Lady Anne Scott of Buccleuch' and 'The Mermaid') as consecutive items in a section of 'Miscellaneous Poems' in *James Hogg: Selected Poems* (Oxford: Clarendon Press, 1970), pp. 72–91, noting (pp. 165–66) that they are among the poems in the 1822 *Midsummer Night Dreams* volume of *Poetical Works*. David Groves reconstructs what he believes to have been the completed collection of 1814, consisting of *The Pilgrims of the Sun* with dedication, 'Connel of Dee', and 'Superstition' only, in *James Hogg: Selected Poems and Songs* (Edinburgh: Scottish Academic Press, 1986), pp. 31–95, with a textual note on pp. 211–14.

Introduction

Midsummer Night Dreams, the collection in the second volume of James Hogg's four-volume *Poetical Works* of 1822, reveals a poet sceptical of the social foundations of his world and troubled about the sources of his art. It reflects Hogg's worries about the impotence and corruption of long-trusted institutions and the fading vitality of his own imaginative roots. Although only three of the poems are set at specific times, and the others take place in some unidentifiable past, the entire volume is unified by a disquieting sense of loss and diminution. Hogg accompanies this pervasive melancholy with a compensatory search for redeeming alternatives, testing each of them within the contexts of various poems.

For Hogg, unlike many of his contemporary poets, the world after Waterloo provided little to praise. His discontent with things as they are permeates *Midsummer Night Dreams*, both in the occasional poems and in those that derive from no particular event. Even 'The Field of Waterloo', which one might expect to celebrate great victory, actually deconstructs military glory and undermines the widely-accepted ethic of sacrifice. Similarly, *The Pilgrims of the Sun* literally turns the cosmos upside down and, in so doing, discards received notions of God, redemption, sanctity, and good and evil. The established church appears in the person of a brutal and greedy monk, while the institutions of civil society—the law, the military, even the arts—are in like manner dismissed as devoid of purpose and merely self-serving.

Other less angry poems advocate resignation, a kind of wise passiveness in the face of hopeless aspiration. Lamenting the disappearance of 'What Scotland had, and now has not!' the poet reluctantly acquiesces in the reality of a modern Scotland bereft of its folkloric heritage.[1] Connel of Dee forsakes the joys and risks of marital bliss for the comforts of safety, plain water, and the beauties of nature; and no matter how touching her lamentation, the Mermaid will never be reunited with her mortal lover. At the end of 'The Powris of Moseke' Robene the mighty horn-player reluctantly abandons his dream of dancing with the fairy maidens but reserves his right to tell 'lees' in a lesser role as tavern minstrel.

As one might expect from the title, the poems of *Midsummer Night Dreams* invoke a world in which the bonds of civil society, both institutional and imaginative, are badly in need of reinvigoration. Theseus and Hippolyta, Puck and the young lovers, kingdom and wood, are all absent; but Hogg knew what he was doing when he named the collection.[2] As in Shakespeare's play, the stability of the political establishment draws its strength from the vitality of the folk imagination. When that tradition is placed at risk or rationalism shakes our sustaining contact with it, we must find alternative food for the imagination and the body politic alike.

1. 'Idiot Kings': 'The Field of Waterloo' and the Ideology of Sacrifice

Hogg's letter to Scott of 16 November [1815] shows that 'The Field of Waterloo' was written soon after the battle that is its subject:

> By the by since ever I saw you and heard your enthusiastic sentiments about the great events of late taken place in the world and of our honour and glory as a nation lately won I have been busily engaged with a poem on Waterloo as a small tribute to our heros which I think not unbecomes every British Bard. It has no connection with yours either in plan or matter but as far as I am gone I am rather pleased with it. With your approval I intend inscribing it to you in one single stanza acknowleding [*sic*] its source and my noble emulation of my master.[3]

(Hogg apparently changed his mind about dedicating it to Scott, or possibly Scott declined the honour.) However, there is no recorded instance of its publication until the 1822 *Poetical Works*, when Hogg inserted it toward the end of the second, or *Midsummer Night Dreams* volume, by which time it may have seemed slightly out-dated. At first sight 'The Field of Waterloo' seems to have little or nothing in common with the other *Midsummer Night Dreams* poems. In 1815–16, of course, everyone with any pretence to the name of poet wrote something on this subject, and most of them are execrable. Even Scott's offering is craven, and Southey's is an aesthetically as well as politically reprehensible celebration of imperialism. It could be that Hogg failed to publish his poem on 'The Field of Waterloo' in the immediate post-Napoleonic climate of triumphant jingoism because it calls into serious question so many of the values celebrated by the other poems and by the press.

In his essay 'Three Poets on Waterloo', Carl Woodring distinguishes between 'exploitation, which confirms an audience in its oversimplifications' and 'propaganda, which endeavors to increase the number of adherents to a given oversimplification'.[4] Woodring places Scott's and Southey's poems on Waterloo in the first category, and Byron's in the second. He does not deal with Hogg's; but according to his definitions, it is neither one nor the other. On the contrary, it expresses revulsion at the prevailing ideology of sacrifice and the immediate post-Waterloo glorification of Wellington and all things military, and it attempts to demythologise both of them.

The multi-media propaganda barrage accompanying the Napoleonic wars was extraordinarily thorough; it took the form of tracts, broadsheets, sermons, ballads, and caricatures. As early as 1793, William Windham, who became Secretary of War the following year, urged the House of Commons to involve all men in universal defence training: 'you must put the country in a situation in which its patriotic zeal, its native courage, its various and abundant energies may have a way to operate and produce their natural effects'.[5] Ten years later, passage of the Militia Service Bill elicited a huge outpouring of broadsheets, 'the earliest attempt at recruitment of active popular support for government and war by means of "mass" propaganda'.[6] The need to recruit enormous numbers of men led to ever-increasing onslaughts of propaganda, which defined patriotism as loyalty to the government as well as steadfast resistance to any change in the social order. Attempting to obscure both class and national differences, the propaganda focused on the commonality of constitutional blessings: 'In defence of his native land, an Englishman, a Scotchman, a Welshman, and an Irishman, are one and the same people', claimed a broadsheet from 'John Bull to Brother Patrick in Ireland'.[7] The Glasgow poet John Mayne pointedly invoked 'English, Scots, and Irishmen' in his bloody-minded 'Patriotic Address to the Inhabitants of the United Kingdom', warning his fellow citizens of three nations about the Napoleonic atrocities to come:

> Then, when the Land is all defil'd,
> He'll butcher woman, man and child—
> He'll turn your gardens to a wild—
> Your Courts to caves of misery![8]

Propaganda aimed at the mass audience stressed the shared benefits *all* British citizens stood to lose from revolution. It minimised class differences and emphasised that only the lowest of the low stood to profit from the destruction of historical continuity and social order. This was no time for the 'unrestrained pursuit of equality'.[9] A mock-epitaph on Napoleon in an 1814 broadside exemplifies this appeal:

BRITON!

Ere you pass by,
Kneel and thank thy God,
For all the Blessings of thy glorious Constitution;
Then return into the peaceful Bosom of the Family and continue
In the practice of those virtues
By which thy Ancestors
Have obtained the Favour of the Almighty.[10]

Propagandists appealed both to the pragmatic fear of invasion and to the more lofty ideology of sacrifice; motivated by love of country as supreme allegiance, the patriot would gladly choose to offer his own life in her cause.[11]

At the same time, the propaganda denigrated the French, constructing a national stereotype quite opposed to the traditional British strengths and virtues. Richard Mant's 'War Song' of 1803 begins with Bonaparte crowing in triumph:

Bow, Britons, bow the haughty head!
  Bend, Britons, bend the stubborn knee!
Own your ancient virtue fled,
  And know not that you once were free.
  Think not as your fathers thought;
  Speak no more, as Britons ought;
  Act no more the Britons' part,
  With valiant hand and honest heart;
  What indignation bids you feel,
  Dare not, dare not to reveal;[12]

Caricaturists, notably Gillray and Rowlandson, depicted the French as less-than-human creatures, often monkeys, who, having repudiated God, deserved no Christian mercy. Voltaire was regarded as the 'mastermind of universal atheism and pan-European revolution', and a copy of *Candide* within a sketch invariably signified depravity.[13] This demonised Other of the broadsheets and caricatures came to be represented as the morally-acceptable target for hatred and extermination. Who better to do it than the British, time-honoured guardians of law and order and Europe's providentially-designated deliverer? As invasion fears coalesced public opinion behind the wars, popular conservatism flourished as 'a spontaneous reaction to genuine and widespread fears of the consequences of [...] failing to resist French aggression'. Loyalist opinion thrived as long as it could be 'linked with the anarchy of the French revolution and the military aggression of Napoleon'.[14] Strangely enough, much of the propaganda had an oddly materialist flavour; some of it bolstered the standard appeals to British liberty by disdaining the supposed French diet of 'soupe maigre' in favour of the gustatory pleasures of roast beef and ale.

During the Napoleonic period, the chivalric model remained the accepted literary and public paradigm for war; it would continue to do so (witness Tennyson's 'The Charge of the Light Brigade' of 1854) until irretrievably shattered by the horrors of the Great War. Based upon an ideology of voluntary individual sacrifice in the service of a greater good—that of king, church, and constitution—the chivalric model privileged the ennobling experience of battle, which Hogg in his poem relegates to the merely instinctive self-defence of animals. The chivalric model necessarily evaded realism, both the brutal details of individual suffering in war and the unsettling questions of ultimate purpose. Wordsworth's 1816 sonnet 'Occasioned by the Battle of Waterloo' exemplifies this ideology of duty and willing sacrifice:

> Intrepid sons of Albion! not by you
> Is life despised; ah no, the spacious earth
> Ne'er saw a race who held, by right of birth,
> So many objects to which love is due:
> Ye slight not life—to God and Nature true;
> But death, becoming death, is dearer far,
> When duty bids you bleed in open war:
> Hence hath your prowess quelled that impious crew.
> Heroes!—for instant sacrifice prepared;
> Yet filled with ardour and on triumph bent
> 'Mid direst shocks of mortal accident—
> To you who fell, and you whom slaughter spared
> To guard the fallen, and consummate the event,
> Your Country rears this sacred Monument![15]

Hogg abhorred the abstraction of human suffering and the celebration of sacrifice which mark this sonnet and so many of the formulaic poems engendered by Waterloo. In Number IV of the *Lay Sermons* (1834) he laments the senselessness of war and the futility of sacrifice:

> Look at all the wars of Europe for hundreds of years, and you will see, that, after millions of human beings had been sacrificed, at the end all things were settled the same as when the war began, and the same boundaries remained to be peo-

pled anew.[16]

Hogg similarly deplores the insidious propaganda which blinds us to war's 'barbarous acts of destruction':

> We never stop to consider how horrible these scenes are, because what we know of them we generally learn at an age when the mind receives ideas implicitly, admires every thing that appears great, and never loses those early impressions, which remain indelibly fixed in it for ever.[17]

Granted, Hogg wrote these passages many years later, and their quality of righteous indignation is absent from the earlier poem. Nevertheless, to a considerable extent even in 'The Field of Waterloo' he deconstructed the ideology of heroic sacrifice, one reason, perhaps, why his dying hero fails to grasp that he is dying until, two-thirds of the way through the narrative, he recalls an ominous prophecy.

Hogg's 'The Field of Waterloo' differs in several respects from other versions by major poets. Most obviously, while the others made their pilgrimages to Belgium within a year of the battle, Hogg never visited the site. While Scott and Byron meditate upon the scene and Southey entangles himself in dream-vision, Hogg employs dramatic form, structuring most of his poem as a conversation. He eschews the privileged positions of the other personae and employs a narrator of decidedly humble origins.

Early in the poem, Hogg clearly conveys his low opinion of the thought-control offensive that accompanied the French Revolution in Britain. Though clad in regimental tartan, his hero is a Borderer who hails from a place that combines both pastoral beauty and 'warlike fame':

> That Border land, so nobly blent
> With hill, and dale of green extent,
> With camp, and tower, and battlement. (ll. 31–33)

Most notably, however, this is a place resistant to propaganda:

> That is a land, full well 'tis known,
> Where cottage maid, and matron brown,
> Where shepherd boy, or peasant elf,
> Reads, thinks, and judges for himself. (ll. 34–37)

Our hero has enlisted in the army, not to battle for king, country, and constitution, but in response to unrequited love.

> There had our soldier spent his youth,
> In ways of happiness and truth,
> Till scorn cast from a maiden's eye
> Drove him in distant fields to die. (ll. 44–47)

Unless he has been later consoled by a second lover who is the mother of his child, he has fathered a child out of wedlock and fled the scene. He is humanly imperfect, and his character may reinforce the poem's clear link between the war's devastation and 'human guilt'.

Hogg structures the body of the poem as a debate on war, honour, and sacrifice among three voices: the dying Borderer, the fiercely patriotic Russian veteran of the battles of Borodino and Moscow, and the Prussian officer, an 'Enlightenment' stoic who disdains both petty nationalism and traditional religion in favour of the voice of reason. The brave but not-very-reflective Scottish soldier recites the usual catalogue of battlefield horrors and minimises his own role in the fray:

> E'er since I bore the onset's shock,
> And was involved in fire and smoke,
> I've had no knowledge what hath been,
> Nor thought, nor mind—a mere machine.
> I only viewed it as my meed,
> To stand or fall, as Heaven decreed;
> For honour's cause to do my best,
> And to the Almighty leave the rest. (ll. 154–61)

Having accepted the ideology of sacrifice, or 'honour's cause', he has been reduced to 'a mere machine' by the fog of war. Although he contemplates glorious future narratives of 'What heroes fell, what lions fought' (l. 182), the soldier's own mechanistic metaphor implicitly deprecates the distinction of his behaviour. The Russian attributes the conquest of Bonaparte to his own countrymen and to God; while the Prussian, 'of Voltaire's and of Frederick's school', ignores national loyalties and credits victory to 'the love of freedom, given | To man as his prerogative,–' (ll. 413, 426–27). Hogg grants to the Prussian, with his teleological faith in human progress, this contemptuous dismissal of Napoleon:

> He came with words of specious guise,
>   The hearts of men were on his side.
> O he might conquer idiot kings,
>   These bars in nature's onward plan!
> But fool is he the yoke that flings

O'er the unshackled soul of man! (ll. 432–37)

Thus, in the colloquy that composes the body of the poem, it is the
foreigner, the enlightenment sceptic, the disciple of the despised
Voltaire, who apparently speaks for the poet. The dying prayer of
the Scottish soldier provides a sweet and touching but conventional
afterthought, the discourse one might expect from this brave admirer
of 'doughty deeds' and 'honour's cause'.

Ultimately, however, Hogg retreats from iconoclasm, and his poem
on 'The Field of Waterloo', like so many of the others, becomes an
affirmation of the status quo, what Gilbert and Gubar see in the
aftermath of a later war as a reinscription of patriarchy and of the
male-dominated community.[18] Only in death and only as an
unthreatening guardian spirit may the hero return to his humble
Border origins, somewhat incongruously described in impeccable
standard English. His prayer is irreproachably orthodox, pronounc-
ing both his faith in God's providential plan and in the ideology of
sacrifice Hogg had earlier questioned:

> The victory is thine, we nothing abate,
> But thou gavest it the good as well as the great;
> And their names are registered with thee
> Who have bled for the cause of liberty. (ll. 573–76)

In the Borderer's prayer, the questioning voices fall silent, the estab-
lished order prevails, and Hogg evades political statement, supplant-
ing the carnage of Waterloo, not with the renewal of nature noted by
both Scott and Southey, but with the even-less-threatening iconic peace
of mother and child. The poem concludes on a humanely generative
rather than a sacrificial note, and it is the 'stoic Prussian' who has the
last word, even if that last word consists of the sceptic's wistful yearning
to believe:

> "What's this?" said he, "who can conceive?
> I cannot fathom, nor believe
> The substance of this Christian faith;
> But 'tis a steadfast hold in death!
> I never saw its hideous door
> Entered with such a mien before!" (ll. 691–96)

Unfortunately, however, this is not absolutely the last word. Hogg
elects to leave unsettled the debate among scepticism, nationalism,
and faith, and he withdraws to the safe and familiar ground of Bor-
der legend. The narrator confirms the presence of the soldier's spirit,
'Sent there to roam the lonely wild, | To guard the mother and the

child' (ll. 725–26); and the reader is left with a pleasing *frisson*, perhaps, but also with a disappointing evasion of difficult issues which the poem raises but declines to resolve.

2. The Anthropology of Pilgrimage and *The Pilgrims of the Sun*

The lead poem of the *Midsummer Night Dreams* collection, *The Pilgrims of the Sun*, first published in December 1814, also expresses uncertainties, in this case relating rather to religious than political orthodoxy. The four-part narrative presents a jarring *mélange* of forms and styles written within the frame of a traditional dream-vision. A rhymed gothic tale at the end can be felt as a relief from the inconsistent theological and political pronouncements of Parts First through to Third. Formally Hogg draws upon a wide but seemingly arbitrary array of styles and models: at various times the narrative voice reverts to his 'hill-harp', appeals to the Biblical harp of David, and invokes the muse of the 'Imperial England' of Dryden and Pope, while promising to endow the latter with a distinctly Scottish flavour. Behind it all reverberates the voice of *Paradise Lost*, or at least Hogg's version thereof, rife with elaborate Miltonic similes and a panoramic view of a fantastic cosmology.

   The poem begins in iambic tetrameter quatrains with Hogg's heroine, Mary Lee, who, like the Kilmeny of *The Queen's Wake*, is beautiful, virginal, and humble before God:

> On form so fair, or face so mild,
>   The rising sun did never gleam;
> On such a pure untainted mind
>   The dawn of truth did never beam.
>   (Part First, ll. 21–24)

A mind oblivious to the 'dawn of truth' is, perhaps, a dubious compliment; but then Mary Lee indulges herself in 'books of deep divinity' (Part First, l. 34), which render her severely sceptical of received religious truths. Tormented by doubt, she is confronted by a white-robed apparition, a handsome young spirit called Cela, who guides her on a heavenly journey. As Mary Lee's apparently-dead body is left behind, the 'naked form' (l. 79) of her soul is newly clothed, and she and Cela ascend on a scenic flight. Along the way, they lean on a rainbow to watch the sunrise and eventually abandon the 'firmament of air' for space, a realm where there 'was no up, there was no down' (ll. 251–53). They travel toward the sun, the seat of divinity,

passing several worlds on their journey, most notably a green planet
of youthful immortality, similar in climate to a mild Scottish summer
but dissimilar in that it is totally devoid of churches. Mary asks Cela
if they might stay, but he demurs; they cannot remain there:

> Thou art a visitant beloved
>   Of God, and every holy one;
> And thou shalt travel on with me,
>   Around the spheres, around the sun,
> To see what maid hath never seen,
>   And do what maid hath never done.
>   (Part First, ll. 283–88)

Having thus promised the full cosmological itinerary, the narrative
voice accompanies them as far as the sun and then turns to himself.
Hanging up his 'hill-harp' as incompatible with what is to follow, in
its place he invokes the 'ethereal timbrel' of the Psalmist (l. 313).

Hogg switches to blank verse in Part Second. Appealing to the
'Harp of Jerusalem' he ponders how to find a style appropriate to
his exalted material—the answer: keep it soft and simple, 'Then will
the harp of David rise with thee' (Part Second, l. 14). Imitating with
varying success the descriptive techniques of *Paradise Lost*, Hogg po-
sitions his travellers on the periphery of the sun to watch 'the mo-
tioned universe' revolve around it. This is a Miltonic cosmos; the
planets hang from the sun, the seat of divinity, from whence the
enthroned God can observe the minutest detail of Creation. Mary
experiences an array of new and delightful sensations, suggesting a
sort of spiritual deflowering if not a physical one. She believes she
sees the earth, a world 'far more extensive 'tis and fair | Than all the
rest' (Part Second, ll. 90–91). But Cela upbraids her provincialism
and her fancied view of Ettrick and Yarrow; earth is actually 'yon
cloudy spot [...] a sphere | Unseemly and forbidding' (ll. 137, 141–
42).

Still somewhat conventional in her theological assumptions, Mary
enquires if the beings inhabiting all these other worlds have fallen
and been redeemed. Once again Cela corrects her: 'Thou talkest
thou know'st not what' (l. 157). He deflects her query, promising
more enlightenment anon, but responds for the moment with a doc-
trine of human-centred Divine beneficence:

> This truth conceive, that God must ever deal
> With men as men—Those things by him decreed,
> Or compassed by permission, ever tend
> To draw his creatures, whom he loves, to goodness;

> For he is all benevolence, and knows
> That in the paths of virtue and of love
> Alone, can final happiness be found.
> (Part Second, ll. 160–66)

To replace the doctrine of redemption through Christ, Cela offers a
vaguely Eastern series of thousand-year incarnations, each one bring-
ing a being closer to heaven. At this point the travellers are still on
the periphery of the sun, and they proceed to travel inward, first
toward the dwellings of the saints and martyrs, then of the angels,
and ultimately of God. This is a politically correct heaven, and Mary
is suitably impressed by its diversity:

> Child that I was, ah! could my stinted mind
> Harbour the thought, that the Almighty's love,
> Life, and salvation, could to single sect
> Of creatures be confined, all his alike!
> (Part Second, ll. 233–36)

The narrator then proposes a teleological vision of 'all created na-
ture' in which the hierarchy of beings 'all were in progression–mov-
ing on | Still to perfection', a model for the human soul 'hoping still |
In something onward!' (ll. 249, 253–54, 255–56). Here the essence
of humanity seems to be spiritual aspiration; the soul

> shall hope, and yearn,
> And grasp, and gain, for times and ages, more,
> Than thought can fathom, or proud science climb!
> (Part Second, ll. 258–60)

As Mary and Cela approach the pyramidal meeting hall of heaven,
she is overcome by a glorious angelic chorus; Cela transports her
back to the periphery, where, having regained consciousness, Mary
and her guide converse with the saints about the 'ways of God with
man' (l. 378). Leaning on 'the brink of heaven' (l. 391), this blessed
damosel notices a wandering world, long ago cut loose by God,
hurled into the void, and now returned as a comet. Such, Mary learns,
will some day be the fate of earth.

Having indulged his Miltonic longings, Hogg drops blank verse
in favour of iambic pentameter couplets for Part Third. In a presci-
ently post-colonial entreaty, he invokes the harp of Imperial Eng-
land–'Well may'st thou lend what erst was not thine own' (Part
Third, l. 8)–and promises to transport it to a Border setting:

> Thou shalt be strung where green-wood never grew,

> Swept by the winds, and mellowed by the dew.
>   (Part Third, ll. 21–22)

Cela and Mary then embark on a tour of the created cosmos. Each
world, Cela explains, is inhabited by human souls. The planets fur-
thest from the sun are 'nurseries', and souls progress through vari-
ous worlds toward 'perfection'; to understand this is to understand
'the ways of God' (ll. 96–97). The two pilgrims visit planets popu-
lated by ever-young lovers, ruinous warriors, egotistical poets, un-
scrupulous lawyers, hypocritical clerics, and vain beaux and belles.
While Cela's opinion of most of these souls is decidedly negative,
his angry pacifism is particularly noteworthy:

> What is the soldier but an abject fool—
> A king's, a tyrant's, or a statesman's tool!
> Some patriot few there are—but ah! how rare!
> For vanity or interest still is there;
> Or blindfold levity directs his way—
> A licensed murderer that kills for pay!
>   (Part Third, ll. 323–28)

Finally Cela and Mary look in on the 'downward realms' (l. 391), a
region of homelessness where the wicked wander.

   Leaving nothing to chance, Cela pronounces the poem's theologi-
cal dictum:

> Therefore no more let doubts thy mind enthral,
> Through nature's range thou see'st a God in all:
>   (Part Third, ll. 399–400)

Mary has learned her lesson well:

> By all, the earth-born virgin plainly saw
> Nature's unstaid, unalterable law;
> That human life is but the infant stage
> Of a progressive, endless pilgrimage
> To woe, or state of bliss, by bard unsung,
> At that eternal fount where being sprung.
>   (Part Third, ll. 405–10)

Finally at the end of Part Third, the voyagers return to Mary's home
to find her mother in mourning. Cela then leads Mary to the church-
yard of old Lindeen, the 'hoary pile' or 'hoary fane', and leaves her
in a freshly-dug grave, but with the promise, 'Soon we shall meet,
and never part again' (l. 454). Thus Part Third, by far the weakest
part of the narrative, ends.

Part Fourth, written in tetrameter couplets, recurs to the search for Mary just after she has gone missing. Her body is discovered and buried, and then her grave is robbed by an evil monk. Just as he attempts to cut off her finger, her soul returns from its wanderings, her body arises, and the grave-robber is permanently deprived of his wits. This part represents Hogg at his tale-telling best, evoking terror through inexorable detail, suspending the disbelief of the happily-complicit reader. Wrapped in her bloody shroud, Mary knocks on the door of her home as all its inhabitants successively keel over. She recounts her wanderings to her mother, but at this point the narrator inserts a disclaimer; he has merely related the tale and can vouch only for the part that 'relates to earth' (Part Fourth, l. 261).

Although the Borderers believe Mary's story, the priests may discredit its implicit egalitarianism (since 'up and down' can refer to more than the effects of gravity):

> For the mass-men said, with fret and frown,
> That through all space it well was known,
> By moon, or stars, the earth or sea,
> An up and down there needs must be:
>
> (Part Fourth, ll. 266–69)

Mary ignores them and thrives. In harmony with nature, she worships the sun. More beautiful than ever, she politely rejects all suitors until the appearance of Cela in the guise of one Hugo of Norroway, a peaceful harper and shepherd who shuns war. Hugo's ecological consciousness, however, leaves much to be desired: he deforests Ettrick for grazing land, apparently with the Ettrick Shepherd's blessing. Hugo and Mary marry, have children, and live happily until old age. Mary dies a grandmother and is borne to her grave by '[f]ive gallant sons' (l. 430). Hugo mysteriously disappears, rumoured to have been buried by fairies, and Hogg concludes with a graceful nod to the memory of his patroness, the Duchess of Buccleuch, who died in 1814.

Hogg's title is not an afterthought. He summons the Biblical admonition that we are strangers and pilgrims in this world, that pilgrimage is the defining condition of humankind. For Hogg, as for Bunyan, the metaphor suggests inevitable suffering, struggle, and anxiety in a world of mutability. As a good pilgrim, Mary Lee resists the temptation of *curiositas*, an unseemly concern with the things and people of the temporal realm, to focus on the ways of God.[19] For her, as for all good pilgrims, the pilgrimage functions as a ritual of transformation, operating through myths which 'relate how one state of affairs became another', for example, the formation of cosmos from chaos.[20] Mary returns home from her cosmic journey to raise children and grandchildren in keeping with the double focus of pilgrimage, first on the spiritual value of temporary withdrawal from the world and then on 'the restoration of stability and order' that ensues upon return.[21] *Peregrinatio* implies a destination and a circular journey; in contrast to the wandering *viator*, the pilgrim first turns away from the world and then returns to it.[22] Unlike traditional pilgrims, however, Mary has no sense of purpose or direction and remains the passive wayfarer rather than the determined pilgrim. Nor does she return with a visible 'trace' in hand (usually a badge or cheap trinket), a repository of the holiness of the shrine. Like Bunyan's Christian, she receives her edification neither through ineffable presence nor perceived miracle but through verbal discourse. Suitably, then, her first conscious act is narration.

Among anthropologists, Victor and Edith Turner have engaged in the most extensive studies of pilgrimage. They argue that pilgrimage is a liminoid (or transitional) experience involving, first, loss of individual attributes and status, followed by the formation of 'communitas' or a bond transcending normal social classifications. This sense of 'communitas' enables the individual reception of sacred knowledge and translates into mythic signifiers the common categories of culture and society.[23] In this experience of 'exteriorized mysticism' (p. 7), the initiand enters 'a new, deeper level of existence than he has known in his accustomed milieu' (p. 8). He or she attains temporary 'liberation from profane social structures that are symbiotic with a specific religious system' (p. 9). A pilgrim, then, separates himself from the mundane elements of his faith in order to confront its basic elements in a faraway place, returning only after 'a spiritual step forward' (p. 15).

Toward the end of the pilgrimage, symbolic structures—'religious buildings, pictorial images, statuary and sacralized features of the topography'—circumscribe this new-found freedom from profane categories (p. 10). Hence in Part Second Mary only *thinks* she sees the Eildon hills and Yarrow valley from the edge of the sun, but by the end of Part Third the familiar landscape forcefully reasserts itself:

> When these wild wanderings all were past and done,
> Just in the red beam of the parting sun,
> Our pilgrims skimmed along the light of even,
> Like flitting stars that cross the nightly heaven,
> And lighting on the verge of Phillip plain,

They trode the surface of the world again.
(Part Third, ll. 411–16)

Fittingly, Part Third concludes with poor Mary buried alive beside old Lindeen, the church structure both literal and symbolic which exemplifies all the errors revealed in the course of her journey.

The Turners find 'something inveterately populist, anarchical, even anticlerical, about pilgrimages' in keeping with their nature as liminoid experience (p. 32). Some pilgrimages even approximate ceremonies of national identity, as in the Purgatory of Saint Patrick at Loch Derg in Ireland. Obviously by Chaucer's time, pilgrimage had become inextricably intertwined with tourism and, as such, with the reinforcement of national and ethnic identities.[24] Thus the reassertion of Hogg's highly localised imagination in the traditional Border tale of Part Fourth does not jolt the reader as much as it might. Mary Campbell notes the 'scenic emptiness' of medieval pilgrimage narratives, in that landscape becomes a place where someone did or said something; geography is historicised and 'description then comes in the form of narration'.[25] Although Hogg fills his poem with elaborate descriptions of both feelings and scenery, he deftly captures this material emptiness upon Mary's return to Ettrick, where at first she remembers nothing of her soul's voyage through the extra-terrestrial landscape. However, she comes home to a very familiar place, as well-known and domesticated as the other had been exotic. Despite the mad monk and the mind-forg'd manacles of the clerics of Carelha', the traditional return home of the pilgrimage reinforces Hogg's nationalist and theological agenda. Alan Morinis stresses that pilgrimage 'reflects the social and cultural environment that generates and sustains it'.[26] This expedition, then, has been a national and cultural construct all along, and the peculiar form of gradualist perfectibility it preaches clearly springs from the same doctrinal matrix which will bring forth Hogg's justified sinner.

By furnishing Mary with a guide, Hogg places his poem even more firmly in the pilgrimage tradition. Throughout the journey, Mary remains an outsider but not merely a passive gazer. Like Augustine, Dante, and Bunyan, Hogg provides an interpreter 'to tie the experiences and episodes along the journey into a unity'.[27] However, the goal of their pilgrimage, traditionally associated with an identifiable individual, remains impersonal, unspecified, and thus unreachable. Cela promises Mary, 'What thou misconstruest I shall well explain' (Part Third, l. 76), but unfortunately overindulges his pedagogical inclination to verge upon the tedious. The poem's *longeurs*, then, occur when Hogg forgets that the insights of pilgrimage must be experienced, rather than merely processed.

Although Peter beseeches pilgrims to 'abstain from fleshly lusts, which war against the soul' (I Peter 2. 11), Hogg, like Dante, endows his interpreter with strong erotic attraction. Incarnated in Part Fourth as Hugo of Norroway—the outlander, the handsome hero, and the only man capable of winning Mary's affections—Cela underscores the essential earthiness of this pilgrimage. His eroticism functions as the 'trace' of the pilgrimage, the 'phenomenon of an invisible reality made visible in the world', the magnetism of the shrine acquired by the pilgrim and carried home to render change in the community.[28] Although this change would appear to function primarily for Mary's benefit—her fulfilment is very earthly indeed—her spirit retains a beneficent influence upon the folk:

> And whenever that beauteous shade was seen
> To visit the walks of the Forest green,
> The joy of the land ran to excess,
> For they knew that it boded them happiness!
> Peace, love, and truth, for ever smiled
> Around that genius of the wild.
>   (Part Fourth, ll. 472–77)

Despite the unorthodox theology, Hogg constructed his poem of cosmic pilgrimage along very traditional lines. The conventional pilgrimage moves towards the sacred centre, in numinous terms the spring of holiness, in cultural terms the origin of the constructed social order. The power of the centre (or shrine) attracts pilgrims as a source of blessing, enlightenment, spiritual transformation, and healing. The essence of that power, however, is necessarily Other—indescribable, incomprehensible, unattainable. So the pilgrim first ascends, geographically and spiritually, from the periphery towards the centre and then inevitably returns.[29] In this it resembles Eliot's 'Little Gidding', another poem about 'the spirit unappeased and peregrine', Hogg leaves Mary Lee knowing that 'the end of all our exploring | Will be to arrive where we started | And know the place for the first time'.[30]

3. Hogg and the Uses of Enchantment
in *Midsummer Night Dreams*

Although it is possible that Hogg included some of the poems in the *Midsummer Night Dreams* volume of his 1822 *Poetical Works* in order to make up the required length of the volume, the gathering is by no means arbitrary. The collection as a whole constitutes an elegy for the lost folklore of Scotland and a search for a viable alternative.

The story of the fairies' departure is at least as old as the Wife of Bath's tale:

> IN th'olde dayes of the king Arthour,
> Of which that Britons speken greet honour,
> Al was this land fulfild of fayerye.
> The elf-queen, with hir joly companye,
> Daunced ful ofte in many a grene mede;
> This was the olde opinion, as I rede.
> I speke of manye hundred yeres ago;
> But now can no man see none elves mo.
> For now the grete charitee and prayeres
> Of limitours and othere holy freres,
> That serchen every lond and every streem,
> As thikke as motes in the sonne-beem,
> Blessinge halles, chambres, kitchenes, boures,
> Citees, burghes, castels, hye toures,
> Thropes, bernes, shipnes, dayeryes,
> This maketh that ther been no fayeryes.[31]

While the Wife of Bath's account seems primarily designed to scold the Friar for his presumptuous interruption rather than to present historical fact, the traditional story in Scotland of 'The Fairies' Farewell' carried considerably more popular credence. It exists in multiple versions, but the particulars remain consistent:

> ABOUT the year 1850 a Galloway roadman refused point-blank to obey the County Council's order to widen the highway at a certain point between Glenluce and Newton Stewart by cutting down an ancient thorn reputed to be fairy property. Authority was tolerant, and the tree remained, standing well out on the road and impeding traffic for another seventy years, a witness to the fear of uncanny reprisals.
>
> But Galloway was exceptional. In less isolated parts of the Lowlands the fairies' day was done by the late eighteenth century. Brooding on their disappearance, an old woman came to the regretful conclusion that 'there was sae much preaching, and folk reading the Bible that they got frichted', and no doubt this was one reason, though the Reformation seems scarcely to have daunted them [...]. It was with the agricultural revolution that the hour struck: their dancing rings ploughed, their green hills sown with grain, their existence

not so much denied as ignored.

> Where the scythe cuts and the sock rives
> Hae done wi' fairies and bee dykes ...

It was total defeat; and yet the fairies contrived to surrender on their own terms, staging a ceremonial departure, widely observed and pinned firmly to the margin of history by a date which—apart from Galloway—is roughly the same throughout Scotland. Whatever took place, or was imagined, round about the year 1790, descriptions of it recorded as far apart as Nithsdale and Caithness are detailed, vivid and surprisingly alike. Invested with a curious atmosphere of mystery and regret, it is known as the Fairies' Farewell.[32]

Hogg's version of this traditional tale comes in the ballad of 'Old David' in *The Queen's Wake*, which tells how the fairies deserted Ettrick, depriving its bard of inspiration:

> O, Ettrick! shelter of my youth!
> Thou sweetest glen of all the south!
> Thy fairy tales, and songs of yore,
> Shall never fire my bosom more.[33]

While this regret may seem at first merely formulaic Romantic nostalgia, it looms large in the artistic self-consciousness of a writer who distinguished himself from Scott as 'the king o' the mountain and fairy school'.[34] The departure of the fairies, and of those who communed and celebrated with them, provides the unifying theme of *Midsummer Night Dreams* and accounts for the tone of wistful diminution in so many of its poems.

Two theoretical texts illuminate this collection. The first is Bruno Bettelheim's *The Uses of Enchantment*, which can offer an alternative reading of *The Pilgrims of the Sun*.[35] This poem has been interpreted above as a pilgrimage narrative, but Bettelheim's study of 'the meaning and importance of fairy tales' seems to offer an additional dimension. He argues that fairy tales teach children that struggle is unavoidable, 'that the source of much that goes wrong in life is due to our very own natures', and that nonetheless a happy ending is attainable (p. 7). Fairy tales, then, encourage healthy development in children, helping to overcome their separation anxieties and fears of growing up by representing the value of going out into the world and establishing independent identity. The fairy-story looks forward to the child's development; it 'gives hope for the future, and holds out the promise of a happy ending' (p. 26). This theory can equally well be applied to the developing nation or culture.

Pilgrims of the Sun follows this pattern. Its heroine, Mary Lee, has led a protected life untouched by doubt, but she begins to question her faith when she reads works of theology. Mary Lee's spiritual guide, Cela, forcibly removes her from the familiar and compels her to venture forth with him into the cosmos, where she undergoes a mysterious transformation and attains a radically widened perspective. Only then may she return to Ettrick to be reunited with her mother, to raise a family, and to shower beneficent influence upon her neighbours. Similarly, according to Bettelheim, the child finds solace in fairy tales when he first doubts his own immortality and the permanence of his bond to his parents. However, the fairy tale promise of living happily ever after must be earned by trial and error and sometimes even by terror. In like manner, Mary's spiritual guide and vision of cosmic harmony are metamorphosed into domestic bliss and temporal paradise, but not until her pilgrimage out of and back into the familiarity of the body entails dismay and even fear.

In her excellent book, *At the Bottom of the Garden*, Diane Purkiss notes that fairies are generally associated with borders; they are liminal creatures linked to boundaries in space or time or to moments of transition.[36] Mircea Eliade connects fairy tales to initiation rituals, rites of passage from which a new self is born or attains a higher level of existence.[37] Thus fairy tales and pilgrimage narratives share in common that they are accounts of transformation with a promised happy ending. As the first and longest poem in the *Midsummer Night Dreams* volume, *Pilgrims of the Sun* defines the problem posed by many of the other component poems. Given a culture in transition, as exemplified in the story of 'The Fairies' Farewell', how does the poet respond to an apparently diminished earth and a lost frame of reference? In *Midsummer Night Dreams* Hogg explores several possible solutions.

While the conventions of fairy tales and pilgrimage narratives assure happy endings, other poems in *Midsummer Night Dreams* are less sanguine about possible resolutions to the cultural crisis at the centre of this volume. The second theoretical text that illuminates Hogg's dilemma is Fredric Jameson's 1988 essay on 'The Vanishing Mediator'.[38] In his commentary on Max Weber, Jameson describes Romanticism 'as a coming to consciousness of some fundamental loss in shock and rage, a kind of furious rattling of the bars of the prison, a helpless attempt to recuperate lost being by posing and assuming one's fatality in "interesting" ways'. The soul of the Romantic writer 'register[s] its shock and distress at the new and barren world in which it finds itself' (p. 7), and 'It is as though the meaningfulness of the world remained intact only so long as some portion of that world [...] hung beyond human reach' (p. 10). For Hogg, that portion of the world is the traditional folklore of rural Scotland, which had sacralised each lowland hill and glen with tales of supernatural inhabitants. Although he candidly acknowledges this body of charmed wisdom as superstition, the poems of *Midsummer Night Dreams* mourn its vanishing and interrogate the implications of its absence in a disenchanted world.

The dispossession Hogg laments affects both individual creative momentum and the sense of national identity. Once again Jameson's essay is apposite. He identifies Calvinism's 'otherworldly thisworldliness', as, in a sense, a 'vanishing mediator' which permits the 'rationalization of innerworldly life' (p. 25) and demands that mythic systems whose usefulness is over be jettisoned. Enlightenment scepticism further dwindled the influence of the old lore, and it is this combined erosion which Hogg deplores in 'Superstition':

> Those were the times for holiness of frame;
> Those were the days when fancy wandered free;
> That kindled in the soul the mystic flame,
> And the rapt breathings of high poesy;
> Sole empress of the twilight–Woe is me!
> That thou and all thy spectres are outworn;
> For true devotion wanes away with thee,
> All thy delirious dreams are laughed to scorn,
> While o'er our hills has dawned a cold saturnine morn.
>
> (ll. 91–99)

While Hogg freely avows that superstition occasionally brought what he delicately called its 'attendant ills' in the form of witchcraft trials and other mass hysteria, on the whole he deems its influence gracious upon both the credulous and the creative. This poem is a strange one. Its carefully wrought Spenserian stanzas seem highly inconsistent with the dirge for a wilder mode of spirituality, but the chosen form does suggest a certain alienation of the Scottish bard from his native matter and proper *métier*. Under the rubric of 'Superstition', Hogg invokes both fairy lore and pre-Reformation Christianity in a strange *mélange* that, he would have us believe, once graciously interceded between the simple people of Scotland and their harsh environment. The 'sceptic leveller' of rationalism and the 'grovelling creed' of Calvinism, however, have dispossessed both them and the 'visionary bard' of their rightful inherited mediators.

The narratives of *Midsummer Night Dreams*, then, explore an imaginatively diminished earth. In 'The Mermaid', a traditional ballad that approaches perfection, the mermaid's song poignantly asserts unending love in a declining mortal world:

> In domes beneath the water-springs
> No end hath my sojourning;
> An' to this land of fading things
> Far hence be my returning;
>
> For spirits now have left the deep,
> Their long last farewell taking:
> Lie still, my love, lie still an' sleep,
> Thy day is near the breaking!
>
> When my loved flood from fading day
> No more its gleam shall borrow,
> Nor heath-fowl from the moorland grey
> Bid the blue dawn good-morrow;
>
> The Mermaid o'er thy grave shall weep,
> Without one breath of scorning:
> Lie still, my love, lie still an' sleep!
> And fare thee well till morning! (ll. 89–104)

In 'this land of fading things', the departure of the spirits is akin to the fairies' farewell, the reluctant bequest of a forsaken earth to its mortal inhabitants, who must now content themselves with only its natural embellishments.

Even the two comic narratives of *Midsummer Night Dreams* share this theme of loss in a world now deprived of its natural and supernatural magic. 'The Powris of Moseke', the funniest poem in the volume, is an amusing tale of a blind horn-player who seeks to summon the fairies. Hogg comically juxtaposes Blynde Robene's fantasies of Elfinland with the distinctly more earthly realities of a child's empty stomach and an angry bull, who mistakes the horn-player's discordant notes for the mating call of 'ane kindlye cowe | Rowtyng for gentil lofe' (ll. 299–300). All finally ends well, the child consumes 'his morning broz' (l. 519), and deceived Robin persists in believing that he has successfully invoked the fairies and banished the devil. Hogg's concluding 'Moralitas', however, playfully but firmly disowns the deception and admonishes the reader to provide himself with more mundane consolations:

Och, nefer bydde ane bad mynstrelle playe,
  Nor seye his mynstrelsye,
Onlesse your wyne be in your hande,
  And your ladye in your ee.

Ane singil say will set him on,
  And simpil is the spelle;
But he nefer will gif ofer againe,
  Not for the deuill himselle. (ll. 521–28)

In 'Connel of Dee' the hormonally-driven protagonist forsakes
his wholesome Deeside home for an alluring and wealthy but bloody-
minded bride, whose supernatural mode of existence is readily ob-
vious to everyone but him. In classic fairy tale fashion, the callow
youth endures a harrowing ordeal to learn that magical luxury and
bewitching sex are pricey and inadequate substitutes for natural sim-
plicity. Connel's tale humorously affirms the uses of enchantment as
Bettelheim describes them. His rite of passage from a sheltered fam-
ily circle into and out of the menacing fairy tale realm teaches him to
celebrate gowans and laverocks in a world unthreatened, but also
unadorned, by the peculiar, the strange, and the mysteriously desir-
able. Connel survives, leaving the reader with a smile as well as the
sense that something has been undeniably forfeited.

In the last poem of the volume, the 'Verses Addressed to the Right
Honourable Lady Anne Scott of Buccleuch', Hogg once again takes
up the idea of irrevocably lost inspiration. Here he conflates the
absent fairy lore with a bygone patriarchalism anachronistically
representative of national identity. It is an equation one would think
more congenial to Scott than to Hogg. The poem, however, addresses
the daughter of his patron, the Duke of Buccleuch, which perhaps
explains its somewhat surprising version of the theme of bardic dis-
possession. As in *The Queen's Wake*, Hogg wistfully recalls the folktales
imprinted upon his childhood:

I learned them in the lonely glen,
The last abodes of living men;
Where never stranger came our way
By summer night or winter day;
Where neighbouring hind or cot was none;
Our converse was with Heaven alone,
With voices through the cloud that sung,
And brooding storms that round us hung. (ll. 49–56)

Here this body of knowledge somehow becomes transmuted into

what Hogg aggrandises as the 'patriarchal days of yore' (l. 210).
Lamenting that contemporary Scotland no longer enjoys the natural
supernaturalism that once permeated the landscape, Hogg nonethe-
less conjures it at the end of the poem in a cosy domestic vignette, in
which he venerates 'A family's and a nation's ties– | Bonds which the
Heavens alone can rend, | With Chief, with Father, and with Friend'
(ll. 213–15). Simultaneously poignant and servile, and with no trace
of his usual irony, Hogg fantasises replacing 'what Scotland had'
(i.e. the living folk memory) with a model of national coherence
based on a complex of allegiances, ancestral ties and loyalties which
surely he realised was similarly absent, if, indeed, it ever existed at
all.

    This peculiar scene at Bowhill constructs an unfortunate conclu-
sion to *Midsummer Night Dreams*. The collection has explored the uses
of enchantment and mourned its passing. The human heart requires
a mediator between itself and the temporality and inexplicability of
the world, a necessity that had been nicely met for Hogg by the tradi-
tional lore of the Borders, what he calls in this poem 'What Scotland
had, and now has not!' (l. 150). His reluctance to accept the finality
of the fairies' farewell is almost palpable. They and all they repre-
sent have well served the Bard of Ettrick. Now he must find an alter-
native, and the class-based one that he seems to propose here at the
end is singularly unsatisfactory. Ensconced in the aristocratic par-
lour at Bowhill, the poor shepherd expresses smug satisfaction that
he can claim as friend the Duke of Buccleuch, 'The proudest Cal-
edonian name' (l. 221).

    So concludes *Midsummer Night Dreams*, reminding us yet again that
Hogg speaks in many voices. This volume is no exception. What
makes it remarkable, however is the astonishing thematic unity un-
derlying what at first appear radically disparate poems with little
in common. They scrutinise the uses of enchantment, search for its
vanished visionary gleam, and come to terms with its disappearance
in diverse ways. As is almost always true of Hogg, the beauty and
humour of the successful poems outweigh the clumsiness of the less
auspicious ones and bring considerable pleasure to the reader.

4. The Reception of *Midsummer Night Dreams* and its Component Poems

Hogg's decision in 1814 to publish *The Pilgrims of the Sun* outside the
context he had originally conceived for it as one of a series of *Mid-
summer Night Dreams*, has had a prolonged influence upon the recep-

tion both of that particular poem and some of the other poems he clustered around it when he reinstated the *Midsummer Night Dreams* context in 1822. Inevitably, *Pilgrims of the Sun* has had a separate reception history, as one of the sequence of long narrative poems Hogg published in the 1810s, following immediately after his break-through success with *The Queen's Wake* in 1813.

Hogg was naturally anxious to capitalise on the success of *The Queen's Wake* when ushering his next narrative poem before the world. He presented *The Pilgrims of the Sun* to his prospective publisher John Murray as an expansion of the ballad of 'Kilmeny', one of the most popular parts of *The Queen's Wake* (see the 'Essay on the Genesis of the Texts' above), and the resemblance was inevitably picked up for comment by the first reviewers of the poem. The *Critical Review*, for instance, noted, 'The same recorded superstition that served for the basis of that very fanciful composition ['Kilmeny'], is made the ground-work of the present poem'.[39] Within that context Hogg's adoption of the verse forms of Milton, Dryden, and Pope and his evocation of Dante's cosmic journeying was viewed as a risky strategy for an Ettrick Shepherd, since 'he brings himself into an immediate com-parison with the very greatest poets that have written in various ages and in various languages'.[40] Critics who had appreciated the dream-like narrative of 'Kilmeny' judged the change of versification in each part of *Pilgrims* 'a very silly conceit' since 'such violent and abrupt differences wake the mind from its illusion'.[41] The poem had a '*patch-work* appearance' and 'a man of taste and talent should rest his claims to admiration on more solid and worthy foundations than the tricks of metre and rhyme'. Nevertheless, several critics commented on 'the powerful brilliancy of his fancy', or that his poem was 'full of poetic excellency' which breathed in many passages 'the true spirit of descriptive poetry'.[42] Many of the reviews published in 1815 were distinctly favourable, particularly (as Hogg himself noted in his 'Memoir') that of the *Eclectic Review*, which declared, 'We have re-ceived so much gratification from the volume before us, that were we to express our opinion of its merits, under the warm impulse of the feelings it awakened, we fear that our praise would be thought partial or inordinate'. This reviewer compared Hogg favourably with Byron and Scott, the two leading poets of the age:

> after the gloomy scepticism through which we have lately been constrained to follow the course of one highly gifted genius, and the absolute barrenness of moral sentiment which deforms the descriptive romances of a popular northern poet, it is a peculiar relief to open upon passages similar to that we

are transcribing [...] the natural association of ideas in a simple and devout mind.[43]

The Champion, which considered *The Pilgrims of the Sun* a failure, nevertheless acknowledged 'many passages of great beauty' as evidence that if Hogg 'will but be faithful to his mountain muse, we do not think it likely that he or the public will have cause to regret the engagement he has made with Poetry'. The *Scots Magazine* concurred:

> We must frankly own, though every part bears the stamp of the author's genius, we were best pleased with those in which he has not quite lost sight of his native earth. For this reason, the first and last parts were those which most gratified us. It is true, the delineation of supernatural beings may be considered as even a peculiar talent of Mr Hogg; but rather those founded upon the mythology of his own country, than sought for in such lofty regions as the present. In his future publications, therefore, we would rather meet him, we confess, in his old accustomed haunts.[44]

Francis Jeffrey may also have made an unspoken comparison with 'Kilmeny' in telling the author that *Pilgrims* showed 'great powers of imagination and composition' but was 'too *stretchy* and desultory—the public estimation of your powers will lose nothing by it [but] of your judgement it may'. Behind many of these contemporary verdicts lies the assumption that Hogg, while displaying great powers of imagination, has overstepped the bounds proper to a peasant poet. The review in the *New Universal Magazine* opens with a general discussion of labouring-class poets, judging that Hogg 'though vastly inferior to Burns, stands somewhat higher than Bloomfield', and concludes:

> From these extracts, our readers will perceive that Mr. Hogg is gifted with no ordinary powers, for the delineation of what has been termed pure poetry. His fancy is creative, and though too often wild and inconsistent, yet it carries the marks of native force and originality. When the circumstances of his birth, education, and present condition are considered, we have no hesitation in pronouncing him an extraordinary man, but not a miracle.[45]

Some of these adverse critical reactions had been anticipated by the publishers Hogg had selected for *The Pilgrims of the Sun* (for details see the 'Essay on the Genesis of the Texts' above). In the close-knit, gossip-ridden world of literary Edinburgh the news that Manners and Miller had stopped the presses to send Hogg's manuscript out among a succession of advisors was probably known to many. William Blackwood might well have told others than John Murray that only the first part of the poem was of interest and that Hogg's 'Miltonic soaring into the empyreal heavens will not do'. Hogg himself certainly felt that Murray's removal of his prestigious name from the title-page of the London copies of the first edition would adversely affect its reception, telling him in a letter of 18 January 1815, 'this was not generous to a poor Shepherd I considered your name of greater importance to the success of the work than mine'.[46] Hogg was probably unwise to draw attention in the version of his 'Memoir' prefacing the 1821 edition of *The Mountain Bard* to the lack of faith shown in his poem by the publishing trade, since this subsequently filtered into comment on the poem in published articles about his life and literary output. John Wilson in his scathing attack on the 'Memoir' in *Blackwood's Edinburgh Magazine* for August 1821 does not fail to note that 'Miller seems to have intended to publish the Pilgrims of the Sun, but got frightened at Hogg's uncouth appearance, and the universal rumours of his incapacity. Murray seems to have awoke out of a dream, and on recovering his senses, to have cut the Shepherd in his easiest manner'.[47] However, the timing of the publication close to the appearance of a highly favourable review by Francis Jeffrey himself of *The Queen's Wake* in the prestigious *Edinburgh Review* was in its favour, and to begin with *The Pilgrims of the Sun* met with a moderate success.[48] Hogg was obliged to request more copies for him to dispose of personally on the day of publication in Edinburgh. Blackwood reported a month later, 'The Pilgrims are moving off', and Murray seems to have willingly paid Hogg his author's share of the profits in full in April 1815, judging that this was only anticipating by a few days the time when it would have become due.[49] David Laing, writing in 1821, remembered reading the poem on its first appearance and 'how much we were gratified with the powers which it evinced'. Hogg reported to Southey on publication that 'the publick opinion of it is high'. Hogg's overall assessment that it was then 'rather well received' appears to be accurate.[50]

During the years that followed, however, *The Pilgrims of the Sun* continued to be viewed as a flawed twin to the 'Kilmeny' of *The Queen's Wake*. Even Hogg's close friend James Gray made a sustained comparison of the two in his article 'On the Life and Writings of James Hogg' published in the *Edinburgh Magazine* in March 1818. He argued that 'Mary Lee [...] is not a twin sister of Kilmeny, but Kilmeny herself, in the very same circumstances, yet treated in a far less interesting way'. His verdict is 'that Mr Hogg's reputation would not have been so high as it is, if the Pilgrims of the Sun had been his first work, and would not suffer any great diminution if all were deducted from it which this production ever gained him'.[51]

The calls of the first reviewers of *The Pilgrims of the Sun* to Hogg to be faithful to his mountain muse partly reflected his reputation as an effective poet of superstition and the supernatural, a position which he subsequently described to Scott as that of 'the king o' the mountain and fairy school'. In his 1821 'Memoir' Hogg indirectly reflects on the advantages of removing the poem from the context of a series of long narrative poems of the 1810s to one which would emphasise this perceived poetic strength, commenting, 'Among other wild and visionary subjects, the Pilgrims of the Sun would have done very well, and might at least have been judged one of the best'.[52] Shortly afterwards David Laing advised Hogg publicly to 'revert to an old project, that of filling up a volume with those delightful subjects which he contemplated for his MIDSUMMER'S NIGHT DREAMS'.[53] Hogg appears to have taken his advice, but unfortunately the 'Midsummer Night Dreams' heading was concealed in 1822 within the main publication title of *The Poetical Works of James Hogg*, and the new context seems to have achieved little during Hogg's lifetime and to have been largely overlooked by the generations that followed.

The other poems in the second volume of Hogg's 1822 *Poetical Works* were also received separately by his contemporaries, and met with varying degrees of success. Unsurprisingly, the 'Verses Addressed to the Right Honourable Lady Anne Scott of Buccleuch' were highly regarded by the *Blackwood's* Tory circle for their emphasis on the bonds of faith and loyalty between peasant, landlord, and nation. They were showcased in *Blackwood's Edinburgh Magazine* soon after their first publication as the dedication to *The Brownie of Bodsbeck; And Other Tales*, and cited by the fictional Dr Morris in the ideologically-charged portrait of Scotland presented by Lockhart in *Peter's Letters to his Kinsfolk*.[54] Hogg's 'Verses to the Comet of 1811' also seem to have been regarded highly from the number of surviving manuscript presentation copies, and its two publications previous to 1822. Hogg's friend James Gray particularly admired 'The Gyre Caryl' in its previous incarnation as 'The Harper's Song' of *Mador of the Moor*, citing it at length in his 1818 article on Hogg's life and work as evidence that 'in the regions of pure fancy, even in this age of great poets, he has no rival, and the themes in which he is most at home, is fairy superstition'.[55] At the other extreme, 'The Field of Waterloo' was received so badly in Edinburgh at the end of 1815 that it was never published until its insertion in the 1822 *Poetical Works*.[56] The quality of two of the very best of Hogg's *Edinburgh Magazine* contributions in the *Midsummer Night Dreams*, 'The Mermaid' and 'The Powris of Moseke' appear to have gone unrecognised, probably because as a collected works (rather than a fresh publication) the four-volume *Poetical Works of James Hogg* did not attract much attention from periodical reviewers. One exception to this rule may be the *Literary Speculum*, which in 1822 followed the publication of *Poetical Works* with an article 'On the Genius of Hogg', assessing his poetical career. The reviewer made the interesting suggestion that *The Pilgrims of the Sun*, dedicated to Lord Byron, in which Mary Lee takes a cosmological journey with the angelical Cela, might have been a forerunner of the similar journey made by Byron's eponymous *Cain* (1821) with Satan.[57]

'Superstition' enjoyed something of a vogue in the second half of the twentieth century, critics following Louis Simpson's lead that in this poem Hogg had described witches 'with deep understanding and pity' and that 'Hogg's instincts, being more deeply rooted in popular tradition than Scott's, brought him closer to the essential truth'.[58] In his anthology of Hogg's poetry of 1970 Douglas Mack concurred that 'Superstition' achieves 'a level of deep seriousness' and 'is of particular interest as it is a meditation on a recurring theme of Hogg's work both in poetry and prose—his complex and ambiguous attitude towards the supernatural and the cult of witchcraft'. With 'Superstition' Mack also reprinted 'The Mermaid' and 'Verses to Lady Anne Scott' under the heading 'Miscellaneous Poems', but his editorial note treats them together as forming a part of the 'Midsummer Night Dreams' volume of the 1822 *Poetical Works*. It was left to David Groves in his 1986 anthology to reinstate the 'Midsummer Night Dreams' heading within the body of his text, although he emphasised Hogg's abandoned conception of 1814 and therefore included only *The Pilgrims of the Sun* with its dedication to Byron, 'Connel of Dee', and 'Superstition'.[59]

A serious treatment of *The Pilgrims of the Sun* as a major Hogg poem was provided by Nelson Smith in his study *James Hogg* of 1980, where he bracketed it with the *Confessions of a Justified Sinner* as one of Hogg's two most successful extended narratives, judging it 'central to an understanding of Hogg's notions of perfectibility and attitudes toward religion'. Smith seems to have persuaded Douglas Gifford, previously inclined to be dismissive of the poem, that a serious reassessment of it was due.[60] David Groves in his 1988 study, *James Hogg: The Growth of a Writer* pushed hard for a reinstatement of the

Midsummer Night Dreams grouping, seeing 'Connel of Dee' as a complement to *The Pilgrims of the Sun* in the same way that in *The Queen's Wake* 'The Witch of Fife' complements 'Kilmeny'. Taken together, he argued, 'the two main poems of *Midsummer Night Dreams* form a ring or cycle'. The idea of the journey, central to his study, was exemplified in *Midsummer Night Dreams* as 'mature myth-making'.[61] Although Groves's conception was limited to the partially-completed collection of 1814 and did not extend to the reconfiguration of 1822, it is indeed largely due to his advocacy that the present volume of the Stirling/South Carolina Edition takes the form that it does.

Critics since Groves have extended our knowledge of the component poems of *Midsummer Night Dreams* in various ways. Karl Miller, for instance, interprets 'Connel of Dee' as an expression of Hogg's problems with literary Edinburgh and places 'The Mermaid' as among those of Hogg's writings 'which deal with the half-submerged subject of venereal infection'.[62] Sharon Alker and Holly Nelson have opened up the topic of Hogg and war by discussing the figure of the soldier in various works, including 'The Field of Waterloo', demonstrating how his characters acknowledge unbridled violence yet seek to modify it by a capacity for sympathy.[63] There have been interpretations of *The Pilgrims of the Sun* as a 'cerebral journey, anchored in science' and as 'a complex and important poem' demonstrating Hogg's regret for the old pre-Reformation Scotland. Kate McGrail recognises the influence of Dunbar on the 1814 conception of *Midsummer Night Dreams*, described as a group of 'poems about poetry'.[64] Valentina Bold, in her recent study of Hogg as an autodidact poet, includes an extended discussion of *The Pilgrims of the Sun* in a chapter on 'Fantastic Journeys and Royal Adventures', placing it alongside *Mador of the Moor* and *Queen Hynde*. In this she follows the assessment of the poem by Hogg's contemporaries as part of a sequence of his long narrative poems, but her subsequent discussion of 'Connel of Dee' and 'Superstition' recognises the *Midsummer Night Dreams* collection as envisaged in 1814. Her index, however, includes entries under *Poetical Works* for all except three of the poems in the second, or *Midsummer Night Dreams* volume of the 1822 collection and none for poems from the other volumes.[65] Perhaps she may be more open to the 1822 *Midsummer Night Dreams* grouping than she at first appears to be?

The present edition, it is hoped, will both confirm the standing of *The Pilgrims of the Sun* as one of Hogg's more interesting long narrative poems and place it firmly within the *Midsummer Night Dreams* context. The collection as a whole confirms Hogg's versatility of mood and technique, ranging from the stately seriousness of 'Superstition' through the dream-like ballad perfection of 'The Mermaid' to the absurd comic gusto of 'The Powris of Moseke'. It provides much to enjoy even within the rich context of the Stirling/South Carolina Research Edition of the Collected Works of James Hogg.

Notes

1. 'Verses Addressed to the Right Honourable Lady Anne Scott of Buccleuch', l. 150. Quotations from the component poems of Hogg's *Midsummer Night Dreams* volume of 1822 are taken from the text in the present volume and referenced in this introduction by line number. The Introduction also employs the list of abbreviations for commonly-cited works provided at the start of the 'Editorial Notes' below.

2. See the editorial note on Midsummer night as 'traditionally a celebration for lovers' in *James Hogg: Selected Poems and Songs*, ed. by David Groves (Edinburgh: Scottish Academic Press, 1986), p. 212.

3. *Letters*, I, 256.

4. Carl Woodring, 'Three Poets on Waterloo', *The Wordsworth Circle*, 18 no. 2 (Spring 1987), 54–57 (p. 54).

5. Quoted in Stella Cottrell, 'The Devil on Two Sticks: Franco-phobia in 1803', in *Patriotism: The Making and Unmaking of British National Identity*, ed. by Raphael Samuel, 3 vols (London and New York: Routledge, 1989), I, 259–74 (p. 259).

6. Cottrell, p. 260.

7. Quoted in Cottrell, p. 261.

8. John Mayne, 'English, Scots, and Irishmen. A Patriotic Address to the Inhabitants of the United Kingdom, July, 1803', quoted in Betty T. Bennett, *British War Poetry in the Age of Romanticism: 1793–1815* (New York and London: Garland, 1976), pp. 311–12.

9. H. T. Dickinson, 'Popular Conservatism and Militant Loyalism 1789–1815', in *Britain and the French Revolution, 1789–1815*, ed. by H. T. Dickinson (Basingstoke: Macmillan Education, 1989), pp. 103–25 (p. 107).

10. Quoted by Vic Gammon, 'The Grand Conversation: Napoleon and British Popular Balladry', originally published in *RSA Journal*, 137 (September 1989), 645–73, and cited from http://www.mustrad.org.uk/articles/boney.htm.

11. Cottrell, p. 261.

12. Rev. R. Mant, 'War Song. Written in May, 1803, on the Publication of the Negotiation Papers', quoted in Bennett, pp. 288–90 (p. 289).

13. Gerald Newman, *The Rise of English Nationalism: A Cultural History 1740–1830* (New York: St Martin's Press, 1997), p. 232.

14. See Dickinson, pp. 120, 124.

15. 'Occasioned by the Battle of Waterloo', in *William Wordsworth: Poems, Volume II*, ed. by John O. Hayden (Harmondsworth: Penguin, 1977), p. 334.

16. *A Series of Lay Sermons on Good Principles and Good Breeding*, ed. by Gillian Hughes with Douglas S. Mack (S/SC, 1997), p. 41.

17. *Lay Sermons*, p. 40.

18. Sandra M. Gilbert and Susan Gubar, *No Man's Land: The Place of the Woman Writer in the Twentieth Century*, 3 vols (New Haven and London: Yale University Press, 1988–94).

19. The theoretical distance between pilgrimage and curiosity is the thesis of

Christian K. Zacher in *Curiosity and Pilgrimage: The Literature of Discovery in Fourteenth-Century England* (Baltimore and London: John Hopkins Press, 1976).

20. See Marinus H. F. van Uden and Joseph Z. T. Pieper, building on the work of Victor Turner's *Image and Pilgrimage in Christian Culture* (1978), in their 'Christian Pilgrimage Motivational Structures and Ritual Functions', in *Current Studies on Rituals: Perspectives for the Psychology of Religion*, ed. by Hans-Günter Heimbrock and H. Barbara Boudewijnse (Amsterdam and Atlanta, GA: Rodopi, 1990), pp. 165–76 (p. 175).

21. Zacher, p. 49.

22. Leonard J. Bowman, '*Itinerarium*: The Shape of the Metaphor', in *Itinerarium: The Idea of Journey*, ed. by Leonard J. Bowman (Salzburg: Institut für Anglistik und Amerikanistik, Universität Salzburg, 1983), pp. 3–33 (p. 31).

23. Victor Turner and Edith Turner, *Image and Pilgrimage in Christian Culture. Anthropological Perspectives* (New York: Columbia University Press, 1978).

24. James J. Preston, 'Spiritual Magnetism: An Organizing Principle for the Study of Pilgrimage', in *Sacred Journey: The Anthropology of Pilgrimage*, ed. by Alan Morinis (Westport, Connecticut and London: Greenwood Press, 1992), pp. 31–46 (pp. 36–37).

25. Mary B. Campbell, ' "The Object of One's Gaze": Landscape, Writing, and Early Medieval Pilgrimage', in *Discovering New Worlds: Essays on Medieval Exploration and Imagination*, ed. by Scott D. Westrem (New York and London: Garland Publishing, 1991), pp. 3–15 (pp. 4, 6).

26. Alan Morinis, 'Introduction: The Territory of the Anthropology of Pilgrimage', in *Sacred Journeys*, pp. 1–28 (p. 15).

27. Paul G. Kuntz, 'Man the Wayfarer: Reflections on the Way', in *Itinerarium*, pp. 216–34 (p. 228).

28. Preston, p. 41.

29. Erik Cohen, 'Pilgrimage and Tourism: Convergence and Divergence', in *Sacred Journeys*, pp. 47–61.

30. 'Little Gidding' from *Four Quartets*, in T. S. Eliot, *The Complete Poems and Plays* (London: Faber and Faber, 1969 repr. 1990), pp. 191–98 (pp. 194, 197).

31. See the opening lines of 'The Tale of the Wyf of Bathe' from *The Canterbury Tales* in *Chaucer: Complete Works*, ed. by Walter W. Skeat (London: Oxford University Press, 1912 repr. 1973), pp. 576–81 (p. 576).

32. *A Forgotten Heritage: Original Folktales of Lowland Scotland*, ed. by Hannah Aitken (Edinburgh and London: Scottish Academic Press, 1973), p. 121.

33. *The Queen's Wake*, ed. by Douglas S. Mack (S/SC, 2004), p. 73 (ll. 684–87: 1813 version).

34. See *Anecdotes of Scott*, ed. by Jill Rubenstein (S/SC, 1999), p. 9.

35. Bruno Bettelheim, *The Uses of Enchantment: The Meaning and Importance of Fairy Tales* (Harmondsworth: Penguin, 1991). All page references in the text are to this edition.

36. Diane Purkiss, *At the Bottom of the Garden: A Dark History of Fairies, Hobgoblins, and Other Troublesome Things* (New York: New York University Press, 2000 repr. 2003), pp. 4, 86.

37. Cited in Bettelheim, p. 35.

38. Fredric Jameson, 'The Vanishing Mediator; or, Max Weber as Storyteller', in *The Ideologies of Theory: Essays 1971–1986*, 2 vols (London: Routledge, 1988), II, 3–34.

39. *Critical Review*, fifth series, 1 (April 1815), 399–409 (p. 401).

40. *The Champion*, 12 February 1815, pp. 54–55 (p. 55).

41. *Theatrical Inquirer*, 6 (February 1815), 130–38 (p. 137).

42. *Critical Review*, fifth series, 1 (April 1815), 399–409 (pp. 403, 406); *Salopian*

Magazine, 1 (May and July 1815), 228–31, 273–74 (p. 273); *Theatrical Inquirer*, 6 (February 1815), 130–38 (p. 133).

43. See *Altrive Tales*, p. 39, and *Eclectic Review*, n. s. 3 (March 1815), 280–91 (pp. 281, 286).

44. *The Champion*, 12 February 1815, pp. 54–55 (p. 55); *Scots Magazine*, 76 (December 1814), 930–32 (p. 932).

45. Jeffrey's remarks were reported by Hogg himself in a letter to John Murray of 21 January 1815, in *Letters*, I, 234. See also the *New Universal Magazine*, 2 (February 1815), 116–21 (pp. 116, 121).

46. See William Blackwood's letter to John Murray of 11 December 1814 in the John Murray Archive: NLS, Acc. 12604/1113, and also Hogg's letter to Murray of 18 January 1815, in *Letters*, I, 231.

47. See *Mountain Bard*, pp. 218–21, and 'Familiar Epistles to Christopher North, From an Old Friend with a New Face. Letter I. On Hogg's Memoirs', *Blackwood's Edinburgh Magazine*, 10 (August 1821), 43–52 (p. 48).

48. *The Pilgrims of the Sun* was published in Edinburgh on 12 December 1814 (see 'Essay on the Genesis of the Texts' above) while an advertisement for no. 47 of the *Edinburgh Review*, the issue that included Jeffrey's favourable review of *The Queen's Wake*, appeared in the *Edinburgh Evening Courant* of 22 December 1814. Blackwood reported to Murray in his letter of 1 December 1814 that Hogg 'is in great spirits as he has just seen Jeffrey's Critique upon his poem which is most favourable' (John Murray Archive: NLS, Acc. 12604/1113).

49. See Hogg's letter to Blackwood requesting extra copies of [12 December 1814], in *Letters*, I, 220, Blackwood's letter to Murray of 14 January 1815 (John Murray Archive: NLS, Acc. 12604/1114), and Murray's letter to Hogg of 21 April 1815 (NLS, MS 2245, fols 17–18).

50. For Laing's review of the 1821 edition of *The Mountain Bard* see *Edinburgh Monthly Review*, 5 (June 1821), 662–72 (p. 667). For Hogg's letter to Southey of 15 December 1814 see *Letters*, I, 221, and for his assessment in his 'Memoir' see *Altrive Tales*, p. 39.

51. For Gray's comment see the final instalment of his three-part article on the 'Life and Writings of James Hogg', *Edinburgh Magazine*, 2 (March 1818), 215–223 (p. 216).

52. For Hogg's comment see *Anecdotes of Scott*, ed. by Jill Rubenstein (S/SC, 1999), p. 9, and for his subsequent judgement on the lone publication of *The Pilgrims of the Sun* see his 'Memoir' in *Mountain Bard*, p. 218.

53. See the conclusion to Laing's review of the 1821 edition of *The Mountain Bard* in *Edinburgh Monthly Review*, 5 (June 1821), 662–72 (p. 672).

54. *Blackwood's Edinburgh Magazine*, 4 (October 1818), 74–76. Dr Morris's citation occurs in *Peter's Letters to his Kinsfolk*, 3 vols (Edinburgh: William Blackwood; London: T. Cadell and W. Davies, 1819), II, 312.

55. For details of presentation manuscript copies and previous printings of the 'Verses to the Comet of 1811' see the relevant entry in 'Note on the Texts' below. For James Gray's praise and citation of 'The Harper's Song' ('The Gyre Caryl') see 'Life and Writings of James Hogg', *Edinburgh Magazine*, 2 (March 1818), 215–23 (pp. 220–21).

56. See the entry for 'The Field of Waterloo' in 'Note on the Texts' below.

57. 'On the Genius of Hogg', *Literary Speculum*, 2 (December 1822), 433–43 (p. 441). See also Meiko O'Halloran's discussion of the influence of *The Pilgrims of the Sun* on Byron's poem in her essay in the present volume, '"Circling the pales of heaven": Hogg and Otherworld Journeys from Dante to Byron' (pp. xcvi–xcviii).

58. Louis Simpson, *James Hogg: A Critical Study* (Edinburgh and London: Oliver

& Boyd, 1962), p. 64.

59. *James Hogg: Selected Poems*, ed. by Douglas S. Mack (Oxford: Clarendon Press, 1970), pp. xviii, 165–67; *James Hogg: Selected Poems and Songs*, ed. by David Groves (Edinburgh: Scottish Academic Press, 1986), pp. 31–95.

60. Nelson Smith, *James Hogg*, Twayne's English Authors 311 (Boston: Twayne Publishers, 1980), pp. 62, 168. In his own *James Hogg* (Edinburgh: Ramsay Head Press, 1976) Douglas Gifford had dismissed *The Pilgrims of the Sun* as 'interesting only in that it shows that success in a poem or song or parody for Hogg meant that he would ever after repeat the style and content in the vain hope of recapturing the glory of the original' (p. 62). Reviewing Smith's book, however, he declared that Smith 'makes out a strong case for re-assessment'—see *Scottish Literary Journal*, Supplement 17 (Winter 1982), 84–89 (p. 87).

61. David Groves, *James Hogg: The Growth of a Writer* (Edinburgh: Scottish Academic Press, 1988), pp. 62, 65, 80.

62. Karl Miller, *Electric Shepherd: A Likeness of James Hogg* (London: Faber and Faber, 2003 repr. 2005), pp. 109–10, 61–62.

63. Sharon Alker and Holly Faith Nelson, '"Ghastly in the Moonlight": Wordsworth, Hogg and the Anguish of War', *SHW*, 15 (2004), 76–89.

64. See Valentina Bold, 'The Magic Lantern: Hogg and Science', *SHW*, 7 (1996), 5–17 (p. 16); Douglas S. Mack, 'Hogg and the Blessed Virgin Mary', *SHW*, 3 (1992), 68–75 (p. 69); Kate McGrail, 'Re-making the Fire: James Hogg and the Makars', *SHW*, 7 (1996), 26–36 (p. 33).

65. Valentina Bold, *James Hogg: A Bard of Nature's Making* (Bern: Peter Lang, 2007), pp. 153–71, 348.

'Circling the pales of heaven': Hogg and Otherworld Journeys from Dante to Byron

Meiko O'Halloran

When James Hogg composed *The Pilgrims of the Sun* between February and July 1814, he had every reason to hope that the new poem would surpass the success of his previous otherworld adventures. Drawing on supernatural crossings in Border ballads and tropes of pilgrimage from Puritan spiritual autobiography, Hogg's most celebrated ballads from *The Queen's Wake* (1813), 'Kilmeny' and 'The Witch of Fife', had presented mortals whose heavenly and nightmarish journeys changed their lives forever. Although Hogg expressed confidence in his new poem, declaring shortly after *The Pilgrims of the Sun* was published, 'I will risk my fame on it to all eternity', it proved much less successful than the earlier imaginative flights which had helped to secure his reputation as a poet.[1] The shifting forms of *The Pilgrims of the Sun*, showcasing Hogg's imitation of the verse styles of Scott, Milton, Dryden and Pope, positively ask for the poem to be read in response to a 'high' canonical tradition, but William Blackwood was not alone in thinking that Hogg's 'Miltonic soaring into the empyreal heavens will not do'.[2] The reader for the *Critical Review* was one of several reviewers who, after admiring the 'unearthly aerial charm' of the poem, took issue with Hogg's 'vanity' in mingling verse styles. Despite noting his 'dexterity', the reviewer recommended that Hogg 'keep to his old poetical habits', remarking that 'ballad-measure' was 'most natural to him'.[3] In attempting to follow 'Kilmeny' with a poem in pursuit of more erudite literary masters, Hogg was judged by some to have overreached, and, like Icarus, found his limits.

It was easy for Hogg's contemporary critics to assume that an autodidact shepherd must have a limited grasp of 'high' culture, but as I hope to demonstrate, Hogg's engagement with well-known literary predecessors is more intricate, multi-layered and complex than has been fully recognised. David Groves's reading of *The Pilgrims of the Sun* as the voyage of two readers through a literary universe and his recognition of the 'strong Romantic influence' in the poem has opened the way for further investigation.[4] My essay aims to re-situate *The Pilgrims of the Sun*, Hogg's most ambitious journey in *Midsummer Night Dreams*, as part of a rich array of otherworld travel writings—which included the dream visions of Dante and Chaucer, Milton's biblical paradigm, Bunyan's Christian allegory, Robert Paltock's utopia, and the dark compulsive journeys of Romantic poets such as Coleridge and Byron. By interweaving the ballad tradition of supernatural journeys with a 'high' poetic tradition of spiritual flight and pilgrimage, Hogg made an important contribution to journeys of the imagination in Romantic literature. In *The Pilgrims of the Sun*, he creates a journey which not only rescues the mortal traveller from earth and enables her to experience other worlds, but crucially also allows her to be reintegrated with her community on earth. As Jill Rubenstein remarks, the use of pilgrimage allows for 'a circular journey' and a return to the familiar with new understanding (Introduction, p. lvii). This essay begins by considering Hogg's departure from his earlier imaginative journeys, before going on to examine his innovative transformation of tropes from the otherworld journeys of an array of poets from Dante to Byron. The main part of my essay explores the *The Pilgrims of the Sun* as a Romantic response to the work of Dante and Milton, in which Hogg allows his pilgrims to see God in the sun. In the final part, I contrast the optimism of Hogg's poem with the disturbing journeys into the unknown in *The Rime of the Ancient Mariner* (1798) and *Cain* (1821), in which other realms are symbolic sites of self-interrogation and conflict for their male protagonists. Hogg was adept at delving into the hellish or comically grotesque (as in 'The Witch of Fife' or 'Connel of Dee'), but he was especially unusual for his day in also offering redeeming otherworld journeys which are given to pure young women as a privileged glimpse of the world to come. In an inversion of the Dantean circles of hell, Hogg's pilgrims, 'circling the pales of heaven', paradoxically experience an unorthodox universe which deepens their Christian faith.[5] Mary rediscovers the earth through a kind of pantheism.

With their folk motifs and antiquated language, Hogg's most successful poems, 'Kilmeny' and 'The Witch of Fife', captured a *Zeitgeist* for otherworldly experience. To readers who were familiar with verse narratives of fatal journeys such as 'Sir Patrick Spens' and *The Rime of the Ancient Mariner*, or of enigmatic loss, as in Wordsworth's Lucy poems in *Lyrical Ballads*, the moral ambivalence of 'Kilmeny' must have appealed. Set apart from other women by her chaste disinterest in 'Duneira's men', the eponymous young heroine is transported from her quiet rural life in pre-Reformation Scotland to a heavenly 'land of love, and ane land of lychte'. In this 'land of veizion' and

'everlestyng dreime', she is given an allegorical view of the future of
Scotland, which compounds her separation from home–finding that
she no longer belongs in her mother's house, she returns to the 'land
of the spiritis'.[6] Although it is clear from the beginning that Kilmeny
is already detached from the rhythms of her community, there is
something poignantly unsettling about her removal from the circle
of familial love to an anonymous society of spirits. In the same way
that Coleridge's pseudo-antiquated language and later marginal gloss
heighten the fantastical, remote, and dream-like qualities of the An-
cient Mariner's voyage, so Hogg's use of pseudo-medieval Scots
enhances the mysteriousness of Kilmeny's experience, making it lin-
guistically strange and full of wonder for readers. This opaque effect
of clouding one's moral co-ordinates contributes to the difficulty of
finding contentment in Kilmeny's end. Despite her redemption from
the turmoil of mortality, it is hard not to feel that Kilmeny's absorp-
tion into a visually opulent but emotionally muted realm has de-
prived her of the fullness of life on earth. In a characteristic melding
of poetic traditions, Hogg's revisiting of medieval Scots poetry re-
veals his indebtedness to the stylistic simplicity and enigmatic end-
ings of recently revived ballads of supernatural abduction such as
'Thomas the Rhymer'.[7]

In the darkly humorous 'Witch of Fife', the supernatural journey
is used to explore domestic strife rather than an alternative world.
In contrast to Kilmeny's delicate election to another realm, the hus-
band of the Witch of Fife embarks on a rebellious flight only to be
bound by his human weakness. Jealous of his wife's adventures among
fairies in Lapland and her raiding of a bishop's wine cellar, he re-
peats her flying spell and follows her and her cronies on their flight
by cockle shell to Carlisle Castle. Transporting his petty struggles
for marital power to the feudal castle, he competes with his wife's
raucous appreciation for fine wine, but after a night of carousing, he
misses the flying spell for their return and is left behind, drunk. In
the first edition of *The Queen's Wake*, the luckless husband suffers a
gruesome punishment for his more-than-mortal aspirations, being
tortured till 'the reid blude ran' and burnt at the stake for his theft,
but thanks to Scott's good-humoured objection, he received a comic
reprieve in the third edition.[8] Hogg's revised ending has the over-
reaching husband rescued by his wife, whose flamboyance, it is im-
plied, he will henceforth respect in the domestic sphere. These bal-
lads of supernatural journeys with their uneasy ideas of spiritual
election and punishment were singled out for praise by Hogg's early
readers and came to characterise the 'high' and 'low' otherworldly

possibilities of his poetry in the public imagination.

Francis Jeffrey's review of *The Queen's Wake* in *Blackwood's* of November 1814 makes clear that Hogg's success was bound up with the 'high' Romantic ideal of poetry inspired by the imagination. For Jeffrey, Hogg's 'richness of language' and 'exaltation of fancy' carried him to 'the borders of a very high species of poetry'.[9] 'Kilmeny' was 'pure poetry' (borrowing Thomas Warton's phrase), which Jeffrey went on to define:

> that is, poetry addressed almost exclusively to the imagination, and inspired rather by the recollection of its most fantastic and abstracted visions, than by any observation of the characters, the actions, or even the feelings of mortal men.

According to Jeffrey, this 'high species of poetry', woven from the artist's visions, was the work of 'original genius' and characterised by its separation from the everyday world.[10] In this and other reviews, 'Kilmeny' emerges as a fine example of the prevailing Romantic values of originality, spontaneity, and otherworldly inspiration, partly derived from mid-eighteenth-century reinventions of the poet such as Gray's 'The Bard' and Macpherson's Ossian. By Jeffrey's definition, instead of revealing lost epic worlds, this 'species of poetry' was 'difficult' and 'dangerous' because it required a more inviting creative instinct—'not only a certain fairy brightness and purity in the colouring—but an entire novelty'. Promoting a reassuringly tasteful idea of the supernatural, Jeffrey admired the 'great delicacy and beauty' and 'wild and unearthly charm' of Hogg's poem, which was 'without any of the vulgar horrors or exaggerations of the German school of incantation'.[11] In his most successful poetic treatment of fantastic subject matter, then, Hogg had trumped the extravagance of the Gothic with an enchanting 'unearthly' possibility.

Other readers were similarly struck by Hogg's imaginative scope. In his private correspondence with Hogg in December 1814, Robert Southey praised the two ballads: 'each is excellent in its way, but Kilmeny is of the highest character: The Witch of Fife is a rich work of fancy,—Kilmeny a fine one of imagination,—which is a higher and rarer gift'.[12] Southey's distinction between the 'higher and rarer' work of imagination and the 'rich work of fancy' anticipates the hierarchical terms of Coleridge's definitions of the primary and secondary imagination and the fancy in *Biographia Literaria* (1817), while also sharing Coleridge's emphasis on the transcendent poetic imagination. The recognition of Hogg's 'high' imaginative powers in 1814 certainly helped to strengthen his poetic persona as an inspired 'Mountain

Bard'.[13] The second and third editions of *The Queen's Wake*, published that year, carried laudatory verses by Bernard Barton, extolling the 'Heaven-taught Shepherd' as a follower of Burns, while asserting his originality: 'What urged thee thus a flight to dare | Through realms by former bards unsought?'.[14] Hogg had boldly claimed his place in the literary market as a poet at home in the realms of fairies and witches. Where would he fly to next?

Even as he promoted his poetic image as a '*Naturæ Donum*' or 'gift of nature',[15] Hogg sought to align himself with a highbrow line of literary originals. The otherworld journeys he composed for his projected collection, *Midsummer Night Dreams*, and the Shakespearean title, make clear that he hoped to appeal to a wider audience, gradually following his highly-regarded poetic predecessors into a position of greater material security and artistic freedom. Shakespeare provided a model for Hogg's fairy world in 'The Haunted Glen', but there were other prominent influences for his forays into the unknown.

1. Approaching the 'light sublime': *Pilgrims of the Sun* in Response to Dante and Milton

When Kilmeny awakes in the land of thought having been transported by unknown means, she has little sense of the universe beyond the two terrestrial and celestial worlds, and no guide. By contrast, the heroine of *The Pilgrims of the Sun*, Mary Lee, whose purity also sets her apart from her local community, is taken on an edifying spiritual tour of the universe by a celestial companion. Released from her body, Mary's spirit ascends with Cela and together they visit 'the Eternal's throne of light sublime' (the palace of God in the sun) and a series of worlds, through which they witness the pilgrimage of spirits progressing towards perfection (Part First, l. 234). They even observe the 'cloudy spot' of earth and dark purgatorial worlds before returning to Carterhaugh, where Mary is painfully reunited with her body (Part Second, l. 137). Hogg's introduction of a cosmic journey was clearly influenced by Satan's survey of the universe on his flight to Eden in the early books of *Paradise Lost*, but the introduction of a spiritual guide for Mary was most likely inspired chiefly by Dante, whose progress from earth to Paradiso in the *Commedia* involves his intellectual and emotional re-education by Virgil and Beatrice, as he traverses the circles of hell, ascends Mount Purgatory, and enters the heavens—significantly including a visit to the sun before meeting God himself.

Mary Lee's spiritual flight is a dramatic variation on Dante's and Milton's journeys from the depths of hell, not least because Hogg's innocent traveller sees God in the sun, rather than paradise, and glimpses purgatorial places only from a distance, before returning to her native district. In the final part of the poem, Hogg literally returns to ballad territory since Carterhaugh is the setting of the famous 'Tam Lin'. At this point he draws on a local legend about the reanimation of a woman's corpse at her own funeral. As Mary Lee's spirit is restored to her body, she shrieks into life and finds herself resurrected in the grave where her body has been buried. Thus, Hogg frames Mary's spiritual flight with local tradition while aspiring to a host of 'high' poets in the central otherworld journey. That the same reviewer who recommended Hogg keep to 'ballad-measure' went on to acknowledge that in Part Second of the poem, Hogg not only managed to 'avoid imitating, the genius of Milton and Dante', but also demonstrated 'the powerful brilliancy' of his own imagination, suggests that although readers appreciated the 'high' Miltonic and 'low' ballad traditions he used, they saw Hogg's melding of them as incongruous.[16] This was certainly the case for the publishers, John Murray and William Blackwood, who welcomed the Kilmeny-like opening passages, but later reacted against the journey towards God's celestial light along the lines of Dante and Milton.

Strikingly, Hogg's composition of *Pilgrims of the Sun* coincided with the introduction of Dante's *Commedia* in Britain through the Reverend Henry Cary's blank-verse translation, *The Vision*. Published on 1 January 1814, *The Vision* appeared perhaps only a matter of weeks before Hogg began his poem. Cary's work played a crucial role in establishing the *Commedia* in Britain's cultural consciousness, giving Dante a far wider currency and popularity in Britain than previous translations by Charles Rogers (1782) and Henry Boyd (1785, 1802).[17] Yet the humble appearance and slow success of *The Vision* make it uncertain whether Hogg read it. Printed at Cary's own expense in three tiny volumes, and circulated in a small print run, the translation attracted little attention until Cary's meeting with Coleridge in the autumn of 1817 resulted in the publication of a larger second edition.[18] Hogg may have encountered Dante through Cary's earlier translations, *Purgatorio* (1805) and *Inferno* (1806), but it was clearly Paradiso which captured his imagination. In *The Pilgrims of the Sun*, Hogg contrasts the freedom of his 'aerial travellers' (Part First, l. 173) with the hardships of earthly pilgrimage in a circling movement which recalls Dante:

> Far far away, thro' regions of delight
> They journeyed on–not like the earthly pilgrim,
> Fainting with hunger, thirst, and burning feet,
> But, leaning forward on the liquid air,
> Like twin-born eagles, skimmed the fields of light,
> Circling the pales of heaven. (Part Second, ll. 175–80)

Here, Mary and Cela, gracefully 'circling the pales of heaven', emerge as virtuous counterparts to the adulterous lovers, Paolo and Francesca, whose spirits must spiral endlessly in the second circle of Dante's underworld. As Hogg's image of the 'twin-born eagles' suggests, they also enjoy more freedom of movement and equality than Dante and Beatrice. In his powerfully personal pre-Reformation spiritual autobiography, Dante the poet-protagonist is rescued from the dark forest by the shade of Virgil and summoned to heaven at Beatrice's request–so that she becomes his angelic saviour. Dante's epic journey through the Inferno and Purgatorio under the guidance of the Roman master brings him into harrowing encounters with characters from history and classical mythology as well as his own political enemies. Crucially he also discovers at the threshold of Paradiso that there are limitations to salvation which are beyond intellectual wisdom or virtue. With profound shock and sadness, Dante sees that his guide, Virgil, a pagan belonging to a pre-Christian age, is forever beyond the pale of heaven. Finding that Virgil has returned to Limbo, Dante weeps, but Beatrice leads him into the heavens to everlasting love and peace. In contrast to the physical hardship of Dante's journey and Beatrice's superior power, Mary Lee's circular progress towards God highlights her spiritual freedom and equality with Cela before they are united on earth.

Mary Lee's pilgrimage may begin with the blindness of intellectual enquiry on earth, but as an epitome of purity, more akin to the angelic Beatrice than Dante, she is far from being 'lost'. Her pious restlessness to see the next world is prompted by her scepticism of church teaching. After poring over 'books of deep divinity' and meditating on 'the life that is, and the life to be', she begins to doubt the truth of the beadsmen:

> And the more she thought, and the more she read
>   Of the ways of Heaven and Nature's plan,
> She feared the half that the bedesmen said
>   Was neither true nor plain to man.
>   (Part First, ll. 37–40)

Aptly, Mary's scepticism gives rise to an unorthodox pilgrimage.

Throughout *The Pilgrims of the Sun*, Hogg defies the rational enquiry of book-learning, and destabilises his readers' expectations by employing the conventions of spiritual rescue only to depart from them. Although Cela is conventionally 'sent' by 'Heaven in pity' to liberate Mary, she is already uniquely qualified by her virtue and set apart from society by her sexual innocence. Her summoning therefore becomes reminiscent of the Annunciation, while her flight to heaven invites comparisons with the Assumption of the Virgin Mary (Part First, l. 55). Mary is so pure that when her spirit rises from her body to take flight with Cela, she is 'more lightsome, pure, and fair than he' (Part First, l. 80). But at the same time, Hogg refuses the mould of Catholicism by introducing the pagan trope of sun-worship at the heart of the poem. Placing God at the centre of the sun and resurrecting Mary on earth, Hogg both pursues and resists biblical, Dantean and Miltonic precedents.

Whereas Dante makes painful progress through the topography of the Catholic belief system, Hogg transports Mary directly and joyously from the Scottish Borders to heaven, giving her an exhilarating ease of movement and an exquisite accuracy of vision which befit her purity and goodness. Mary's affinity with heaven and her feeling of belonging are gradually enhanced as Cela takes her around the 'glorious heaven, till by degrees | Thy frame and vision are so subtilized | As that thou may'st the inner regions near' to walk among angels (Part Second, ll. 168–70). Even as he appropriates Dante's use of circularity in the circles of hell and the celestial spheres, the idea of Hogg's pilgrim's vision being 'subtilized' as she circles the outskirts of heaven perhaps owes something to the subtle visual effects of Milton's poetry. Critics from Warton onwards had praised Milton's visual shadowiness over Dante's pictorial detail, with Burke particularly admiring Milton's 'judicious obscurity' in creating the sublime.[19] Although Hogg allows Mary and Cela unlimited vision, he follows Milton in not delineating his other worlds too precisely. This Romantic interest in liberating the imagination from the constraints of detail makes Hogg's admiration of Milton very much of its time. In his introduction to the second edition of *The Vision* in 1819, Cary went on to praise Milton's 'sublimity' in contrast to Dante, who sometimes lapsed into the grotesque by attempting 'to define all his images in such a manner as to bring them distinctly within the circle of our vision'.[20] As Ralph Pite explains, for many late eighteenth- and early nineteenth-century British readers, Dante simply made hell too visible.[21] In his poem, Hogg often preserves the numinous in a delicate way, but he also pokes fun at sublimity–

some of his images for concealing God are irresistibly comic, as in the 'unapproached pavilion, framed | Of twelve deep veils, and every veil composed | Of thousand thousand lustres' which houses God at the beginning of the Miltonic second part of the poem (ll. 6–8). In many ways, then, Hogg is careful to leave his readers with enough scope for imagining heaven.

In addition to Hogg's probable knowledge of critical comparisons of Dante and Milton, his familiarity with essays by Johnson, Addison and Steele in his weekly paper, *The Spy* (1810–11), suggests his keen awareness of Milton's eighteenth-century reception. For his aesthetic use of obscurity and the journey to the sun in *Pilgrims*, Hogg may have recalled Addison's essay on *Paradise Lost* from *The Spectator* of 1 March 1712, in which Addison specifically admires the 'shadowy Nature' of Satan's 'Roaming upon the Frontiers of the Creation', which 'strikes the Imagination with something astonishingly great and wild'.[22] For Addison, Milton's elusive treatment of this episode seems to heighten the reader's impression of Satan's lawless strength as he pits himself against the divine Creation. Addison's praise for the 'luxuriant Imagination' with which Milton presented Satan's 'Flight between the several Worlds that shined on every Side of him, with the particular Description of the Sun' and the poet's 'finely contrived' idea 'of directing *Satan* to the Sun [...] and the placing in it an Angel' perhaps contributed to make this episode from *Paradise Lost* a stimulus for Hogg's imaginative flight.[23] As Hogg turned his attention to the sun, he distinguished his traveller from Milton's as a morally pure and privileged young woman–in Cela's words, 'a visitant beloved' of heaven (Part First, l. 283)–whose flight and vision his readers were invited to share imaginatively, but, as Jeffrey had observed of 'Kilmeny', in an enchanting rather than threateningly sublime way.

Hogg's closest debt to Dante emerges as Mary and Cela draw near the sun early in their celestial tour. Leaving the night sky with its 'light of the waning moon' to perch 'above the beams of the breaking day', Hogg's 'aerial travellers' take a panoramic survey of the cosmos (Part First, ll. 174, 186, 173). As they rest in the liminal space between night and day, Mary is astonished to see Cela bowing to the sun–a pivotal moment which strongly recalls Dante and Beatrice pausing on the verge of Paradiso. When the exhausted poet-narrator of the *Commedia* approaches the threshold of Paradiso with Beatrice, having crossed the circles of Hell and scaled the heights of Purgatorio, he pauses at the border between the mortal and divine to observe the prevalent influence of the sun. Here, in the words of Cary's translation, Dante sees that the 'world's bright lamp' not only sheds light for mankind, as we perceive from earth, but the sun itself has a creative power in imprinting its character upon the earth: 'to the worldly wax best giv[ing] | It's temper and impression' [*sic*].[24] Standing before a vista in which the darkness of night and brightness of day are dramatically juxtaposed, he sees Beatrice turn to the sun:

> Morning there,
> Here eve was by almost such passage made;
> And whiteness had o'erspread that hemisphere,
> Blackness the other part; when to the left
> I saw Beatrice turn'd, and on the sun
> Gazing, as never eagle fix'd his ken.
> (Paradise, Canto I, 41–46)

With instinctive sympathy, the poet-narrator becomes equally mesmerised as he absorbs the sight of Beatrice watching the sun and follows her line of vision. In a characteristically intricate Dantean metaphor, Beatrice's reverent gaze–figured symbolically as a ray of light–gives rise to a second, reflected beam of light (the poet's gaze) which is compared to a pilgrim hurrying home to God:

> As from the first a second beam is wont
> To issue, and reflected upwards rise,
> E'en as a pilgrim bent on his return,
> So of her act, that through the eyesight pass'd
> Into my fancy, mine was form'd; and straight,
> Beyond our mortal wont, I fix'd mine eyes
> Upon the sun.
> (Paradise, Canto I, 47–53)

The pilgrim's journey to God, figured through Dante's joining Beatrice in gazing at the sun, serves as a microcosmic image of Dante's journey. In keeping with Christian convention, the far-reaching clarity of Dante's vision 'beyond our mortal wont' not only signals that the pilgrim is spiritually ready to meet his maker, but that he is now made physically fit to see the light of heaven. This anticipates their progress in Paradise X–XIV, when Dante and Beatrice climb into the sun (the fourth heaven after the moon, Mercury, and Venus) and converse with two circles of blessed spirits, before continuing through the Ptolemaic system to Mars, Jupiter, Saturn, the Fixed Stars, the Primum Mobile, and the Empyrean, where Dante comes face to face with God. Although Hogg parallels this pre-celestial scrutiny of the sun during Mary's journey with Cela, similarly associating sunlight with heavenly light and giving Mary keener vision as she nears the sun, he departs from Dante and Milton in preserving far more mystery about the purpose of their journey. As Jill Rubenstein observes, Mary differs from traditional pilgrims in having 'no sense of purpose or direction' (Introduction, p. lvii). Hogg's universe is heliocentric (like Milton's) according to the Copernican revolution, but when he parallels the pilgrims' focus on the sun from the *Commedia*, he gives the sun an increased significance.

In the dramatic moment of Mary's nearing the sun with Cela, she sees angels in the sun pulling its curtains away to create a new day. For Hogg's travellers, this revelation comes at the beginning of their journey and shapes Mary's later pantheistic sun-worship. In keeping with Dante's fascinated mirroring of Beatrice staring at the sun, Mary's attention is arrested by her guide's pious respect for the solar temple:

> And they saw the chambers of the sun,
>   And the angels of the dawning ray,
> Draw the red curtains from the dome,
>   The glorious dome of the God of Day.
>
> And the youth a slight obeisance made,
>   And seemed to bend upon his knee:
> The holy vow he whispering said
>   Sunk deep in the heart of Mary Lee.
>   (Part First, ll. 187–94)

Crucially for Hogg, the light of the sun not only represents God's benevolence and truth; it emanates from the reality of God's physical presence in the sun. In his primary source, the book of Revelation, the apostle John likens Christ's face to 'the sun shining in all its brilliance' (2. 16) and later, the appearance of the Rider whose 'name is the Word of God' is followed by John's testimony: 'And I saw an angel standing in the sun, who cried in a loud voice to all the birds flying in mid-air, "Come, gather together for the great supper of God [...]"' (19. 17). But there is no obvious precedent for Hogg's remarkable fusion of Christian belief with pagan sun-worship, for neither in Revelation, nor in *Commedia*, nor in *Paradise Lost*, does God physically occupy the sun. When Milton's Satan passes the sun on his way to Eden and 'Saw within ken a glorious angel stand, | The same whom John saw also in the sun', the 'regent of the sun' who guards the 'radiant light' is Uriel.[25] In *The Pilgrims of the Sun*, Mary's revelation surpasses the apostle's since the regent is the Creator himself, the sun his 'throne of light sublime'.

Hogg's image of the sun as 'the glorious dome of the God of Day' also partly recalls James Thomson's personification of the sun as 'the powerful King of Day' in *The Seasons* (1730).[26] But whereas Thomson's admiration for Newtonian science supports the doctrine of divine creation, Hogg flirts with a pagan idea. For Thomson, the intricate cycles of *The Seasons* exemplify God's intelligent design; his image of the sun as a monarch conveys the Creator's benign power to rule his universe. In *Pilgrims*, the sun does not represent God figuratively, nor is it majestic itself—it is 'glorious' simply because it is God's home. By locating God in the body of the sun (perhaps a play on 'son') and making this a moment of epiphany in his heroine's spiritual journey, Hogg seems intent on reconciling two opposing belief systems—the biblical association of light with goodness (Jesus as 'the light of the world' or the word of God as 'a lamp unto our feet')[27] and the ancient pagan practice of sun-worship, associated with sun gods from Baal to Apollo.

   This is perhaps the most intriguing of Hogg's ventures into other worlds for its close echoing of and departures from Dante and Milton, and the daring implied marriage of Christian and pagan beliefs. Although Dante's first-person narrator speaks with the intensity of personal experience while Hogg's narrator is outside Mary's situation, Hogg's narrator treats Cela's sun-worship sympathetically, preserving its secret as reverently as Dante followed Beatrice's attention to the sun:

> I may not say the prayer he prayed,
>   Nor of its wondrous tendency;
> But it proved that the half the bedesmen said
>   Was neither true nor ever could be.
>   (Part First, ll. 195–98)

This harks back to Mary's scepticism at the beginning of the poem, but, moving from the local to the cosmic, the narrative perspective soon expands dramatically into an image of Hogg's virgin Mary literally hovering over the world. Whereas once she saw the sunrise over the local spots of Harlaw cairn and Yarrow, Mary Lee now has a visual command of the earth:

> O! think how glowed the virgin's breast
>   Hung o'er the profile of the world;
>
> On battlement of storied cloud
>   That floated o'er the dawn serene,
> To pace along with angel tread,
>   And on the rainbow's arch to lean.
>   (Part First, ll. 205–10)

In keeping with the shifting ideas of the poem, the Catholic iconography of the Assumption of the Virgin Mary is soon displaced as Hogg affirms explicitly that in this universe God dwells in the sun. Although Mary and Cela survey Edenic 'blossom-loaded trees, | And gardens of perennial blow', 'the scenes of glory' which occupy their attention are emphatically not the biblical site of genesis, but the sun (Part First, ll. 219–220, 225):

> It was the dwelling of that God
>   Who oped the welling springs of time;
> Seraph and cherubim's abode;
>   The Eternal's throne of light sublime.
>   (Part First, ll. 231–34)

Cela's repeated turning to the sun becomes an important motif in Mary's spiritual education, gradually bringing about her recognition of God's presence. Her fear that Cela is heathen is dispelled in Part Second when she sees his worship mirrored by all the planets and led by the heavenly assembly collected around God himself.

As in Dante's and Milton's otherworld journeys, Hogg uses his characters' expanding and contracting abilities and perceptions at particular points on their journey to reflect the dynamics of being inside or outside, belonging to or being exiled from, celestial places. Just as Mary's effortless guided flight to the sun highlights her freedom and grace in contrast to Satan's difficult solitary flight from the dark depths of Pandemonium to the empyrean, so her innocent admiration for God's 'light sublime' is an inversion of Satan's guilty view of the sun in *Paradise Lost*. Moments before he sees the angel Uriel in the sun, the accursed Satan sees, as Dante did with Beatrice, that the rays of the 'golden sun' give keener vision and direct the traveller upwards:

> Here matter new to gaze the devil met
> Undazzled, far and wide his eye commands,
> For sight no obstacle found there, nor shade,
> But all sunshine, as when his beams at noon
> Culminate from the equator, as they now
> Shot upward still direct, whence no way round
> Shadow from body opaque can fall, and the air,
> Nowhere so clear, sharpened his visual ray
> To objects far (III, 613–21)

Dante's view of the sun reaffirmed his ultimate destination to the light of God, but Satan's expansive visual command and moment of

clarity recall his former brightness only to renew his corruptive pur-
pose. For the outcast Satan on his subversive mission to spy on God's
new creation, the sunlight is a bitter reminder of his downfall. Soon
afterwards, he metamorphoses into a cherub to obtain Uriel's direc-
tions to Paradise. Hogg's heroine has no such need for subterfuge or
spying—she experiences her otherworld journey in her purest spir-
itual form and is more at ease in heavenly realms than on earth.
Mary not only views but stands upon the sun—and 'saw the plan | Of
God's fair universe'; she not only sees angels in the sun but also
God 'Himself enthroned | In light' at its centre (Part Second, ll. 63–
65).

    Satan's and Mary's cosmic flights each prompt a re-assessment of
their place in the universe. As Satan turns his destructive attention to
the 'pendent world' (II, 1052), no bigger than a star beside the moon—
so on Mary's journey, there is a moment for pausing to contemplate
the fragile world to which she belongs. Despite hovering above the
earth, Mary reveals her limited sight in a way that is reminiscent of
Chaucer's dream visions—especially the poet's flight with the eagle
as his guide in *The House of Fame*, the account of Scipio's Dream in
The Parliament of Fowls, and the elevation of Troilus's soul at the end
of *Troilus and Criseyde*. In the same way that Scipio's flight and Troilus's
death enable them to see how small and trivial the earth is, Mary is
made to recognise the narrowness of her world-view from a cosmic
vantage point. Cela reveals that she is wrong to imagine that she can
see her beloved Bowhill and Carterhaugh on the most beautiful of
the planets, for earth is the 'cloudy spot' she had overlooked (Part
Second, l. 137). When Hogg prepared *The Pilgrims of the Sun* for inclu-
sion in his *Poetical Works* of 1822, he strengthened its thematic allu-
sions to the genre of dream vision by claiming that Mary's journey
was not physical: 'The erratic pilgrimage is given merely as a dream
or vision of a person in a long trance'.[28] His cautious emphasis on
the visionary nature of the journey stemmed chiefly from his embar-
rassment about the poem's mixed reception in 1815 and particularly
John Murray's decision to revoke his agreement to publish it. Nev-
ertheless, Hogg's appeal to an imaginative flight within the heroine's
subconscious draws attention to a medieval tradition of dream vi-
sion which is especially apropos for the *Pilgrims* and the projected
Midsummer Night Dreams. As the title of Cary's translation, *The Vision*,
emphasises, Dante had presented the *Commedia* as his vision, dated
to Good Friday 1300. Moreover, Dante's fainting and taking refuge
in dreams during his journey is perhaps echoed in *Pilgrims* when
Mary faints at the heavenly assembly and revives in a state of 'dream-

ing melody' (Part Second, l. 343).

Attending to Hogg's use of Dante's and Milton's otherworld journeys helps to illuminate *The Pilgrims of the Sun* as part of the Romantic reception of the two poets. Some of Hogg's appropriations are cosmetic, as in the double allusion of Cela and Mary conversing with the saints and inhabitants of heaven, as Dante and Beatrice did when they climbed into the sun—of 'the ways of God with man' (Part Second, l. 378), echoing Milton's justifying 'the ways of God to men' (I, 26). But Hogg's use of Dante and Milton goes beyond the ornamental appropriation of visual tropes to reveal his admiration for the scope, energy, and freedom with which these predecessors used their imaginations to explore the universal and transcendent. Hogg's intricate response to Dante's use of pilgrimage and the sun in 1814 makes him an early respondent in the enthusiastic nineteenth-century British reception of Dante. By 1818, the *Commedia* was so well-known in Britain that in that year Hazlitt and Coleridge gave public lectures on Dante in Surrey and London, Ugo Foscolo's articles on Dante appeared in the *Edinburgh Review*, and in Peacock's *Nightmare Abbey* (1818), Mr Listless remarked that Dante was growing fashionable. Among Romantic readers of *The Vision*, Coleridge, Hazlitt, Shelley, and Keats were impressed by different facets of Dante's poetry—his bold use of epic, his vivid imagery, his personal reader-writer dynamic, his ideals of liberty, or the purifying effect of love.[29] Dante clearly inspired Hogg's use of the sun as a focal point for a shared spiritual journey of the heavens between innocent lovers—contrasting with Milton's hero's guilty view of the sun. Yet Hogg's careful balancing of Christian and pagan possibilities ensures that Mary's spiritual flight with Cela is at once a quest for the truth of Christian doctrine, in keeping with the *Commedia*, *Paradise Lost*, and later spiritual allegories such as *The Pilgrim's Progress* (1678)—and a mysterious exploration of alternative worlds that appealed to the Romantic preoccupation with the liberated imagination.

Hogg's whimsical preoccupation with seeing God in the sun aligns *The Pilgrims of the Sun* with William Blake's colour-printed etching, *Glad Day, or Albion Rose* (c. 1796), in which a young man triumphantly steps out of the sun in a cruciform pose—at once suggesting Christ's glory and the dawn of a new day. Blake's *The Ancient of Days* (1794) is another powerful image which places God in the sun—here the huge bearded figure of the creator, Urizen, reaches down from the red sun with his architectural tools, against a dramatically black sky.[30] Although the select circulation of Blake's work among London radicals makes it unlikely that Hogg ever saw these prints, Hogg's blending of the pagan and Christian is intriguingly close to Blake. Their shared interest in the mystical possibilities of the sun seems to anticipate J. M. Turner's later painting, *The Angel Standing in the Sun* (exhibited at the Royal Academy in 1846), illustrating the source passage from Revelation.[31]

In contemplating ideas of apocalypse, Hogg may have recalled his mystified reaction to reading Thomas Burnet's *Sacred Theory of the Earth* (1684) while working as a shepherd in his youth: 'All the day I was pondering on the grand millennium, and the reign of the saints; and all the night dreaming of new heavens and a new earth; the stars in horror, and the world in flames!'[32] From Burnet, however, comes this suggestive passage about a 'great Being' in the sun:

> This glorious Body, which now we can only gaze upon and admire, will be then better understood. A mass of Light and Flame, and Ethereal matter, ten thousand times bigger than this Earth: Enlightning and enlivening an Orb that exceeds the bulk of our Globe [...] may reasonably be presum'd to have some great Being at the Centre of it. But what that is, we must leave to the enquiries of another life.[33]

In *The Pilgrims of the Sun*, Hogg gives Mary Lee a unique opportunity to see the 'glorious Body' and 'great Being' of the sun, and, in an important departure from 'Kilmeny', he insists on taking the otherworld experience back to the folkloric setting and integrating it with the human community. When Mary returns to Carterhaugh, she feels for the first time that she is part of a harmonious marriage of nature, her neighbourhood, God, and the sun. The final part of this essay examines the way in which Hogg's benign use of the sun and his celebration of God's presence refute the distorted perceptions of the sun and a hostile universe in Coleridge's *Rime of the Ancient Mariner* and Byron's *Manfred* and *Cain*. I suggest that Hogg's optimistic pursuit of the elusive and unorthodox, and his union of the cosmic and local in *The Pilgrims of the Sun*, challenge the oppressive other worlds imagined by his Romantic contemporaries—by implicitly absorbing the optimism of eighteenth-century utopia and romance, and embracing a form of Coleridgean pantheism.

2. Seeing God in the Sun: *Pilgrims of the Sun* in Response to Coleridge and Byron

The third part of the *Pilgrims*, in which Hogg uses Mary's tour of the worlds around the sun to critique his society, draws on a legacy of

eighteenth-century satire, travel-writing, and romance about alterna-
tive worlds. The degeneracy of Hogg's society is implied when Mary
and Cela see a series of worlds inhabited by scoundrels, among
whom are lawyers, beadsmen, 'snarling critics' and patriots (Part
Third, l. 366), but although he imitates Pope's verse style, the social
satire here is far more general than in *The Dunciad* (1728) or Swift's
Gulliver's Travels (1726). With its emphasis on heavenly purity and
the distancing of evil from good, Hogg's otherworld journey is es-
sentially utopian, perhaps closer in spirit to Pope's *An Essay on Man*
(1732–34), in which the chaotic universe is found to be: 'All discord,
harmony, not understood; | All partial evil, universal good'.[34] The
combination of Mary Lee's unrivalled virtue and her mortal flight
may be more specifically indebted to Robert Paltock's popular ro-
mance, *The Life and Adventures of Peter Wilkins, A Cornish Man* (1751), in
which the shipwrecked hero falls in love with an ideal winged woman
and is welcomed by her native flying people, the innately good
Gawries and Glumms. Like Paltock, Hogg is interested in trans-
porting a local hero to an unfamiliar imaginative space and finding
out what happens when s/he returns home. Paltock's novel was es-
pecially influential on Coleridge's Mariner's voyage to the South
Pole; it also impressed Charles Lamb and Leigh Hunt and became a
direct source for Southey's flying Glendoveers, 'the loveliest race of
all of heavenly birth', in *The Curse of Kehema* (1810), which Hogg had
read.[35]

Mary Lee's flight to the sun also provides an intriguing contrast to
eighteenth-century utopian narratives about moon travel, which in-
cluded Pythagorlunster's *A Journey to the Moon* (*c.* 1740), William
Thomson's *The Man in the Moon; or, Travels into the Lunar Regions* (1783),
and Aratus's *A Voyage to the Moon Strongly Recommended to All Lovers of
Real Freedom* (1793).[36] But Hogg's moon imagery specifically recalls
the ballad of 'Sir Patrick Spens' and Coleridge's poetry. When, early
in her flight, Mary sees 'the wraith of the waning moon' 'cradled on
the wave' as 'a line of silver light' (Part First, ll. 155, 159, 161), the
image partly recalls the new moon, 'circled with a silver Thread',
with the old moon cradled in her arms, from the opening of
Coleridge's 'Dejection: An Ode' (1802).[37] Similarly, when 'the halo
of the evening star | Sank like a crescent on the sea' (Part First, ll.
129–30), its swift movement invites comparisons with the acceler-
ated cycles of the sun and moon, and the albatross which 'sank |
Like lead into the sea' in *The Rime of the Ancient Mariner*—especially since it
is followed by a ship 'speed[ing] swiftly o'er the faem' (Part First, l.
168).[38] These allusions highlight that in Hogg's poem there is noth-

ing ominous about the waning moon or the sinking crescent—they are simply part of a splendid succession of sights glimpsed by Mary and Cela as they move 'ten thousand times' beyond the speed of the ship, enjoying unparalleled views of the coastlines and skies before ascending into the heavens (Part First, l. 171).

Mary's and Cela's view of the sun as a hospitable set of 'chambers' lit up by a benevolent God, and Mary's survey of the universe at the pinnacle of their journey provide a powerful contrast to Coleridge's Godless realm in *The Rime of the Ancient Mariner*. Hogg and Coleridge each explore an unorthodox universe which eludes the laws of logic and cause and effect, and in which the poet's imagination is the driving force—indeed Coleridge later emphasised his ballad to Mrs Barbauld as a 'work of [...] pure imagination'.[39] But whereas Hogg's pilgrimage to the sun is exuberantly unconventional in its insistence on God's munificent presence, the Mariner who experiences intense physical, emotional, and psychological suffering, seems haunted by God's absence (a world 'so lonely [...] that God himself | Scarce seemed there to be').[40] After killing the albatross, an act which he perceives as a crime against God and Nature, the Mariner sees a ghost-ship on the horizon against the sun. His perception of the sun as a prisoner now reflects his guilty perception of himself:

> And straight the sun was flecked with bars,
> (Heaven's mother send us grace!)
> As if through a dungeon grate he peered
> With broad and burning face.[41]

The persecuted imagery of the sun, projected through the Mariner's sin and self-loathing, seems to exemplify the isolation and confinement of his otherworld journey. In the world of the poem everything is arbitrary, extreme, and disproportionate—the death of the albatross seems to entail the death of two hundred men, while the Mariner's fate is determined by a roll of the dice when Death and Life-in-Death gamble for his life. The Mariner's guilt even weighs on him physically, blinding and imprisoning him within a tightly constructed but unpredictable framework of rhymes:

> I closed my lids and kept them close,
> Till the balls like pulses beat;
> For the sky and the sea, and the sea and the sky
> Lay like a load on my weary eye,
> And the dead were at my feet.[42]

Hemmed in by a crew of corpses, his eyeballs beating against the

insides of his eyelids and the sky and seascape bearing down from
without, the Mariner's claustrophobia and blindness could hardly
be more extreme. By contrast, Mary Lee is blessed beyond all mortals
with uninhibited movement and vision. It is not just that Hogg's trav-
ellers have more fun on their otherworld journey, but that their uni-
verse releases them from the consistency of any single belief system.
Hogg not only mingles Catholic and pagan ideas, but contradicts his
own claims in different parts of the poem. For example, the eternal
progression towards perfection, whereby spirits journey 'from world
to world more pure—till by degrees | After a thousand years' pro-
gression' they attain 'bliss unspeakable' (Part Second, ll. 198–99,
121) is complicated by the existence of 'accursed' and hellish places
for atheists. Later it emerges that the 'progressive, endless pilgrim-
age' is not a refining journey towards spiritual perfection—but '*to
woe, or state of bliss*' (my emphasis, Part Third, ll. 408, 409). This con-
ceptual changeability makes it impossible to read the journey in *The
Pilgrims of the Sun* as propounding any particular belief system, real or
imagined. Nevertheless, the variable universe Hogg creates is suffi-
cient to accommodate the pious curiosity of his guiltless heroine.
There are no harrowing Dantean encounters with the spirits of peo-
ple she knows and none of the terrifying unpredictability endured
by the Mariner.

As well as offering an uplifting antidote to the stifling constraints
and suffering of Coleridge's Ancient Mariner, Hogg's emphasis on
boundless vision and flight in *Pilgrims* suggests a possible dialogue
with Byron. When Mary reaches the sun (the pinnacle of heaven),
she stands with Cela on a mount of 'wreathy light' and watches 'the
motioned universe' which is animated in an invigorating rather than
claustrophobic way (Part Second, ll. 28, 31):

> Raised as they were now
> To the high fountain-head of light and vision,
> Where'er they cast their eyes abroad, they found
> The light behind, the object still before;
> And on the rarefied and pristine rays
> Of vision borne, their piercing sight passed on
> Intense and all unbounded—Onward!—onward!
> No cloud to intervene! no haze to dim!
> Or nigh, or distant, it was all the same;
> For distance lessened not.—O what a scene,
> To see so many goodly worlds upborne!
> (Part Second, ll. 32–42)

The energising exclamations of this passage aptly capture the excitement of seeing a host of worlds with pristine clarity. Here, God is benevolently present and engaged in loving sight–'He viewed the whole, and with a father's care | Upheld and cherished' (Part Second, ll. 66–67). Hogg's dedication of *The Pilgrims of the Sun* to Byron explicitly invokes the younger poet's fearless spirit and artistic flight– his 'bold and native energy' and 'soul that dares each bound to overfly, | Ranging through Nature on erratic wing–'.[43] Yet in contrast to Hogg's joyful celebration of Mary's freedom and 'piercing sight', Byron's dramatic poem, *Manfred* (1817), presents the static condition and limited view of the mortal over-reacher who is 'half dust, half deity'.

Soliloquizing upon the cliffs of the Jungfrau, Manfred contrasts the soaring flight and 'pervading vision' of a passing eagle with his own confinement:

> Thou art gone
> Where the eye cannot follow thee; but thine
> Yet pierces downward, onward, or above
> With a pervading vision.–Beautiful!
> How beautiful is all this visible world!
> How glorious in its action and itself;
> But we, who name ourselves its sovereigns, we,
> Half dust, half deity, alike unfit
> To sink or soar, with our mix'd essence make
> A conflict of its elements, and breathe
> The breath of degradation and of pride,
> Contending with low wants and lofty will
> Till our mortality predominates[44]

The momentum and expansiveness of Hogg's 'Onward!–onward! | No cloud to intervene! no haze to dim!' at first appear to be matched by Manfred's stirring 'Beautiful! | How beautiful is all this visible world!' but the effect is rapidly diminished by the unravelling of his godlike aspirations. Although he has outstripped his fellow men through the pursuit of forbidden knowledge, Manfred can never transcend his mortality. As he stands poised between heaven and earth, his sensitivity to the natural beauty around him makes his condition even more unbearable since he is aware of contaminating its purity with 'the breath of degradation and of pride'. Knowing that he can neither live more fully nor resume ordinary life, he prepares to leap from the mountain summit to the rocks below as the only means of escape–and even then he is thwarted by the chamois hunter.

Manfred may speak of the mind's power 'to comprehend the universe' but in Byron's '*mental theatre*' the mind must war against itself; limitation and constraint are always encountered.[45]

If Manfred's speech partly responds to Mary's edifying spiritual journey in *Pilgrims of the Sun*, the dark intellectual flight of Byron's controversial drama, *Cain: A Mystery* (1821), perhaps offers a more developed reply. At least one reader recognised Hogg's poem as a source for *Cain*. Writing of Hogg's achievements, an anonymous critic for the *Literary Speculum* in December 1822 observed that 'the Pilgrims of the Sun, is chiefly remarkable for its fable, which Lord Byron in his Cain, and Shelley in his Queen Mab, have palpably imitated'.[46] In fact Shelley had composed his verse narrative about a young girl who is transported across time and space and educated about atheism by the fairy queen as early as 1812–13; otherworld journeys were evidently a Romantic preoccupation. With its dedication to Scott, Byron's *Cain* won the support of a strong literary protector who was prepared to defend his exploration of unorthodox ideas—yet Cain's cosmic tour with Lucifer through 'the abyss of eternity' and Hades responds less to Scott's work than to *The Pilgrims of the Sun*, the poem that Hogg dedicated to Byron. *Cain* is far more metaphysically and topographically complex than Hogg's poem, and critics such as Truman Guy Steffan have suggested a number of possible sources for its otherworld journey—including Fontenelle's *Conversations on the Plurality of Worlds* (1686).[47] Here I suggest that *The Pilgrims of the Sun* might usefully be considered among the sources for *Cain*. Following on from Manfred's overreaching plight of being 'half dust, half deity', Cain's dissatisfaction with his parents' fall from Eden is easily exacerbated by Lucifer, who offers to show him 'Worlds greater than thine own'.[48] But in contrast to the finality of Manfred's self-destruction, or the serene conclusion of Shelley's poem, in which the heroine, Ianthe, awakes from her dream, in *Cain* Byron shares Hogg's interest in the mortal hero or heroine who must resume life on earth after seeing the universe.

While Hogg's ever-evolving poetic styles in *The Pilgrims of the Sun* aptly support Mary Lee's liberation from any single belief system, Byron uses the constraints of verse to reinforce his hero's sense of limitation. In a provocative challenge to conventional Christian doctrine, the incestuous family life of Adam and Eve's offspring, who can only procreate among themselves, is broken apart by Lucifer—a Promethean defender of intellectual freedom who feeds Cain's suspicion of God's tyranny. The characters' carefully measured speeches heighten the intense emotions they express by their very compression.

At first, Cain's tour with Lucifer, like Mary's with Cela, yields an empowering boundlessness. Contemplating 'an aerial universe of endless | expansion', Cain feels 'Intoxicated with eternity'.[49] But Lucifer's presentation of the earth as 'but the wreck' of a previous world, and his revelation that Cain and his kin will share the fate of the 'superior' pre-Adamites, now reduced to 'mighty phantoms', has the effect of diminishing Cain in his own eyes.[50] After gazing upon eternity, Cain feels more insignificant than before ('Alas! I seem | Nothing') and upon returning to earth, he laments: 'I feel | My littleness again'.[51] Manfred and Cain discover that the knowledge they have gained is in itself limited and confining, neither satisfying their intellectual appetites nor fulfilling their expectations of liberty and power, but bringing isolation, inner turmoil and self-disgust. This internal annihilation precipitates the final catastrophe, in which Cain murders his brother and is exiled with his wife and sister, Adah. By contrast, Mary Lee is resurrected to a new life on earth–first reunited with her body in the grave and then restored to her family home.

Ultimately Mary's otherworld journey makes her life on earth more fulfilling. After returning to Carterhaugh, Mary not only makes her vows to the sun as Cela did, but participates in a sun-worship which brings her into communion with all of nature. She notices that flowers, birds, and children turn to the sun instinctively, and that through the child's innocent gaze, the sun shapes the infant mind:

> She saw the new born infant's eye
> Turned to that light incessantly;
> Nor ever was that eye withdrawn
> Till the mind thus carved began to dawn.
> All Nature worshipped at one shrine,
> Nor knew that the impulse was divine.
>   (Part Fourth, ll. 316–21)

Here Hogg offers a harmonious resolution to the oppressive other worlds of many Romantic poems–by drawing on the Pantheistic beliefs expressed by Wordsworth and Coleridge, whose early poetry repeatedly evokes God's immanence in the natural world. Hogg's tableau of the child's mind being 'carved' by God as he watches the sun is especially reminiscent of Coleridge's conversation poems of 1798–'The Nightingale' in which the poet's son, though 'capable of no articulate sound', hushes responsively to behold the moon, and 'Frost at Midnight', in which the poet imagines his son imbibing the 'eternal language' of God through the intelligence and beauty of the natural forms around him.[52] Here Coleridge figures the child wandering 'like a breeze' by lakes, shores and mountains, and receiving God's teaching through his sense impressions:

> so shalt thou see and hear
> The lovely shapes and sounds intelligible
> Of that eternal language, which thy God
> Utters, who from eternity doth teach
> Himself in all, and all things in himself.[53]

Turning away from his own sense of restriction, Coleridge expresses an intense desire for his child to enjoy a God-given love, blessing and freedom. In the poet's imagination his child is freed from 'the stern preceptor' of his own cloistered schooling and instead moulded by the 'Great universal Teacher' who is at once embodied in nature and represented by it.[54]

In *The Pilgrims of the Sun*, Hogg similarly liberates Mary Lee from the blind authority of the beadsmen and re-educates her to perceive God's presence by emotional instinct. Poignantly, Hogg is able to share his heroine's journey in a way that Coleridge and Byron could not. By the end of the poem it is clear that, unlike Dante, Hogg identifies with both the mortal pilgrim and her guide. In a humorous twist, Cela reappears in human form as Hugo the Harper, an avatar of Hogg himself, to marry Mary and father a line of minstrels—making their union artistically nurturing for the nation. Through Mary's otherworld journey and her return to the community, Hogg achieves a different kind of imaginative freedom to his predecessors and contemporaries. Drawing on 'high' and 'low' poetic traditions and transforming them with his own distinctive topoi, in *The Pilgrims of the Sun* Hogg allows himself and Mary the benediction that Coleridge wanted to bestow on his son. He not only circles heaven and sees God in the sun, but lives more fully on earth.

Notes

Warmest thanks to Gill Hughes for inviting me to write this essay and for kindly allowing me to see all the editorial apparatus which she and Jill Rubenstein prepared for this volume. I would also like to thank both Kate Davies and Gill Hughes for their very helpful comments and suggestions on a draft of this essay. I am grateful to the Trustees of the National Library of Scotland for permission to quote from manuscripts in their collection. For the list of abbreviations employed here please see the 'Note on the Texts' below (pp. 177–78).

1. Hogg to John Murray, 21 January 1815, in *Letters*, I, 234.
2. William Blackwood to John Murray, 11 December 1814. John Murray Archive: National Library of Scotland (hereafter NLS), Acc. 12604/1113.

3. *Critical Review*, fifth series, 1 (April 1815), 399–409 (pp. 399, 403).

4. David Groves, *James Hogg: The Growth of a Writer* (Edinburgh: Scottish Academic Press, 1988), pp. 58–62 (p. 61).

5. *Pilgrims*, Part Second, l. 180. All subsequent quotations are from the present edition and references are given in parentheses.

6. 'Kilmeny', in *The Queen's Wake, A Legendary Poem* [1813], ed. by Douglas S. Mack (S/SC, 2004), Night the Second, ll. 1348, 1392, 1396, 1397, 1436.

7. See Suzanne Gilbert, 'Hogg's "Kilmeny" and the Ballad of Supernatural Abduction', *SHW*, 8 (1997), 42–55.

8. 'The Witch of Fife', in *The Queen's Wake* [1813], ed. Mack, Night the First, l. 879.

9. See the review of the third edition of *The Queen's Wake*, in *Edinburgh Review*, 24 (November 1814), 157–74 (p. 162).

10. *Ibid*, pp. 163–64.

11. *Ibid*, p. 164.

12. Robert Southey to James Hogg, 1 December 1814 (NLS, MS 2245, fols 7–8).

13. Hogg's first major published collection of poems was *The Mountain Bard* (Edinburgh: Archibald Constable; London: John Murray, 1807).

14. For Barton's lines see *The Queen's Wake*, ed. Mack, pp. 391–93 (p. 392).

15. *The Queen's Wake*, ed. Mack, p. 63 (Night the Second, l. 302).

16. *Critical Review*, p. 406.

17. See Michael Caesar's introduction to *Dante: the Critical Heritage* (London: Routledge, 1989), pp. 1–88 (p. 53). *The Vision* became the principal text through which British readers read Dante in the Romantic era.

18. See Ralph Pite's introduction to *The Divine Comedy: The Vision of Dante*, trans. by Henry Cary, ed. by Ralph Pite (London: Everyman, 1994), pp. xix–xxviii (p. xxiii).

19. Edmund Burke, *A Philosophical Enquiry into the Origin of our Ideas of the Sublime and Beautiful*, ed. by Adam Phillips (Oxford: Oxford University Press, 1998), p. 55.

20. Henry Francis Cary, 'The Life of Dante' in *The Vision; or Hell, Purgatory, and Paradise, of Dante Alighieri*, 2nd edn, 3 vols (London: Taylor and Hessey, 1819), I, i–lii (pp. xliv, xliii).

21. See Ralph Pite, *The Circle of Our Vision: Dante's Presence in English Romantic Poetry* (Oxford: Clarendon Press, 1994), pp. 12–17.

22. See Addison's no. 315 of *The Spectator* for 1 March 1712, in *The Spectator*, ed. by G. Gregory Smith, 4 vols (London: J. M. Dent & Sons Ltd., 1907), II, 448–453 (pp. 451, 450, 451).

23. *Ibid*, p. 453.

24. Dante Alighieri, *The Divine Comedy, The Vision of Dante*, trans. by Henry Cary, ed. by Ralph Pite (London: Everyman, 1994), Paradise, Canto I, 40–41. All subsequent quotations are from this edition and references are given in parentheses.

25. John Milton, *Paradise Lost*, ed. by Alastair Fowler, 2nd edn (London: Longman, 2007), III, 622–23, 690, 594. All subsequent quotations from *Paradise Lost* are from this edition and references are given in parentheses.

26. James Thomson, *The Seasons*, ed. by James Sambrook (Oxford: Clarendon Press, 1981), 'Summer', l. 81.

27. John 8. 12 and Psalm 119. 105.

28. See p. 148 of the present edition.

29. See Michael Caesar's introduction to *Dante: the Critical Heritage*, p. 54, and Ralph Pite's introduction to *The Divine Comedy: The Vision of Dante*, p. xxiv.

30. I am grateful to Mark Crosby for suggesting *The Ancient of Days* in this

context.

31. For a brief comparison of Blake's *Glad Day* and Turner's painting, see Gerald Finley, *Angel in the Sun: Turner's Vision of History* (Montreal: McGill's-Queen's University Press, 1999), p. 177.

32. James Hogg, 'Memoir of the Life of James Hogg' [1807 version], in *The Mountain Bard*, ed. by Suzanne Gilbert (S/SC, 2007), pp. 7–17 (p. 11).

33. Thomas Burnet, *The Sacred Theory of the Earth*, ed. by Basil Willey (London: Centaur Press Ltd, 1965), p. 368.

34. *An Essay on Man*, in *Alexander Pope: The Major Works*, ed. by Pat Rogers (Oxford: Oxford University Press, 2006), Epistle I, 291–92.

35. Robert Southey, *The Curse of Kehama* (London: Longman, Hurst, Rees, Orme, and Browne, 1810), pp. 47 and 258. Hogg mentions Southey's poem in a letter to the poet of 17 September 1811 (see *Letters*, I, 114–15).

36. See *Modern British Utopias 1700–1850*, ed. by Gregory Claeys, 8 vols (London: Pickering & Chatto, 1997), volumes II and IV.

37. 'Dejection: An Ode' (l. 12), in *Samuel Taylor Coleridge: The Major Works*, ed. by H. J. Jackson (Oxford: Oxford University Press, 2000). Unless otherwise stated, all subsequent quotations from Coleridge are from this edition.

38. 'The Ancient Mariner: A Poet's Reverie', in William Wordsworth and Samuel Taylor Coleridge, *Lyrical Ballads: Second Edition*, ed. by Michael Mason, 2nd edn (London: Pearson Longman, 2007), IV, 284–85. All subsequent quotations from 'The Ancient Mariner' are from this edition, which uses the 1805 text of *Lyrical Ballads* which was available to Hogg when he composed *Pilgrims*.

39. See the entry for [31 May 1830], in Coleridge's *Table Talk*, in *Coleridge*, ed. H. J. Jackson, p. 593.

40. 'The Ancient Mariner', stanza VII, ll. 593–94.

41. 'The Ancient Mariner', stanza III, ll. 171–74.

42. 'The Ancient Mariner', stanza IV, ll. 242–46.

43. For more on Hogg and Byron, see Gillian Hughes, '"Native Energy": Hogg and Byron as Scottish Poets', *The Byron Journal*, 34 no 2 (2006), 133–42.

44. *Manfred*, in *Byron*, ed. by Jerome J. McGann (Oxford: Oxford University Press, 1986), I. 2. 32–47. All subsequent quotations from Byron are from this edition.

45. *Manfred*, II. 2. 111. Byron to John Murray, 23 August 1821, in *Byron's Letters and Journals*, ed. by Leslie A. Marchand, 13 vols (London: John Murray, 1973–94), VIII, 187 (original emphasis).

46. 'On the Genius of Hogg', *Literary Speculum*, 2 (December 1822), 433–43 (p. 441).

47. Truman Guy Steffan, *Lord Byron's Cain: Twelve Essays and a Text With Variants and Annotations* (Austin: University of Texas Press, 1968), pp. 300–03.

48. *Cain*, II. 2. 44.

49. *Cain*, II. 1. 107–08, 109.

50. *Cain*, II. 2. 153, and II. 2. 69, 44.

51. *Cain*, II. 2. 420–21, and III. 1. 67–68.

52. 'The Nightingale', l. 92.

53. 'Frost at Midnight', ll. 54, 58–62.

54. 'Frost at Midnight', ll. 37, 63.

To the Right Hon.
Lord Byron

NOT for thy crabbed state-creed, wayward wight,
Thy noble lineage, nor thy virtues high,
(God bless the mark!) do I this homage plight;
No—'tis thy bold and native energy;
Thy soul that dares each bound to overfly,
Ranging through Nature on erratic wing—
These do I honour—and would fondly try
With thee a wild aërial strain to sing:
Then, O! round Shepherd's head thy charmed mantle fling.

The Pilgrims of the Sun

PART FIRST

OF all the lasses in fair Scotland,
   That lightly bound o'er muir and lee,
There's nane like the maids of Yarrowdale,
   Wi' their green coats kilted to the knee.

O! there shines mony a winsom face,   5
   And mony a bright and beaming ee;
For rosy health blooms on the cheek,
   And the blink of love plays o'er the bree.

But ne'er by Yarrow's sunny braes,
   Nor Ettrick's green and wizard shaw,   10
Did ever maid so lovely won
   As Mary Lee of Carelha'.*

O! round her fair and sightly form
   The light hill-breeze was blithe to blow,
For the virgin hue her bosom wore   15
   Was whiter than the drifted snow.

The dogs that wont to growl and bark,
   Whene'er a stranger they could see,
Would cower, and creep along the sward,
   And lick the hand of Mary Lee.   20

On form so fair, or face so mild,
   The rising sun did never gleam;
On such a pure untainted mind
   The dawn of truth did never beam.

She never had felt the stounds of love,   25
   Nor the waefu' qualms that breed o' sin;
But ah! she shewed an absent look,
   And a deep and thoughtfu' heart within.

---

* Now vulgarly called Carterhaugh.

She looked with joy on a young man's face,
   The downy chin, and the burning eye,   30
Without desire, without a blush,
   She loved them, but she knew not why.

She learned to read, when she was young,
   The books of deep divinity;
And she thought by night, and she read by day,   35
   Of the life that is, and the life to be.

And the more she thought, and the more she read
   Of the ways of Heaven and Nature's plan,
She feared the half that the bedesmen said
   Was neither true nor plain to man.   40

Yet she was meek, and bowed to Heaven
   Each morn beneath the shady yew,
Before the laverock left the cloud,
   Or the sun began his draught of dew.

And when the gloaming's gouden veil   45
   Was o'er Blackandro's summit flung,
Among the bowers of green Bowhill
   Her hymn she to the Virgin sung.

And aye she thought, and aye she read,
   Till mystic wildness marked her air;   50
For the doubts that on her bosom preyed
   Were more than maiden's mind could bear.

And she grew weary of this world,
   And yearned and pined the next to see;
Till Heaven in pity earnest sent,   55
   And from that thraldom set her free.

One eve when she had prayed and wept
   Till daylight faded on the wold–
The third night of the waning moon!
   Well known to hind and matron old;   60

For then the fairies boun' to ride,
   And the elves of Ettrick's greenwood shaw;
And aye their favourite rendezvous
   Was green Bowhill and Carelha'–

There came a wight to Mary's knee,   65
    With face, like angel's, mild and sweet;
His robe was like the lily's bloom,
    And graceful flowed upon his feet.

He did not clasp her in his arms,
    Nor showed he cumbrous courtesy;   70
But took her gently by the hand,
    Saying, "Maiden, rise and go with me.

"Cast off, cast off these earthly weeds,
    They ill befit thy destiny;
I come from a far distant land   75
    To take thee where thou long'st to be."

She only felt a shivering throb,
    A pang defined that may not be;
And up she rose, a naked form,
    More lightsome, pure, and fair than he.   80

He held a robe in his right hand,
    Pure as the white rose in the bloom;
That robe was not of earthly make,
    Nor sewed by hand, nor wove in loom.

When she had doned that light seymar,   85
    Upward her being seemed to bound;
Like one that wades in waters deep,
    And scarce can keep him to the ground.

Tho' rapt and transient was the pause,
    She scarce could keep to ground the while;   90
She felt like heaving thistle-down,
    Hung to the earth by viewless pile.

The beauteous stranger turned his face
    Unto the eastern streamers sheen,
He seemed to eye the ruby star   95
    That rose above the Eildon green.

He spread his right hand to the heaven,
    And he bade the maid not look behind,
But keep her face to the dark blue even;
    And away they bore upon the wind.   100

She did not linger, she did not look,
    For in a moment they were gone;
But she thought she saw her very form
    Stretched on the greenwood's lap alone.

As ever you saw the meteor speed,   105
    Or the arrow cleave the yielding wind,
Away they sprung, and the breezes sung,
    And they left the gloaming star behind;

And eastward, eastward still they bore,
    Along the night's grey canopy;   110
And the din of the world died away,
    And the landscape faded on the ee.

They had marked the dark blue waters lie
    Like curved lines on many a vale;
And they hung on the shelve of a saffron cloud,   115
    That scarcely moved in the slumbering gale.

They turned their eyes to the heaven above,
    And the stars blazed bright as they drew nigh;
And they looked to the darksome world below,
    But all was grey obscurity.   120

They could not trace the hill nor dale,
    Nor could they ken where the greenwood lay;
But they saw a thousand shadowy stars,
    In many a winding watery way;
And they better knew where the rivers ran   125
    Than if it had been the open day.

They looked to the western shores afar,
    But the light of day they could not see;
And the halo of the evening star
    Sank like a crescent on the sea.   130

Then onward, onward fast they bore
    On the yielding winds so light and boon,
To meet the climes that bred the day,
    And gave the glow to the gilded moon

Long had she chambered in the deep,   135
    To spite the maidens of the main,

But now frae the merman's couch she sprung,
  And blushed upon her still domain.

When first from out the sea she peeped,
  She kythed like maiden's gouden kemb,   140
And the sleepy waves washed o'er her brow,
  And belled her cheek wi' the briny faem.

But the yellow leme spread up the lift,
  And the stars grew dim before her ee,
And up arose the Queen of Night   145
  In all her solemn majesty.

O! Mary's heart was blithe to lie
  Above the ocean wastes reclined,
Beside her lovely guide so high,
  On the downy bosom of the wind.   150

She saw the shades and gleams so bright
  Play o'er the deep incessantly,
Like streamers of the norland way,
  The lights that danced on the quaking sea.

She saw the wraith of the waning moon,   155
  Trembling and pale it seemed to lie;
It was not round like golden shield,
  Nor like her moulded orb on high.

Her image cradled on the wave,
  Scarce bore similitude the while;   160
It was a line of silver light,
  Stretched on the deep for many a mile.

The lovely youth beheld with joy
  That Mary loved such scenes to view;
And away, and away they journeyed on,   165
  Faster than wild bird ever flew.

Before the tide, before the wind,
  The ship speeds swiftly o'er the faem;
And the sailor sees the shores fly back,
  And weens his station still the same: 170

Beyond that speed ten thousand times,
    By the marled streak and the cloudlet brown,
Past our aerial travellers on
    In the wan light of the waning moon.

They keeped aloof as they passed her bye,   175
    For their views of the world were not yet done;
But they saw her mighty mountain form
    Like Cheviot in the setting sun.

And the stars and the moon fled west away,
    So swift o'er the vaulted sky they shone;   180
They seemed like fiery rainbows reared,
    In a moment seen, in a moment gone.

Yet Mary Lee as easy felt
    As if on silken couch she lay;
And soon on a rosy film they hung,   185
    Above the beams of the breaking day.

And they saw the chambers of the sun,
    And the angels of the dawning ray,
Draw the red curtains from the dome,
    The glorious dome of the God of Day.   190

And the youth a slight obeisance made,
    And seemed to bend upon his knee:
The holy vow he whispering said
    Sunk deep in the heart of Mary Lee.

I may not say the prayer he prayed,   195
    Nor of its wondrous tendency;
But it proved that the half the bedesmen said
    Was neither true nor ever could be.

Sweet breaks the day o'er Harlaw cairn,
    On many an ancient peel and barrow,   200
On braken hill, and lonely tarn,
    Along the greenwood glen of Yarrow.

Oft there had Mary viewed with joy
    The rosy streaks of light unfurled:
O! think how glowed the virgin's breast   205
    Hung o'er the profile of the world;

On battlement of storied cloud
   That floated o'er the dawn serene,
To pace along with angel tread,
   And on the rainbow's arch to lean.   210

Her cheek lay on its rosy rim,
   Her bosom pressed the yielding blue,
And her fair robes of heavenly make
   Were sweetly tinged with every hue.

And there they lay, and there beheld   215
   The glories of the opening morn
Spread o'er the eastern world afar,
   Where winter wreath was never borne.

And they saw the blossom-loaded trees,
   And gardens of perennial blow   220
Spread their fair bosoms to the day,
   In dappled pride, and endless glow.

These came and passed, for the earth rolled on,
   But still on the brows of the air they hung;
The scenes of glory they now beheld   225
   May scarce by mortal bard be sung.

It was not the hues of the marbled sky,
   Nor the gorgeous kingdoms of the East,
Nor the thousand blooming isles that lie
   Like specks on the mighty ocean's breast: 230

It was the dwelling of that God
   Who oped the welling springs of time;
Seraph and cherubim's abode;
   The Eternal's throne of light sublime.

The virgin saw her radiant guide   235
   On nature look with kindred eye;
But whenever he turned him to the sun,
   He bowed with deep solemnity.

And ah! she deemed him heathen born,
   Far from her own nativity,   240
In lands beneath the southern star,
   Beyond the sun, beyond the sea.

And aye she watched with wistful eye,
   But durst not question put the while;
He marked her mute anxiety,   245
   And o'er his features beamed the smile.

He took her slender hand in his,
   And swift as fleets the stayless mind,
They scaled the glowing fields of day,
   And left the elements behind.   250

When past the firmament of air,
   Where no attractive influence came;
There was no up, there was no down,
   But all was space, and all the same.

The first green world that they passed bye   255
   Had 'habitants of mortal mould;
For they saw the rich men, and the poor,
   And they saw the young, and they saw the old.

But the next green world the twain past bye
   They seemed of some superior frame;   260
For all were in the bloom of youth,
   And all their radiant robes the same.

And Mary saw the groves and trees,
   And she saw the blossoms thereupon;
But she saw no grave in all the land,   265
   Nor church, nor yet a church-yard stone.

That pleasant land is lost in light,
   To every searching mortal eye;
So nigh the sun its orbit sails,
   That on his breast it seems to lie.   270
And, though its light be dazzling bright,
   The warmth was gentle, mild, and bland,
Such as on summer days may be
   Far up the hills of Scottish land.

And Mary Lee longed much to stay   275
   In that blest land of love and truth,
So nigh the fount of life and day;
   That land of beauty, and of youth.

"O maiden of the wistful mind,
    Here it behoves not to remain;   280
But Mary, yet the time will come
    When thou shalt see this land again.

"Thou art a visitant beloved
    Of God, and every holy one;
And thou shalt travel on with me,   285
    Around the spheres, around the sun,
To see what maid hath never seen,
    And do what maid hath never done."

Thus spoke her fair and comely guide,
    And took as erst her lily hand;   290
And soon in holy ecstasy
    On mountains of the sun they stand.

Here I must leave the beauteous twain,
    Casting their raptured eyes abroad,
Around the valleys of the sun,   295
    And all the universe of God:

And I will bear my hill-harp hence,
    And hang it on its ancient tree;
For its wild warblings ill become
    The scenes that oped to Mary Lee.   300

Thou holy harp of Judah's land,
    That hung the willow boughs upon,
O leave the bowers on Jordan's strand,
    And cedar groves of Lebanon;

That I may sound thy sacred string,   305
    Those chords of mystery sublime,
That chimed the songs of Israel's King,
    Songs that shall triumph over time.

Pour forth the trancing notes again,
    That wont of yore the soul to thrill,   310
In tabernacles of the plain,
    Or heights of Zion's holy hill.

O come, ethereal timbrel meet,
    In Shepherd's hand thou dost delight;

On Kedar hills thy strain was sweet,   315
   And sweet on Bethlehem's plain by night;

And when thy tones the land shall hear,
   And every heart conjoins with thee,
The mountain lyre that lingers near
   Will lend a wandering melody.   320

END OF PART FIRST

The Pilgrims of the Sun

PART SECOND

Harp of Jerusalem! how shall my hand
Awake thy Hallelujahs!—How begin
The song that tells of light ineffable,
And of the dwellers there, the fountain pure,
And source of all—Where bright Archangels dwell,   5
And where, in unapproached pavilion, framed
Of twelve deep veils, and every veil composed
Of thousand thousand lustres, sits enthroned
The God of Nature!—O thou harp of Salem,
Where shall my strain begin!   10

   Soft let it be,
And simple as its own primeval airs;
And, Minstrel, when on angel wing thou soar'st,
Then will the harp of David rise with thee.

   In that fair heaven the mortal virgin stood,   15
Beside her lovely guide, Cela his name.
Yes, deem it heaven, for not the ample sky,
As seen from earth, could slight proportion bear
To those bright regions of eternal day,
Once they are gained—So sweet the breeze of life   20
Breathed through the groves of amarynth—So sweet
The very touch of that celestial land.
Soon as the virgin trode thereon, she felt

Unspeakable delight–Sensations new
Thrilled her whole frame–As one, who his life long   25
Hath in a dark and chilly dungeon pined,
Feels when restored to freedom and the sun.

  Upon a mount they stood of wreathy light
Which cloud had never rested on, nor hues
Of night had ever shaded–Thence they saw   30
The motioned universe, that wheeled around
In fair confusion–Raised as they were now
To the high fountain-head of light and vision,
Where'er they cast their eyes abroad, they found
The light behind, the object still before;   35
And on the rarefied and pristine rays
Of vision borne, their piercing sight passed on
Intense and all unbounded–Onward!–onward!
No cloud to intervene! no haze to dim!
Or nigh, or distant, it was all the same;   40
For distance lessened not.–O what a scene,
To see so many goodly worlds upborne!
Around!–around!–all turning their green bosoms
And glittering waters to that orb of life
On which our travellers stood, and all by that   45
Sustained and gladdened! By that orb sustained!
No–by the mighty everlasting One
Who in that orb resides, and round whose throne
Our journeyers now were hovering. But they kept
Aloof upon the skirts of heaven; for, strange   50
Though it appears, there was no heaven beside.
They saw all nature–All that was they saw;
But neither moon, nor stars, nor firmament,
Nor clefted galaxy, was any more.
Worlds beyond worlds, with intermundane voids,   55
That closed and opened as those worlds rolled on,
Were all that claimed existence: Each of these,
From one particular point of the sun's orb,
Seemed pendent by some ray or viewless cord,
On which it twirled and swung with endless motion.   60

  O! never did created being feel
Such rapt astonishment, as did this maid
Of earthly lineage, when she saw the plan

Of God's fair universe!—Himself enthroned
In light she dared not yet approach!—From whence   65
He viewed the whole, and with a father's care
Upheld and cherished.—Wonder seemed it none
That Godhead should discern each thing minute
That moved on his creation, when the eyes
Which he himself had made could thus perceive   70
All these broad orbs turn their omniferous breasts,
And sun them in their Maker's influence.
O! it was sweet to see their ample vales,
Their yellow mountains, and their winding streams,
All basking in the beams of light and life!   75
    Each one of all these worlds seemed the abode
Of intellectual beings; but their forms,
Their beauty, and their natures, varied all.
And in these worlds there were broad oceans rolled,
And branching seas.—Some wore the hues of gold,   80
And some of emerald or of burnished glass.
And there were seas that keel had never plowed,
Nor had the shadow of a veering sail
Scared their inhabitants—for slumbering shades
And spirits brooded on them.   85

    "Cela, speak,"
Said the delighted but inquiring maid,
"And tell me which of all these worlds I see
Is that we lately left? For I would fain
Note how far more extensive 'tis and fair   90
Than all the rest—little, alas! I know
Of it, save that it is a right fair globe,
Diversified and huge, and that afar,
In one sweet corner of it lies a spot
I dearly love—where Tweed from distant moors   95
Far travelled flows in murmuring majesty;
And Yarrow rushing from her bosky banks,
Hurries with headlong haste to the embrace
Of her more stately sister of the hills.
Ah! yonder 'tis!—Now I perceive it well,"   100
Said she with ardent voice, bending her eye
And stretching forth her arm to a broad globe
That basked in the light—"Yonder it is!
I know the Caledonian mountains well,

And mark the moony braes and curved heights 105
Above the lone Saint Mary.–Cela, speak;
Is not that globe the world where I was born;
And yon the land of my nativity?"
She turned around her beauteous earnest face
With asking glance, but soon that glance withdrew, 110
And silent looked abroad on glowing worlds;
For she beheld a smile on Cela's face,
A smile that might an angel's face become,
When listening to the boasted, pigmy skill,
Of high presuming man.–She looked abroad, 115
But nought distinctly marked–nor durst her eye
Again meet his, although that way her face
So near was turned, one glance might have read more;
But yet that glance was staid. Pleased to behold
Her virgin modesty, and simple grace, 120
His hand upon her flexile shoulder pressed,
In kind and friendly guise, he thus began:–

   "My lovely ward, think not I deem your quest
Impertinent or trivial–well aware
Of all the longings of humanity 125
Toward the first, haply the only scenes
Of nature e'er beheld or understood;
Where the immortal and unquenched mind
First oped its treasures; and the longing soul
Breathed its first yearnings of eternal hope. 130
I know it all; nor do I deem it strange,
In such a wilderness of moving spheres,
Thou shouldst mistake the world that gave thee birth.
Prepare to wonder, and prepare to grieve:
For I perceive that thou hast deemed the earth 135
The fairest, and the most material part
Of God's creation. Mark yon cloudy spot,
Which yet thine eye hath never rested on;
And though not long the viewless golden cord
That chains it to this heaven, ycleped the sun, 140
It seems a thing subordinate–a sphere
Unseemly and forbidding–'Tis the earth.
What think'st thou now of thy Almighty maker,
And of this goodly universe of his?"

Down sunk the virgin's eye—her heart seemed wrapped 145
Deep deep in meditation—while her face
Denoted mingled sadness.—'Twas a thought
She trembled to express. At length, with blush,
And faltering tongue, she mildly thus replied:—

"I see all these fair worlds inhabited   150
By beings of intelligence and mind.
O! Cela, tell me this—Have they all fallen,
And sinned like us? And has a living God
Bled in each one of all these peopled worlds!
Or only on yon dank and dismal spot   155
Hath one Redeemer suffered for them all?"
     "Hold, hold;—No more!—Thou talkest thou knowest not what,"
Said her conductor with a fervent mien;
"More thou shalt know hereafter.—But meanwhile
This truth conceive, that God must ever deal   160
With men as men—Those things by him decreed,
Or compassed by permission, ever tend
To draw his creatures, whom he loves, to goodness;
For he is all benevolence, and knows
That in the paths of virtue and of love   165
Alone, can final happiness be found.
More thou shalt know hereafter—Pass we on
Around this glorious heaven, till by degrees
Thy frame and vision are so subtilized
As that thou may'st the inner regions near   170
Where dwell the holy angels—where the saints
Of God meet in assembly—seraphs sing,
And thousand harps, in unison complete,
With one vibration sound Jehovah's name."

Far far away, through regions of delight   175
They journeyed on—not like the earthly pilgrim,
Fainting with hunger, thirst, and burning feet,
But, leaning forward on the liquid air,
Like twin-born eagles, skimmed the fields of light,
Circling the pales of heaven. In joyous mood,   180
Sometimes through groves of shady depth they strayed,
Arm linked in arm, as lovers walk the earth;
Or rested in the bowers where roses hung,
And flowerets holding everlasting sweetness.

And they would light upon celestial hills   185
Of beauteous softened green, and converse hold
With beings like themselves in form and mind;
Then, rising lightly from the velvet breast
Of the green mountain, down upon the vales
They swooped amain by lawns and streams of life;   190
Then over mighty hills an arch they threw
Formed like the rainbow.—Never since the time
That God outspread the glowing fields of heaven
Were two such travellers seen!—In all that way
They saw new visitants hourly arrive   195
From other worlds, in that auspicious land
To live for ever.—These had sojourned far
From world to world more pure—till by degrees
After a thousand years' progression, they
Stepped on the confines of that land of life,   200
Of bliss unspeakable and evermore.

    Yet, after such probation of approach,
So exquisite the feelings of delight
Those heavenly regions yielded, 'twas beyond
Their power of sufferance.—Overcome with bliss,   205
They saw them wandering in amazement on,
With eyes that took no image on their spheres,
Misted in light and glory, or laid down,
Stretched on the sward of heaven in ecstasy.

    Yet still their half-formed words, and breathings, were 210
Of one that loved them, and had brought them home
With him in full felicity to dwell.

    To sing of all the scenes our travellers saw
An angel's harp were meet, which mortal hand
Must not assay.—These scenes must be concealed   215
From mortal fancy, and from mortal eye,
Until our weary pilgrimage is done.

    They kept the outer heaven, for it behoved
Them so to do; and in that course beheld
Immeasurable vales, all colonized   220
From worlds subjacent.—Passing inward still
Toward the centre of the heavens, they saw
The dwellings of the saints of ancient days

And martyrs for the right—men of all creeds,
Features, and hues! Much did the virgin muse,   225
And much reflect on this strange mystery,
So ill conform to all she had been taught
From infancy to think, by holy men;
Till looking round upon the spacious globes
Dependent on that heaven of light—and all   230
Rejoicing in their God's beneficence,
These words spontaneously burst from her lips:
"Child that I was, ah! could my stinted mind
Harbour the thought, that the Almighty's love,
Life, and salvation, could to single sect   235
Of creatures be confined, all his alike!"
      Last of them all, in ample circle spread
Around the palaces of heaven, they passed
The habitations of those radiant tribes
That never in the walks of mortal life   240
Had sojourned, or with human passions toiled.
Pure were they framed; and round the skirts of heaven
At first were placed, till other dwellers came
From other spheres, by human beings nursed.
Then inward those withdrew, more meet to dwell   245
In beatific regions. These again
Followed by more, in order regular,
Neared to perfection. It was most apparent
Through all created nature, that each being,
From the archangel to the meanest soul   250
Cherished by savage, caverned in the snow,
Or panting on the brown and sultry desert,
That all were in progression—moving on
Still to perfection. In conformity
The human soul is modelled—hoping still   255
In something onward! Something far beyond
It fain would grasp!—Nor shall that hope be lost!
The soul shall hold it—she shall hope, and yearn,
And grasp, and gain, for times and ages, more
Than thought can fathom, or proud science climb!   260

      At length they reached a vale of wondrous form
And dread dimensions, where the tribes of heaven
Assembly held, each in its proper sphere
And order placed. That vale extended far

Across the heavenly regions, and its form   265
A tall gazoon, or level pyramid.
Along its borders palaces were ranged,
All fronted with the thrones of beauteous seraphs,
Who sat with eyes turned to the inmost point
Leaning upon their harps; and all those thrones   270
Were framed of burning crystal, where appeared
In mingled gleam millions of dazzling hues!

    Still, as the valley narrowed to a close,
These thrones increased in grandeur and in glory,
On either side, until the inmost two   275
Rose so sublimely high, that every arch
Was ample as the compass of that bow
That, on dark cloud, bridges the vales of earth.

    The columns seemed ingrained with gold, and branched
With many lustres, whose each single lamp   280
Shone like the sun as from the earth beheld;
And each particular column, placed upon
A northern hill, would cap the polar wain.
There sat, half-shrouded in incessant light
The great Archangels, nighest to the throne   285
Of the Almighty—for—O dreadful view!
Betwixt these two, closing the lengthened files,
Stood the pavilion of the eternal God!
Himself unseen, in tenfold splendours veiled,
The least unspeakable, so passing bright,   290
That even the eyes of angels turned thereon
Grow dim, and round them transient darkness swims.

    Within the verge of that extended region
Our travellers stood. Farther they could not press,
For round the light and glory threw a pale,   295
Repellent, but to them invisible;
Yet myriads were within of purer frame.

    Ten thousand thousand messengers arrived
From distant worlds, the missioners of heaven,
Sent forth to countervail malignant sprites   300
That roam existence. These gave their report,
Not at the throne, but at the utmost seats
Of these long files of throned seraphim,

By whom the word was passed. Then fast away
Flew the commissioned spirits, to renew   305
Their watch and guardship in far distant lands.
They saw them, in directions opposite,
To every point of heaven glide away
Like flying stars; or, far adown the steep,
Gleam like small lines of light.   310

         Now was the word
Given out, from whence they knew not, that all tongues,
Kindreds, and tribes, should join, with one accord,
In hymn of adoration and acclaim,
To him that sat upon the throne of heaven,   315
Who framed, saved, and redeemed them to himself!

   Then all the countless hosts obeisance made,
And, with their faces turned unto the throne,
Stood up erect, while all their coronals
From off their heads were reverently upborne.   320
Our earth-born visitant quaked every limb.
The angels touched their harps with gentle hand
As prelude to begin—then, all at once,
With full o'erwhelming swell the strain arose;
And pealing high rolled o'er the throned lists   325
And tuneful files, as if the sun itself
Welled forth the high and holy symphony!
All heaven beside was mute—the streams stood still
And did not murmur—the light wandering winds
Withheld their motion in the midst of heaven,   330
Nor stirred the leaf, but hung in breathless trance
Where first the sounds assailed them!—Even the windows
Of God's pavilion seemed to open wide
And drink the harmony!

         Few were the strains   335
The virgin pilgrim heard, for they o'erpowered
Her every sense; and down she sunk entranced
By too supreme delight, and all to her
Was lost—She saw nor heard not!—It was gone!

   Long did she lie beside a cooling spring   340
In her associate's arms, before she showed
Motion or life—and when she first awoke

It was in dreaming melody—low strains
Half sung half uttered hung upon her breath.

"O! is it past?" said she; "Shall I not hear   345
That song of heaven again?—Then all beside
Of being is unworthy—Take me back,
Where I may hear that lay of glory flow,
And die away in it.—My soul shall mix
With its harmonious numbers, and dissolve   350
In fading cadence at the gates of light."

Back near the borders of that sacred vale
Cautious they journeyed; and at distance heard
The closing anthem of that great assembly
Of saints and angels.—First the harps awoke   355
A murmuring tremulous melody, that rose
Now high—now seemed to roll in waves away.
And aye between this choral hymn was sung,
"O! holy! holy! holy! just, and true,
Art thou, Lord God Almighty! thou art he   360
Who was, and is, and evermore shall be!"
Then every harp, and every voice, at once
Resounded *Haleluiah!* so sublime,
That all the mountains of the northern heaven,
And they are many, sounded back the strain.   365

O! when the voices and the lyres were strained
To the rapt height, the full delirious swell,
Then did the pure elastic mounds of heaven
Quiver and stream with flickering radiance,
Like gossamers along the morning dew.   370
Still paused the choir, till the last echo crept
Into the distant hill—O it was sweet!
Beyond definement sweet! and never more
May ear of mortal list such heavenly strains,
While linked to erring frail humanity.   375

After much holy converse with the saints
And dwellers of the heaven, of that concerned
The ways of God with man, and wondrous truths
But half revealed to him, our sojourners
In holy awe withdrew. And now, no more   380
By circular and cautious route they moved,

But straight across the regions of the blest,
And storied vales of heaven, did they advance,
On rapt ecstatic wing; and oft assayed
The seraphs' holy hymn. As they passed bye,   385
The angels paused; and saints, that lay reposed
In bowers of paradise, upraised their heads
To list the passing music; for it went
Swift as the wild-bee's note, that on the wing
Bombs like unbodied voice along the gale.   390

    At length upon the brink of heaven they stood;
There lingering, forward on the air they leaned
With hearts elate, to take one parting look
Of nature from its source, and converse hold
Of all its wonders. Not upon the sun,   395
But on the halo of bright golden air
That fringes it, they leaned, and talked so long,
That from contiguous worlds they were beheld
And wondered at as beams of living light.

    There all the motions of the ambient spheres   400
Were well observed, explained, and understood.
All save the mould of that mysterious chain
Which bound them to the sun—that God himself,
And he alone, could comprehend or wield.

    While thus they stood or lay (for to the eyes   405
Of all, their posture seemed these two between,
Bent forward on the wind, in graceful guise,
On which they seemed to press, for their fair robes
Were streaming far behind them) there passed bye
A most erratic wandering globe, that seemed   410
To run with troubled aimless fury on.
The virgin, wondering, inquired the cause
And nature of that roaming meteor world.

    When Cela thus:—"I can remember well
When yon was such a world as that you left;   415
A nursery of intellect, for those
Where matter lives not.—Like these other worlds,
It wheeled upon its axle, and it swung
With wide and rapid motion. But the time
That God ordained for its existence run.   420

Its uses in that beautiful creation,
Where nought subsists in vain, remained no more!
The saints and angels knew of it, and came
In radiant files, with awful reverence,
Unto the verge of heaven where we now stand,   425
To see the downfall of a sentenced world.
Think of the impetus that urges on
These ponderous spheres, and judge of the event.
Just in the middle of its swift career,
The Almighty snapt the golden cord in twain   430
That hung it to the heaven—Creation sobbed!
And a spontaneous shriek rang on the hills
Of these celestial regions. Down amain
Into the void the outcast world descended,
Wheeling and thundering on! Its troubled seas   435
Were churned into a spray, and, whizzing, flurred
Around it like a dew.—The mountain tops,
And ponderous rocks, were off impetuous flung,
And clattered down the steeps of night for ever.

     "Away into the sunless starless void   440
Rushed the abandoned world; and through its caves,
And rifted channels, airs of chaos sung.
The realms of night were troubled—for the stillness
Which there from all eternity had reigned
Was rudely discomposed; and moaning sounds,   445
Mixed with a whistling howl, were heard afar
By darkling spirits:—Still with stayless force,
For years and ages, down the wastes of night
Rolled the impetuous mass!—of all its seas
And superfices disencumbered,   450
It boomed along, till by the gathering speed,
Its furnaced mines and hills of walled sulphur
Were blown into a flame—When meteor-like,
Bursting away upon an arching track,
Wide as the universe, again it scaled   455
The dusky regions.—Long the heavenly hosts
Had deemed the globe extinct—nor thought of it,
Save as an instance of Almighty power:
Judge of their wonder and astonishment,
When far as heavenly eyes can see, they saw,   460
In yon blue void, that hideous world appear,

Showering thin flame, and shining vapour forth,
O'er half the breadth of heaven!–The angels paused!
And all the nations trembled at the view.

"But great is he who rules them!–He can turn   465
And lead it all unhurtful through the spheres,
Signal of pestilence, or wasting sword,
That ravage and deface humanity.

"The time will come, when, in like wise, the earth
Shall be cut off from God's fair universe;   470
Its end fulfilled.–But when that time shall be,
From man, from saint, and angel, is concealed."

Here ceased the converse.–To a tale like this
What converse could succeed?–They turned around,
And kneeling on the brow of heaven, there paid   475
Due adoration to that holy One
Who framed and rules the elements of nature.
Then like two swans that far on wing have scaled
The Alpine heights to gain their native lake,
At length, perceiving far below their eye   480
The beauteous silvery speck–they slack their wings,
And softly sink adown the incumbent air:
So sunk our lovely pilgrims, from the verge
Of the fair heaven, down the streamered sky;
Far other scenes, and other worlds to view.   485

END OF PART SECOND

The Pilgrims of the Sun

PART THIRD

IMPERIAL England, of the ocean born,
Who from the isles beyond the dawn of morn,
To where waste oceans wash Peruvia's shore,
Hast from all nations drawn thy boasted lore!
Helm of the world, whom seas and isles obey,   5

Though high thy honours, and though far thy sway,
Thy harp I crave, unfearful of thy frown;
Well may'st thou lend what erst was not thine own.

Come, thou old bass—I loved thy lordly swell,
With Dryden's twang, and Pope's malicious knell;   10
But now, so sore thy brazen chords are worn,
By peer, by pastor, and by bard forlorn;
By every grub that harps for venal ore,
And crabbe that grovels on the sandy shore:
I wot not if thy maker's aim has been   15
A harp, a fiddle, or a tambourine.

Come, leave these lanes and sinks beside the sea;
Come to the silent moorland dale with me;
And thou shalt pour, along the mountain hoar,
A strain its echoes never waked before;   20
Thou shalt be strung where green-wood never grew,
Swept by the winds, and mellowed by the dew.

Sing of the globes our travellers viewed, that lie
Around the Sun, enveloped in the sky;
Thy music slightly must the veil withdraw,   25
From lands they visited, and scenes they saw;
From lands, where love and goodness ever dwell;
Where famine, blight, or mildew never fell;
Where face of man is ne'er o'erspread with gloom,
And woman smiles for ever in her bloom: 30
And thou must sing of wicked worlds beneath,
Where flit the visions, and the hues of death.

The first they saw, though different far the scene,
Compared with that where they had lately been,
To all its dwellers yielded full delight;   35
Long was the day, and long and still the night;
The groves were dark and deep, the waters still;
The raving streamlets murmured from the hill:
It was the land where faithful lovers dwell,
Beyond the grave's unseemly sentinel;   40
Where, free of jealousy, their mortal bane,
And all the ills of sickness and of pain,
In love's delights they bask without alloy—

The night their transport, and the day their joy.
The broadened sun, in chamber and alcove,   45
Shines daily on their morning couch of love;
And in the evening grove, while linnets sing,
And silent bats wheel round on flittering wing,
Still in the dear embrace their souls are lingering.

"O! tell me, Cela," said the earthly maid,   50
"Must all these beauteous dames like woman fade?
In our imperfect world, it is believed
That those who most have loved the most have grieved;
That love can every power of earth controul,
Can conquer kings, and chain the hero's soul;   55
While all the woes and pains that women prove,
Have each their poignance and their source from love:
What law of nature has reversed the doom,
If these may always love, and always bloom?"

"Look round thee, maid beloved, and thou shalt see,   60
As journeying o'er this happy world with me,
That no decrepitude nor age is here;
No autumn comes the human bloom to sere;
For these have lived in worlds of mortal breath,
And all have passed the dreary bourn of death: 65
Can'st thou not mark their purity of frame,
Though still their forms and features are the same?"

Replied the maid: "No difference I can scan,
Save in the fair meridian port of man,
And woman fresh as roses newly sprung: 70
If these have died, they all have died when young."

"Thou art as artless as thy heart is good;
This in thy world is not yet understood:
But wheresoe'er we wander to and fro,
In heaven above, or in the deep below,   75
What thou misconstruest I shall well explain,
Be it in angel's walk, or mortal reign,
In sun, moon, stars, in mountain, or in main.

"Know then, that every globe which thou hast seen,
Varied with valleys, seas, and forests green,   80
Are all conformed, in subtilty of clime,

To beings sprung from out the womb of time;
And all the living groups, where'er they be,
Of worlds which thou hast seen, or thou may'st see,
Wherever sets the eve and dawns the morn,   85
Are all of mankind—all of woman born.
The globes from heaven which most at distance lie,
Are nurseries of life to these so nigh;
In those, the minds for evermore to be,
Must dawn and rise with smiling infancy.   90

    "Thus 'tis ordained—these grosser regions yield
Souls, thick as blossoms of the vernal field,
Which after death, in relative degree,
Fairer, or darker, as their minds may be,
To other worlds are led, to learn and strive,   95
Till to perfection all at last arrive.
This once conceived, the ways of God are plain,
But thy unyielding race in errors will remain.

    "These beauteous dames, who glow with love unstained,
Like thee were virgins, but not so remained.   100
Not to thy sex this sere behest is given;
They are the garden of the God of heaven:
Of beauties numberless and woes the heir,
The tree was reared immortal fruit to bear;
And she, all selfish chusing to remain,   105
Nor share of love the pleasures and the pain,
Was made and cherished by her God in vain;
She sinks into the dust a nameless thing,
No son the requiem o'er her grave to sing.
While she who gives to human beings birth,   110
Immortal here, is living still on earth;
Still in her offspring lives, to fade and bloom,
Flourish and spread through ages long to come.

    "Now mark me, maiden—why that wistful look?
Though woman must those pains and passions brook,   115
Beloved of God, and fairest of his plan,
Note how she smiles, superior still to man;
As well it her behoves; for was not he
Lulled on her breast, and nursed upon her knee?
Her foibles and her failings may be rife,   120

While toiling through the snares and ills of life,
But he who framed her nature, knows her pains,
Her heart dependant, and tumultuous veins,
And many faults the world heap on her head,
Will never there be harshly visited.   125
Proud haughty man, the nursling of her care,
Must more than half her crimes and errors bear;
If flowerets droop and fade before their day;
If others sink neglected in the clay;
If trees, too rankly earthed, too rathly blow,   130
And others neither fruit nor blossom know,
Let human reason equal judgment frame,
Is it the flower, the tree, or gardener's blame?

    "Thou see'st them lovely—so they will remain;
For when the soul and body meet again,   135
No 'vantage will be held of age, or time,
United at their fairest fullest prime.
The form when purest, and the soul most sage,
Beauty with wisdom shall have heritage,
The form of comely youth, the experience of age.   140

    "When to thy kindred thou shalt this relate,
Of man's immortal and progressive state,
No credit thou wilt gain, for they are blind,
And would, presumptuous, the Eternal bind,
Either perpetual blessings to bestow,   145
Or plunge the souls he framed in endless woe.

    "This is the land of lovers, known afar,
And named the Evening and the Morning Star:
Oft, with rapt eye, thou hast its rising seen,
Above the holy spires of old Lindeen;   150
And marked its tiny beam diffuse a hue
That tinged the paleness of the morning blue;
Ah! did'st thou deem it was a land so fair?
Or that such peaceful 'habitants were there?

    "See'st thou yon gloomy sphere, thro' vapours dun, 155
That wades in crimson like the sultry sun?
There let us bend our course, and mark the fates
Of mighty warriors, and of warriors' mates;
For there they toil 'mid troubles and alarms,

The drums and trumpets sounding still to arms;   160
Till by degrees, when ages are outgone,
And happiness and comfort still unknown,
Like simple babes, the land of peace to win,
The task of knowledge sorrowful begin:
By the enlightened philosophic mind,   165
More than a thousand ages left behind.

   "O what a world of vanity and strife!
For what avails the stage of mortal life!
If to the last the fading frame is worn,
The same unknowing creature it was born!   170
Where shall the spirit rest? where shall it go?
Or how enjoy a bliss it does not know?
It must be taught in darkness and in pain,
Or beg the bosom of a child again.
Knowledge of all, avails the human kind,   175
For all beyond the grave are joys of mind."

   So swift and so untroubled was their flight,
'Twas like the journey of a dream by night;
And scarce had Mary ceased, with thought sedate,
To muse on woman's sacred estimate,   180
When on the world of warriors they alight,
Just on the confines of its day and night;
The purple light was waning west away,
And shoally darkness gained upon the day.

   "I love that twilight," said the pilgrim fair,   185
"For more than earthly solemness is there.
See how the rubied waters winding roll;
A hoary doubtful hue involves the pole!
Uneasy murmurs float upon the wind,
And tenfold darkness rears its shades behind!   190

   "And lo! where, wrapt in deep vermilion shroud,
The daylight slumbers on the western cloud!
I love the scene!–O let us onward steer,
The light our steeds, the wind our charioteer!
And on the downy cloud impetuous hurled,   195
We'll with the twilight ring this warrior world!"

Along, along, along the nether sky!
The light before, the wreathed darkness nigh!
Along, along, through evening vapours blue,
Through tinted air, and racks of drizzly dew,   200
The twain pursued their way, and heard afar
The moans and murmurs of the dying war;
The neigh of battle-steeds by field and wall,
That missed their generous comrades of the stall,
Which, all undaunted, in the ranks of death,   205
Yielded, they knew not why, their honest breath;
And, far behind, the hill-wolf's hunger yell,
And watchword passed from drowsy sentinel.

Along, along, through mind's unwearied range,
It flies to the vicissitudes of change.   210
Our pilgrims of the twilight weary grew,
Transcendent was the scene, but never new;
They wheeled their rapid chariot from the light,
And pierced the bosom of the hideous night.

So thick the darkness, and its veil so swarth,   215
All hues were gone of heaven and of the earth!
The watch-fire scarce like gilded glow-worm seemed;
No moon nor star along the concave beamed;
Without a halo flaming meteors flew;
Scarce did they shed a sullen sulphury blue;   220
Whizzing they passed, by folded vapours crossed,
And in a sea of darkness soon were lost!

Like pilgrim birds that o'er the ocean fly,
When lasting night and polar storms are nigh,
Enveloped in a rayless atmosphere,   225
By northern shores uncertain course they steer;
O'er thousand darkling billows flap the wing,
Till far is heard the welcome murmuring
Of mountain waves, o'er waste of waters tossed,
In fleecy thunder fall on Albyn's coast.   230

So passed the pilgrims through impervious night,
Till, in a moment, rose before their sight
A bound impassable of burning levin!
A wall of flame, that reached from earth to heaven!
It was the light shed from the bloody sun,   235

In bootless blaze upon that cloud so dun;
Its gloom was such as not to be oppressed,
That those perturbed spirits might have rest.

Now oped a scene, before but dimly seen,
A world of pride, of havock, and of spleen;   240
A world of scathed soil, and sultry air,
For industry and culture were not there;
The hamlets smoked in ashes on the plain,
The bones of men were bleaching in the rain,
And, piled in thousands, on the trenched heath,   245
Stood warriors bent on vengeance and on death.

"Ah!" said the youth, "we timely come to spy
A scene momentous, and a sequel high!
For late arrived, on this disquiet coast,
A fiend, that in Tartarian gulf was tossed,   250
And held in tumult, and commotion fell,
The gnashing legions through the bounds of hell,
For ages past—but now, by heaven's decree,
The prelude of some dread event to be,
Is hither sent like desolating brand,   255
The scourge of God, the terror of the land!
He seems the passive elements to guide,
And stars in courses fight upon his side.

"On yon high mountain will we rest, and see
The omens of the times that are to be;   260
For all the wars of earth, and deeds of weir,
Are first performed by warrior spirits here;
So linked are souls by one eternal chain,
What these perform, those needs must do again:
And thus the Almighty weighs each kingdom's date,   265
Each warrior's fortune, and each warrior's fate,
Making the future time with that has been,
Work onward, rolling like a vast machine."

They sat them down on hills of Alpine form,
Above the whirlwind and the thunder storm: 270
For in that land contiguous to the sun,
The elements in wild obstruction run;
They saw the bodied flame the cloud impale,
Then river-like fleet down the sultry dale.

While, basking in the sun-beam, high they lay,   275
The hill was swathed in dark unseemly gray;
The downward rainbow hung across the rain,
And leaned its glowing arch upon the plain.

While thus they staid, they saw in wondrous wise,
Armies and kings from out the cloud arise;   280
They saw great hosts and empires overrun,
War's wild extreme, and kingdoms lost and won:
The whole of that this age has lived to see,
With battles of the East long hence to be,
They saw distinct and plain, as human eye   285
Discerns the forms and objects passing by.
Long yet the time, ere wasting war shall cease,
And all the world have liberty and peace!

The pilgrims moved not—word they had not said,
While this mysterious boding vision staid;   290
But now the virgin, with disturbed eye,
Besought solution of the prodigy.

"These all are future kings of earthly fame;
That wolfish fiend, from hell that hither came,
Over thy world, in ages yet to be,   295
Must desolation spread and slavery,
Till nations learn to know their estimate;
To be unanimous is to be great!
When right's own standard calmly is unfurled,
The people are the sovereigns of the world!   300

"Like one machine a nation's governing,
And that machine must have a moving spring;
But of what mould that moving spring should be,
'Tis the high right of nations to decree.
This mankind must be taught, though millions bleed,   305
That knowledge, truth, and liberty, may spread."

"What meant the vision 'mid the darksome cloud?
Some spirits rose as from unearthly shroud,
And joined their warrior brethren of the free;
Two souls inspired each, and some had three?"   310

"These were the spirits of their brethren slain,
Who, thus permitted, rose and breathed again;
For still let reason this high truth recall,
The body's but a mould, the soul is all:
Those triple minds that all before them hurled,   315
Are called Silesians in this warrior world."

"O tell me, Cela, when shall be the time,
That all the restless spirits of this clime,
Erring so widely in the search of bliss,
Shall win a milder happier world than this?"   320

"Not till they learn, with humbled hearts, to see
The falsehood of their fuming vanity.
What is the soldier but an abject fool—
A king's, a tyrant's, or a statesman's tool!
Some patriot few there are—but ah! how rare!   325
For vanity or interest still is there;
Or blindfold levity directs his way—
A licensed murderer that kills for pay!
Though fruitless ages thus be overpast,
Truth, love, and knowledge, must prevail at last!"   330

The pilgrims left that climate with delight,
Weary of battle and portentous sight.

It boots not all their wanderings to relate,
By globes immense, and worlds subordinate;
For still my strain in mortal guise must flow,   335
Though swift as winged angels they might go;
The palled mind would meet no kind relay,
And dazzled fancy wilder by the way.

They found each clime with mental joys replete,
And all for which its 'habitants were meet: 340
They saw a watery world of sea and shore,
Where the rude sailor swept the flying oar,
And drove his bark like lightning o'er the main,
Proud of his prowess, of her swiftness vain;
Held revel on the shore with stormy glee,   345
Or sung his boisterous carol on the sea.

They saw the land where bards delighted stray,
And beauteous maids that love the melting lay;
One mighty hill they clomb with earnest pain,
For ever clomb, but higher did not gain: 350
Their gladsome smiles were mixed with frowns severe;
For all were bent to sing, and none to hear.

Far in the gloom they found a world accursed,
Of all the globes the dreariest and the worst!
But there they could not sojourn, though they would,   355
For all the language was of mystic mood,
A jargon, nor conceived, nor understood;
It was of deeds, respondents, and replies,
Dark quibbles, forms, and condescendencies:
And they would argue, with vociferous breath,   360
For months and days, as if the point were death;
And when at last enforced to agree,
'Twas only how the argument should be!

They saw the land of bedesmen discontent,
Their frames their god, their tithes their testament!   365
And snarling critics bent with aspect sour,
T' applaud the great, and circumvent the poor;
And knowing patriots, with important face,
Raving aloud with gesture and grimace—
Their prize a land's acclaim, or proud and gainful place. 370
Then by a land effeminate they passed,
Where silks and odours floated in the blast;
A land of vain and formal compliment,
Where won the flippant belles, and beaux magnificent.

They circled nature on their airy wain,   375
From God's own throne, unto the realms of pain;
For there are prisons in the deep below,
Where wickedness sustains proportioned woe,
No more nor less; for the Almighty still
Suits to our life the goodness and the ill.   380

O! it would melt the living heart with woe,
Were I to sing the agonies below;
The hatred nursed by those who cannot part;
The hardened brow, the seared and sullen heart;
The still defenceless look, the stifled sigh,   385

The writhed lip, the staid despairing eye,
Which ray of hope may never lighten more,
Which cannot shun, yet dares not look before.
O! these are themes reflection would forbear,
Unfitting bard to sing, or maid to hear;   390
Yet these they saw in downward realms prevail,
And listened many a sufferer's hapless tale,
Who all allowed that rueful misbelief
Had proved the source of their eternal grief;
And all the Almighty punisher arraigned   395
For keeping back that knowledge they disdained.

   "Ah!" Cela said, as up the void they flew,
"The axiom's just—the inference is true;
Therefore no more let doubts thy mind enthral,
Through nature's range thou see'st a God in all: 400
Where is the mortal law that can restrain
The atheist's heart, that broods o'er thoughts profane?
Soon fades the soul's and virtue's dearest tie,
When all the future closes from the eye."—
By all, the earth-born virgin plainly saw   405
Nature's unstaid, unalterable law;
That human life is but the infant stage
Of a progressive, endless pilgrimage
To woe, or state of bliss, by bard unsung,
At that eternal fount where being sprung.   410

   When these wild wanderings all were past and done,
Just in the red beam of the parting sun,
Our pilgrims skimmed along the light of even,
Like flitting stars that cross the nightly heaven,
And lighting on the verge of Phillip plain,   415
They trode the surface of the world again.

   Arm linked in arm, they walked to green Bowhill;
At their approach the woods and lawns grew still!
The little birds to brake and bush withdrew,
The merl away unto Blackandro flew;   420
The twilight held its breath in deep suspense,
And looked its wonder in mute eloquence!

   They reached the bower, where first at Mary's knee
Cela arose her guide through heaven to be.

All, all was still–no living thing was seen!   425
No human footstep marked the daisied green!
The youth looked round, as something were unmeet,
Or wanting there, to make their bliss complete.
They paused–they sighed–then with a silent awe,
Walked onward to the halls of Carelha'.   430

 They heard the squires and yeomen, all intent,
Talking of some mysterious event!
They saw the maidens in dejection mourn,
Scarce daring glance unto a yeoman turn!
Straight to the inner chamber they repair,   435
Mary beheld her widowed mother there,
Flew to her arms, to kiss her and rejoice;
Alas! she saw her not, nor heard her voice,
But sat unmoved with many a bitter sigh,
Tears on her cheek, and sorrow in her eye!   440
In sable weeds her lady form was clad,
And the white lawn waved mournful round her head!
Mary beheld, arranged in order near,
The very robes she last on earth did wear;
And shrinking from the disregarded kiss,   445
"Oh, tell me, Cela!–tell me, what is this?"

 "Fair maiden of the pure and guileless heart,
As yet thou knowest not how, nor what thou art;–
Come, I will lead thee to yon hoary pile,
Where sleep thy kindred in their storied isle: 450
There I must leave thee, in this world below;
'Tis meet thy land these holy truths should know:
But, Mary, yield not thou to bootless pain,
Soon we shall meet, and never part again."

 He took her hand, she dared not disobey,   455
But, half reluctant, followed him away.
They paced along on Ettrick's margin green,
And reached the hoary fane of old Lindeen:
It was a scene to curdle maiden's blood–
The massy church-yard gate wide open stood!   460
The stars were up!–the valley steeped in dew!
The baleful bat in silent circles flew!
No sound was heard, except the lonely rail,

Harping his ordinal adown the dale;
And soft, and slow, upon the breezes light,   465
The rush of Ettrick breathed along the night!
Dark was the pile, and green the tombs beneath!
And dark the gravestones on the sward of death!

    Within the railed space appeared to view
A grave new opened–thitherward they drew;   470
And there beheld, within its mouldy womb,
A living, moving tenant of the tomb!
It was an aged monk, uncouth to see,
Who held a sheeted corse upon his knee,
And busy, busy, with the form was he!   475
At their approach he uttered howl of pain,
Till echoes groaned it from the holy fane,
Then fled amain–Ah! Cela, too, is gone;
And Mary stands within the grave alone!
With her fair guide, her robes of heaven are fled,   480
And round her fall the garments of the dead!

    Here I must seize my ancient harp again,
And chaunt a simple tale, a most uncourtly strain.

END OF PART THIRD

The Pilgrims of the Sun

PART FOURTH

    THE night-wind is sleeping–the forest is still,
The blare of the heath-cock has sunk on the hill,
Beyond the gray cairn of the moor is his rest,
On the red heather-bloom he has pillowed his breast;
There soon with his note the gray dawning he'll cheer,   5
But Mary of Carel' that note will not hear!

    The night-wind is still, and the moon in the wane,
The river-lark sings on the verge of the plain;

So lonely his plaint, by the motionless reed,
It sounds like an omen or tale of the dead;   10
Like a warning of death, it falls on the ear
Of those who are wandering the woodlands in fear;
For the maidens of Carelha' wander, and cry
On their young lady's name, with the tear in their eye.
The gates had been shut, and the mass had been sung,   15
But Mary was missing, the beauteous and young;
And she had been seen in the evening still,
By woodman, alone, in the groves of Bowhill.

   O, were not these maidens in terror and pain?
They knew the third night of the moon in the wane!   20
They knew on that night that the spirits were free;
That revels of fairies were held on the lea;
And heard their small bugles, with eirysome croon,
As lightly they rode on the beam of the moon!
O! woe to the wight that abides their array!   25
And woe to the maiden that comes in their way!

   The maidens returned all hopeless and wan;
The yeomen they rode, and the pages they ran;
The Ettrick and Yarrow they searched up and down,
The hamlet, the cot, and the old borough town;   30
And thrice the bedesman renewed the host;
But the dawn returned–and Mary was lost!

   Her lady mother, distracted and wild,
For the loss of her loved, her only child,
With all her maidens tracked the dew–   35
Well Mary's secret bower she knew!
Oft had she traced, with fond regard,
Her darling to that grove, and heard
Her orisons the green bough under,
And turned aside with fear and wonder.   40

   O! but their hearts were turned to stone,
When they saw her stretched on the sward alone;
Prostrate, without a word or motion,
As if in calm and deep devotion!
They called her name with trembling breath;   45
But ah! her sleep was the sleep of death!

They laid their hands on her cheek composed;
But her cheek was cold and her eye was closed:
They laid their hands upon her breast,
But the playful heart had sunk to rest;   50
And they raised an eldritch wail of sorrow,
That startled the hinds on the braes of Yarrow.

    And yet, when they viewed her comely face,
Each line remained of beauty and grace;
No death-like features it disclosed,   55
For the lips were met, and the eyes were closed.
'Twas pale—but the smile was on the cheek;
'Twas modelled all as in act to speak!
It seemed as if each breeze that blew,
The play of the bosom would renew;   60
As nature's momentary strife
Would wake that form to beauty and life.

    It is borne away with fear and awe
To the lordly halls of Carelha',
And lies on silken couch at rest—   65
The mother there is constant guest,
For hope still lingers in her breast.

    O! seraph Hope! that here below
Can nothing dear to the last forego!
When we see the forms we fain would save   70
Wear step by step adown to the grave,
Still hope a lambent gleam will shed
Over the last, the dying bed:
And even, as now, when the soul's away,
It flutters and lingers o'er the clay!   75
O Hope! thy range was never expounded!
'Tis not by the grave that thou art bounded!

    The leech's art, and the bedesman's prayer,
Are all mispent—no life is there!
Between her breasts they dropped the lead,   80
And the cord in vain begirt her head;
Yet still on that couch her body lies,
Though another moon has claimed the skies;
For once the lykewake maidens saw,
As the dawn arose on Carelha',   85

A movement soft the sheets within,
And a gentle shivering of the chin!

   All earthly hope at last outworn,
The body to the tomb was borne;
The last pale flowers in the grave were flung;   90
The mass was said, and the requiem sung;
And the turf that was ever green to be,
Lies over the dust of Mary Lee.

   Deep fell the eve on old Lindeen!
Loud creaked the rail in the clover green!   95
The new moon from the west withdrew—
O! well the monk of Lindeen knew
That Mary's winding-sheet was lined
With many fringe of the gold refined!
That in her bier behoved to be   100
A golden cross and a rosary;
Of pearl beads full many a string,
And on every finger a diamond ring.
The holy man no scruples staid;
For within that grave was useless laid   105
Riches that would a saint entice—
'Twas worth a convent's benefice!

   He took the spade, and away he is gone
To the church-yard, darkling and alone;
His brawny limbs the grave bestride,   110
And he shovelled the mools and the bones aside;
Of the dust, or the dead, he stood not in fear,
But he stooped in the grave and he opened the bier;
And he took the jewels, of value high,
And he took the cross, and the rosary,   115
And the golden heart on the lid that shone,
And he laid them carefully on a stone.

   Then down in the depth of the grave sat he,
And he raised the corse upon his knee;
But in vain to gain the rings he strove,   120
For the hands were cold, and they would not move:
He drew a knife from his baldrick gray,
To cut the rings and fingers away.

He gave one cut—he gave but one—
It scarcely reached unto the bone: 125
Just then the soul, so long exiled,
Returned again from its wanderings wild;
By the stars and the sun it ceased to roam,
And entered its own, its earthly home.
Loud shrieked the corse at the wound he gave, 130
And, rising, stood up in the grave.

The hoary thief was chilled at heart,
Scarce had he power left to depart;
For horror thrilled through every vein;
He did not cry, but he roared amain; 135
For hues of dread and death were rife
On the face of the form he had woke to life:
His reason fled from off her throne,
And never more dawned thereupon.

Aloud she called her Cela's name, 140
And the echoes called, but no Cela came!
O! much she marvelled that he had gone,
And left her thus in the grave alone.
She knew the place, and the holy dome;
Few moments hence she had thither come; 145
And through the hues of the night she saw
The woods and towers of Carelha'.
'Twas mystery all—She did not ween
Of the state or the guise in which she had been;
She did not ween that while travelling afar, 150
Away by the sun and the morning star,
By the moon, and the cloud, and aerial bow,
That her body was left on the earth below.

But now she stood in grievous plight;
The ground was chilled with the dews of the night; 155
Her frame was cold and ill at rest,
The dead-rose waved upon her breast;
Her feet were coiled in the sheet so wan,
And fast from her hand the red blood ran.

'Twas late, late on a Sabbath night! 160
At the hour of the ghost, and the restless sprite!
The mass at Carelha' had been read,

And all the mourners were bound to bed,
When a foot was heard on the paved floor,
And a gentle rap came to the door.   165

O God! that such a rap should be
So fraught with ambiguity!
A dim haze clouded every sight;
Each hair had life, and stood upright;
No sound was heard throughout the hall,   170
But the beat of the heart and the cricket's call;
So deep the silence imposed by fear,
That a vacant buzz sung in the ear.

The lady of Carelha' first broke
The breathless hush, and thus she spoke:–   175
"Christ be our shield!–who walks so late,
And knocks so gently at my gate?
I felt a pang–it was not dread–
It was the memory of the dead!
O! death is a dull and dreamless sleep!   180
The mould is heavy, the grave is deep,
Else I had weened that foot so free
The step and the foot of my Mary Lee!
And I had weened that gentle knell
From the light hand of my daughter fell!   185
The grave is deep, it may not be!
Haste, porter–haste to the door and see."

He took the key with an eye of doubt,
He lifted the lamp and he looked about;
His lips a silent prayer addressed,   190
And the cross was signed upon his breast;
Thus mailed within the armour of God,
All ghostly to the door he strode.
He wrenched the bolt with grating din,
He lifted the latch–but none came in!   195
He thrust out his lamp, and he thrust out his head,
And he saw the face and the robes of the dead!
One sob he heaved, and tried to fly,
But he sunk on the earth, and the form came bye.

She entered the hall, she stood in the door,   200
Till, one by one, dropt on the floor

The blooming maiden, and matron old,
The friar gray, and the yeoman bold.
It was like a scene on the Border green,
When the arrows fly and pierce unseen;   205
And nought was heard within the hall,
But Aves, vows, and groans withal.
The lady of Carel' stood alone,
But moveless as a statue of stone.

"O! lady mother, thy fears forego;   210
Why all this terror and this woe?
But late when I was in this place,
Thou wouldest not look me in the face;
O! why do you blench at sight of me?
I am thy own child, thy Mary Lee."   215

"I saw thee dead and cold as clay;
I watched thy corpse for many a day;
I saw thee laid in the grave at rest;
I strewed the flowers upon thy breast;
And I saw the mould heaped over thee—   220
Thou art not my child, my Mary Lee."

O'er Mary's face amazement spread;
She knew not that she had been dead;
She gazed in mood irresolute:
Both stood aghast, and both were mute.   225

"Speak, thou loved form—*my* glass is run,
I nothing dread beneath the sun,
Why comest thou in thy winding-sheet,
Thy life-blood streaming to thy feet?
The grave-rose that my own hands made,   230
I see upon thy bosom spread;
The kerchief that my own hands bound,
I see still tied thy temples round;
The golden rings, and bracelet bands,
Are still upon thy bloody hands.   235
From earthly hope all desperate driven,
I nothing fear beneath high heaven;
Give me thy hand and speak to me,
If thou art indeed my Mary Lee."

That mould is sensible and warm,   240
It leans upon a parent's arm:
The kiss is sweet, and the tears are sheen,
And kind are the words that pass between;
They cling as never more to sunder—
O! that embrace was fraught with wonder!   245

    Yeoman, and maid, and menial poor,
Upraised their heads from the marble floor;
With lengthened arm, and forward stride,
They tried if that form their touch would bide;
They felt her warm!—they heard!—they saw!   250
And marvel reigns in Carelha'!

    The twain into their chamber repair;
The wounded hand is bound with care;
And there the mother heard with dread
The whole that I to you have said,   255
Of all the worlds where she had been,
And of all the glories she had seen.
I pledge no word that all is true,
The virgin's tale I have told to you;
But well 'tis vouched, by age and worth,   260
'Tis real that relates to earth.

    'Twas trowed by every Border swain,
The vision would full credence gain.
Certes 'twas once by all believed,
Till one great point was misconceived;   265
For the mass-men said, with fret and frown,
That through all space it well was known,
By moon, or stars, the earth or sea,
An up and down there needs must be:
This error caught their minds in thrall;   270
'Twas dangerous and apocryphal!
And this nice fraud unhinged all.
So grievous is the dire mischance
Of priestcraft and of ignorance!

    Belike thou now can'st well foresee,   275
What after happ'd to Mary Lee—
Then thou mayest close my legend here:
But ah! the tale to some is dear!

For though her name no more remains,
Her blood yet runs in Minstrel veins.   280

    In Mary's youth, no virgin's face
Wore such a sweet and moving grace;
Nor ever did maiden's form more fair
Lean forward to the mountain air;
But now, since from the grave returned,   285
So dazzling bright her beauty burned,
The eye of man could scarcely brook
With steady gaze thereon to look:
Such was the glow of her cheek and eyes,
She bloomed like the rose of paradise!   290

    Though blither than she erst had been,
In serious mood she oft was seen.
When rose the sun o'er mountain grey,
Her vow was breathed to the east away;
And when low in the west he burned,   295
Still there her duteous eye was turned.
For she saw that the flowerets of the glade
To him unconscious worship paid;
She saw them ope their breasts by day,
And follow his enlivening ray,   300
Then fold them up in grief by night,
Till the return of the blessed light.
When daylight in the west fell low,
She heard the woodland music flow,
Like farewell song, with sadness blent,   305
A soft and sorrowful lament:
But when the sun rose from the sea,
O! then the birds from every tree
Poured forth their hymn of holiest glee!
She knew that the wandering spirits of wrath   310
Fled from his eye to their homes beneath,
But when the God of glory shone
On earth, from his resplendent throne,
In valley, mountain, or in grove,
Then all was life, and light, and love.   315
She saw the new born infant's eye
Turned to that light incessantly;
Nor ever was that eye withdrawn
Till the mind thus carved began to dawn.

All Nature worshipped at one shrine,   320
Nor knew that the impulse was divine.

The chiefs of the Forest the strife begin,
Intent this lovely dame to win;
But the living lustre of her eye
Baulked every knight's pretensions high;   325
Abashed they sunk before her glance,
Nor farther could their claims advance;
Though love thrilled every heart with pain,
They did not ask, and they could not gain.

There came a Harper out of the east;   330
A courteous and a welcome guest
In every lord and baron's tower—
He struck his harp of wondrous power;
So high his art, that all who heard
Seemed by some magic spell ensnared;   335
For every heart, as he desired,
Was thrilled with woe—with ardour fired;
Roused to high deeds his might above,
Or soothed to kindness and to love.
No one could learn from whence he came,   340
But Hugo of Norroway hight his name.

One day, when every Baron came,
And every maid, and noble dame,
To list his high and holy strain
Within the choir of Melrose fane,   345
The lady of Carelha' joined the band,
And Mary, the flower of all the land.

The strain rose soft—the strain fell low—
O! every heart was steeped in woe!
Again as it pealed a swell so high,   350
The round drops stood in every eye;
And the aisles and the spires of the hallowed fane,
And the caves of Eildon, sung it again.

O Mary Lee is sick at heart!
That pang no tongue can ever impart!   355
It was not love, nor joy, nor woe,
Nor thought of heaven, nor earth below;

'Twas all conjoined in gleam so bright—
A poignant feeling of delight!
The throes of a heart that sought its rest,   360
Its stay—its home in another's breast!
Ah! she had heard that holy strain
In a land she hoped to see again!
And seen that calm benignant eye
Above the spheres and above the sky!   365
And though the strain her soul had won,
She yearned for the time that it was done,
To greet the singer in language bland,
And call him Cela, and clasp his hand.

  It was yon ancient tombs among   370
That Mary glided from the throng,
Smiled in the fair young stranger's face,
And proffered her hand with courteous grace.
He started aloof—he bent his eye—
He stood in a trance of ecstasy!   375
He blessed the power that had impelled
Him onward till he that face beheld;
For he knew his bourn was gained at last,
And all his wanderings then were past.

  She called him Cela, and made demand   380
Anent his kindred, and his land;
But his hand upon his lip he laid,
He lifted his eye, and he shook his head!
"No—Hugo of Norroway is my name,
Ask not from whence or how I came: 385
But since ever memory's ray was borne
Within this breast of joy forlorn,
I have sought for thee, and only thee;
For I ween thy name is Mary Lee.
My heart and soul with thine are blent,   390
My very being's element—
O! I have wonders to tell to thee,
If thou art the virgin Mary Lee!"

  The Border chiefs were all amazed,
They stood at distance round and gazed;   395
They knew her face he never had seen,
But they heard not the words that past between.

They thought of the power that had death beguiled;
They thought of the grave, and the vision wild!
And they found that human inference failed,   400
That all in mystery was veiled,
And they shunned the twain in holy awe;–
The flower of the Forest, and Carelha',
Are both by the tuneful stranger won,
And a new existence is begun.   405

   Sheltered amid his mountains afar,
He kept from the bustle of Border war;
For he loved not the field of foray and scathe,
Nor the bow, nor the shield, nor the sword of death;
But he tuned his harp in the wild unseen,   410
And he reared his flocks on the mountain green.

   He was the foremost the land to free
Of the hart, and the hind, and the forest tree;
The first who attuned the pastoral reed
On the mountains of Ettrick, and braes of Tweed;   415
The first who did to the land impart
The shepherd's rich and peaceful art,
To bathe the fleece, to cherish the dam,
To milk the ewe, and to wean the lamb;
And all the joys ever since so rife   420
In the shepherd's simple, romantic life.
More bliss, more joy, from him had birth,
Than all the conquerors of the earth.
   They lived in their halls of Carelha'
Until their children's sons they saw;   425
There Mary closed a life refined
To purity of soul and mind,
And at length was laid in old Lindeen,
In the very grave where she erst had been.
Five gallant sons upbore her bier,   430
And honoured her memory with a tear;
And her stone, though now full old and grey,
Is known by the hinds unto this day.

   From that time forth, on Ettrick's shore,
Old Hugo the harper was seen no more!   435
Some said he died as the morning rose;
But his body was lost ere the evening close!

He was not laid in old Lindeen;
For his grave or his burial never were seen!

    Some said that eve a form they saw   440
Arise from the tower of Carelha'
Aslant the air, and hover a while
Above the spires of the hallowed pile,
Then sail away in a snow-white shroud,
And vanish afar in the eastern cloud.   445

    But others deemed that his grave was made
By hands unseen in the greenwood glade.
Certes that in one night there grew
A little mound of an ashen hue,
And some remains of gravel lay   450
Mixed with the sward at the break of day:
But the hind past bye with troubled air,
For he knew not what might be slumbering there;
And still above that mound there grows,
Yearly a wondrous fairy rose.   455

    Beware that cairn and dark green ring!
For the elves of eve have been heard to sing
Around that grave with eldritch croon,
Till trembled the light of the waning moon!
And from that cairn, at midnight deep,   460
The shepherd has heard from the mountain steep
Arise such a mellowed holy strain
As if the Minstrel had woke again!

    Late there was seen, on summer tide,
A lovely form that wont to glide   465
Round green Bowhill, at the fall of even,
So like an angel sent from heaven,
That all the land believed and said
Their Mary Lee was come from the dead;
For since that time no form so fair   470
Had ever moved in this earthly air:
And whenever that beauteous shade was seen
To visit the walks of the Forest green,
The joy of the land ran to excess,
For they knew that it boded them happiness!   475

Peace, love, and truth, for ever smiled
Around that genius of the wild.

Ah me! there is omen of deep dismay,
For that saintlike form has vanished away!
I have watched her walks by the greenwood glade,   480
And the mound where the Harper of old was laid;
I have watched the bower where the woodbine blows,
And the fairy ring, and the wondrous rose,
And all her haunts by Yarrow's shore,
But the heavenly form I can see no more!   485
She comes not now our land to bless,
Or to cherish the poor and the fatherless,
Who lift to heaven the tearful eye
Bewailing their loss—and well may I!
I little weened when I struck the string,   490
In fancy's wildest mood to sing,
That sad and low the strain should close,
'Mid real instead of fancied woes!

END OF THE PILGRIMS OF THE SUN

Connel of Dee

1.

CONNEL went out by a blink of the moon
    To his light little bower in the deane;
He thought they had gi'en him his supper owre soon,
    And that still it was lang until e'en.
      Oh! the air was so sweet, and the sky so serene,   5
        And so high his soft languishment grew–
That visions of happiness danced o'er his mind;
He longed to leave parent and sisters behind;
For he thought that his Maker to him was unkind,
      For that high were his merits he knew.   10

2.

Sooth, Connel was halesome, and stalwart to see,
    The bloom of fayir yudith he wore;
But the lirk of displeasure hang over his bree,
    Nae glisk of contentment it bore;
      He langed for a wife with a mailen and store;   15
        He grevit in idless to lie;
Afar from his cottage he wished to remove,
To wassail and waik, and unchided to rove,
And beik in the cordial transports of love
      All under a kindlier sky.   20

3.

O sweet was the fa' of that gloaming to view!
    The day-lighte crap laigh on the doon,
And left its pale borders abeigh on the blue,
    To mix wi' the beams of the moon.
      The hill hang its skaddaw the greinwud aboon,   25
        The houf of the bodyng Benshee;
Slow o'er him were sailing the cloudlets of June,
The beetle began his wild airel to tune,
And sang on the wynde with ane eirysome croon,
      Away on the breeze of the Dee!   30

4.

With haffat on lufe poor Connel lay lorn!
    He languishit for muckle and mair!

His bed of greine hether he eynit to scorn,
  The bygane he doughtna weel bear!
  Attour him the greine leife was fannyng the air,   35
    In noiseless and flychtering play;
The hush of the water fell saft on his ear,
And he fand as gin sleep, wi' her gairies, war near,
Wi' her freaks and her ferlies and phantoms of fear,
    But he eidently wysit her away.   40

5.
Short time had he sped in that sellible strife
  Ere he saw a young maiden stand by,
Who seemed in the bloom and the bell of her life;
  He wist not that ane was sae nigh!
  But sae sweet was her look, and sae saft was her eye,   45
    That his heart was all quaking with love;
And then there was kything a dimple sae sly,
At play on her cheek, of the moss-rose's dye,
That kindled the heart of poor Connel on high
    With ravishment deadlye to prove.   50

6.
He deemed her a beautiful spirit of night,
  And eiry was he to assay;
But he found she was mortal with thrilling delight,
  For her breath was like zephyr of May;
  Her eye was the dew-bell, the beam of the day,   55
    And her arm it was softer than silk;
Her hand was so warm, and her lip was so red,
Her slim taper waiste so enchantingly made!
And some beauties moreover that cannot be said—
    Of bosom far whiter than milk!   60

7.
Poor Connel was reaved of all power and of speech,
  His frame grew all powerless and weak;
He neither could stir, nor caress her, nor fleech,
  He trembled, but word couldna speak!
  But O, when his lips touched her soft rosy cheek,   65
    The channels of feeling ran dry,
He found that like emmets his life-blood it crept,
His liths turned as limber as dud that is steeped,

He streekit his limbs, and he moaned and he wept;
   And for love he was just gaun to die.   70

8.

The damsel beheld, and she raised him so kind,
   And she said, "My dear beautiful swain,
Take heart till I tell you the hark of my mind,
   I'm weary of lying my lane;
     I have castles, and lands, and flocks of my ain,   75
       But want ane my gillour to share;
A man that is hale as the hart on the hill,
As stark, and as kind, is the man to my will,
Who has slept on the heather and drank of the rill,
       And, like you, gentle, amorous, and fair.   80

9.

"I often hae heard, that like you there was nane,
   And I aince gat a glisk of thy face;
Now far have I ridden, and far have I gane,
   In hopes thou wilt nurice the grace,
     To make me thy ain—O come to my embrace!   85
       For I love thee as dear as my life!
I'll make thee a laird of the boonmost degree,
My castles and lands I'll give freely to thee,
Though rich and abundant, thine own they shall be,
       If thou wilt but make me thy wife."   90

10.

Oh! never was man sae delighted and fain!
   He bowed a consent to her will,
Kind Providence thankit again and again,
   And 'gan to display his rude skill
     In leifu' endearment, and thought it nae ill   95
       To kiss the sweet lips of the fair,
And press her to lie, in that gloamin sae still,
Adown by his side in the howe of the hill,
For the water flowed sweet, and the sound of the rill
       Would sooth every sorrow and care.   100

11.

No—she wadna lie by the side of a man
   Till the rites of the marriage were bye.
Away they hae sped; but soon Connel began,

For his heart it was worn to a sigh,
  To fondle, and simper, and look in her eye,   105
    Oh! direful to bear was his wound!
When on her fair neck fell his fingers sae dun—
It strak through his heart like the shot of a gun!
He felt as the sand of existence were run:
    He trembled, and fell to the ground.   110

12.

O Connel, dear Connel, be patient a while!
  These wounds of thy bosom will heal,
And thou with thy love mayest walk many a mile
  Nor transport nor passion once feel.
  Thy spirits once broke on electeric wheel,   115
    Cool reason her empire shall gain;
And haply, repentance in dowy array,
And laithly disgust may arise in thy way,
Encumbering the night, and o'ercasting the day,
    And turn all those pleasures to pain.   120

13.

The mansion is gained, and the bridal is past,
  And the transports of wedlock prevail;
The lot of poor Connel the shepherd is cast
  'Mid pleasures that never can fail;
  The balms of Arabia sweeten the gale,   125
    The tables for ever are spread
With damask, and viands, and heart-cheering wine,
Their splendour and elegance fully combine,
His lawns they are ample, his bride is divine,
    And of goud-fringed silk is his bed.   130

14.

The transports of love gave rapture, and flew;
  The banquet soon sated and cloyed;
Nae mair they delighted, nae langer were new,
  They could not be ever enjoyed!
  He felt in his bosom a fathomless void,   135
    A yearning again to be free:
Than all that voluptuous sickening store,
The wine that he drank and the robes that he wore,
His diet of milk had delighted him more
    Afar on the hills of the Dee.   140

15.

O oft had he sat by the clear springing well,
  And dined from his wallet full fain!
Then sweet was the scent of the blue heather-bell,
  And free was his bosom of pain;
    The laverock was lost in the lift, but her strain   145
      Came trilling so sweetly from far,
To rapture the hour he would wholly resign,
He would listen, and watch, till he saw her decline,
And the sun's yellow beam on her dappled breast shine,
      Like some little musical star.   150

16.

And then he wad lay his blue bonnet aside,
  And turn his rapt eyes to the heaven,
And bless his kind Maker who all did provide,
  And beg that he might be forgiven,
    For his sins were like crimson!—all bent and uneven   155
      The path he had wilsomely trode!
Then who the delight of his bosom could tell?
O sweet was that meal by his pure mountain well;
And sweet was its water he drank from the shell,
      And peaceful his moorland abode.   160

17.

But now was he deaved and babbled outright,
  By gossips in endless array,
Who thought not of sin nor of Satan aright,
  Nor the dangers that mankind belay;
    Who joked about heaven, and scorned to pray,   165
      And gloried in that was a shame.
O Connel was troubled at things that befell!
So different from scenes he had once loved so well,
He deemed he was placed on the confines of Hell,
      And fand like the sa'ur of its flame!   170

18.

Of bonds and of law-suits he still was in doubt,
  And old debts coming due every day;
And a thousand odd things he kend naething about
  Kept him in continued dismay.
    At board he was awkward, nor wist what to say,   175

Nor what his new honours became;
His guests they wad mimic and laugh in their sleeve;
He blushed, and he faltered, and scarce dought believe
That men were so base as to smile and deceive;
    Or eynied of him to make game!   180

19.

Still franker and freer his gossippers grew,
    And preyed upon him and his dame;
Their jests and their language to Connel were new,
    It was slander, and cursing, and shame!
    He groaned in his heart, and he thought them to blame   185
        For revel and rout without end;
He saw himself destined to pamper and feed
A race whom he hated, a profligate breed,
The scum of existence to vengeance decreed!
    Who laughed at their God and their friend.   190

20.

He saw that in wickedness all did delight,
    And he kendna what length it might bear;
They drew him to evil by day and by night,
    To scenes that he trembled to share!
    His heart it grew sick, and his head it grew sair,   195
        And he thought what he dared not to tell!
He thought of the far distant hills of the Dee;
Of his cake, and his cheese, and his lair on the lea;
Of the laverock that hung on the heaven's ee-bree,
    His prayer, and his clear mountain well!   200

21.

His breast he durst sparingly trust wi' the thought
    Of the virtuous days that were fled!
Yet still his kind lady he loved as he ought,
    Or soon from that scene he had fled.
    It now was but rarely she honoured his bed–   205
        'Twas modesty, heightening her charms!
A delicate feeling that man cannot ween!
O Heaven! each night from his side she had been–
He found it at length—Nay, he saw't with his een,
    She slept in a paramour's arms!!!   210

22.

It was the last pang that the spirit could bear!
   Destruction and death was the meed:
For forfeited vows there was nought too severe;
   Even conscience applauded the deed.
    His mind was decided, her doom was decreed;   215
      He led her to chamber apart,
To give her to know of his wrongs he had sense,
To chide and upbraid her in language intense,
And kill her, at least, for her heinous offence–
    A crime at which demons would start!   220

23.

With grievous reproaches, in agonized zeal,
   Stern Connel his lecture began,
He mentioned her crime!—She turned on her heel
   And her mirth to extremity ran.
    "Why that was the fashion!–no sensible man   225
      Could e'er of such freedom complain.
What was it to him? there were maidens enow
Of the loveliest forms, and the loveliest hue,
Who blithely would be his companions, he knew,
    If he wearied of lying his lane."   230

24.

How Connel was shocked!–but his fury still rose,
   He shivered from toe to the crown!
His hair stood like heath on the mountain that grows,
   And each hair had a life of its own!
    "O thou most"–But whereto his passion had flown   235
      No man to this day can declare,
For his dame, with a frown, laid her hand on his mouth,
That hand once as sweet as the breeze of the south!
That hand that gave pleasures and honours and routh,
    And she said, with a dignified air,–   240

25.

"Peace, booby! if life thou regardest beware,
   I have had some fair husbands ere now;
They wooed, and they flattered, they sighed and they sware,
   At length they grew irksome like you.
    Come hither one moment, a sight I will show   245

That will teach thee some breeding and grace."
She opened a door, and there Connel beheld
A sight that to trembling his spirit impelled,
A man standing chained, who nor 'plained, nor rebelled,
    And that man had a sorrowful face.   250

26.

Down creaked a trap-door, on which he was placed,
   Right softly and slowly it fell;
And the man seemed in terror, and strangely amazed,
   But why, Connel could not then tell.
   He sunk and he sunk as the vice did impel;   255
     At length, as far downward he drew,
Good Lord! In a trice, with the pull of a string,
A pair of dread shears, like the thunderbolt's wing,
Came snap on his neck, with a terrible spring,
    And severed it neatly in two.   260

27.

Adown fell the body—the head lay in sight,
   The lips in a moment grew wan;
The temple just quivered, the eye it grew white,
   And upward the purple threads span!
   The dark crooked streamlets along the boards ran, 265
    Thin pipings of reek could be seen;
Poor Connel was blinded, his lugs how they sung!
He looked once again, and he saw like the tongue,
That motionless out 'twixt the livid lips hung,
    Then mirkness set over his een.   270

28.

He turned and he dashed his fair lady aside;
   And off like the lightning he broke,
By staircase and gallery, with horrified stride,
   He turned not, he staid not, nor spoke;
   The iron-spiked court-gate he could not unlock, 275
    His haste was beyond that of man;
He stopped not to rap, and he staid not to call,
With ram-race he cleared at a bensil the wall,
And headlong beyond got a grievous fall,
    But he rose, and he ran, and he ran!   280

29.

As stag of the forest, when fraudfully coiled,
  And mured up in barn for a prey,
Sees his dappled comrades dishonoured and soiled
  In their blood, on some festival day,
    Bursts all intervention, and hies him away,   285
      Like the wind over holt, over lea;
So Connel pressed on, all encumbrance he threw,
Over height, over hollow, he lessened to view:
It may not be said that he ran, for he flew,
    Straight on for the hills of the Dee.   290

30.

The contrair of all other runners in life,
  His swiftness increased as he flew,
But be it remembered, he ran from a wife,
  And a trap-door that sunk on a screw.
    His prowess he felt and decidedly knew,   295
      So much did his swiftness excel,
That he skimmed the wild paths like a thing of the mind,
And the stour from each footstep was seen on the wind,
Distinct by itself for a furlong behind,
    Before that it mingled or fell.   300

31.

He came to a hill, the ascent it was steep,
  And much did he fear for his breath;
He halted, he ventured behind him to peep,
  The sight was a vision of death!–
    His wife and her paramours came on the path,   305
      Well mounted, with devilish speed;
O Connel, poor Connel, thy hope is a wreck!
Sir, run for thy life, without stumble or check,
It is thy only stake, the last chance for thy neck,
    Strain Connel, or death is thy meed!   310

32.

O wend to the right, to the woodland betake;
  Gain that, and yet safe thou may'st be;
How fast they are gaining!–O stretch to the brake!
  Poor Connel, 'tis over with thee!
    In the breath of the horses his yellow locks flee,   315

The voice of his wife's in the van;
Even that was not needful to heighten his fears,
He sprang o'er the bushes, he dashed thro' the breers,
For he thought of the trap-door and damnable shears,
    And he cried to his God, and he ran.   320

33.

Through gallwood and bramble he floundered amain,
  No bar his advancement could stay;
Though heels-over-head whirled again and again,
  Still faster he gained on his way.
    This moment on swinging bough powerless he lay, 325
    The next he was flying along;
So lightly he scarce made the green leaf to quake,
Impetuous he splashed through the bog and the lake,
He rainbowed the hawthorn, he needled the brake,
    With power supernaturally strong. 330

34.

The riders are foiled, and far lagging behind,
  Poor Connel has leisure to pray,
He hears their dread voices around on the wind,
  Still farther and farther away:
    "O Thou who sit'st throned o'er the fields of the day, 335
    Have pity this once upon me,
Deliver from those that are hunting my life,
From *traps* of the wicked that round me are rife,
And O, above all, from the rage of a wife,
    And guide to the hills of the Dee! 340

35.

"And if ever I grumble at Providence more,
  Or scorn my own mountains of heath;
If ever I yearn for that sin-breeding ore,
  Or shape to complaining a breath,
    Then may I be nipt with the scissors of death,"– 345
    No farther could Connel proceed,
He thought of the snap that he saw in the nook,
Of the tongue that came out, and the temple that shook,
Of the blood and the reek, and the deadening look;
    He lifted his bonnet and fled. 350

36.

He wandered and wandered thro' woodlands of gloom,
  And sorely he sobbed and he wept;
At cherk of the pyat, or bee's passing boomb,
  He started, he listened, he leaped.
   With eye and with ear a strict guardship he kept;   355
    No scene could his sorrows beguile;
At length he stood lone by the side of the Dee,
It was placid and deep and as broad as a sea;
O could he get over, how safe he might be,
  And gain his own mountains the while.   360

37.

'Twas dangerous to turn, but proceeding was worse,
  For the country grew open and bare,
No forest appeared, neither broomwood nor gorse,
  Nor furze that would shelter a hare.
   Ah! could he get over how safe he might fare;   365
    At length he resolved to try;
At worst, 'twas but drowning, and what was a life
Compared to confinement in sin and in strife,
Beside a trap-door, and a scandalous wife?
    'Twas nothing–he'd swim, or he'd die.   370

38.

Ah! he could not swim, and was loath to resign
  This life for a world unknown,
For he had been sinning, and misery condign
  Would sure be his portion alone.
   How sweetly the sun on the green mountain shone,   375
    And the flocks they were resting in peace,
Or bleating along on each parallel path;
The lambs they were skipping on fringe of the heath,
How different might kythe the lone valleys of death,
   And cheerfulness evermore cease.   380

39.

All wistful he stood on the brink of the pool,
  And dropt on its surface the tear;
He started at something that boded him dool,
  And his mouth fell wide open with fear.
   The trample of galloppers fell on his ear,   385

One look was too much for his eye,
For there was his wife, and her paramours twain,
With whip and with spur coming over the plain,
Bent forward, revengeful, they gallopped amain,
    They hasten, they quicken, they fly!   390

40.

Short time was there now to deliberate, I ween,
    And shortly did Connel decree;
He shut up his mouth, and he closed his een,
    And he pointed his arms like a V,
    And like a scared otter, he dived in the Dee,   395
      His heels pointed up to the sky;
Like bolt from the firmament downward he bears,
The still liquid element startled uprears,
It bubbled, and bullered, and roared in his ears,
    Like thunder that gallows on high.   400

41.

He soon found the symptoms of drowning begin,
    And painful the feeling be sure,
For his breath it gaed out, and the water gaed in,
    With drumble and mudwart impure;
    It was most unpleasant, and hard to endure,   405
      And he struggled its inroads to wear;
But it rushed by his mouth, and it rushed by his nose,
His joints grew benumbed, all his fingers and toes,
And his een turned, they neither would open nor close,
    And he found his departure was near.   410

42.

One time he came up, like a porpoise, above,
    He breathed and he lifted his eye,
It was the last glance of the land of his love,
    Of the world, and the beautiful sky:
    How bright looked the sun from his window on high, 415
      Through furs of the light golden grain!
O Connel was sad, but he thought with a sigh,
That far above yon peaceful vales of the sky,
In bowers of the morning he shortly might lie,
    Though very unlike it just then.   420

43.

He sunk to the bottom, no more he arose,
The waters for ever his body enclose;
The horse-mussel clasped on his fingers and toes,
   All passive he suffered the scathe.
But O there was one thing his heart could not brook,   425
Even in his last struggles his spirit it shook,
The eels, with their cursed equivocal look,
   Redoubled the horrors of death.
O, aye since the time that he was but a bairn,
When catching his trouts in the Cluny, or Gairn,   430
At sight of an eel he would shudder and darn!
   It almost deprived him of breath.

44.

He died, but he found that he never would be
   So dead to all feeling and smart,
No, not though his flesh were consumed in the Dee,   435
   But that eels would some horror impart.
   With all other fishes he yielded to mart,
      Resistance became not the dead;
The minnow, with gushet sae gowden and braw,
The siller-ribbed perch, and the indolent craw,   440
And the ravenous ged, with his teeth like a saw,
      Came all on poor Connel to feed.

45.

They rave and they rugged, he cared not a speal,
   Though they preyed on his vitals alone;
But, Lord! when he felt the cold nose of an eel,   445
   A quaking seized every bone;
   Their slid slimy forms lay his bosom upon,
      His mouth that was ope, they came near;
They guddled his loins, and they bored thro' his side,
They warped all his bowels about on the tide.   450
   *   *   *   *   *

46.

Young Connel was missed, and his mother was sad,
   But his sisters consoled her mind;
And said, he was wooing some favourite maid,
   For Connel was amorous and kind.   455

Ah! little weened they that their Connel reclined
  On a couch that was loathful to see!
'Twas mud!—and the water-bells o'er him did heave,
The lampreys passed through him without law or leave,
And windowed his frame like a riddle or sieve,   460
  Afar in the deeps of the Dee!

47.

It was but a night, and a midsummer night,
  And next morning when rose the red sun,
His sisters in haste their fair bodies bedight,
  And, ere the day's work was begun,   465
  They sought for their Connel, for they were undone
    If ought should their brother befall:
And first they went straight to the bower in the deane,
For there he of late had been frequently seen;
For nature he loved, and her evening scene   470
  To him was the dearest of all.

48.

And when within view of his bourack they came,
  It lay in the skaddow so still,
They lift up their voices and called his name,
  And their forms they shone white on the hill;   475
  When, trow you, that hallo so erlisch and shrill
    Arose from those maids on the heath?
It was just as poor Connel most poignant did feel,
As reptiles he loved not of him made a meal,
Just when the misleered and unmannerly eel   480
  Waked him from the slumbers of death.

49.

He opened his eyes, and with wonder beheld
  The sky and the hills once again;
But still he was haunted, for over the field
  Two females came running amain.   485
  No form but his spouse's remained on his brain;
    His sisters to see him were glad;
But he started bolt upright in horror and fear,
He deemed that his wife and her minions were near,
He flung off his plaid, and he fled like a deer,   490
  And they thought their poor brother was mad.

50.

He 'scaped; but he halted on top of the rock;
  And his wonder and pleasure still grew;
For his clothes were not wet, and his skin was unbroke,
  But he scarce could believe it was true   495
    That no eels were within; and too strictly he knew
      He was married and buckled for life.
It could not be a dream; for he slept and awoke;
Was drunken, and sober; had sung, and had spoke;
For months and for days he had dragged in the yoke   500
      With an unconscientious wife.

51.

However it was, he was sure he was there,
  On his own native cliffs of the Dee:
O never before looked a morning so fair,
  Or the sun-beam so sweet on the lea!   505
    The song of the merl from her old hawthorn tree,
      And the blackbird's melodious lay,
All sounded to him like an anthem of love,
A song that the spirit of nature did move,
A kind little hymn to their Maker above,   510
      Who gave them the beauties of day.

52.

So deep the impression was stamped on his brain,
  The image was never defaced;
Whene'er he saw riders that gallopped amain,
  He darned in some bush till they passed.   515
    At kirk or at market sharp glances he cast,
      Lest haply his wife might be there;
And once, when the liquor had kindled his ee,
It never was known who or what he did see,
But he made a miraculous flight from Dundee,   520
      The moment he entered the fair.

53.

But never again was his bosom estranged
  From his simple and primitive fare;
No longer his wishes or appetite ranged
  With the gay and voluptuous to share.   525
    He viewed every luxury of life as a snare;

He drank of his pure mountain spring;
He watched all the flowers of the wild as they sprung;
He blessed his sweet laverock, like fairy that sung,
Aloft on the hem of the morning cloud hung,   530
    Light fanning its down with her wing.

54.

And oft on the shelve of the rock he reclined,
    Light carolling humoursome rhyme,
Of his midsummer dream, of his feelings refined,
    Or some song of the good olden time.   535
    And even in age was his spirit in prime,
      Still reverenced on Dee is his name!
His wishes were few, his enjoyments were rife,
He loved and he cherished each thing that had life,
With two small exceptions, an eel and a wife,   540
    Whose commerce he dreaded the same.

Superstition

1.

In Caledonia's glens there once did reign
A Sovereign of supreme unearthly eye;
No human power her potence could restrain,
No human soul her influence deny:
Sole Empress o'er the mountain homes, that lie   5
Far from the busy world's unceasing stir:
But gone is her mysterious dignity,
And true Devotion wanes away with her;
While in loose garb appears Corruption's harbinger.

2.

Thou sceptic leveller—ill-framed with thee   10
Is visionary bard a war to wage:
Joy in thy light thou earth-born Sadducee,
That earth is all thy hope and heritage:
Already wears thy front the line of age;
Thou see'st a heaven above—a grave before;   15
Does that lone cell thy wishes all engage?
Say, does thy yearning soul not grasp at more?
Woe to thy grovelling creed—thy cold ungenial lore!

3.

Be mine to sing of visions that have been,
And cherish hope of visions yet to be;   20
Of mountains clothed in everlasting green,
Of silver torrent and of shadowy tree,
Far in the ocean of eternity.
Be mine the faith that spurns the bourn of time;
The soul whose eye can future glories see;   25
The converse here with things of purer clime,
And hope above the stars that soars on wing sublime.

4.

But she is gone that thrilled the simple minds
Of those I loved and honoured to the last;
She who gave voices to the wandering winds,   30
And mounted spirits on the midnight blast:
At her behest the trooping fairies past,

And wayward elves in many a glimmering band;
The mountains teemed with life, and sore aghast
Stood maid and matron 'neath her mystic wand,   35
When all the spirits rose and walked at her command.

5.

And she could make the brown and careless boy
All breathless stand, unknowing what to fear;
Or panting deep beneath his co'erlet lie,
When midnight whisper stole upon his ear.   40
And she could mould the vision of the seer
To aught that rankled breast of froward wight;
Or hang the form of cerement or of bier
Within the cottage fire—O woful sight!
That called forth many a prayer and deepened groan by night.   45

6.

O! I have bowed to her resistless sway,
When the thin evening vapours floated nigh;
When the grey plover's wailings died away,
And the tall mountains melted into sky:
The note of gloaming bee that journeyed by   50
Sent through my heart a momentary knell;
And sore I feared in bush or brake might lie
Things of unearthly make—for I knew well
That hour with danger fraught more than when midnight fell.

7.

But O! if ancient cemetery was near,   55
Or cairn of harper murdered long ago,
Or wandering pedlar for his hoarded gear,
Of such, what glen of Scotland doth not know?
Or grave of suicide, upon the brow
Of the bleak mountain, withered all and grey;   60
From these I held as from some deadly foe:
There have I quaked by night and mused by day;
But chiefly where I weened the bard or warrior lay.

8.

For many a wild heart-thrilling Scottish bard,
In lowland dale the lyre of heaven that wooed,   65
Sleeps 'neath some little mound or lonely sward,
Where humble dome of rapt devotion stood;

'Mid heathy wastes by Mary's silent flood,
Or in the moorland glen of dark Buccleuch;
There o'er their graves the heath-fowl's mottled brood,   70
Track with light feathery foot the morning dew;
There plays the gamesome lamb, or bleats the yeaning ewe.

9.

Yet there still meet the thoughtful shepherd's view
The marble fount-stone, and the rood so grey;
And often there he sees with changeful hue   75
The snow-white scull washed by the burn away:
And O! if 'tis his chance at eve to stray,
Lone by the place where his forefathers sleep;
At bittern's whoop or gor-cock's startling bay,
How heaves his simple breast with breathings deep!   80
He mutters vow to Heaven, and speeds along the steep.

10.

For well he knows, along that desert room,
The spirits nightly watch the sacred clay;
That, cradled on the mountain's purple bloom,
By him they lie, companions of the day,   85
His guardian friends, and listening to his lay:
And many a chant floats on the vacant air,
That spirit of the bard or warrior may
Hear the forgotten names perchance they bare:
For many a warrior wight, and nameless bard, lies there!   90

11.

Those were the times for holiness of frame;
Those were the days when fancy wandered free;
That kindled in the soul the mystic flame,
And the rapt breathings of high poesy;
Sole empress of the twilight—Woe is me!   95
That thou and all thy spectres are outworn;
For true devotion wanes away with thee,
All thy delirious dreams are laughed to scorn,
While o'er our hills has dawned a cold saturnine morn.

12.

Long did thy fairies linger in the wild,   100
When vale and city wholly were resigned;
Where hoary cliffs o'er little holms were piled,

And torrents sung their music to the wind:
The darksome heaven upon the hills reclined,
Save when a transient sun-beam, through the rain,   105
Past, like some beauteous phantom of the mind,
Leaving the hind in solitude again—
These were their last retreats, and heard their parting strain.

13.

But every vice effeminate has sped,
Fast as the spirits from our hills have gone,   110
And all these light unbodied forms are fled,
Or good or evil, save the ghost alone.
True, when the kine are lowing in the loan,
An evil eye may heinous mischief brew;
But deep enchantments to the wise are known,   115
That certainly the blasted herd renew,
And make the eldron crone her cantrips sorely rue.

14.

O! I have seen the door most closely barred;
The green turf fire where stuck was many a pin;
The rhymes of incantation I have heard,   120
And seen the black dish solemnly laid in
Amid the boiling liquid—Was it sin?
Ah! no—'twas all in fair defence of right.
With big drops hanging at her brow and chin,
Soon comes the witch in sad and woeful plight;   125
Is cut above the breath, and yelling takes her flight!!

15.

And I have seen, in gaunt and famished guise,
The brindled mouser of the cot appear;
A haggard wildness darted from her eyes;
No marvel was it when the truth you hear!   130
That she is forced to carry neighbour near,
Swift through the night to countries far away;
That still her feet the marks of travel bear;
And her broad back, that erst was sleek and grey,
O, hapless beast!—all galled where the curst saddle lay.   135

16.

If every creed has its attendant ills,
How slight were thine!—a train of airy dreams!

No holy awe the cynic's bosom thrills;
Be mine the faith diverging to extremes!
What though, upon the moon's distempered beams,   140
Erewhile thy matrons gallopped through the heaven,
Floated like feather on the foaming streams,
Or raised the winds by tenfold fury driven,
Till ocean blurred the sky, and hills in twain were riven.

17.

Where fell the scathe?—The beldames were amused,   145
Whom eild and poverty had sorely crazed.
What, though their feeble senses were abused
By gleesome demon in the church-aisle raised,
With lion tail, and eyes that baleful blazed,
Whose bagpipe's blare made all the roof to quake!   150
But ages yet unborn will stand amazed
At thy dread power, that could the wretches make
Believe these things all real, and swear them at the stake.

18.

But ah! thou filled'st the guilty heart with dread,
And brought the deeds of darkness to the day!   155
Who was it made the livid corse to bleed
At murderer's touch, and cause the gelid clay
By fancied movement all the truth betray?
Even from dry bones the drops of blood have sprung!
'Twas thou, Inquisitor!—whose mystic sway   160
A shade of terror over nature hung;
A feeling more sublime than poet ever sung.

19.

Fearless the shepherd faced the midnight storm
To save his flocks deep swathed amid the snow;
Though threatening clouds the face of heaven deform,   165
The sailor feared not o'er the firth to row;
Dauntless the hind marched forth to meet the foe:
For why? they knew, though earth and hell combined,
In heaven were registered their days below;
That there was one well able and inclined   170
To save them from the sword, the wave, and stormy wind.

20.

O! blissful thought to poverty and age,
When troubles press and dangers sore belay!
This is their only stay, their anchorage;
"It is the will of Heaven, let us obey!   175
"Ill it befits the creatures of a day
"Beneath a father's chastening to repine."
This high belief in Providence's sway,
In the eye of reason wears into decline;
And soon that heavenly ray must ever cease to shine.   180

21.

Yet these were days of marvel—when our king,
As chronicles and sapient sages tell,
Stood with his priests and nobles in a ring,
Searching old beldame for the mark of hell,
The test of witchcraft and of devilish spell: 185
And when I see a hag, the country's bane,
With rancorous heart and tongue of malice fell,
Blight youth and beauty with a burning stain,
I wish for these old times, and Stuarts back again.

22.

Haply 'tis weened that Scotland now is free   190
Of witchcraft, and of spell o'er human life;
Ah me!—ne'er since she rose out of the sea,
Were they so deep, so dangerous, and so rife:
The heart of man, unequal to the strife,
Sinks down before the lightning of their eyes.   195
O! it is meet that every maid and wife
Some keen exorcist still should scrutinize,
And bring them to the test, for all their sorceries.

23.

Much have I owed thee—Much may I repine,
Great Queen! to see thy honours thus decay.   200
Among the mountain maids the power was thine,
On blest Saint Valentine's or Hallow Day.
Ours was the omen—theirs was to obey:
Firm their belief, or most demurely feigned!
Each maid her cheek on lover's breast would lay,   205
And, sighing, grant the kiss so long refrained;—
'Twas sin to counteract what Providence ordained!

24.

O! I remember, as young fancy grew,
How oft thou spokest in voice of distant rill;
What sheeted forms thy plastic finger drew,   210
Throned on the shadow of the moonlight hill;
Or in the glade so motionless and still
That scarcely in this world I seemed to be;
High on the tempest sing thine anthem shrill;
Across the heaven upon the meteor flee;   215
Or in the thunder speak with voice of majesty!

25.

All these are gone—The days of vision o'er;
The bard of fancy strikes a tuneless string.
O! if I wist to meet thee here no more,
My muse should wander, on unwearied wing,   220
To find thy dwelling by some lonely spring,
Where Norway opes her forests to the gale;
The dell thy home, the cloud thy covering,
The tuneful sea maid, and the spectre pale,
Tending thy gloomy throne, amid heaven's awful veil.   225

26.

Or shall I seek thee where the Tana rolls
Her deep blue torrent to the northern main;
Where many a shade of former huntsman prowls,
Where summer roses deck the untrodden plain,
And beauteous fays and elves, a flickering train,   230
Dance with the foamy spirits of the sea?
O! let me quake before thee once again,
And take one farewell on my bended knee,
Great ruler of the soul, which none can rule like thee!

The Gyre Caryl

THERE wals ane auld caryl wonit in yon howe,
   Lemedon! lemedon! ayden lillelu!
His face was the geire, and his hayre was the woo,
   Sing Ho! Ro! Gillan of Allanhu!
But och! quhan the mure getis his cuerlet gray, &c.   5
Quhan the gloamyng hes flauchtit the nychte and the day, &c.
Quhan the crawis haif flowin to the greinwode schaw,
And the kydde hes blet owr the Lammer Law;
Quhan the dewe hes layde the klaiver asteep,
And the gowin hes fauldit hir buddis to sleep;   10
Quhan nochte is herde but the merlinis mene—
Och! than that gyre caryl is neuir his lene!

   Ane bonnye baby, se meike and mylde,
Aye walkis wythe him the dowie wylde:
The gowlin getis of sturt and stryffe,   15
And wearie wailis of mortyl lyffe,
Wald all be hushit till endless pece
At ane blynke of that babyis fece!

   Hir browe se fayre, and her ee se meike,
And the damysk roz that blumis on her cheike;   20
Hir lockis, and the bend of hir bonnye bree,
And hir smyle mochte waukin the deide to see!

   Hir snoode, befryngit with mony a geme,
Wals stouin fra the raynbowe's brychtest beme;
And hir raile, mair quhyte than snawye dryfte,   25
Was neuir woven anethe the lyfte;
It keust sikn lychte on hill and gaire,
It shawit the wylde deer til hir laire;
And the fayries wakinit fra their beddis of dewe,
And they sang ane hyme, and the hyme was new!   30
List, lordyngs, list! for neuir agayne
Shalt' heire sikn wylde wanyirdlye strayne.
For they sang the nychte-gale in ane swoone,
And they sang the goud lockes fra the moone;
They sang the reidbreiste fra the wud,   35
And the laueroke out of the merlit clud;

And sum wee feres of bludeless byrthe
Cam out of the wurmholes of the yirthe,
And swoofit se lychtlye round the lee,
That they waldna kythe to mortyl ee; 40
But their erlisch sang it rase se shill,
That the waesum tod youlit on the hill!
O lordyngs, list the cronach blande!
The flycherynge songe of Fayrie-land!

The Song of the Fairies

SING AYDEN! AYDEN! LILLELU! 45
Bonnye bairne, we sing to you!
Up the Quhyte, and doune the Blak,
No ane leuer, no ane lak,
No ane shado at ouir bak;
No ane stokyng, no ane schue, 50
No ane bendit blever blue,
No ane traissel in the dewe!
Bonnye bairne, we sing to you,
AYDEN! AYDEN! LILLELU! &c.

Speile! speile! 55
  The moone-rak speile!
Warre the rowan, warre the steile,
Throu the rok and throu the reile,
Rounde about lyke ane spynning wheile;
Throu the libbert, throu the le, 60
Rounde the yirde and rounde the se,
Bonnye bairne, we sing to thee,
Rounde the blumis and bellis of dewe,
AYDEN! AYDEN! LILLELU!

Speide! speide! 65
  Lyving or deide!
Faster than the fyirie gleide,
Biz throu Laplin's tyrling dryfte!
Rounde the moone, and rounde the lyfte,
Aye we ring, and aye we sing 70
Our hune! hune!
And ante-tune!
Neuir! neuir! neuir dune!

Up the Leider and doune the Dye
Aye we sing our lullabye!   75
Bonnye bairne, we sing to you,
AYDEN! AYDEN! LILLELU!

    Ryng! ryng!
     Daunce and sing!
Hiche on the brume yer garlandis hyng!   80
For the bairnis sleipe is sweite and sure,
And the maydenis reste is blest and pure
Throu all the lynkis of Lammer-mure;
Sen our bonnye baby was sent fra heven.
Scho comis owr-nychte withe the dewe of even,   85
And quhan the sone keikes out of the maine,
Scho swawis withe the dewe to heven again.
But the lychte shall dawne and the houlat flee,
The deide shall ake, and the day shall be
Quhan scho shall smyle in the gladsum noone,   90
And sleipe and sleipe in the lychte of the moone!
Than shall our luias weke anewe,
With herpe and vele and ayril too,
TO AYDEN! AYDEN! LILLELU!

    Hyde! hyde!   95
     Quhateuir betyde,
Elfe and dowle that ergh to byde!
The littil wee burdie mai cheipe in the wa,
The plevir mai sing, and the coke mai craw;
For neuir ane spyrit derke and doure   100
Dar raike the creukis of Lammer-mure;
And everilke gaiste of gysand hue
Shall melt in the breize our baby drew!
But we ar left in the grein-wud glen,
Bekaus we luf the chylder of men,   105
Sweitlye to sing our flawmand new;
Bonnye bairne, we sing to you,
AYDEN! AYDEN! LILLELU!

    Pace! pace!
     Spyritis of grace!   110
Sweite is the smyle of our babyis face!
The kelpye dernis, in dreide and dule,

Deipe in the howe of his eirye pule;
Gil-Moules frehynde the hallen mene fle,
Throu the dor-threshil, and throu the dor-ke,   115
And the mer-mayde mootes in the saifrone se.
But we ar left in the grein-wud glen,
Bekaus we luf the chylder of men,
Sweitlye to sing and neuir to rue,
Sweitlye to sing ouir last adue;   120
Bonnye bairne, we sing to you,
AYDEN! AYDEN! LILLELU!

      Sing! sing!
    How shall we sing
Rounde the bairne of the spyritis Kyng!   125
Lillelu! lillelu! mount in a ryng!
Fayries away! away on the wyng!
We too maune flytt to ane land of blisse!
To ane land of holy silentnesse!
To ane land quhair the nychte-wynd neuir blewe!   130
But thy fayre spryng shall euir be newe!
Quhan the moone shall waik ne mayre to wane,
And the clud and the raynbowe baithe ar gane,
In bowirs aboone the brik of the day
We'll sing to our baby for ever and aye!   135

      Than the caryl he saw them swoof alang,
And he herde the wordis of thair leifu sang;
They seemit to lyng asklent the wynde,
And left ane streamourie trak behynde;
But he heirit them singyng as they flewe,   140
AYDEN! AYDEN! LILLELU!

      Than the caryl liftit the babe se yung,
And nemit hir with ane tremilous tung;
And the lychte of God strak on his face
As he nelit on the dewe, and callit her Grace: 145
And he barrit the day of sorrowe and reuth
To flee fra the bairne of Hevenly Truthe;
And he barrit the deidis that nurice paine
Euir to thrall the worild again.
Than he claspit his handis, and wepit ful sair,   150

Quhan he bade hir adue for evirmaire.
O neuir wals babyis smyle se meike
Quhan scho fand the teir drap on her cheike!
And neuir wals babyis leuke se wae
Quhan scho saw the leal auld caryl gae!   155
But all his eiless ouphen trayne,
And all his gaistis and gyis war gane;
The gleides that gleimit in the derksome schaw,
And his fayries had flown the last of a':
Than the puir auld caryl was blythe to fle   160
Away fra the emerant isle of the se,
And neuir mayre seikis the walkis of men,
Unless in the diske of the gloamyng glen.

The Haunted Glen

DRAMATIS PERSONÆ

———————

LU, *a Scottish Prince, carried off by the Fairies, and afterwards chosen their King*

KNIGHT

SPIRIT

PHILANY,
DEW,
SNOWFLAKE,   *Fairies.*
FOAMBELL,
RUE,
MOTHE,

LULA, *a Princess living in concealment*

The Haunted Glen
SCENE I.–*A Dell, by moon-light, with a distant view behind.*

———————

A FAIRY *enters, winding swiftly among the trees.*
VOICE *above.*

Voice. Fairy, fairy, whither away?

Fairy. Come down and see;
It fits not thee
To hide in the bud of the chesnut tree,
And scare with yelp and eldritch croon   5
The spirits that pass by the light of the moon.

Voice. I heard a sound come through the wood,
I feared it came from flesh and blood;
But I'll be with thee for evil or good.

SPIRIT *enters.*
Now, fairy, tell me whither away,   10

For I have much to thee to say,
And much to do ere the break of day.

Fairy. I know thee not—I cannot tell
Whether thou art from heaven or hell.
In Scottish glen, since the days of old,   15
I have watched the hamlet and the fold;
Long have I sojourned by mountain and dale,
I have sailed on the moon-beam, and rode on the gale
For a thousand years, and a thousand more;
But, Spirit, I never saw thee before.   20

Spirit. Here am I sent a while to dwell;
Tell me thy nature, and mine I'll tell.

Fairy. This form was made when the rose first grew,
Of an odour dissolved in the falling dew,
When first from the heaven it 'gan to distil   25
Above the top of the highest hill:
And if I may judge from the moment I came
There's a germ of the rainbow in my frame;
For my being grew, I remember well,
When first the bow on the rose-bud fell;   30
And the very first scene that met my view
Was its pale blossom, tinged anew
With stripes of the green, the red, and the blue.
But I am a spirit of joy and love,
For the breath that formed me was from above.   35

Spirit. Then, gladsome spirit, list to me,
For we may meet by tower and tree:
When first the fires of vengeance and wrath
Were kindled in a world beneath,
They from their boundaries burst on high,   40
And flashed into the middle sky;
From these a thin blue vapour came,
Something between a smoke and flame,
And it journeyed on through the firmament,
Till with a sun-beam it was blent: 45
Of that I was framed, and in my mood
There is something evil and something good.
But I have been busy since I came here,
There's a comely corse lies stretched near—
Within yon wood of alders grey   50

There was murder done at the close of day.
O, I ne'er saw so lovely a sight
As a maiden's corse in the pale moonlight!

Fairy. Ah! spirit of stern and ill intent,
The land may rue that thou wast sent.   55

Spirit. 'Tis true, I love to seek and see
The evils of humanity,
And the woes and the plagues of the human lot!
But I cannot hurt where sin is not.
Come, trifling fay, I'll consort you   60
The relics of mortal beauty to view;
The writhed limb you there may see,
And the stripes of blood upon the lea;
Half open is her still blue eye;
Her face is turned unto the sky;   65
The shadows sleep on her bosom bare,
And the dew-weft on her raven hair,
And never again shall spirit see
Such picture of sorrow and sanctity!

Fairy. Get thee away,   70
Thou elfin grey,
Thou art not fit with fairies to stay!
For me I am sent by the still moonlight,
Each floweret's bosom to bedight,
For the fairies revel here o'er-night.   75
The time draws on when Lu of Kyle,
Who in Fairyland hath sojourned a while,
Must be crowned, by a virgin's hand,
The king of the fairies of fair Scotland:
And fairies have ridden, and fairies have run,   80
From the evening set till the morning sun,
The first of mortal maidens to find,
Fairest of body, and purest of mind;
For she must be chaste as the snow-drop at noon,
Stately as cherubim, mild as the moon,   85
Sweet as the rose-bud, and fresh as the dew,
That sets the crown on the head of King Lu.

Spirit. If right I judge, you will only miss
Your aim in travelling far for this;
For in this glen there dwells a dame,   90

The fairest of human form and name;
But if I get sway of this woodland scene,
This matchless maid shall be, ere e'en,
What many a maiden before has been.

Fairy. Get thee away,   95
Thou elfin grey,
Thou art not fit with fairies to stay!
The fairies of Scotia are mild as the even,
Jocund and blithe as the laverock in heaven;
Tender to childhood, gentle to age,   100
Pesterous to priest, and freakish to sage;
But whatever they do, or wherever they go,
They grieve aye for human failings and woe.
Get thee away, over brake, over thorn,
Woo thy dead corse till the break of the morn,   105
For I hear the sound of the fairies' horn.
    [*Spirit vanishes.*

SCENE *continues.*

*Endless trains of Fairies, clothed in green, and riding
on white steeds, are seen in the distance.*

Song within.
Sweet is the mountain breeze of night,
  To fairy troopers blithly riding,
Over holt, and holm, and height,
  Through the links of greenwood gliding.   110

CHORUS.
  Ara Lu! Ora Lu!
  Who shall man and fairy sever?
  Ara Lu! Ora Lu!
  They are knit, and knit for ever.
Lu is prince of Fairyland,   115
  Vales of light and fairy fountains;
Lu shall wield the regal wand
  Over Scotia's heathy mountains.

CHORUS.
  Ara Lu! Ora Lu! &c.

Enter LU *and* FEMALE FAIRIES.

First Fairy. Our names, prince,—Our new names.   120

   Lu. Come hither, beauteous trifle.
Thy name be hence Philany, and thy charge
The nestlings of the birds, that sing at eve
And ere the morning sun. And thou, pale blossom,
Thy name is Snowflake; and thy envied charge   125
The walks and couch of virgin purity.
O guard that well! If e'er thou markest the eye
Beaming with more than earthly lustre, then
Thy sickening opiates use, to dim the ray
Too bright for man to look on. In the night   130
By maiden's bosom watch; and if she dream,
Lay thy cold hand upon her youthful breast;
Hang on her waving locks by day, and watch
Her sweet and mellow breath; and as it heaves
And rocks thee to and fro, thou shalt discern   135
The slightest workings of the soul within;
The rest thy wisdom and thy care direct.

   Kiss me, thou little sweet and humid thing,
Bright as the orient—thy name be Dew;
Thy care the wild flowers of the hill and dale,   140
To pearl the rose and weave the heavenly bow.
And thou, her sister, guard the rivulets,
And silver pools where little fishes dwell,
And sport them in the sun—thou hast a flock
Full wayward and exposed—so be thy care—   145
Thy name is Foambell, brook thou well the name.
And thine is Rue—thy charge, declining life.
And thou, that hast a pathos in thy looks
Bespeaking mould of tenderness and love,
Be guardian thou of playful infancy;   150
Watch o'er the imps, and when the comely boy
Nears to the precipice, where blossoms wave,
Or to the pool, where green inverted hills,
And trees, and shrubs betray—then flutter thou
Close by his foot like gilded butterfly,   155
To lure the rosy lubber from the snare
Of adders young, and from the slow-worm's den.
Thy name is Mothe, the joy of doing good
Be thy reward.

Thou downy dancing thing,   160
Fond as the nestling, playful as the fawn,
Thy dwelling be the mountain, and thy task
To guard the young deer and the leveret
And tender lamb—thy name is Gossamer.
Embrace me all, then bound you on your way,   165
To sport and revel till the dawn of day.
                    [*He embraces them all.*
Sweet gladsome beings! sweet you are, and kind,
And well I love you. But my mortal frame
Is not so subtilized and pure, but that
I feel in your communion something short   170
Of true felicity. In all your rounds,
And wanderings wild, search for the mortal maid
Of purity and beauty so refined
That spirits may consort with; and no stain
Of human love or longing intervene.   175

   Dew. Prince, here I met with a spirit stern,
Who said that by this forest dern,
There dwells the fairest, loveliest dame,
That ever wore the human frame;
But wicked men and fiends below   180
Have both combined to work her woe.
Prince, watch this glen, and if you see
A knight of comely courtesy
Lead a fair maiden to the wood,
Of lady mien, and mournful mood;   185
Be sure that knight's intent is ill,
For the blood is on his corslet still!

   Lu. Hie you away, by valley and brae,
Attend to your tasks, by night and by day;
And each take a thousand fays along,   190
To tend your behests for right or for wrong;
And here will I watch till the rising sun,
For fear more guilty deeds be done.

The Fairies dance slowly round him in a circle, and sing.

The baby's rest shall be sweet and sure,
The maiden's slumber blest and pure;   195
The grey-haired sire shall rejoice in mind,
And look before, and not behind;

The flowers shall blow, and the rainbow beam,
The fishes sport in the sunny stream;
Young Love and Peace shall go hand in hand,   200
And Sin and Sorrow flee the land;
The lamb beside the fox shall stray,
The kid and fawn round the martin play,
And the child shall dance by the adder's den,
Since spirits pure are conjoined with men.   205

CHORUS.
   Then hie away, fairies, hie away,
   Light over flower and tender spray,
   Light over moonbeam and midnight dew,
   Our blithsome gambols to renew.

The Haunted Glen
SCENE II.–*A Wood.*

Enter LU.

  Lu. Another day is past, and it has been
To me a day of such delight, and pain,
And new sensations mingled, as I never
Deemed consonant with being.–I have seen
The peerless maid of this romantic glen,   5
Have watched her every motion, word, and look,
With lover, and alone. Such beauty, truth,
And purity of soul, I did not ween
This sinful world contained! I love her so,
That I would yield this incorporeal frame,   10
This state of mental energy, attained
By seven years' penance, and again assume
My former state of gross humanity,
Rather than lose that virgin's fellowship,
Her confidence, and love. I watched her steps,   15
Led by that treacherous, that decoying fiend,
That demon in the guise of man, and heard
His smooth deceitful tale. I took the form
Of redbreast, and I hopped upon the spray
Close to her cheek, and sung my plaintive note;   20

And she called me "sweet Robin," and I saw
A kindness in her looks. "Sir Knight," said she,
"List to that Robin's note. Methinks he says,
'Beware, young simple Lula.'" "On my faith,"
The knight replied, "'tis very like these words!"   25
"I wish I were that Robin's mate," said she,
"To fly away with him o'er many lands,
And live in innocence!" And then I sung
"Would that you were, sweet Lula." Her blue eyes
Turned doubtfully up to the sky, when this   30
She heard sung by a bird; her lovely face
Was stamped with sweet amazement and deep thought.

   Then I became a coney, and I stole
From out the brake, and hitched around their seat,
Mounching the herbs, and raised up my long ears   35
As listening in dismay, and looked full wise,
Making my cloven lip and wiry beard
Move with grimace.–Back to the thicket then
Amain I scudded, and as quick returned,
And cowered, and mounched the grass–She laughed at me,   40
And praised my antic tricks, but little weened
I was a fairy lover, and far less
A mortal prince rid of his mortal nature.
I must retire and take some other form,
For here my loved and beauteous Lula comes,   45
Led by the wretch that woos her to her fate.
                       [*Exit.*

Enter LULA *and* KNIGHT.

   Lula. Where do you lead me, Knight? I may not go
Farther into the glen: have you not heard
How it is haunted?

   Knight. Fear not, gentle Lula;   50
No spirit may do harm to innocence
And beauty such as thine.–Come, let us stray
Deeper into this dell, and watch the rise
Of the full moon. See how her radiant verge
Streams through the broken cliffs of yon far hill,   55
Like fragments of a moon. The Queen of heaven
Smiles from her lattice! Has it not a cast
Of sweet sublimity that scene, my Lula?

Lula. It has.—O, I could list and look for ever,
And muse upon these goings on of nature! 60

Knight. 'Tis a fit scene for love.—Will you not hear
The man that loves you to distraction, breathe
The vows of constancy and endless love?

Lula. Nay, then I'm gone; I loathe the very name
Of love, and every baneful consequence 65
That follows in its train. Why talk to me
Of love, when Emma's lost?—Emma, who loved you
With fondness never equalled! Tell me, Knight,
Where think you Emma's gone?

Knight. How can I know? 70
Woe's me, poor Emma! She is fled, I fear,
With false deceiver, or some base-born hind;—
Let us not think of her.

Lula. Yet you grow pale
At mention of her name—I honour you 75
For this.—'Tis true she loved you!—What is here?
There's blood upon your basnet, Knight!—Your hilt
And arm are stained with it.—What blood is this?

Knight. It is the blood of my white steed, which I
Slew in a rage, that now I sore repent. 80

Lula. Your steed is whole and standing in his stall;
I saw him; ask your groom.

Knight. It was my hound,
My milk-white hound—Woe's me that she is slain!

Lula. Your hound is well, and hunting through the wood. 85

Knight. It was a deer that held the hound at bay,
'Twas that I meant.

Lula. You have not slain a deer
For months and days, nor is it hunting time;
You rave! or do not think of what you say.— 90
But here's our gentle Robin come again,
To cheer us with his homely note.—O, Knight,
Let us return.—Hear what the Robin sings!

Knight. Come, let us dive into the dell, my Lula,
And see the moon lie bathing in the stream, 95

Deep in the centre of the wood; it is
A scene will charm you.–Let us go, my love.

   Lula. I never farther leave my home at eve;
That glen is dangerous, for spirits there
Hold nightly rendezvous.–Poor Emma loved   100
Thoughtful to stray in it;–now, where, alas!
Is simple Emma? Knight, though I nought fear,
Strange fancies crowd on me.–Ah, might it be
As I now deem!–Do guardian spirits ever
Take form of beast or bird?   105

   Knight. So sages say.
But wherefore ask? Come, let us go, my love,
Down that sweet winding glen.–You cannot fear
To walk that space with me?–I know the scene
Hath that in't will delight you. You shall see   110
The moonbeam streaming o'er the shadowy hill,
To kiss the winding wave, and deck the trees
In golden foliage.–You shall see the shades
Of hills, and trees, and rocks, lie stretched afar,
Bathing in liquid crystal, till you lose   115
Sense which is the true world, the stars and moon,
And which the elemental imagery.
Oh! I beseech you, let us go, sweet Lula.

   Lula. Well, I will go, for when I hear you talk
Of nature I am charmed–'tis so unlike   120
The converse of these simple cottagers;
But talk of that alone, and not of love,
Else I'll not list, nor answer deign to you.
Why am I plagued with language which I loathe?
                            [*Going, stops short.*
Protect my senses, Heaven!–Can it be?   125
Look at that bird, Sir Knight–Is it not changed
In form and hue since last we looked at it?

   Knight. What is it?

   Lula. See! it grows and changes still;
Waylays and threatens us–I will not go   130
Farther upon that path for will of man.

   Knight. Then my resolve is fixed–Dame, you *shall* go,
Return home as you may.

Lula. What do you mean?

Knight. Only that you shall go into that glen   135
Far as I list to lead you—if you prove
As coy when you return, my well-earned skill
In woman I give up. Nay, struggle not,
Nor pule, nor cry, for neither shall avail.

      Lu *enters, and by a wave of his hand lays the*
             Knight *flat on his back.*

Lula. O comely stranger, spare my helpless youth!   140
Protect and guard me! here I throw myself
Into your arms.

Lu. And from all brutal force
And insult shall these arms protect thee, maid.

Lula. Yes, I can trust you, there is in your look   145
And your embrace, that chastened dignity,
That calm pure sympathy, which I have longed
And pined so much to look on. Whence are you?
From what blest land or kingdom came you thus
To my deliverance?   150

Lu. These lands were mine,
Far as the soaring eagle's eye can reach;
But I resigned them for a dynasty
Wild and ethereal. Could you love me, Lula?

Lula. I know not—If your touch and looks were aye   155
As pure as they are now—methinks I could.

Lu. Then I'll be aught for thee—I'll be again
The thing I was, that I may be caressed
And loved by you; though pain, and woe, and death,
And spirits' vengeance on the issue wait.   160
Come with me, gentle maid; and while I lead you
Home to your cot, I will a tale unfold
Shall make your ears to tingle, and your thoughts
Wander into delirious mystery.
        [*Exeunt* Lu *and* Lula. *The* Knight *rises.*

Knight. What can this mean? How was I struck to earth,   165
And chained as by some spell? Curse on the stripling!
Who can he be, or whither did he come
To brave me in this guise? 'Tis like a dream;

And yet I saw them go, arm linked in arm,
While I not moved a finger or a limb.   170

   Might I believe that I some thing have seen
Not of this world, that with one wave of 's hand
Could strike me motionless, then do I strive
In vain for the possession of the maid.
But here I swear above this craven sword,   175
That for the first time slept within its sheath
Beneath the eye of insult, not to brook
Life without Lula. Never shall I see
Another filch that precious morsel, placed
Thus in my reach! Arm, thou wast never wont   180
To lie in dull and nerveless apathy
When will called "Strike." Ah! couldst thou do it now,
When the most delicate and luscious cup
That ever mocked Desire's pale parching lip
Was rudely dashed away! Blood and revenge   185
Be hence thy meed, or scornful Lula mine!

The Haunted Glen
SCENE III.—*The Glen.—Twilight.*

LU *and* FAIRY *meeting.*

Lu. Welcome, my little Foambell, here:
How fare thy flocks by frith and meer,
By river, pool, and streamlet clear?

Foam. O, Prince, my charge I yield again!
My little breast is rent with pain!   5
No happy thing on earth may be
While ruthless man holds sovereignty.
I chose the sweetest stream that fell
From mountain glen, and moorland well,
Where happy, gay, and innocent,   10
My finny tribes were in thousands blent;
And I rejoiced and smiled to see
Each awkward beck and courtesy,
How downward turned each full set eye,
As I, their Queen, went sailing bye.   15

One day I spied upon the strand,
A carl that waved a sounding wand
Of marvellous length, whom I did deem
Some earthly guardian of the stream;
But coming nigh I wept full sore   20
To see my people dragged ashore,
One after one, and two by two,
And welcomed forth with murderous blow,
While their dying throes rejoiced his sight,
For his ugly face had the grin of delight.   25

   This scene my feelings could not bear,
I tried to wile them from the snare;
The form of a fisherman I took,
And I angled before him in the brook;
But they wearied of my phantom fly,   30
And the carl he thrashed and waded nigh;
I could not scare them from his hook,
For I cast no shadow on the brook;
Though boardly my frame, as man's might be,
"The sun shone through my thin bodye."   35
I wist not what to do or say,
For still the carl he plashed away;
And his rod, that stretched o'er half the flood,
It sounded through the air so loud,
That it made me start and pant for breath,   40
For I knew the sough was the sound of death.
No minute passed but one or more
Was dragged forth struggling to the shore;
I saw them flutter in wild affright,
And shiver and gasp in piteous plight;   45
Their silvery sides, that in the flood
Shone bright and pure, were striped with blood;
Yet no remorse did the carl feel,
But thrust them in his wicker creel.

   Then I bethought me of a plan,   50
Of turning pike instead of man;
And aye where his hook the angler threw
I chased away my harmless crew:
Oh! how astonished were the throng
When I came gaping them among!   55
Away they fled to ward the scathe,

Fast I pursued with threat of death.
Most gleesome sport I had the while,
But wondered at the carl's wile,
For o'er the ripple he swam his fly,   60
So sleek and so provokingly,
That scarcely could I myself restrain
From springing at that bait amain;
For, though by sage it be denied,
Nature and form are still allied.   65

    Amazement marked the fisher's look,
Another fish he could not hook;
He changed his tackle, he changed his fly,
And blamed the colour of the sky;
But, baulked for once, he went away,   70
Cursing the fish and hateful day.

    Full six times twelve away he bore,
I saw him count them on the shore;
All reft of life withouten law,
To gorge a miscreant's ravenous maw.   75
Then sooth, while man has sway below,
My watery charge I must forego.

    _Lu._ But here comes slender Gossamer,
Like shred of silver through the air.—
What news, thou gentle, pitying child,   80
From mountain, glen, and pathless wild?

    Gos. Ah, woeful news! my heart's in pain!
All would be joy in my domain,
The kid and lamb would sport in peace,
The young deer dwell in happiness;   85
But man—remorseless ravenous man,
Kills and devours; and stay who can!
The life-blood and the trembling limb
Of parting life are joy to him:
That rank devourer hence restrain,   90
Or take from me my charge again.

    _Lu._ Woe's me, that those we so much love
Such troublers should of nature prove:
But here comes one whose placid face
Speaks better things of the human race.   95
Welcome, sweet Snowflake, back to me;

How thrives sweet virgin purity?

Snow. Ah, Prince, decline the woeful theme!
Give it not thought,–give it not name!
Else first restrain or quench the blood   100
Of man, the defacer of all good!
The maiden is pure without a stain,
And pure in mind would aye remain,
But man–I sicken at the thought
Of all the shame that he hath wrought;   105
There is no art–there is no wile
That may the maiden heart beguile,
And cloud for aye the joyous smile,
Which this destroyer scorns to prove,–
This recreant in the paths of love.   110
Thousands to shame and ruin driven,
Debased on earth–debarred from heaven–
Of human forms and souls divine,
Yearly at Love's unholy shrine,
On bloated altar doomed to lie,   115
Unblest to weep, unwept to die.

Without regret, or wish t' atone,
He boasts his feats and urges on;
And when no other schemes remain
To give the virtuous bosom pain,   120
To Beauty's walks he wends his way,
With shameless stare in open day,
To check the step, abash the eye,
And tint the cheek of modesty.
O Prince, my charge I must disclaim,   125
While man's rude nature is the same.

And more, a baleful imp, I fear,
Is lately come to sojourn here;
A stranger spirit, bent on ill,
Whom I have watched o'er vale and hill;   130
His purposes we must gainsay,
Else shame may be ere break of day.
Yon cot I marked him prying round,
But scared him thence, and there I found
The loveliest maid of mortal race,   135
In dangerous and in helpless case;
A clown had crept her door within,

And left it open to the gin;
A dark knight stood her casement nigh,
With burning cheek, and greedy eye,   140
While the unweeting simple maid
Kneeled on the floor and inly prayed.
Her light locks o'er her shoulders swung,
Her night-robe round her waist was flung;
Her eyes were raised—her breast of snow   145
Heaved with devotion's grateful glow;
The speaking lip, the brow erect,
The movement on the polished neck,
The blooming cheek, the fervent mien,
Were all so comely, so serene,   150
The breeze of earth did ne'er embrace
Such pure angelic loveliness.

   The peasant's rugged form I took,
And braved the blood-hound's surly look;
At me he flew with horrid bay;   155
I fled, provoked, and led the way
Straight to the base and wicked clown—
The ban-dog seized and pulled him down;
Aloud he cried, and fought for life,
And rough and bloody was the strife.   160

   Then in the maiden's form so light,
Forthwith I glided by the knight,
Who followed fast, and begged and prayed,
But still I flew along the glade;—
Just when his arms were stretched to press   165
My waist with hellish eagerness,
A quagmire deep I led him in,
And left him struggling to the chin.

   Thus far full deftly have I sped,
Protecting maidhood's guiltless bed;   170
But ah, if man, the lord below,
Continue still as he is now,
Alas! my Prince, my toils will prove
Light balance in the scales of love.

   But who would strive?—Last night I spied   175
The loveliest flower on Leven side
In her bed-chamber laid to rest,

A sweet babe cradled on her breast;
Such fondness melted in her eye—
Affection's holiest purity!—   180
When with her breast the elfin played,
His round cheek to that bosom laid,
That I was moved, and weened if bliss
Be found in life's imperfectness,
If pure affection's from above,—   185
If "Love is Heaven, and Heaven is Love,"
All love, all fondness is outdone
By mother's o'er her only son:
That glow is bright, its workings kind,
Calm, chastened, ardent, yet refined.   190
Then let me roam, as heretofore,
And think of guarding maids no more.

Song by Lu.

Never, gentle spirits, never
    Yield your cares of human kind!
Can you leave the lonely river,   195
From the moonlight valley sever,
    All your guardian love resigned?
Thrown aside and scorned the giver?
Never, gentle spirits, never!

Chorus of FAIRIES.

Never till the dawn of day,   200
    Dawn of truth that shine shall ever,
Will we quit our polar way;
Over greenwood, glen, and brae,
        Over tree,
        Over lea,   205
Over fell and forest free,
Over rock, and over river,
Over cairn and cloud to quiver;
    Never, gentle spirits, never!
        Never!—Never!   210

The Haunted Glen
SCENE IV.–*A deep Dell.*

KNIGHT *sitting disconsolate.*

Knight. Sure there's some power unseen, unmeet for man
To cope with, watches o'er that witching thing.
First by a stripling I was stunned, and laid
Flat without motion; next to slough decoyed,
Bayed by a madman–by a blood-hound torn.   5
If I escape infection from the fangs
Of that outraged monster, I shall never
Strive for possession of that maiden more,
Though my heart burn within me.

SPIRIT *enters, and speaks and sings aside.*

Spirit. Then my sport will all be done: 10
Knight, before the rising sun,
Wet and weary, racked with pain,
You shall seek that maid again.

Sings.

My love's blithe as the bird on the tree;
My love's bonnie, as bonnie can be;   15
Though she loves another far better than me,
    Yet the dream wears kind in the morning.

Then I will steal to my love's bed-side,
And I will kiss my bonnie, bonnie bride;
And I'll whisper a vow, whatever betide,   20
    To my little flower in the morning.

Her breath is as sweet as the fragrant shower
Of dew that is blown from the rowan-tree flower;
O never were the sweets of roseate bower
    Like my love's cheeks in the morning!   25

Her eye is the blue-bell of the spring,
Her hair is the fleece of the raven's wing,
To her bonnie breast O how I'll cling,
    While sleeping so sound in the morning.

Enter Lu *and* Fairies.

  Lu. Fairies, the night wears on apace;   30
There's a paleness spread on the heaven's face,
A silvery haze so mild to see,
As lambent and as pure as we.
Soon will we mount with blithsome sway
Through these bright paths on our spiral way,   35
On the locks of the morning star to swing,
Or the veil of the sky for dew to wring;
To gallop the blue so lightsome and boon,
  Or braid the fair tresses of beauty so bright,
That wanton and wave at the horns of the moon,   40
  They are half of them ether, and half of them light.
But ere we depart from the morning ray,
To follow the moonlight west away,
O Spirits, advise what shall be done,
This loveliest flower beneath the sun,   45
From shame, from sin, and from sorrow to win.

  Dew. Bear her away,
'Twixt the night and the day;
We spirits have might
When we work for the right,   50
And each of us as much can bear
Of aught corporeal through the air,
As the swallow can carry on wing opprest,
Or the merle upbear to her downy nest.
Then bear her away   55
'Twixt the night and the day,
For she is too pure in the world to stay.

  Lu. That may not be—By rite divine,
In holy church and at holy shrine,
She has been washed with prayer and vow,   60
And named by a name to which we bow.
Or she must change with free good will,
Or be as she is for good or for ill;
Should I her gain, say, shall she be
The Queen of the Fairies, and Queen to me?   65

  Dew. Treason and pain!
Speak not again!
Trial and penance must long remain!

Bonnie Philany, Snowflake, and Foam;
Rainbow, Rainbow, blink and go home!   70

    Phil. (Aside.) Regard not, Prince, that freakish thing,
From jealousy her ravings spring;
One we must have, whatever befall,
To-morrow is our great festival,
And nought but mortal virgin's hand   75
Must crown thee King of Fairyland;
And then thy fate is fixed for ever,
From us and ours no more to sever.

    Lu. Would that the time were not so soon!
It is not yet the wane of the moon.   80

    Phil. Prince, I have a word to say to thee—
Your troubled mind and eye I see;
But if you dare to harbour a thought
Of yielding a crown so dearly bought,
With all the joys of the moonlight dell,   85
And the fervent beings that love you so well,
For the sake of a flower that will soon decay,
A piece of fair well-moulded clay,
We'll pick these bright eyes from your head,
And there we'll fix two eyes of lead;   90
We'll pull the heart from thy breast-bone,
And there we'll lodge a heart of stone:
So take thou care, lest some espy
The thoughts that in thy bosom lie.

    Lu. Sweet friendly fay, 'tis all too true;   95
Nor thought nor wish I'll hide from you:
Either that maiden here I must have,
Or return to the world, to death, and the grave.
O haste thee, Snowflake, haste and glide
To yon little cot by the greenwood side,   100
And watch yon maid till the break of day,
For I hear the watch-dog's angry bay;
Watch by her pillow, and look to her bed,
For I fear that beauty is hard bested.

    Then hie you away, fairies, hie you away!   105
Lean to the breeze, and ride in array
Over the land and the sea so fleet,
Over the rain, and the hail, and the sleet,

Keep aye the sun far under your feet,
The morning behind and the stars by your side,   110
The moonbeam your path, and her crescent your guide;
For O, her mild and humid flame
Suits best with the fairy's airy frame!
And meet we again to-morrow at even,
When the first star peeps through the veil of heaven; 115
And here such a palace of light shall be
As the world ne'er saw and never will see:
For there shall be lamps and glories in store,
And a thousand stars and a thousand more;
And there shall the ruby and onyx be seen,   120
The amethyst blue, and the emerald green,
With millions of gems of varied flame,
That have no likeness and have no name.
And our columns shall reach to the middle sky,
And the throne shall stand as the pine tree high;   125
Soft music shall flow of the spheres above,
The songs of gladness and songs of love;
And our feast shall begin with glory and glee—
But little we know what the end shall be!

Song.

  O weel befa' the guileless heart   130
    In cottage, bught, or pen!
And weel befa' the bonnie May
    That wons in yonder glen;
Wha loes the good and true sae weel—
Wha's aye sae kind and aye sae leal,   135
And pure as blooming asphodel
    Amang sae mony men;
O weel befa' the bonnie thing
    That wons in yonder glen.

There's beauty in the violet's vest,   140
    There's hinny in the haw,
There's dew within the rose's breast,
    The sweetest o' them a'.
The sun may rise and set again,
And lace wi' burning gowd the main,   145
The rainbow bend attour the plain
    Sae lovely to the ken;

But there's naething like my bonnie thing
   That wons in yonder glen.

'Tis sweet to hear the music float   150
   Alang the gloaming lea;
'Tis sweet to hear the blackbird's note
   Come pealing frae the tree;
To see the lambkin's lightsome race;
The speckled kid in wanton chase;   155
The young deer cower in lonely place
   Deep in his flowery den;
But what is like the bonnie face
   That smiles in yonder glen!

     *   *   *   *

The Mermaid

"O WHERE won ye, my bonnie lass,
   Wi' look sae wild an' cheery?
There's something in that witching face
   That I lo'e wonder dearly."

"I live where the hare-bell never grew,   5
   Where the streamlet never ran,
Where the winds o' heaven never blew;
   Now find me gin you can."

"'Tis but your wild an' wily way,
   The gloaming maks you eirie,   10
For ye are the lass o' the Braken-Brae,
   An' nae lad maun come near ye:

"But I am sick, an' very sick
   Wi' a passion strange an' new,
For ae kiss o' thy rosy cheek   15
   An' lips o' the coral hue."

"O laith, laith wad a wanderer be
   To do your youth sic wrang,
Were you to reave a kiss from me
   Your life would not be lang.   20

"Go, hie you from this lonely brake,
   Nor dare your walk renew;
For I'm the Maid of the Mountain Lake,
   An' I come wi' the falling dew."

"Be you the Maid of the Crystal Wave,   25
   Or she of the Braken-Brae,
One tender kiss I mean to have;
   You shall not say me nay.

"For beauty's like the daisy's vest
   That shrinks from the early dew,   30
But soon it opes its bonnie breast,
   An' sae may it fare wi' you."

"Kiss but this hand, I humbly sue,
    Even there I'll rue the stain;
O the breath of man will dim its hue,   35
    It will ne'er be pure again.

"For passion's like the burning beal
    Upon the mountain's brow,
That wastes itself to ashes pale;
    An' sae will it fare with you."   40

          ————

"O mother, mother, make my bed,
    An' make it soft and easy;
An' with the cold dew bathe my head,
    For pains of anguish seize me:

"Or stretch me in the chill blue lake,   45
    To quench this bosom's burning;
An' lay me by yon lonely brake,
    For hope there's none returning.

"I've been where man should not have been
    Oft in my lonely roaming,   50
And seen what man should not have seen
    By greenwood in the gloaming.

"O, passion's deadlier than the grave,
    A human thing's undoing!
The Maiden of the Mountain Wave   55
    Has lured me to my ruin!"

          ————

'Tis now an hundred years an' more,
    An' all these scenes are over,
Since rose his grave on yonder shore,
    Beneath the wild wood cover;   60

An' late I saw the Maiden there,
    Just as the day-light faded,
Braiding her locks of gowden hair,
    An' singing as she braided:–

Mermaid's Song

Lie still, my love, lie still and sleep,   65
    Long is thy night of sorrow;
Thy Maiden of the Mountain Deep
    Shall meet thee on the morrow.

But oh, when shall that morrow be,
    That my true love shall waken?   70
When shall we meet, refined an' free,
    Amid the moorland braken?

Full low and lonely is thy bed,
    The worm even flies thy pillow;
Where now the lips, so comely red,   75
    That kissed me 'neath the willow?

O I must laugh, do as I can,
    Even 'mid my song of mourning,
At all the fuming freaks of man
    To which there's no returning.   80

Lie still, my love, lie still an' sleep–
    Hope lingers o'er thy slumber;
What though thy years beneath the steep
    Should all its stones outnumber?

Though moons steal o'er, an' seasons fly   85
    On time's swift wing unstaying,
Yet there's a spirit in the sky
    That lives o'er thy decaying!

In domes beneath the water-springs
    No end hath my sojourning;   90
An' to this land of fading things
    Far hence be my returning;

For spirits now have left the deep,
    Their long last farewell taking:
Lie still, my love, lie still an' sleep,   95
    Thy day is near the breaking!

When my loved flood from fading day
   No more its gleam shall borrow,
Nor heath-fowl from the moorland grey
   Bid the blue dawn good-morrow;   100

The Mermaid o'er thy grave shall weep,
   Without one breath of scorning:
Lie still, my love, lie still an' sleep!
   And fare thee well till morning!

Verses to the Comet of 1811

How lovely is this wildered scene,
   As twilight from her vaults so blue
Steals soft o'er Yarrow's mountains green,
   To sleep embalmed in midnight dew!

All hail, ye hills, whose towering height,   5
   Like shadows, scoops the yielding sky!
And thou, mysterious guest of night,
   Dread traveller of immensity!

Stranger of Heaven! I bid thee hail!
   Shred from the pall of glory riven,   10
That flashest in celestial gale,
   Broad pennon of the King of Heaven!

Art thou the flag of woe and death,
   From angel's ensign-staff unfurled?
Art thou the standard of his wrath   15
   Waved o'er a sordid sinful world?

No, from that pure pellucid beam,
   That erst o'er plains of Bethlehem shone,[*]
No latent evil we can deem,
   Bright herald of the eternal throne!   20

Whate'er portends thy front of fire,
   Thy streaming locks so lovely pale,–
Or peace to man, or judgments dire,
   Stranger of Heaven, I bid thee hail!

Where hast thou roamed these thousand years?   25
   Why sought these polar paths again,
From wilderness of glowing spheres,
   To fling thy vesture o'er the wain?

[*] It was reckoned by many that this was the same Comet which appeared at the birth of our Saviour.

And when thou scalest the milky way–
   And vanishest from human view,   30
A thousand worlds shall hail thy ray
   Through wilds of yon empyreal blue!

Oh! on thy rapid prow to glide!
   To sail the boundless skies with thee,
And plough the twinkling stars aside,   35
   Like foam-bells on a tranquil sea!

To brush the embers from the sun,
   The icicles from off the pole;
Then far to other systems run,
   Where other moons and planets roll!   40

Stranger of Heaven! O let thine eye
   Smile on a rapt enthusiast's dream;
Eccentric as thy course on high,
   And airy as thine ambient beam!

And long, long may thy silver ray   45
   Our northern arch at eve adorn;
Then, wheeling to the east away,
   Light the grey portals of the morn!

The Powris of Moseke,

Ane Rychte Plesant Ballaunt,
Maide be Maistere Jamis Hougge

BLYNDE Robene sat on Bowman Lawe,
   And houlit upon his horne;
And aye he bummit, and he strummit,
   Quhille patience wals foreworne.

And the verye hillis in travail seemit,   5
   Thoche noe yung hillis were borne!
For they yellit and youtit soe yirlischly
   Als their bouellis hald bene torne.

And by him sat ane byzenit boi,
   Ane brat of brukit breide;   10
His moder wals ane weirdlye witche
   Of Queen's foreste the dreide;

But whether the deuill did him bygette,
   Or ane droiche of Elfinlande,
Or ane water-kelpie horrible,   15
   I colde not understande.

But he hald not tastit broz that dai,
   Nor kirne-mylke, wheye, nor brede;
So hunger raif at his yung herte,
   And wals like to be his dede.   20

And aye he said, "Dere maistere mine,
   What spring is that you playe?
For there are listeniris gadderyng rounde,
   And I wish we were awaye."

"Quhat doste thou se, my bonnie boi,   25
   I pray thee tell to mee?
I won these notis frae the fairye folke
   Beneth the grene wode tre;

"And I weenit it wals ane charmed spring,
   By its wilde melodye: 30

Och wo is mee that I am blynde!
   Littil boi, quhat doste thou se?"

"I se the hartis but and the hyndis,
   Stand quaking to the morne,
And wildlye snouke the westlyn wyndis,   35
   And shaike the braken horne:

"And the littil wee raeis they cour betwene,
   With their backis of dapplit greye:
And the gaitis they are waggyng their auld greye berdis—
   Lorde, gin we were awaye!"   40

"Sit still, sit still, my bonnie boi;
   I haif shawit you, with gode wille,
Ane littil of the Powris of Grande Moseke,
   I will shaw you greater stille.

"Lend me thine eire, and thou shalt heire   45
   Some thrillyng fallis I wis,
By minstrelis maide, and eithlye playit
   In oder worldis than this."

Blynde Robene liftit his stokel horne
   And brushit it all full cleine;   50
It wals laide with the eevorye and the goude,
   And glancit with the sylver sheine;

He heezit the horne intil his muthe,
   And soundit the airel hole,
And the melodye that that horne spake   55
   His herte it colde not thole!

For the soundis went hie and the soundis went lowe,
   Sae laigh and sae hie did they spryng,
That the laigh anes bummit in the world belowe,
   And the hie maide the heavinis ryng.   60

"Och holde thine hande, mine deire maistere!
   Thou maikest mine herte to blede,
And holde that heavinly braith of thine,
   Or the soundis will be mine dede."

"Ha! sayest thou soe, mine bonnie boi? 65
    To me thou art still more deire!
I trowit not of thy taiste before,
    Nor of thine blessit eire.

"But looke thee rounde, my bonnie boi,
    And looke to holme and heathe, 70
And caste thine eyne to heavin above,
    And to the yird benethe;

"And note the shadowis and the shapis
    That hover on hille and gaire;
And tell me trowlye, my bonnie boi, 75
    Of all thou seest there."

The elfin stoode up on his feite,
    And Robenis breiste he saynit;
And aye he chatterit with his tethe,
    And grefously he grainit: 80

And the sobbis that rase fra his stamocke
    Wolde birste ane herte of claye;
But neuir ane worde he saide but this—
    "Lorde, gin we were awaye!"

Blynde Robene stymit him rounde about, 85
    And he gapit gastrouslye—
"Och, tell me, tell me, littil boi,
    Of all that thou doste se."

"I se the cloudis creipe up the hille,
    And down the hille likewise; 90
And there are spyritis gadderyng rounde
    Fra baith the yird and skyis;

"The ghastis are glyming with their dede eyne
    Lapperit with mist and claye,
And they are fauldyng out their windyng shetis, 95
    And their flesche is faidyng awaye."

"If that be true, my bonnie boi,
    Strainge visiteris are rife!
Well, we moste gif them ane oder spring
    To sweiten their waesome life. 100

"I never kennit, soe helpe me Heavin,
   The ghastis had had soche skille,
Or knewe soe well ane maisteris hande,
   Sothe they moste haif their fille.

"For come they up, or come they downe,   105
   The ghaste or the elfin greye,
Till the fairyis come and heire their spring
   I cannot goe away."

"Och deire! och deire!" thochtis the littil boi,
   The teire blindyng his ee,   110
"We are far fra ony meite or drynk,
   Quhat will become of me?

"Och, holde thine hand, deire maistere mine,
   For pitye's saike now stay,
Or helle will sone be about our luggis,   115
   And deirlye we shall paye:

"The bullis are booyng in the wode,
   The deiris stande all abreiste;
You haif wakenit the dede out of their graifs–
   Lorde! quhat shall you do neiste?"   120

"Taik thou noe caris, my littil boi,
   Quhateuir thou mayest vewe,
For sholde ane elf or fairye rise
   From every belle of dewe,–

"Sholde all the fiendis that euir gowlit   125
   Downe in the deipis for paine,
Spiele up, and stande in thousandis rounde,
   I wolde playe them downe again."

"Faithe, that is strainge!" then thochtis the boi,
   But yet he said no thing: 130
"Och, Moseke is grande, my bonnie boi,
   We'll haif ane oder spring."

The boyis lip curlit to his noz,
   Als bende als ony bowe,
And syne his muthe begoude to thrawe–   135
   Quhat colde the hurchon doo?

His fastyng spittol he swallowit downe,
   With rattlyng, rhattyng dynne;
But hit hardlye wet the gyzenit throte,
   For all wals toome withynne.   140

Blynde Robene set his horne to his muthe,
   And wet his airel hole;
"Tout-tout! tout-tout!" quod blynde Robene,
   Quhille the very rockis did yolle.

But the boi he said unto himself,   145
   Als bitterlye als colde be,
"Gin I hald but my mornyng broz,
   Deuill fetche the spring and thee!"

He lookit to hille, he lookit to daille,
   Then rose with joyous speide–   150
"The fairyis moste come there is noe doubte,
   Or death is all my meide;

"Now holde thine hande, deire maistere mine,
   And fly rychte speidilye,
There are seventy-seven belted knychtes   155
   Comyng rankyng downe the le.

"There are fire and furye in their lookis
   Als they tredde on the wynde;
And there are seventy-seven bonnie damis
   All dauncyng them behynde.   160

"The fairye knychtis haif sordis and sheldis,
   Like chrystal spleetis to se;
And the damis are cledde in grass-grene sylke,
   And kyltit abone the kne."

"Quhat's that you say, mine bonnie boi?"   165
   Och Robenis muthe grew wyde!
And he poukit the hurchon with his hande,
   And helde his lug asyde.
And aye he glymit him rounde about,
   And strainit his dim quhyte eyne;   170
For he grenit to see the dapper limbis
   All quidderyng on the grene.

"Ochon! ochon!" quod blynde Robene,
 "My blyndnesse I may rewe!
But quhat it wals to want mine sychte   175
 Till now I neuir knewe!

"For ae glance of the bonnie damis
 Dauncyng soe blythe on le,
Each with her sailyng grene seymar
 Soe far abone the kne!"   180

"Och, not soe far, mine deire maistere,
 It is modeste all and meite;
And like the wynde on sunnye hillis
 Shimmer their lovelye feite.

"But the knychtis are in ane awsum raige, 185
 Raumpaugyng on the le;
For lofe of lyfe, now blynde Robene,
 Come let us rise and fle."

"And can I leife the winsum damis,
 All fryskyng on the grene?   190
Och noe! och noe! mine littil boi,
 More manneris I haif sene.

"I will gyf them ane spring will gar them skyppe,
 And rise with mychte and maine,
Quhille they dyng their hedis agynst the sternis, 195
 And bob on the yird againe.

"I will gar them jompe sae merrilye hie,
 The blythsum seventy-seven;
Quhille they coole their littil bonnie brestis
 Amid the cloudis of heavin.   200

"Liloo–liloo"–quod blynde Robene,
 (Heavinis mercye! als he blewe!)
"Now I shall gar the fairye folkis
 The Powris of Moseke vewe."

But the boi he weepit rychte piteouslye, 205
 And downward sore did bowe,
And helde his middis with both his handis,
 For feire he sholde fall through.

Saint Bothan! als blynde Robene blewe,
    Sae yirlisch and sae cleire! 210
And aye he turnit his stokel horne,
    That fairyis all mochte heire.

And aye he glymit with his quhyte eyne,
    Thoche sore the horne colde jar;
For he longit to see the lily limbe 215
    And kyltit grene seymar.

"Looke yet againe, my bonnie boi,
    At the fairye damis anewe,
And tell me how their robis appeire
    In texture and in hewe!" 220

"Och, they are lychtlye cledde, maistere,
    Soe lychte I dare not showe,
For I se their lovelye tiny formis,
    Als pure as mountaine snowe.

"Their robis are made of the gossamere, 225
    Wove of the misty sheine,
And dyit in the rainbowis gaudye gaire
    Sae glauncyng and sae grene."

Blynde Robene clewe his tufted heide,
    And raif his auld greye hayre, 230
And the teiris wolde haif fallen from his eyne,
    Had anie eyne bene there;

He turnit up his cleire face for braith,
    And to eisse his crouchand backe;
And then he toutit and he blewe 235
    Quhille bethe his luggis did cracke.

"Och, holde your hande, deire maistere mine!"
    Cryit the boi with yirlisch screime,
"For there is the deuill comyng on
    With his eyne like fiery gleime; 240

"His fingeris are like lobster taeis,
    And long als barrowe tramis;
His tethe are reide-hot tedderstakis,
    And barkit are his hammis:

"His tayle it is ane fierye snaike   245
    Aye wrything far behynde,
Its fangis are two clothe yardis in length,
    And it is coolyng them in the wynde."

Blynde Robenis face grewe lang and blanke,
    And his lyppe begoude to fall;–   250
"That is ane gueste, my littil boi,
    I like the worst of all!

"The fairyis are mine own deire folkis;
    The ghastis are glydyng geire;
But the deuill is ane oder chappe!   255
    Lorde! quhat's he sekyng here?"

Blynde Robene maide als he wolde rise,
    To flye als he were faine;
But the fairye damis came in his mynde,
    And he crouched him downe againe.   260

"Come well, come woe, I shall not goe,"
    Said Robene manfullye,
"I will play to my welcome fairye folkis,
    And the deuill may rayre for me!"

Againe the notis knellit through the ayre   265
    Sae mychtye and sae deivin,
For ilkane burel hole wals loosit,–
    Ane hole wals blawn in heavin:

And the soundis went in, and the soundis went ben,
    Quhille the folkis abone the skie   270
And the angelis caperit ane braif corante
    Als they went stroamyng bye.
The Powris of Moseke wals sae greate,
    Sae mychtie and devyne,
That Robene ravit for very joi   275
    Quhille his quhyte eyne did shyne;

And his cleire countenance wals blente
    With a joi and a pryde sublyme–
"There is no hope," quod the littil boi,
    "He will playe quhille the end of tyme!"   280

———————

But in the grenewode ower the hill,
  There graissit ane herde of kyne,
Waidyng in grene gerse to the knes,
  And grofellyng lyke to swyne.

For they snappit it with their muckil mouis   285
  Quhille sullenlye they lowit,
And aye they noddit their lang quhite hornis,
  And they chumpit and they chowit.

Och, they were fierce! and nefer fedde
  At mainger nor at stalle;   290
But among them there wals ane curlye bulle,
  The fiercete of them all.

His hornis were quhite als driven snowe,
  And sharpe als poyntit pole;
But his herte wals blacker than his hyde,   295
  Thoche that wals lyke ane cole.

This bulle he heirit blynde Robenis notis
  Passe ower his heide abofe,
And he thochte it wals ane kindlye cowe
  Rowtyng for gentil lofe.   300

And this bulle he thochtis into himselle
  How this braife courteous cowe
Might haif passit far for lofe that dai,
  And travellit faustyng too.
"I will goe and meite her," thochtis the bulle,   305
  "Als gallante brote sholde doo."

And this bulle he thochtis into himselle,
  "This dame rowtis mychtye loude!
I will sende furth ane voyce shall maike her quaile,
  And she shall not be soe proude!"   310

And ower the hille and downe the hille,
  The bulle came roaryng furth,
And with his hofe but and his horne
  He ture the shaikyng yirth;

And aye he brullyit and he bruffit,   315
  Quhille his braith it singit the grasse;

And then he raisit his noz and squeelit
    Rychte lyke ane coddye asse.

But the woefulle boi he laye acrosse
    And grofellit on the grounde,   320
And with the blare of Robenis horne
    He nefer heirde the sounde!

But the soundis they percit blynde Robenis eire,
    For ane sherpe eire had hee:
"Is that the deuill, my littil boi,   325
    That rayris soe boysterouslye?"

"Och, maistere, it is ane great black bulle
    Comyng foamyng madlye here;
He has fleyit awaye the fairye folkis,
    And the deuill has fledde for feire.   330

"With his hornis sherper than ane speire
    The hillis grene breste is rift,
And his tayle is curlyng up the cloudis,
    And swooping on the lyfte.

"His eyne are two reide colis of fire,   335
    You heire his horryde crie;
The mountaine is quakyng like ane deire,
    Quhen the houndis are yowting bye."

Blynde Robene raisit his face and smylit,
    And shoke his lockis of snow;   340
"Och! great is the Powir of Moseke, boi,—
    Greatir nor ouchtis belowe!

"I haif playit the spyritis fra the deipe,
    And playit them downe againe;
And that is the Bulle of Norrowaye   345
    I haif brochte outower the maine.

"He is something, I haif heirde them saye,
    Betwene ane gode and beiste;
But sit thou still, my bonnie boi,
    I will charme him to the eiste."   350

The bulle now lookit eiste and weste,
    And he lookit unto the northe;
But he colde not se the kyndlye dame
    For quham he hald comit furth.

"Too—too! tee—too!" quod blynde Robene,   355
    Quhille hee raif the herkenyng ayre;
Then the bulle he gallopit lyke ane fiende,
    For he thochte his cowe wals there.

But quhan he came nere to the plaisse,
    Thochtyng his lofe to fynde,   360
And saw nochtis but ane auld mynstrelle,
    He wals nouther to houlde nor bynde!

He ryppit the grounde with hofe and horne,
    And maide the rockis to yelle;
For every rore that the black bulle gae   365
    Wals lyke ane burst of helle.

Blynde Robenis braith begoude to cut,
    His notis begoude to shaike,
These burstis of raige he could not stande,
    They maide his herte to aike.   370

"Och, maistere, maistere!" cryit the boi,
    Squeikyng with yirlisch dynne,
"It is but ane bowshote to the wode
    That overhingis the lynne.

"Let us haiste and won the Bowman Lynne,   375
    And hyde in boshe or tre;
Or, by Saint Fillanis sholder-bone,
    Charme als you lyke for me!"

Blynde Robene bangit him to his feite,
    Alane he dorste not staye,   380
For he thochte, als well as the littil boi,
    It wals tyme he were awaye.

He helde out his lang necke and ranne,
    Quhille low his back did bowe;
And he turnit up his cleire quhite face,   385
    Als blynde men wonte to doo.

And ower rocke, and ower rone,
　　He lyftit his feite full hie;
And ower stocke, and ower stone,
　　Blynde Robene he did flie!　　　　　　　　　390

But Robenis braith is all forespente,
　　He gaspit sore anone!
The bulle is thonderyng at his backe;
　　Blynde Robene he is gone!

For his haiste grewe greatir than his speide,　　　395
　　His bodie it pressit on
Faster than feite colde followe up,
　　And on the grounde he is prone!

But yet to profe blynde Robenis speide
　　Quhen he felle on his face before,　　　　　400
He plowit ane furrowe with his noz
　　For two clothe yardis and more.

Ah! laik-a-day! now, blynde Robene,
　　Thy moseke moste depairte;
That cursit Bulle of Norrowaye　　　　　　　405
　　Is fomyng ower thine herte.

Och, woe betyde that wicked boi
　　Als he sat up on hychte!
I wat he leuch quhille neirlye dede,
　　To se blynde Robenis plychte.　　　　　　410
For the bulle gaed rounde, and the bulle gaed rounde
　　Blynde Robene with horryde dynne;
He hald neuir bene usit to stycke ane man,
　　And he knowit not how to begynne.

And he scraipit ane graif with his fore fute,　　　415
　　With many ane rowte and rayre;
And he borit the truff a thousand tymis
　　Arounde blynde Robenis layre.

Poor Robene hald but ane remeide,
　　Ane trembilyng houpe hald he;　　　　　　420
He set his stokel horne to his muthe
　　And blewe yblastis thre.

"Quhat worme is this," then thochtis the bulle,
   "That mockis my lofe and me?"

He shoke his heide, and he gaif ane prodde,   425
   Quhille his hornis ranne to the brymme;
"I shall bore your bodie," thochtis the bulle,
   "Throu the life-bloode and the limbe."

And out-throu, and out-throu blynde Robene
   He hes maide his quhite hornis gae;   430
But they nouther touchit his skynne nor his bone,
   But his coate and mantil greye.

And he has heivit up blynde Robene,
   And tossit him lyke ane reide;
And aye he shoke his curlye powe,   435
   To drive him from his heide.

And he wals in ane grefous frychte,
   Yet wist not quhat to feire;
But he laye acrosse lyke ane ousen yoke,
   Mervillyng quhat wals asteer.   440

But hald you sene the devilisch boi;
   Ane ill deide mot he de!
He leuch until he tint all powris
   Als he sat on his tre.

Then the bulle he gaif Robene ane toss   445
   By some unchancie fling;
And ower the verge of the Bowman Lynne
   He made the auld man to swing.

At first he flew across the voyde,
   Then downward sank lyke lede,   450
Till he fell into ane hazil boshe,
   Saft als ane fedder bedde.

And there he laye, and there he swung,
   Als lychte als lefe on tre;
He knewe nochtis of his great daingere,   455
   Nor yet of his safetye.

And thc bullc he brullyit and he brooit,
   Outower the Bowman Lynne,
And sore he yernit for life-bloode,
   But dorste not venter in.   460

Poor Robcnc heirde the defenyng noisse,
   And laye full sore aghast;
At length he raisit his forlorne houpe,
   To charme him with ane blaste.

Quheneuir the bulle he heirde the soundis,   465
   His aunger byrnit lyke helle,
And rounde the rocke he raschit in raige,
   But missit his fute and felle.

And downe the bank and downe the brae
   He bumpit and he blewe;   470
And aye he stoattit fra the stonis,
   And flapperit as he flewe.

He wals lyke ane mychtie terre barelle
   Gawn bombyng down the steipe,
Quhille he plungit in the howe of the Bowman Lynne, 475
   Full fiftie faddom deipe.

And the ekois claumb fra rocke to rocke,
   Roryng the dark wode under,
And yollerit, yollerit, fra the hillis,
   Lyke ane ryvyng clappe of thunder.   480
"Holloa! quhat's that?" cryit blynde Robene,
   "Is there anie here to telle?"
"It is the bulle," quod the littil boi,
   "You haif charmit him down to helle.

"The mychtie featis that you haif done,   485
   This beatis them all to-daye!
Rise up, rise up, deire maistere mine,
   I will guide you on your waye."

Och Robene wals ane braife proude man
   That day on Bowman brae,   490
And he braggit of that mornyngis featis
   Until his dying dai.

And aye his quhite face glowit sublyme,
　　And aye his brente browe shone;
And thoche he tould ane store of les,　　495
　　To helpe it there wals none.

He saide that he drewe the dapplit raeis
　　Fra out the dingillye delle,
The nut-browne hart, but and the hynde,
　　Downe fra the hedder belle;　　500

And brochte the gaitis with their greye berdis,
　　Far fra the rockie glenne,
And the fairyis fra some plesaunt lande
　　That Robene did not kenne:

And then he tauld how he raisit the dede,　　505
　　In their windyng shetis soe quhite,
And how the deuill came from his denne,
　　And lystenit with delyte:

How he brochte the Bulle of Norrowaye
　　Outower the sea-waife grene,　　510
And charmit him downe to the pytte of helle,
　　Quhare he nefer more wals sene.

But then the false and wicked boi,
　　He nefer wolde allowe
That he charmit ouchtis but ane wicked bulle,　　515
　　Quha tooke him for ane cowe.

May nefer poore mynstrelle wante the worde
　　That drawis the graitefulle teire,
Nor ane waywarde brat his morning broz,
　　For both are harde to beire.　　520

MORALITAS

Och, nefer bydde ane bad mynstrelle playe,
　　Nor seye his mynstrelsye,
Onlesse your wyne be in your hande,
　　And your ladye in your ee.

Ane singil say will set him on,   525
   And simpil is the spelle;
But he nefer will gif ofer againe,
   Not for the deuill himselle.

The Field of Waterloo,

and

Death-Bed Prayer of a Soldier

THE eventful day had come, and gone,
And the night in majesty drew on,
For just as the twilight shed a ray
On the plains of Belgium west away,
The eastern heaven was all o'erspread   5
With a veil of high and murky red;
And there was awe in the soldier's eye
Whenever it met that lurid sky,
For he thought, as he lifted his visage swarth,
There was blood on the heaven, and blood on the earth!   10

   The day was past, the fateful day!
The pride of the Tyrant prostrate lay;
And the battle-clang, and the trumpet's tone,
Were rolling to the southward on,
When a war-worn soldier, far behind   15
On the verge of a rising height reclined:
A wounded hero, of courage true,
Who of his deadly wound not knew;
For he weened the blood that swathed him so
The blood of a proud and hateful foe;   20
And much he marvelled why he lay
Thus faint and weary by the way.

   Though round his form the tartans hung,
Yet his tall mould, and Doric tongue,
Bespoke his lineage from the scene   25
Of crystal rill and mountain green,
From that fair land of warlike fame
Where Douglas fought, and overcame,—
The land of forays, feuds, and plots,
Of Elliots, and of valiant Scotts,—   30
That Border land, so nobly blent
With hill, and dale of green extent,
With camp, and tower, and battlement.

That is a land, full well 'tis known,
Where cottage maid, and matron brown,   35
Where shepherd boy, or peasant elf,
Reads, thinks, and judges for himself.
Deep there of hcavcn's awards the sense,
And trust in sacred Providence;
The old, the young, deep reverence pay   40
To God's own blessed and holy day;
'Tis there, by hamlet and by hill,
A day of holy resting still.

There had our soldier spent his youth,
In ways of happiness and truth,   45
Till scorn cast from a maiden's eye
Drove him in distant fields to die.
Now on that height he lay forlorn,
Where Gallia's troops, at break of morn,
Did first with ready wheel combine,   50
And form the mighty crescent line;
And then he saw, and heard, and felt
The dire effects of human guilt.
O, such a day of dole and pain
May human nature ne'er again   55
Behold, while earth and heaven remain!

Soon as the gloaming drew her screen
Over the red and rueful scene,
Then every moan was heard as near,
And every plaint fell on the ear;   60
The parting throb, the smothered sigh,
And shriek of sharpest agony:
But every anathema said
By widowed dame and weeping maid,
Or passed in soldier's dying groan,   65
All cursed one, and one alone.
All tongues and languages were blent,
But all was sorrow and lament,—
Or weeping for the valiant dead,
Or curses on a tyrant's head.   70

Our soldier raised him from the sod,
And lifting up his eyes to God,

He leaned upon his bloody wrist,
And cried aloud, with throbbing breast,
"O grant, thou Being all divine,   75
Such load of guilt be never mine,
As his—that scourge of human life,
Who flies inglorious from the strife.
For since the fields of war were seen,
Such desolation hath not been;   80
Thou knowest why, thy will be done:
Blessed be thy name, the field is won!"

 As thus he said, there by him stood
Two strangers tall, of gentle mood;
Soldiers they were, or late had been,   85
And many a bloody field had seen:
One was from Prussia's forests wide,
And one from Wolga's stormy side;
Their message done, they paused to view
The havoc done on Waterloo.   90

 "Soldier," they said, "why liest thou thus,
As all were peace and quietness?
Such deeds you Scots have ne'er achieved,
Since Wallace fought and Douglas reaved:
Swift flies the foe, as flies the wind,   95
There's fame before, and spoil behind;
O soldier, it befits thee ill
To rest like hind upon the hill."

 "Sore am I grieved, but toil severe,
And drowsy faintness keep me here;   100
My soul is burning to pursue,
And fain would move from Waterloo;
For such a din my ear assails
Of piteous plaint, and dying wails,
Methinks it would be perfect bliss   105
To be in any place but this!"

 "Peace to thy heart, brave soldier—say
How think'st thou of this wondrous day?"

 "How think I?"—From the dust he reared
His ghastly cheek with blood besmeared,   110

"How think I? By this heart forlorn,
An oath I ne'er before have sworn,
I think, that first since human guilt
Provoked to war, and blood was spilt
In battle field, beneath the sun   115
Such doughty deeds were never done,
So boldly fought, so bravely won.
Nay, pardon me; in ardour hot
My darling theme I had forgot,
But sure, of earthly well fought fields,   120
To Bannockburn alone it yields."

The bold Silesian smiled in spite,
He thought of Leipsic's bloody fight;
The Russian cast a glance of flame,
But Borodina scorned to name.   125

"Soldier," they said; "thou saw'st the strife;
Say, sooth, in all thy bypast life
Hast thou not seen, nor read, nor heard
Of ought with this to be compared?"

"I could compare 't with cloud of morn   130
Fleet on the whirlwind's eddies borne,
That, melting denser folds of rain,
Rebounding bursts, and wheels again.
I might compare it with the force
Of mountain river's roaring course,   135
And one small mound raised in its way,
To bear its whole resistless sway,
Which firmly stemmed the whelming tide
That foamed, and fled to either side.
I could compare 't to ocean's roar   140
Against the adamantine shore.
But in all ages that shall spring,
When man shall tell, or poet sing,
Of what he would the most impress
Upon the heart with powerfulness;   145
Of nature's terrors in the cloud,
The tempest's rage, the roaring flood,
Or lightning bursting on the view,
He'll liken it to Waterloo.

I saw it. But to me it seems   150
A train of long-past hideous dreams,
Of things half known, and half forgot,
I know not whether seen or not.
E'er since I bore the onset's shock,
And was involved in fire and smoke,   155
I've had no knowledge what hath been,
Nor thought, nor mind—a mere machine.
I only viewed it as my meed,
To stand or fall, as Heaven decreed;
For honour's cause to do my best,   160
And to the Almighty leave the rest.
Blessed be his hand that swayed the fight
For mankind's and for freedom's right!

   "Glancing along our Scottish files,
I marked our foemen's powerful wiles,   165
And scarcely weened that we could stand
Against such odds of spear and brand,
Of harnessed horse, in column deep,
And red artillery's wasting sweep,
Yet only closed fast as we fell,   170
Without one thought but to repel.
O Scotia, land of old renown,
Thy prowess yet is never known—
I glory that thou art mine own!

   "Methinks I hear, in after time,   175
The hamlet song in rustic rhyme,—
Wove by some shepherd of the dale
Where first I breathed the mountain gale,
And listed first the magic lore
Which I, alas! shall hear no more,—   180
Telling of deeds that here were wrought,
What heroes fell, what lions fought,
Till all the striplings stare and sigh,
With round tears dropping from the eye,
Begging again to hear the song,   185
Though homely be the rhyme and long.

   "O might my name but mentioned be
In land of my nativity,

How would my parting spirit joy,
And spring from earth without alloy!   190
Yes, I will hope that men shall tell
Of all our deeds, and fondly dwell
On every humble soldier's name
That stood on this day's list of fame,
And, at the call of morning roll,   195
Was blotted from the bloody scroll.

  "Of Wellesley these songs shall tell;
And how the gallant Picton fell;
And how the lancer's steady eye
Aimed to the heart of Ponsonby.   200
O Ponsonby, the brave, the just,
A soldier sorrows o'er thy dust!

  "Ah me! the last time e'er I strayed,
Like hermit, in my native glade,
I followed him o'er mountain grey   205
With Border chief of mighty sway,
The heath-fowl from the moor to spring,
And lower the black-cock on the wing;
Then blithe his heart; he little knew
Of such a fate at Waterloo!   210

  "Yet sooth he might, for he heard tell
Of prophecy remembered well.
'Twas a weird dame his fate that read,
The shepherd's and the maiden's dread.
What's this? Ah, well may I repine!   215
For with his death she coupled mine.
And though in wrath she us assailed,
Yet what she says hath never failed.

  "'Avaunt,' she cried, 'thou droich of three!
Thou'rt nought in life; nor thou, nor he,   220
But passing shadows—a mere blot!
Men trowed it was, but it is not.
But mark me—there is thee before
A hideous flood, a tideless shore,
From which a wolf shall turn and run,   225
An eagle fall, and a harper won:
Then down shall sink an angel grim,

But falling, you shall fall with him.
On such an eve of such a day
Thou shalt remember what I say!'   230

    "Ah me! who can his fate controul?
That sibyl's words now shake my soul.
That very day, and hour, she knew
Of this day's doom at Waterloo.
Oh, pardon me! I sink aghast   235
At memory of some visions past.
My doom is sealed; here I must bow
To death's arrest, I know not how."

    "Soldier, take heart, and be advised,
In time to come whene'er thou try'st   240
Of this day's deeds to take the sum,
Of Leipsic think, and then be dumb!"

    "Or heard'st thou ne'er of Moscow's flame?
Nor Borodina's chilling name,
Where slaughtered myriads only gave   245
New ardour to the living brave?
I saw at morn proud Moscow stand
The glory of our northern land,
With gilded spires and turrets blent
That pierced the yielding firmament;   250
But ere the midnight watch was o'er
The ancient Moscow was no more!

    "I saw, through weary wastes of snow,
Thousands of hopeless journeyers go,
O'er all the forests wandering wide,   255
Without a home their heads to hide.
I saw the babe oft hushed to rest
On mother's agonized breast,
But long ere day that breast beloved
The death-bed of its darling proved: 260
There did they rest, in death laid low,
Their grave the drifted wreath of snow.

    "I saw the stripling, worn and bent,
Halting and crying as he went;
Straining his eyes o'er flood and field,   265

Loath his young life so soon to yield:
Weak grew his plaint, his motion slow,
I saw the blood-drops on the snow,
And glad was I, his sufferings o'er,
When down he sunk to rise no more.   270

    "On message sent, I crossed in haste
Kaluga's northmost dreary waste,
Where many a maiden's youthful form
Had sunk beneath the ruthless storm.
I saw the beauteous taper limb,   275
That made the winter wreath look dim;
The young, the fair half moulded breast,
That icicles even gentlier pressed!
The whole so pure, and stretched so low,
Seemed but some mould of lovelier snow.   280
Though all was lost that life held dear,
And all was suffered mind could bear;
Yet not a plaint was heard to fall,
Our country and our cause was all.–
Now, soldier, has that land of thine   285
Done half, or suffered half of mine?

    "On Borodina not alone
The dying and the dead were strewn;
The tyrant's rout was tracked in blood
From Moscow's gate to Niemen's flood;   290
Far as could reach the roving eye
O'er lands that waste and open lie,
I saw myself, and marked it well,
The snow-flakes redden as they fell.
The drifted wreaths were purpled o'er,   295
Crusted and gorged with human gore,
While o'er them rose a forest dim
Of horses' hoof and human limb.

    "Soldier, I tell thee, though I love
Thy ardour, and thy zeal approve,   300
If thou hast seen no field like this,
Thou know'st not yet what warfare is.

    "Say of my country what you will,
And call us rude and savage still;

I'll say't to Europe and to thee,   305
Though left alone, we dared be free,
And stood for death or liberty.

"Yes, Europe cringed to tyrant's might;
'Twas we who turned the scale of right;
'Twas we who bruised the monster's head;–   310
The Germans joined to make him bleed.
What have you Britons done t' avail,
By this defence and bold assail,
But only crushed the severed tail?"

"And, might I judge from what I saw,   315
I would this simple inference draw–
Had it not been *our* brave Bulow
This had to them been day of woe,
And ended in their overthrow."

"What? Veteran Britons overthrown   320
Led on by warlike Wellington?
No! Who can brow the heaven with me
So proud a claim to verify?
They never were. If one knows when,
Let him talk of it–not till then.   325

"But cease, my friends, this poignant strain,
For friends we are, and must remain.
I too might say, in scorn and pride,
With fair pretext upon my side,
That during Russia's vaunted plea   330
She only fought to turn and flee,
And feebly still the strife renewed,
Till Heaven fought–then she pursued.

"And I might say of Prussia's boast,
'Tis right equivocal at most: 335
Her head she raised with martial show,
But stooped the lowest of the low;
Dragged on her chain of galling steel,
And followed at the tyrant's heel;
But when the royal beast grew lame,   340
Then turned the ass, his bulk to maim.
This I might say with courtesy,

For such the taunts you cast on me;
But hard it sounds from friendship's mouth,
To those who list to learn the truth.   345

"In that sweet dale where I was born,
Where green Mount Benger greets the morn,
It is our wont, on either side
Reason to hear, and then decide;
So let us now. For I will stand   350
By the honour of my native land,
While I have tongue t'assert her right,
Or foot to move, or hand to fight.

"I then allow of what befell;
You fought the foe, and fought him well;   355
You fought for home, you fought for life,
For monarch, kinsmen, children, wife;
For very name and being's sake:
Say was not then your all at stake?"

"All was at stake; religion, fame,   360
Nay, more than human tongue can name."

"The less your merit and your meed,
'Twas desperation did the deed;
And where's the creature forced to strife
That will not fight for breath and life?   365
The hunted deer can hold at bay
The gallant hound,—yet who will say
The deer is brave, or yeaning ewe
That drives the fox along the dew?
There is no beast of hill or wood   370
That will not fight to save its brood;
So that the man who shuns such strife,
Is less than ought in brutal life:
Such is the model of your fame,
And such the honours you can claim.   375

"But Britain lay secure and free,
Encircled by her guardian sea,
Her flag of sovereignty unfurled
In every bay that cleaves the world:
One cause alone had she to fight—   380

The glorious cause of human right;
And for that prize to her endeared,
The cause of freedom, long revered,
Where is the foe, say if you can,
That e'er has braved us man to man? 385
And be the leader's name revealed,
That e'er has driven us from the field?

"High be your deeds, to your own thought;
To fight for life I count it nought.
But he, who, seeing friend o'erthrown 390
By sordid guile, and trodden down,
Flies to his aid, and ventures all
At friendship's and at honour's call;
And, by his blood and jeopardy,
Succeeds and sets the injured free– 395
This, this, I say, is bravery!"

The Russian turned his sullen eye,
His silent comrade's mood to spy,
And saw him bent in thought profound,
Moulding wide figures on the ground; 400
"By Heaven!" he cried, as up he threw
His manly eyes of azure blue,
"What the Scots soldier says, is true!"

When this assent our soldier heard,
He moaned and stretched him on the sward; 405
He felt the sand of life near run,
And deemed the day now doubly won.
The strangers friendly aid impart,
Give him to drink, and cheer his heart;
Then down they sat, on converse keen, 410
Beneath the heaven's own starry sheen.

The Prussian was a stoic cool,
Of Voltaire's and of Frederick's school;
And much he said in earnest way,
Of things unfitting poet's lay; 415
Of needful waste of human kind;
Of mankind's late enlightened mind;
How nations first bowed to the yoke;
How furiously the bonds they broke;

And how the soul arose in might,   420
Grasping its own eternal right.

"The time," said he, "is ever gone
    That Europe dreads tyrannic sway;
No more we'll toil in error on,
    Groping at noon to find our way.   425
It was the love of freedom, given
    To man as his prerogative,–
That sacred thing conferred by Heaven,
    The noblest gift that it could give,–
Twas that which made the tyrant rise,   430
    Made kings and kingdoms to divide;–
He came with words of specious guise,
    The hearts of men were on his side.
O he might conquer idiot kings,
    These bars in nature's onward plan!   435
But fool is he the yoke that flings
    O'er the unshackled soul of man!
'Tis like a cobweb o'er the breast
    That binds the giant while asleep,
Or curtain hung upon the east,   440
    The day-light from the world to keep:
The giant wakes in all his might;
    The light of heaven is unconfined;
And man asserts his primal right–
    Thanks to the unconquerable mind!"   445

    The Russian said, it was not so;
What *mind* could do he did not know,
'Twas God, the Russian's guard and guide,
And Alexander, turned the tide.
If these were part of mind or soul,   450
Then that might rule and rein the whole.

    The Scottish soldier raised his eye
As if about to make reply,
But faint from weariness and pain,
He moaned, and laid him down again.   455
The strangers raised him from the ground,
They searched, and found a mortal wound,
"Alas!" they said, "thou gallant youth,

Thou friend to loyalty and truth,
What shall be done some help to give? 460
For short the date thou hast to live."

"And is it so?" said he, "I knew
The sibyl's saying would prove true.
Heaven's will be done! Take ye no heed;
I meet without dismay or dread 465
Man's last great foe—a welcome guest;
I know him conquered like the rest.
One last request I have to make,—
For my departing spirit's sake,
Kneel here, before the eye divine, 470
A dying soldier's prayer to join."

The strangers readily agreed,
Saying, they wished no higher meed,
For though from far and foreign parts,
Yet they were men of gentle hearts. 475
They kneeled amid the ensanguined scene,
Beneath the midnight heaven serene,
While the young gallant soldier lay
Prostrate along the bloody clay;
And as a taper's wasting light 480
In its last glimmer shines more bright,
So was his soul aroused to share,
High energies in his last prayer.

———————

"O thou of existence the fountain and head,
The God of the living, and God of the dead; 485
This world is thine, and the starry frame—
The Lord Jehovah is thy name.
How shall I come my vows to pay?
What offering on thine altar lay?
Alas, my God! if e'er thine eyes 490
Accepted earthly sacrifice,
I bring the last that man can bring;
I am *myself* that offering!
And here I cry from the altar of death,
From the tabernacle of thy wrath, 495

'Mid the cries and the groans of the human race,
O hear in heaven thy dwelling-place!

"Though hid in mystery none can pierce
Thy reign of the ample universe;
Yet he who owns not thy hand alone,   500
In the high events that have come and gone,
Deserves not to possess of thee
The power of the reasoning faculty.

    "When the destroyer left his throne
To brave the eye of the frigid zone,   505
Was there a human head could guess
Or count on probable success?
Or was there a way in nature's course
So to o'erwhelm that cumbrous force,
Which strove the nations to enchain,   510
Or rouse them from their torpor again?
Thy bolts of wrath thou might'st have driven,
Or loosed the artillery of heaven;
Or, as just guerdon of offence,
Sent forth the wasteful pestilence: 515
But not in nature's wide command,
And nature ever is thy hand,
Was other way so to destroy
That armed horde, the world's annoy.

    "Yes, still as the northern patriot bled,   520
When the Russian eagles turned and fled,
Thy arm was seen in the foemen's wrath
That hurried them on to the bourn of death.
When first Iberia spurned the yoke
The judgment was set, and the seals were broke;   525
But when the city of sacred fame
Enwrapt the northern heaven in flame,
Their sentence thou passed'st, ne'er to annul,
For the cup of the Amorite then was full!

    "The spirit of man awoke at thy nod,   530
The elements rose and owned their God;
The sun, and the moon, and the floods below,
And the stars in their courses fought thy foe;
The very heavens and earth seemed blent

In the lowering toiling firmament.   535
The clouds poured swiftly along the sky,
They thickened, they frowned, but they past not by!
The ravens called with boding sound,
The dogs of Moscow howled around;
And the shades of men and of maidens fair,   540
Were seen on the dull and cumbered air.
The storm descended, the tempest blew;
Thy vengeance poured on the ruthless crew.
O God! thy vengeance was never so due!

"I saw thy hand in the coil of the war,   545
I heard thy voice in the thunder afar,
When the Elbe waved slow with the blood of man,
And the Saale scarce gurgled as it ran.
O Father! forgive the insensate heart
That ascribes such wonders to human part.   550
'Twas thou madest the hearts of the nations combine.
Yes, thine is the work, and the glory be thine.

"But chiefly when he, the scourge of the earth,
Was proffered the friendship and hands of the north,
And thus, in that empire, the bane of the day,   555
His dynasty might have been 'stablished for aye;
What counsel of man could the proffer have scorned!
Nor reason, nor madness, could that have suborned!
But the hearts of men are thine own alone,
As the streams of water thou windest them on;   560
And save when thou parted'st Jordan's tide,
And the gates of the Red Sea opened'st wide,
O never so well since time hath been,
Was the governing arm of thy providence seen.

"But the injured still were unavenged,   565
And the men of crimes remained unchanged,
Till thou roused'st them again in triple wrath,
And brought them like beasts to the house of death.
With other kings and armies leagued,
They might have contended or intrigued,   570
But the judgment was passed which they could not shun,
Thou brought'st them here, and the work was done!
The victory is thine, we nothing abate,

But thou gavest it the good as well as the great;
And their names are registered with thee   575
Who have bled for the cause of liberty.

"This morn I bowed above my blade,
I bowed to thee, and for victory prayed;
I prayed that my countrymen might gain,
Though my heart's blood should steep the plain!   580
Thou hast heard my prayer, and answered me,
And with joy I yield my spirit to thee.

"Should I offend thee while yet I live,
A dying man, my God, forgive;
But O, if accordant with thy will,   585
Let that nation of pride be humbled still,
For long hath it moved to commotion and blood,
The pattern of evil, but never of good.

"Nay, now I know I shall answered be,
For I see a dawn of futurity.   590
My soul is parting with the clay,
And it eyes the scenes of a distant day;
Like shadows they come before my sight,
Arising from darkness into light.
That perjured nation of shame and offence,   595
Which mocks at the laws of omnipotence,
Shall rise and trouble the nations again,
And its own bowels tear amain,
Till at length shall rise a devouring flame,
That shall sweep from the earth the nation and name.   600
And then shall the banners of war be furled,
And peace and knowledge pervade the world;
Dear as the purchase hath been to man,
The benefit, ages only may scan.

"And now, O God! the time is near   605
When I may no more address thine ear;
Few moments, and human scrutiny,
Tells me not what I then shall be;
An igneous lamp in the fields below,
A dye of heaven's aërial bow,   610
A stilly vapour on space reclined,
Or a breath of discoloured wandering wind.

But O, while I have speech to say
The thing that I would, I humbly pray
That I for a space may wander free,   615
To visit the scenes of my infancy,
The tiny green where the schoolboys play,
The level pool, with its bridge so grey;
And O, there's a cot by the lonely flood,
With its verdant steep, and its ancient wood,   620
Its willow ring, and its sounding stream,
So like the scene of a fairy dream:
O might I there a while reside,
To rest with the lamb on the mountain's side,
Or stand by the heath-cock's ruby eye,   625
And wonder he cannot my form espy.

   "And in that cot there is a dame,
I cannot, dare not say her name!
O how I long to listen there
To hear that loved one's evening prayer!   630
And in that cot a cradle moves,
Where sleeps the infant that she loves;
O I would like to hover by,
When none but she and that child are nigh,
When her arms stretch to the dear embrace,   635
And the baby smiles her in the face;
Or when she presses him to her heart,
To watch when the holy tear shall start,
And list no other ear to hear,
If she named a name she once held dear.   640

   "O God, if such a thing might be
That a guardian spirit, empowered by thee,
Still round that dwelling linger must,
O may I beg the sacred trust?
I'll do, all evil to cause them shun,   645
More than a spirit before has done;
Against each danger I'll forecast,
And bring them to thyself at last.

   "But wherever my future lot may be,
I have no dread of wrath from thee;   650
For I know thee merciful and good,

Beyond thc fathom of flesh and blood:
And there is a bond 'twixt man and thee,
'Twas sealed and finished on the tree,
Of that, too mystic to unfold,   655
I will not, cannot quit my hold.
Accept me, Lord, that I may bless
Thy name in better world than this.

"I have but one remembrance left,
Before my tongue of speech is reft.—   660
My widowed parent O regard,
And all her love to me reward;
Fondly she nursed my tender years,
With buoyant hopes, and yearning fears;
She weened not, in these hours of bliss,   665
That she reared her child to an end like this.
To save her declining age from woe,
Her darling's fate may she never know,
But still look down the mountain burn
To see her wandering son return,   670
Her parting blessing to receive,
And lay her head in an honoured grave;
That hope may still support her heart,
Till we meet again no more to part."

———————

The light of life blazed not again,   675
He could not say the word AMEN;
But he turned his eye, and spread his hand
To the star above his native land,
Serenely in that posture lay,
And breathed his generous soul away.   680

The Russian heaved a sigh profound,
And gazed insensate on the ground,
The burning tear struck from his eye,
And flung it on the breeze to dry.
The stoic Prussian, in his pride,   685
Unstaidly looked from side to side,
Then fixed on heaven a solemn scowl,
Impelled by his unfathomed soul,
That felt deep yearnings unconfest

For some eternal home of rest.   690
"What's this?" said he, "who can conceive?
I cannot fathom, nor believe
The substance of this Christian faith;
But 'tis a steadfast hold in death!
I never saw its hideous door   695
Entered with such a mien before!"

Onward they passed in moody plight,
Leaving the pale corse on the height,
And said before two British lords
This soldier's prayer and dying words,   700
Who well can vouch this tale is true
Of converse held on Waterloo.

We learned our comrade was no more,
And many an eye for him ran o'er
In friendship's little circle kind,   705
For who not leaves some friends behind?
But yet his prayer was heard in part,
For no one had the cruel heart
His parent of his fate to tell,
She died believing he was well.   710

Ofttimes I visit for his sake
The cottage by the lonely lake,
And I have heard its beauteous dame
With tears pronounce her lover's name;
And once I saw her comely child,   715
It bent its eyes on air and smiled,
Stretching its arms with fervent mien,
As if to reach to something seen.
I've seen the wild-fowl watch and quake,
And cower in terror 'mid the brake,   720
And the mild lamb with steady eye
Gazing intent, I knew not why;
Then chilling thoughts have on me pressed
Of an unbodied heavenly guest,
Sent there to roam the lonely wild,   725
To guard the mother and the child;
For to the death-bed prayer is given
Free passage to the throne of Heaven!

Verses

Addressed to the Right Honourable
Lady Anne Scott of Buccleuch[*]

To HER whose bounty oft hath shed
Joy round the peasant's lowly bed,
When trouble pressed, and friends were few,
And God and angels only knew—
To HER who loves the board to cheer,   5
And hearth of simple cottager;
Who loves the tale of rural hind,
And wayward visions of his mind,
I dedicate, with high delight,
The theme of many a winter night.   10

    What other name on Yarrow's vale
Can Shepherd choose to grace his tale?
There other living name is none
Heard with one feeling—one alone.
Some heavenly charm must name endear   15
That all men love, and all revere!
Even the rude boy of rustic form,
And robes all fluttering to the storm,
Whose roguish lip and graceless eye
Incline to mock the passer by,   20
Walks by the Maid with softer tread,
And lowly bends his burly head,
Following with eye of milder ray
The gentle form that glides away.
The little school-nymph, drawing near,   25
Says with a sly and courteous leer,
As plain as eye and manner can,
"Thou lov'st me—bless thee, Lady Anne!"
Even babes catch the beloved theme,
And learn to lisp their Lady's name.   30

---

[*]   These Verses were published in "THE BROWNIE OF BODSBECK," as the Dedication of that Work.

The orphan's blessing rests on thee;
Happy thou art, and long shalt be!

'Tis not in sorrow, nor distress,
Nor Fortune's power to make thee less.
The heart unaltered in its mood,   35
That joys alone in doing good,
And follows in the heavenly road,
And steps where once an angel trode,–
The joys within such heart that burn,
No loss can quench nor time o'erturn!   40
The stars may from their orbits bend,
The mountains rock, the heavens rend,–
The sun's last ember cool and quiver,
But these shall glow, and glow for ever!

Then thou, who lovest the shepherd's home,   45
And cherishest his lowly dome,
O list the mystic lore sublime
Of fairy tales of ancient time.
I learned them in the lonely glen,
The last abodes of living men;   50
Where never stranger came our way
By summer night or winter day;
Where neighbouring hind or cot was none;
Our converse was with Heaven alone,
With voices through the cloud that sung,   55
And brooding storms that round us hung.

O Lady, judge, if judge you may,
How stern and ample was the sway
Of themes like these, when darkness fell,
And grey-haired sires the tales would tell!   60
When doors were barred, and eldron dame
Plied at her task beside the flame,
That through the smoke and gloom alone
On dim and umbered faces shone–
The bleat of mountain goat on high,   65
That from the cliff came quavering by;
The echoing rock, the rushing flood,
The cataract's swell, the moaning wood,
That undefined and mingled hum–

Voice of the desert never dumb!   70
All these have left within this heart
A feeling tongue can ne'er impart;
A wildered and unearthly flame,
A something that's without a name.

And, Lady, thou wilt never deem   75
Religious tale offensive theme;
Our creeds may differ in degree,
But small that difference sure can be!
As flowers which vary in their dyes,
We all shall bloom in Paradise: 80
As sire who loves his children well,
The loveliest face he cannot tell,–
So 'tis with us–We are the same,
One faith, one Father, and one aim!

And hadst thou lived where I was bred,   85
Amid the scenes where martyrs bled,
Their sufferings all to thee endeared
By those most honoured and revered;
And, where the wild dark streamlet raves,
Hadst wept above their lonely graves,   90
Thou wouldst have felt, I know it true,
As I have done, and aye must do.
And for the same exalted cause,
For mankind's rights, and nature's laws,
The cause of liberty divine,   95
Thy fathers bled as well as mine.

Then be it thine, O noble Maid,
On some still eve these tales to read;
And thou wilt read I know full well,
For still thou lovest the haunted dell;   100
To linger by the sainted spring,
And trace the ancient fairy ring,
Where moonlight revels long were held
In many a lone sequestered field,
By Yarrow den, and Ettrick shaw,   105
And the green mounds of Carterhaugh.

O for one kindred heart that thought
As lady must and minstrel ought,

That loves like thee the whispering wood,
And range of mountain solitude!   110
Think how more wild the greenwood scene,
If times were still as they have been;   .
If fairies at the fall of even,
Down from the eye-brow of the heaven,
Or some aërial land afar,   115
Came on the beam of rising star,
Their lightsome gambols to renew,
From the green leaf to quaff the dew,
Or dance with such a graceful tread
As scarce to bend the gowan's head!   120

    Think if thou wert, some evening still,
Within thy wood of green Bowhill—
Thy native wood!—the forest's pride!—
Lover or sister by thy side;
In converse sweet the hour to improve,   125
Of things below and things above,
Of an existence scarce begun,
And note the stars rise one by one:—
Just then, the moon and day-light blending,
To see the fairy bands descending,   130
Wheeling and shivering as they came,
Like glimmering shreds of human frame;
Or sailing 'mid the golden air,
In skiffs of yielding gossamer.

    O, I would wander forth alone   135
Where human eye hath never shone,
Away o'er continents and isles,
A thousand and a thousand miles,
For one such eve to sit with thee,
Their strains to hear and forms to see!   140
Absent the while all fears of harm,
Secure in Heaven's protecting arm;
To list the songs such beings sung,
And hear them speak in human tongue;
To see in beauty, perfect, pure,   145
Of human face the miniature,
And smile of being free from sin,
That had not death impressed within.

Oh, can it ever be forgot,
What Scotland had, and now has not! 150

 Such scenes, dear Lady, now no more
Are given, or fitted as before,
To eye or ear of guilty dust;
But when it comes, as come it must,
The time when I, from earth set free, 155
Shall turn the spark I fain would be;
If there's a land, as grandsires tell,
Where brownies, elves, and fairies dwell,
There my first visit shall be sped—
Journeyer of earth, go hide thy head! 160
Of all thy travelling splendour shorn,
Though in thy golden chariot borne!
Yon little cloud of many a hue
That wanders o'er the solar blue,—
That do I challenge and engage 165
To be my travelling equipage,
Then onward, onward far to steer,
The breeze of heaven my charioteer;
The soul's own energy my guide,
Eternal hope my all beside. 170
At such a shrine who would not bow!—
Traveller of earth, where art thou now?

 Then let me, for these legends claim,
My young, my honoured Lady's name;
That honour is reward complete, 175
Yet I must crave, if not unmeet,
One little boon—delightful task
For maid to grant, or minstrel ask!—

 One day, thou mayest remember well,
For short the time since it befell, 180
When, o'er thy forest bowers of oak,
The eddying storm in darkness broke;
Loud sung the blast adown the dell,
And Yarrow lent her treble swell;
The mountain's form grew more sublime, 185
Wrapt in its wreaths of rolling rime;
And Newark Cairn, in hoary shroud,

Appeared like giant o'er the cloud;
The eve fell dark, and grimly scowled,
Loud and more loud the tempest howled;   190
Without was turmoil, waste, and din,
The kelpie's cry was in the linn–
But all was love and peace within!
And aye, between, the melting strain
Poured from thy woodland harp amain,   195
Which, mixing with the storm around,
Gave a wild cadence to the sound.

   That mingled scene, in every part,
Hath so impressed thy shepherd's heart
With glowing feelings, kindling bright   200
Some filial visions of delight,
That almost border upon pain,
And he would hear those strains again.
They brought delusions not to last,
Blending the future with the past;   205
Dreams of fair stems in foliage new,
Of flowers that spring where others grew,
Of beauty ne'er to be outdone,
And stars that rise when sets the sun,
The patriarchal days of yore,   210
The mountain music heard no more,
With all the scene before his eyes,
A family's and a nation's ties–
Bonds which the Heavens alone can rend,
With Chief, with Father, and with Friend.   215
No wonder that such scene refined
Should dwell on rude enthusiast's mind!
Strange his reverse!–He never wist–
Poor inmate of the cloud and mist!
That ever he, as friend, should claim   220
The proudest Caledonian name.

ALTRIVE LAKE
April 1, 1818

Notes to
The Pilgrims of the Sun

NOTE I.

THIS poem and the following two were originally written with the intention of their forming part of a volume to be entitled MIDSUMMER NIGHT DREAMS; but having submitted it to the perusal of the late James Park, Esq. of Greenock, a friend in whose good taste and discernment I had the most perfect confidence, he chanced to think so highly of it that he persuaded me, against my own inclination, to publish it as a poem by itself, assuring me of its success. The approbation which the ballad of "Kilmeny" had received, probably influenced him in this opinion; but the poem was no sooner issued to the public, than I perceived a sort of wild unearthly nakedness about it, that rendered it unfit to appear by itself, and I repented of what I had done. It is therefore given in this edition as at first intended, namely, one of a series of *Midsummer Night Dreams*; it being literally so,—the visions of one in a trance, or the wanderings of her disembodied spirit during that oblivious cessation of mortal life.

The poem is founded on a traditionary tale well known over all Scotland, and affirmed to have happened, not only at old Lindeen, but in some lonely and eiry churchyard here and there over the whole country. From these circumstances it appears probable, that the tale has had, at first, some foundation in reality, and that it is exceedingly old. It is sometimes related as having happened to a parish minister's wife,—sometimes to such and such a great man's lady, but most frequently, as in the poem, to a saintly virgin, who was an heiress, but totally disregardful of worldly concerns. The erratic pilgrimage is given merely as a dream or vision of a person in a long trance, while the soul's short oblivious state, as described in pp. 20–21, is supposed to correspond with the symptoms of reanimation, and the "gentle shivering of the chin," noted in the corse at Carelha'.

NOTE II.

And they saw the chambers of the sun,
And the angels of the dawning ray

Draw the red curtain from the dome,
The glorious dome of the God of Day.

And the youth a slight obeisance made,
And seemed to bend upon his knee:
The holy vow he whispering said
Sunk deep in the heart of Mary Lee.

I may not say the prayer he prayed,
Nor of its wondrous tendency; &c.–P. 8.

The extravagant and heterodox position pretended to be established throughout the poem, of the throne of the Almighty being placed in the centre of the sun, must be viewed only as of a piece with the rest of the imaginary scenes exhibited in the work; infinitude and omnipresence being attributes too sacred and too boundless for admission into an enthusiast's dream.

Note III.

When past the firmament of air,
Where no attractive influence came;
There was no up, there was no down,
But all was space, and all the same.–P. 10.

A friend of mine from the country, himself a poet, made particular objections to this stanza, on the ground of its being false and unphilosophical; "For ye ken, Sir," said he, "that wherever a man may be, or can possibly be, whether in a bodily or spiritual state, there maun aye be a firmament aboon his head, and something or other below his feet. In short, it is impossible for a being to be any where in the boundless universe in which he winna find baith an *up* and a *down*." I was obliged to give in, but was so much amused with the man's stubborn incredulity, that I introduced it again in the last part.

Note IV.

"I see all these fair worlds inhabited
By beings of intelligence and mind.
O! Cela, tell me this—Have they all fallen,
And sinned like us? And has a living God
Bled in each one of all these peopled worlds!
Or only on yon dark and dismal spot
Hath one Redeemer suffered for them all?"–P. 16.

It has often been suggested to me that the dangerous doubt expressed in these few lines has proved a text to all Dr Chalmers' sublime astronomical sermons. I am far from having the vanity to suppose this to be literally true; but if it had even the smallest share in turning his capacious and fervent mind to that study, I have reason to estimate them as the most valuable lines I ever wrote.

Note V.

Down amain
Into the void the outcast world descended,
Wheeling and thundering on! &c.–P. 23.

This whole account of the formation of a Comet, from p. 22 to p. 24, has been copied into several miscellaneous works, and has been often loudly censured for its utter extravagance by such as knew not the nature of the work from which it was taken. After all, I cannot help regarding the supposition as perfectly ostensible.

Note VI.

"I saw thee dead and cold as clay;
I watched thy corpse for many a day;
I saw thee laid in the grave at rest;
I strewed the flowers upon thy breast;
And I saw the mould heaped over thee–
Thou art not my child, my Mary Lee," &c.–P. 43.

There is another Border tale resembling this, which would make an excellent subject for a poem of a different description. It likewise relates to the reanimation of a corse; and happened no earlier than in the recollection of several persons yet living. Squire R–y of Burnlee fell deeply in love with the daughter of a worthy magistrate of an ancient Border town,–so deeply indeed, that he declared, and even swore, that he neither could nor would exist without her. This hasty and injudicious resolution was not, however, put fairly to the test; for, after a short but ardent courtship, she became his wife, and the man of course was happy beyond all possible description.

But, as the old song runs,

"It happened ill, it happened worse,
It happened that this lady did dee."

They had not been many months married when the lady fell into fainting fits one morning, and expired suddenly; and, after the usual hurry of gallopping for doctors, rubbing of temples, and weeping of friends, was all fairly over, the body was laid quietly into the bier, and borne away to the churchyard on the shoulders of four stout men in deep mourning, while the long funereal train came slowly up behind.

The distance from Burnlee to the churchyard is not half a mile, but the road winds up by a steep and narrow path, and about mid-way there is an old thorn tree, which throws its long, crabbed, un-yielding branches across the road. The bearers inadvertently press-ing the bier against one of these branches, it came back with a sud-den spring, and threw the coffin from the poles, which, after nearly felling the unfortunate laird, was dashed to pieces in the path. The people gathered all round in great perplexity, but in a few seconds they betook them to their heels and fled. The corse, having been thrown out, rolled down the steep in its dead-clothes, till some of them, laying hold of it, began to lay it decently out on the brae; when, all at once, it sat up among their hands, and fell a struggling to get its arms loose. This struck them with such horror that they could not stand it, but fled precipitately, the laird running as fast as any of them, and without his hat too, which the coffin had knocked off in its fall. Some ran this way, and some that; and when they looked back and saw the dead woman gushing blood at the nose, and tearing the dressings from her face with both hands, they ran still the faster. A smith, of the surname of Walker, was the first to turn the chase, which he did by cursing his flying compeers most manfully. "It was a domned sheame," he said, "to see a hoonder men cheased be a dead woife, and hur never stworring off the beat nwother."

To make a long tale short, the lady walked home on her own legs, wrapped as she was in her winding-sheet, and led by her affec-tionate and rejoiced husband on the one side, and by the parson on the other. She afterwards became a mother, and lived a number of years at Burnlee, though not perhaps so much beloved as she was during the first two or three months: at length she died again even more suddenly than she had done the first time. Every mean was used to bring about resuscitation in vain, and the lady was a second time laid in her bier, and borne away up the strait path to the church-yard. When the procession came to the old tree, the laird looked decently up, and said to the bearers, "I'll thank you to keep off that thorn."

Note VII.

Late there was seen, on summer tide,
A lovely form that wont to glide
Round green Bowhill at the fall of even,
So like an angel sent from Heaven, &c.–P. 49.

These lines, and all to the end, relate to the late Right Honourable Harriet, Duchess of Buccleuch and Queensberry, whose lamented death happened at the very time the first edition of this work was issuing from the press, and cast a gloom over a great proportion of the south of Scotland. Thousands then felt that their guardian angel was indeed departed. Among her latest requests to her noble husband, was one in favour of the humble author of these fairy lays; but that circumstance was not known to me till several years afterwards. It was not however forgotten by him to whom it was made, whose letter to me on that subject I keep as the most affecting thing I ever saw.

Appendix 1:
MS Fragment of
'The Field of Waterloo. A Poem'

Of the manuscript prepared by Hogg in 1815 of his poem 'The Field of Water-loo' all that has apparently survived is a single leaf in National Library of Scotland, MS 582, fol. 182. This contains the title, a motto, and the dedication on one side and the opening lines of the poem itself on the verso, and is written on paper bearing the watermark 'Ivy Mill/ 1813'. The dedication is substan-tially the same as that included in Hogg's letter to Scott of 24 November [1815] (*Letters*, I, 259), and the motto is the same as the one William Blackwood re-ported the poem to bear in his letter to John Murray of [20 December 1815] in the John Murray Archive (NLS, Acc. 12604/1114). The opening lines of the poem correspond to lines 1–39 of 'The Field of Waterloo, and Death-Bed Prayer of a Soldier' in the present text, but there are significant differences which indicate that Hogg had substantially revised his poem between 1815 and 1822. In the transcript below additions are between asterisks and deletions between pointed brackets.

The

Field of Waterloo

A Poem

By James Hogg
——————————

I'll cross it though it blast me
Hamlet

To Walter Scott Esq.

Sore did I deem our ancient lore disgraced
    When thou announced'st theme of modern day
Till once I saw the path thy lays embraced,
    And *heard* thy converse higher far than they;
    Aroused by these, my little mite to pay,
And with my master hand in hand to go,
    I send for thy aproof this trivial lay,
For to that kind approval much I owe,
Those who not know thy heart, but half our minstrel know.

The Field of Waterloo

The eventful day <had> was past and gone,
And the night in majesty drew on;
For just as the twilight shed a ray
On the plains of Belgium west away
The eastern heaven was all o'erspread   5
With a veil of high and murky red;
And there was awe in the soldier's eye,
Whenever it met that lurid sky;
For he thought, as he lifted his visage swarth,
There was blood on the heaven, and blood on the earth. 10
    The day was past, the fateful day;
The pride of the tyrant prostrate lay;
And the battle-clang, and the trumpet's tone,
Were wearing southward, southward, on;
When a war-worn soldier, far behind,   15
On the verge of a rising height reclined;
His wound was deep, but his heart was true,
And of that wound he nothing knew,
For he weened the blood that had ceased to flow,
Was the blood of a proud and a hated foe,   20
And much he wondered why he lay
Thus faint and weary by the way.
    Though round his frame the tartans hung,
Yet his broad word and doric tongue
Bespoke his lineage from the land   25
Where Scotia's southland mountains stand;
That Border land, so beauteous blent,
With hill, and dale, of green extent,
With aged tower and battlement.
    It is a land where every hind   30
Is versed in lore of various kind;
Where shepherd boy or peasant elf,
Thinks, reads, and judges for himself.
Where oft the brown and labouring hind
Displays such energies of mind.   35

Appendix 2:

Hogg's MS Notes to *The Pilgrims of the Sun*

Hogg's manuscript of the notes to *The Pilgrims of the Sun* in the second, or *Midsummer Night Dreams*, volume of his *Poetical Works* of 1822 survives as British Library Add. MS 35,068, fols 110–11. This manuscript consists of a single sheet of woven paper, roughly 31.6 x 38.4 cm, bearing the watermark 'M' and countermark '1820'. The paper has been folded to make one of Hogg's characteristic four-page booklets and paginated [1]–3 by him, the fourth page being left blank. The text, which is discussed in detail in the 'Note on the Texts' (pp. 174–76), is substantially the same as, though not identical to, the printed notes of 1822 (pp. 148–52 above). Before each note Hogg has given an instruction to copy the relevant lines of *The Pilgrims of the Sun*, his page numbers clearly referring to a copy of the first edition of the poem published in December 1814. In the process of drafting his notes Hogg was trying to defend his poem from some of the misconceptions and adverse criticisms made after its first publication, a process which was clearly taken further at the proof stage. It is largely for this reason that the text of Hogg's manuscript is included in the present edition as well as the printed notes.

   Hogg has run his notes on one immediately after another, doubtless trying to be economical with his paper, but for ease of reading and to facilitate comparison with the printed notes in this edition a space has been created between each note in the transcription that follows and the page references in parentheses have been centred. Hogg's additions are given between asterisks and his deletions between pointed brackets.

The Pilgrims of the Sun
Note 1st

   This poem and the following two were originally written with the intention of forming part of a volume to be entitled MIDSUMMER NIGHT DREAMS But having submitted this to the perusal of *the late* James Park Esq. of Greenock a friend in whose *good taste and* discernment I had the most perfect confidence he chanced to think so highly of it that he perswaded me against my own inclination to publish it as a poem by itself assuring me of its success. The approbation which the ballad of Kilmeny had recieved probably influenced him in this opinion but the poem was no sooner issued to the public than I percieved a sort of wild unearthly nakedness about it that rendered it unfit to appear by itself and I repented of what I had done. It is therefore given in this edition as at first intended namely one of a series of *Midsummer Night dreams* this being literally so, the visions of one in a trance, or the wanderings of her disembodied spirit during that oblivious cessation of mortal life

The poem as is well known is founded on a traditionary tale well known over all Scotland and is affirmed not only to have happened at old Lindean but in some lonely and eiry church yard here and there over the whole country. From these circumstances it appears probable that the tale has had at first some foundation in reality and that it is exceedingly old. It is sometimes related as having happened to a parish minister's wife sometimes to such and such a great man's lady but most frequently as in the poem to a saintly virgin who was a great heiress but totally disregardful of worldly concerns The erratic pilgrimage is given merely as a dream or vision of a person in a long trance while the soul's short oblivious state in the heavenly mansions *as described in p. 49* is supposed to correspond with the symptoms of reanimation and the "gentle shivering of the chin" noted in the corpse at Carelha'

(copy p. 14)

The extravagant and heterodox position *pretended to be* established throughout the poem of the throne of the Almighty being placed in the centre of the sun must be viewed only as of a piece with the rest of the imaginary scenes exhibited in the work. But it is an idea of which I never can entirely <rid> *divest* myself in all my contemplations of the glories of nature. Infinitude and omnipresence being attributes too sacred and too boundless for admission into an enthusiast's dream

(copy p. 19)

A friend of mine from the country himself a poet made particular objections to this stanza on the ground of its being false and unphilosophical "For ye ken sir" said he "that wherever a man may be or can possibly be whether in a bodily or spiritual state there maun aye be a firmament aboon his head and some thing or other below his feet. In short it is impossible for a being to be any where in the boundless universe in which he winna find baith an *up* and a *down*." I was obliged to give in but was so much amused with the man's stubborn incredulity that I introduced it again in the last part

(copy p. 36)

It has often been suggested to me that the dangerous doubt expressed in these few lines has proved a text to all Dr. Chambers' [*sic*] sublime astronomical sermons. I am far from having the vanity to suppose this *to be literally true* but if it had even the smallest share in turning his capacious and fervent mind to that study, I have reason to estimate them as the most valuable lines I ever wrote

(copy p. 55)

This whole acount of the formation of a Comet from p. 53 to p. 57 has been copied into several miscellaneous works and has been often loudly censured <as> for its utter extravagance by such as knew not the nature of the work from which it was taken. After all I cannot help regarding the supposition as perfectly ostensible

(copy p. 109)

There is another border tale resembling this which would make an excellent subject for a poem of a different description. It likewise relates to the reanimation of a corpse but happened no earlier than in the reccollection of several persons yet living Squire R—y of Burnlee fell deeply in love with the daughter of a worthy magistrate of an ancient Border <city> town so deeply indeed that he declared and even swore that he neither could nor would subsist without her. This hasty and injudicious resolution was not however put fairly to the test for after a short but ardent courtship she became his wife and the man of course was happy beyond all possible description

But as the old song runs "it happened ill it happened worse It happened that this lady did dee" They had not been many months married when the lady fell into fainting fits one morning and expired suddenly and after the usual hurry and confusion of galloping for doctors rubbing of temples and weeping of friends was all fairly over the body was laid quietly into the bier and borne away to the church yard on the shoulders of four stout men in deep mourning while the long funeral train came slowly up behind

The distance from Burnlee to the churchyard is not half a mile but the road winds up a *by* steep and narrow path and <in> about midway there is an old thorn tree that throws its long crabbed unyielding branches across the road. <Against one of these branches> the bearers inadvertantly [*sic*] pressing the bier against one of these branches it came back with a sudden spring and threw the coffin from the poles which after nearly felling the unfortunate laird was dashed to pieces in the path. The people gathered all round in great perplexity but in a few seconds they betook them to their heels and fled The corpse having been thrown out rolled down the steep in its dead-clothes till some of them laying hold of it began to lay it decently out on the brae when it suddenly sat up amongst their hands and fell a struggling to get its arms loose. This struck them with such horror that they could not stand it and all of them fled precipitately away the laird running as fast as any of them and without his hat too which the coffin had knocked off in its fall. Some ran this way and some that and when they looked back and saw the dead woman gushing blood at the nose and tearing the dressings from her face with both hands they ran still the faster. A smith of the sirname [*sic*] of Walker was the first to turn the chace which he did by cursing his flying compeers most manfully "It was a dom'd sheame he said to see a hoonder men cheased be a dead woife and her never stworring off the beat nwother"

To make a long tale short the lady walked home on her own legs, wrapped <m> as she was in her winding sheet, and led by her affectionate and rejoiced husband on the one hand, and by the parson on the other. She afterwards became a mother, and lived a number of years at Burnlee, though not perhaps so much beloved as she was during the first two or three months; <and> at length she died again even more suddenly than the first time. Every mean [*sic*] was used to bring about resuscitation invain, and the lady was a second time laid in her <p>beir [*sic*] and borne away up the strait path to the church yard. When they came to the old tree the laird looked decently up and said to the bearers "*I'll thank you to keep off that thorn*"

(*copy p. 125*)

These lines and all to the end relate to the late Rt. Hon. Harriet Duchess of Buccleuch and Queensberry whose lamented death happened at the very time the first edition of this poem was issuing from the press and cast a gloom over a great proportion of the south of Scotland. Thousands then felt that their guardian angel was indeed departed. Among her latest requests to her noble husband was one in favours [*sic*] of the humble athor [*sic*] of these fairy lays but that circumstance was not known to him for some years afterward. It was not however forgot by him to whom it was made whose letter to me on that subject I keep as the most affecting thing I ever saw.

Note on the Texts

The Poetical Works of James Hogg was advertised in four volumes by the Constable firm as published that day at £1-10*s* in the *Edinburgh Evening Courant* of 13 June 1822 and in the *Caledonian Mercury* of 15 June. The advertisement drew attention to the fact that Hogg's poetry was 'now first collected' and advertised the set of volumes as containing 'THE QUEEN'S WAKE–PILGRIMS of the SUN–MADOR of the MOOR–POETIC MIRROR–SACRED MELODIES, &c. &c. besides many miscellaneous Poems and Songs, never before published'. As outlined in the 'Essay on the Genesis of the Texts' Hogg then realised an ambition of several years' standing to become a collected author, and *Poetical Works* was also a significant publication for the Constable firm, since it signalled Hogg's abandonment of the rival Edinburgh publisher William Blackwood and his return to the Constable fold of authors that included, for instance, Walter Scott.

Both author and publisher therefore had every incentive to exercise care in the production of the work. Besides having the services of his nephew Robert Hogg, then resident in Edinburgh, to oversee the proofs, Hogg came into town at least twice himself in April and May while production of the edition was underway. Robert Cadell, then the active partner in the Constable firm, seems to have been anxious to meet Hogg's wishes regarding production of *Poetical Works* and the printing was undertaken by the reputable Edinburgh firm of Walker & Greig, who had nearly twelve years previously printed Hogg's *The Forest Minstrel* (1810). The available evidence therefore suggests that Hogg's wishes were respected with regard to the content and production of *Poetical Works* and that Hogg himself was actively involved in the process. The text of the second volume, headed *Midsummer Night Dreams* on the contents page and containing *The Pilgrims of the Sun* as the lead item, appears to have been carefully printed from a mixture of printed and manuscript items and contains very few typographical errors.

With the exception of 'The Field of Waterloo', each component poem in this *Midsummer Night Dreams* volume had been published previously, either in volume form or within a periodical. The history of each item varies, and has been outlined in the individual notes that follow. Robert Cadell in his letter to Hogg of 2 February 1822 (NLS, MS 2245, fols 74–75) had described the objective of *Poetical Works* to Hogg as 'to start you as a collected author', but it failed to do so. No new and updated edition of *Poetical Works* appeared in Hogg's lifetime, and the posthumous five-volume *The Poetical Works of the Ettrick Shepherd* produced by Blackie and Son of Glasgow between 1838 and 1840 (the foundation of Hogg's poetical reputation for the Victorians) abandoned the *Midsummer Night Dreams* grouping. Most of the component poems were published (with others) in the second volume, 'The Powris of Moseke' was included in the third volume, and 'Verses Addressed to the Right Honourable Lady Anne Scott of Buccleuch' in the fourth.

The present volume is the first edition of Hogg's *Midsummer Night Dreams* collection of 1822 since the first. The copy-text for all the component items has been the second volume of *The Poetical Works of James Hogg* of 1822, and any emendations are listed at the end of the textual notes on the individual items below. The same abbreviations are employed in these notes as in the Editorial Notes to the present volume, at the start of which they are listed.

To the Right Hon. Lord Byron

The published dedication, apart from the punctuation added by the printer of *Pilgrims*, differs from Hogg's draft in his letter to Lord Byron of 28 October 1814 (*Letters*, I, 216) only in the penultimate line where the draft's 'In thy inspiring influence to sing' was replaced by 'With thee a wild aërial strain to sing'. Since Byron did not apparently reply to Hogg's letter of 28 October 1814 to approve the dedication before the poem was published (see *Letters*, I, 217), Hogg himself was almost certainly responsible for this change. The dedication was published only once more in Hogg's lifetime, preceding the contents page of the second volume of *Poetical Works* of 1822, the copy-text for this volume of *Midsummer Night Dreams and Related Poems*. Its placement in the volume parallels that of the similar dedication to John Grieve of *Mador of the Moor* in the fourth volume, where the lead poem is followed by a more miscellaneous selection of shorter poems separated from it by appropriate sub-headings. Although it seems probable, therefore, it is not certain that in 1822 Hogg intended to dedicate the whole volume rather than simply the lead poem to Byron. The dedication in the second volume of *Poetical Works* follows that of *Pilgrims*, except for the kind of differences occasioned by the move from the house-style of one printer to that of another. For instance, 'thro' in line 6 has become 'through'.

Hogg's dedication is given here from *Poetical Works* of 1822 without emendation.

The Pilgrims of the Sun (pp. 3–50)

After following a difficult and complex path to publication (outlined in the 'Essay on the Genesis of the Texts' above), *The Pilgrims of the Sun* was published by William Blackwood in Edinburgh in December 1814 and by John Murray in London in January 1815. Hogg's manuscript for *The Pilgrims of the Sun* has not apparently survived, and is likely to have been destroyed in the printing-house of the Caledonian Mercury Press after the printing of the edition had been completed, as was usual in the early nineteenth century. The only other printing of *The Pilgrims of the Sun* in Hogg's lifetime was in the second, or *Midsummer Night Dreams*, volume of Hogg's 1822 *Poetical Works*.

Hogg appears to have supplied the printer of his 1822 *Poetical Works* with a copy of the first edition of *The Pilgrims of the Sun* to use in setting the text of the poem, since his manuscript notes to the poem, freshly composed for *Poetical Works*, indicate which lines of the poem are to be quoted at the head of his individual notes by reference to page numbers in the first edition (see 'Appendix 2' above). A detailed comparison accordingly shows a close correspondence between the two printed texts, even in the punctuation that was normally the province of the printer rather than the author, and does not reveal any corrections or changes that can firmly be ascribed to Hogg himself. The printer of *Poetical Works* regularises some of Hogg's eccentric or old-fashioned spelling that had been transmitted from his manuscript to the first edition: for example, 'wizzard' becomes 'wizard' (Part First, l. 10), 'chrystal' becomes 'crystal' (Part Second, l. 271), 'vallies' becomes 'valleys' (Part Third, l. 80), while 'wonderous'/'wond'rous' is corrected throughout to 'wondrous'. The 1822 printer also displays a house-preference throughout for certain spellings such as 'passed' rather than 'past', and 'through'/'though' rather than 'thro''/'tho''. He occasionally adds missing punctuation, corrects obvious errors of punctuation, adds an initial upper-case letter to words like 'virgin' (Part First, l. 48, where the Virgin Mary is intended), or makes minor changes of punctuation in accordance with his own preferences.

The Pilgrims of the Sun is given in the present volume from *Poetical Works* of 1822 (pp. 1–114), with the following emendations:

p. 16, l. 145 wrapped] warped 1822
  [Editorial: 1822 follows the first edition, but 'warped' with its implications of distortion seems inappropriate]

p. 22, l. 385 seraphs' holy hymn] seraph's holy hymn 1822
[Editorial: 1822 follows the first edition, but all the seraphs
sang]

p. 48, l. 403 flowcr of the Forest] flower of the forest 1822
[Editorial: 1822 follows the first edition, but Ettrick Forest is
meant–compare p. 46, l. 323]

Connel of Dee (pp. 51–66)

According to Hogg's 'Memoir of the Author's Life' 'Connel of Dee'
was the first of the *Midsummer Night Dreams* poems to be written and
was composed immediately after Hogg had finished writing *Mador
of the Moor* in the early spring of 1814–see *Altrive Tales*, p. 35. It was
not published, however, until 1820 in Hogg's *Winter Evening Tales,
Collected Among the Cottagers in the South of Scotland*, 2 vols (Edinburgh:
Oliver & Boyd; London: G. & W. B. Whittaker, 1820), II, 204–22. It
there formed part of the section subtitled 'Country Dreams and
Apparitions'–for Ian Duncan's text of and commentary on this ver-
sion of 'Connel of Dee' see *Winter Evening Tales*, ed. by Ian Duncan
(S/SC, 2002), pp. 410–25, 582. Hogg's manuscript of the poem is
now in the Alexander Turnbull Library, Wellington, New Zealand:
James Hogg Papers (Item 16): MS-Papers-0042-03. As Ian Duncan
points out, it bears a note ('This tale to be inserted in the second vol.
after the Shepherd's Callander and proofs put to me J. H.') demon-
strating that it was used as printer's copy for the first edition of *Win-
ter Evening Tales*, and also has printer's marks indicating new gather-
ings at '205 Vol II' and '217 vol 2', in further confirmation of the fact.
Commenting on the numerous scorings out and alterations Hogg
has made to his manuscript Duncan concludes that 'it is a working
draft, pressed into service as printer's copy, rather than one of Hogg's
fair copy manuscripts, carefully prepared for the printer' (p. 582).
Winter Evening Tales went into a second edition in 1821, but the only
differences to 'Connel of Dee' from the text in the first edition are a
few minor variations in punctuation and orthography and the (pre-
sumably unintentional) omission of the word 'that' in line 429. 'Connel
of Dee' was then reprinted in the second, or *Midsummer Night Dreams*
volume, of the 1822 *Poetical Works* (pp. 115–49), and not otherwise
reprinted in Hogg's lifetime.

The 1822 printing of 'Connel of Dee' reveals minor differences of
spelling and punctuation from the text in *Winter Evening Tales*, and it
seems likely that it may have been set by the printer from a copy of
the earlier collection. The stanza numberings have been changed

from roman to arabic numerals, and the printer displays the same preference for 'through' to 'thro'', for example, that he did in setting *The Pilgrims of the Sun*. In similar fashion, he alters Hogg's archaic or idiosyncratic spellings to conventional ones: 'slieve' becomes 'sleeve' (l. 177), for instance, and 'deem't' becomes 'deemed' (l. 169). He also adds an initial upper-case letter to the exclamation 'Lord!' (l. 445), and expands Hogg's 'd–ble' to 'damnable' (l. 319). The most noteworthy change to 'Connel of Dee' in 1822 is the excision of two lines at the end of Connel's vision (immediately after line 450 in the present text) that imply that the eels consuming Connel's corpse attack his genitals:

> One snapt him on place he no longer would bide.
> It was more than a dead man could bear!

'Connel of Dee' is given in the present volume from *Poetical Works* of 1822 without emendation.

Superstition (pp. 67–73)

Despite what Hogg says in his Notes (see p. 148), 'Superstition' was apparently written after Hogg had abandoned his original and incomplete collection of *Midsummer Night Dreams* in 1814 and decided to publish *The Pilgrims of the Sun* separately. Leaving his manuscript for *The Pilgrims of the Sun* with the Edinburgh publisher Manners and Miller at the end of August 1814, Hogg set out for a holiday in the Lake District and he later recalled that it was during this visit, while staying as John Wilson's guest at Elleray on Windermere, that he composed the poem: 'Mr Wilson and I had a Queen's Wake every wet day–a fair set-to who should write the best poem between breakfast and dinner [...] I wrote the "Ode to Superstition" there, which, to give Mr Wilson justice, he approved of most unequivocally'–see *Songs by the Ettrick Shepherd* (Edinburgh: William Blackwood; London: T. Cadell, 1831), pp. 117–18. Hogg was at Elleray for most of September 1814 and returned to Edinburgh on 8 October–see Gillian Hughes, *James Hogg: A Life* (Edinburgh: Edinburgh University Press, 2007), pp. 126–28.

'Superstition' was first published by William Blackwood in Edinburgh in December 1814 and by John Murray in London in January 1815 in the same volume as *The Pilgrims of the Sun: a Poem* (pp. 131–48), and must therefore have been added (perhaps as a makeweight) while the main poem was being printed in Edinburgh at the Caledonian Mercury Press that autumn. Hogg's manuscript for 'Superstition' has not apparently survived, and may have been destroyed in the printing-house of the Caledonian Mercury Press after printing had been completed. The only other printing of *The Pilgrims of the Sun* in Hogg's lifetime was in the second, or *Midsummer Night Dreams*, volume of Hogg's 1822 *Poetical Works* (pp. 151–66).

It seems likely that the printer of the 1822 *Poetical Works* used a copy of the first edition of *The Pilgrims of the Sun* as his copy for 'Superstition', since there are no significant differences between the two printings. The printer again displays a preference for 'through' to 'thro", gives words like 'Heaven' an initial upper-case letter, conventionalises some of Hogg's spellings such as 'cemetry' to cemetery' (l. 55) and 'lone' to 'loan' (l. 113), and implements his own punctuational preferences. The most noticeable difference is that in the *Poetical Works* printing the earlier pattern of indentation has been abandoned, and each line begins immediately under the start of the preceding one. 'Superstition' is given in the present volume from *Poetical Works* of 1822 without emendation.

The Gyre Caryl (pp. 74–78)

'The Gyre Caryl' had previously appeared under the title of 'The Harper's Song' in *Mador of the Moor* (Edinburgh: William Blackwood; London: John Murray, 1816), pp. 29–37, and its theme is similar to that of 'Superstition', the preceding item in *Midsummer Night Dreams*, the disenchantment of the world. *Mador of the Moor* was written immediately before Hogg began his original *Midsummer Night Dreams* collection, though published after *The Pilgrims of the Sun* and 'Superstition', and provides ample indication that Hogg's mind was turning increasingly to the visionary theme. At one point, indeed, he rebukes his Muse for wandering from the subject because she loves 'amid the burning stars to sail' (as in 'Verses to the Comet of 1811'), 'Or sing with sea-maids' (as in 'The Mermaid'), 'The groves of visionary worlds to hail' (as in *The Pilgrims of the Sun*), and in 'moonlight dells thy fairy rites to keep' (as in 'The Haunted Glen')—see *Mador of the Moor*, ed. by James E. Barcus (S/SC, 2005), p. 52. It was natural enough, then, that when Hogg came to reconstitute the *Midsummer Night Dreams* collection aborted in 1814 for his 1822 *Poetical Works* he should have decided that 'The Harper's Song' formed a natural component of it. It is a lament for the loss of the fairies from Scotland, at the birth of religious grace, and appropriately written in the 'ancient stile' that Hogg used both to evoke a medieval, pre-Reformation Scotland, and to liberate his imagination into freer verse-forms and subject matter. (James E. Barcus has also argued convincingly that it is 'structurally and thematically significant' to *Mador of the Moor* and no mere interlude there—see *Mador*, ed. Barcus, pp. xxxvi, 104–05.) Apart from the change of title (the old one relating to the perform-ance context of *Mador of the Moor*), the only differences between these two versions of the poem are minor variations in spelling and punc-tuation and the correction of one or two mis-spellings in the *Mador* text, which had, for instance, 'rowar' for 'rowan'—see *Mador of the Moor* (Edinburgh: William Blackwood; London: John Murray, 1816), p. 32 (l. 57 of the poem in the present volume).

Hogg had complained on 8 February 1822 to Archibald Consta-ble, who was to publish the 1822 *Poetical Works*, 'I never yet have got an edition without blunders, and most gross ones in my old lan-guage, such as "The Witch o' Fife" "The Gude Greye Catte" "Hymns of the fairies" &c.' (*Letters*, II, 136). 'Hymns of the fairies' must refer to the inset 'The Song of the Fairies' in 'The Gyre Caryl', and the printer has the reader's sympathy, since Hogg's language there is undoubt-edly obscure and a logical meaning hard of access. As James Barcus has shown (*Mador*, p. xvii) at least one reviewer of *Mador of the Moor* felt that the fairy song was 'too long, and difficult to understand'. Peter Garside has demonstrated that Hogg later published a simpli-fied version of 'The Gyre Caryl' under the title of 'Superstition and Grace', firstly in *The Bijou* for 1829 (pp. 129–34), and subsequently in *A Queer Book* (Edinburgh: William Blackwood; London: T. Cadell, 1832), pp. 317–23. In this, Garside notes, 'Hogg thinned out much of his original "ancient stile", transposed certain passages, and also removed some of the more arcane chants in the earlier poem' (*Queer Book*, ed. Garside, p. 264). Barcus, in order to increase the accessi-bility of the earlier version, has printed a parallel text, giving 'The Harper's Song' facing 'Superstition and Grace' page by page, as an appendix in his Stirling/South Carolina volume of *Mador of the Moor* (pp. 87–95). Whether wisely or not in terms of the reception of his work, Hogg seems to have intended 'The Song of the Fairies' to be difficult of access for the reader within the context of his *Midsummer Night Dreams* collection, as an expression of something that, like the fairies themselves, has now vanished. 'The Gyre Caryl' itself is writ-ten in Hogg's 'ancient stile', providing a medieval feel to the narra-tive and 'The Song of the Fairies' deliberately exists at a further re-move even from that. Read aloud it goes with a swing and gives an impression of great energy, replicating the flickering movements of the fairies themselves, and similarly the movement of ideas and im-ages in the song are glancing and associative rather than fixed and logical. The song has meaning, but that meaning has much in com-mon with nursery rhymes and nonsense verse such as that written subsequently by Lewis Carroll or Edward Lear and it depends on the reader being willing to let go. 'The Gyre Caryl' is therefore presented in the present volume as a poem independent of 'Superstition and Grace', and is given from *Poetical Works* of 1822 (II, 167–68) without cmcndation.

The Haunted Glen (pp. 79–100)

A longer version of 'The Haunted Glen' had previously been published in Hogg's *Dramatic Tales*, 2 vols (Edinburgh: John Ballantyne; London: Longmans, 1817), II, 189–271. On the final page Hogg apologises for the fact that it is incomplete by stating that its 'great length' 'rendered its full insertion here inconvenient' (p. 271). However, 'The Haunted Glen' seems to have been composed as *Dramatic Tales* was going through the press and was almost certainly never completed, since Hogg afterwards confessed in his 'Memoir of the Author's Life' that 'the fragment of "The Haunted Glen" was written off-hand, to make the second volume of an equal extent with the first' (*Altrive Tales*, p. 42).

As published in 1817 'The Haunted Glen' mixes scenes concerning Prince Lu, his relationship with the fairies of whom he is about to be crowned king and with the maiden Lula, with comic scenes about a local family of cottars, Eps and Cairney and their uncouth son, Simon. For his *Midsummer Night Dreams* volume Hogg cut the comic subplot from 'The Haunted Glen', shortening his poetic drama and placing the emphasis more firmly on Lu and the fairies. He also made a series of adjustments to cover the disjunction between surviving scenes and to eliminate direct references to elements now removed from the plot. The two acts of Hogg's original play were reduced in the 1822 *Poetical Works* version to four scenes, corresponding as follows to scenes in *Dramatic Tales*:

> *Scene I*: Act First, Scene I in *Dramatic Tales*, II, 190–204
> *Scene II*: Act First, Scene III in *Dramatic Tales*, II, 215–26
> *Scene III*: Act Second, Scene I in *Dramatic Tales*, II, 227–39
> *Scene IV*: lines 1–29 correspond to the opening of Act Second, Scene III, and the remainder of the scene corresponds to Act Second, Scene IV in *Dramatic Tales*, II, 252–54, 263–70

Besides these structural changes there are also a number of instances of local revision by the author for the version of 'The Haunted Glen' in the 1822 *Poetical Works*, in addition to the kind of minor variations in punctuation and spelling that almost certainly reflect the preferences of the printer. For instance, 'that destroying fiend' becomes 'that decoying fiend' (Scene II, l. 16), and 'From mountain, glen, and forest wild?' becomes 'From mountain, glen, and pathless wild?' (Scene III, l. 81). The earlier version of 'The Haunted Glen' will appear in the S/SC volume of *Dramatic Tales*, while the present volume accordingly provides the reader with the shortened version Hogg created for the second, or *Midsummer Night Dreams*, volume of his 1822 *Poetical Works*.

Although 'The Haunted Glen' was not reprinted again during Hogg's lifetime, some of the songs embedded in Hogg's fairy play have an independent publication history. 'O, Weel Befa' the Maiden Gay' seems to have been composed before 'The Haunted Glen' itself, since Hogg later recollected writing it on his visit to John Wilson at Elleray in the Lake District of September 1814—see *Songs by the Ettrick Shepherd* (Edinburgh: William Blackwood; London: T. Cadell, 1831), p. 117. It was subsequently published several times, in two distinct versions. The first version, 'O Weel Befa' the Maiden Gay' was a substantial revision of the song for its appearance in *Blackwood's Edinburgh Magazine*, 20 (July 1826), 108, and from there it passed into *Songs by the Ettrick Shepherd* (Edinburgh: William Blackwood; London; T. Cadell, 1831), pp. 117–20. Another version, closer to that in 'The Haunted Glen', was sent by Hogg to the London music publishing firm of Goulding & D'Almaine in a letter of 24 August 1829 (*Letters*, II, 351–54) as a contribution to the firm's annual, *The Musical Bijou*. It was perhaps from this manuscript that this version of the poem was published as 'Song. By the Ettrick Shepherd' in the short-lived *Monthly Musical and Literary Magazine* of February 1830 (p. 10). For further details of this song's textual history and a text of the *Musical Bijou* version of the song, 'O Weel Befa' the Guileless Heart', see *Contributions to Annuals and Gift-Books*, ed. by Janette Currie and Gillian Hughes (S/SC, 2006), pp. 154, 319–21.

Hogg also reworked two further sections of 'The Haunted Glen' to create a pair of 'Fairy Songs' which he also sent with his letter of 24 August 1829 to Goulding & D'Almaine as a contribution to *The Musical Bijou*. The first of these songs, beginning 'Never, gentle spirits—never' is roughly equivalent to the '*Song by* Lu' that closes Scene III of 'The Haunted Glen' (ll. 193–210 in the present text). It was apparently never published as such. The second song, which was adapted as 'The Song of Oberon' in *The Musical Bijou* for 1830, begins 'Hie you away fairies hie you away' and is essentially a revised and rearranged version of the passage in *Dramatic Tales* that immediately precedes 'O Weel Befa' the Guileless Heart' (equivalent to Scene IV, ll. 105–29 in the present text). For further details of the textual history of both 'Fairy Songs' and an edited text see *Contributions to Annuals and Gift-Books*, ed. by Janette Currie and Gillian Hughes (S/ SC, 2006), pp. 155–57, 321–22.

In the present volume 'The Haunted Glen' is given from the second, or *Midsummer Night Dreams* volume of Hogg's 1822 *Poetical Works* (pp. 179–228) without emendation.

The Mermaid (pp. 101–04)

The composition of 'The Mermaid' can probably be dated to the spring of 1819, when Hogg was paying a visit to his friend John Aitken in Dunbar: in the headnote to 'The Mermaid's Song' in *Songs by the Ettrick Shepherd* (Edinburgh: William Blackwood; London: T. Cadell, 1831) Hogg wrote that the song consists 'only of the singing verses of a long ballad which I wrote many years ago, in the house of Mr Aitken, then living at Dunbar. The original ballad is to be found printed in some work, but where I know not' (p. 87). Hogg visited John Aitken in Dunbar in April 1819, where he was awarded the freedom of the town—see Gillian Hughes, *James Hogg: A Life* (Edinburgh: Edinburgh University Press, 2007), pp. 160–63. 'The Mermaid. A Scottish Ballad' was published shortly afterwards in the *Edinburgh Magazine*, 4 (May 1819), 400–01, and the printing in the second or *Midsummer Night Dreams* volume of the 1822 *Poetical Works* is the only other appearance of the complete work in Hogg's lifetime.

What Hogg referred to as 'the singing verses', namely the inset 'Mermaid's Song', have a separate publication history as a song. A shortened and revised version of the lines in the *Edinburgh Magazine* appeared subsequently set to music by the young Neil Gow in Hogg's song-collection of *A Border Garland* (Edinburgh: Nathaniel Gow and Son, [1819]), pp. 8–9, and to music by James Dewar subsequently in *The Border Garland* (Edinburgh: Robert Purdie, [1828]), pp. 28–30. Finally, Hogg included 'The Mermaid's Song' in *Songs by the Ettrick Shepherd* (Edinburgh: William Blackwood; London: T. Cadell, 1831), pp. 87–89.

In revising 'The Mermaid' for the *Midsummer Night Dreams* volume of 1822 Hogg altered it substantially, particularly 'The Mermaid's Song' in which lines were transposed, added, and excised, changing a forty-eight-line song in six eight-line stanzas to a forty-line song in ten four-line stanzas. Perhaps it was understandable that, in moving from an Edinburgh-based magazine context to the collected edition of poems that he hoped would have a wider British appeal, Hogg should have removed a reference to the superior nature of Scotland as an independent nation in the fifth stanza of the *Edinburgh Magazine* version:

> But on a land so dull and drear
>   No joy hath my attendance;
> Fled all the scenes in Scotia dear,
>   When fled her independence!

It is more difficult to see why he should have deleted the fourth stanza, which appears to fit the visionary theme of *Midsummer Night Dreams* so well.

> No more I'll come at gloaming tide,
>   By this green shore to hover,
> And see the maid cling to the side
>   Of her dismayed lover;
> To meet the fairy by the bower,
>   The kelpy by the river,
> Or brownie by the baron's tower,
>   O vanish'd all for ever!

Although in the *Midsummer Night Dreams* version the mermaid notes that 'spirits now have left the deep, | Their long last farewell taking' (ll. 93–94) the emphasis falls more strongly in the later version of the poem on the personal feeling of the mermaid for her dead lover rather than on the desertion of Scotland by the other spirits. Although the *Edinburgh Magazine* version of Hogg's poem is of great interest, the version relevant to the present volume is that which appeared in 1822. 'The Mermaid' is therefore given in the present volume from the second, or *Midsummer Night Dreams*, volume of Hogg's 1822 *Poetical Works* (pp. 229–37) without emendation.

Verses to the Comet of 1811 (pp. 105–06)

A spectacular comet was visible over much of Europe with the naked eye between April 1811 and January 1812 and Hogg's poem was probably composed at the time of its appearance or shortly afterwards. In his letter to Eliza Izett of 23 March 1813 Hogg states, 'I have no copy of *the Comet* but I have been thinking of it all this day and shall endeavour to make it out' (*Letters*, I, 135). It was first published in 1814 as 'A Night Piece. Written in Autumn, 1811' in the *Poetical Register*, 8 (1810–11), 90–91, and subsequently as 'Stanzas Addressed to a Comet' in *Edinburgh Magazine*, 5 (July 1819), 30. Like 'The Mermaid', therefore, it forms part of a group of 'otherworldly' poems contributed to the magazine of the Constable firm, publishers of Hogg's 1822 *Poetical Works*. Subsequently Hogg thought of using part of the poem in an article for *Blackwood's Edinburgh Magazine*, a projected *Noctes Ambrosianae* set in a hot-air balloon. A surviving manuscript paper of 'Songs for the Baloon!!!' (NLS, MS 4805, fols 101–02) concludes with sixteen lines (equivalent to ll. 25–40 of 'Verses to the Comet' in the present volume) headed 'Please edge in somewhere two of the verses to the Comet in 1811'. Hogg's songs did not, however, appear in *Blackwood's Edinburgh Magazine*, nor was the extract from his comet poem included in the balloon journey subsequently published as 'Dr David Dale's Account of a Grand Aerial Voyage' in the *Edinburgh Literary Journal* of 23 January 1830, pp. 50–54.

Although it was not published subsequent to 1822 during Hogg's lifetime, his comet poem was obviously valued highly by his contemporaries, for several presentation copies in Hogg's hand have survived. One entitled 'The Comet' is now in the Houghton Library, Harvard University (bMS Am 1631(180)), and another entitled 'Verses to the Comet of 1811' in the Bodleian Library, University of Oxford (MS Autogr. c. 9, fol. 125) was made at the request of the Edinburgh journalist and publisher Robert Chambers. An undated manuscript version in NLS, MS 9634, fols 1–2 appears to be a third presentation copy, which closely resembles the poem as published in the *Edinburgh Magazine* but has an additional stanza after the first:

> High on the wold the stars distil
>   Their silver flix of fairy rain,
> Nursing the pure, the parent rill,
>   That rolls a river to the main.

The best-known version of Hogg's poem, however, and the one which was transmitted throughout the nineteenth century by means of the posthumous *The Poetical Works of the Ettrick Shepherd*, 5 vols (Glasgow: Blackie and Son, 1838–40), II, 156–58, is that of 1822.

In revising his poem for the 1822 *Poetical Works* from the *Edinburgh Magazine* Hogg made a number of minor changes, the most interesting of which are perhaps the alteration of 'Teviot's' in the third line to 'Yarrow's', and the change from 'wild enthusiast's dream' in the penultimate stanza to 'rapt enthusiast's dream'.

'Verses to the Comet of 1811' is therefore given in the present volume from the second, or *Midsummer Night Dreams* volume of Hogg's 1822 *Poetical Works* (pp. 239–44) without emendation.

The Powris of Moseke (pp. 107–22)

Hogg published 'The Powris of Moseke, Ane Rychte Plesant Ballaunt' in the *Edinburgh Magazine*, 9 (October 1821), 356–61, not long before the preparation of *Poetical Works*. Its date of composition is unknown, and Hogg's manuscript does not appear to have survived. The poem was not reprinted subsequently in his lifetime after its appearance in the 1822 *Poetical Works*. In preparing his poem for this collected edition, Hogg carefully regularised the spelling of his 'ancient stile' ('boie' becomes 'boi', for instance), and also corrected some misunderstandings of his hand by the magazine printer (for example, 'grapplit' becomes 'grofellit', l. 320). He also made minor changes of wording, so that 'Blynde Robenis face grew lang and brode' becomes 'Blynde Robenis face grewe lang and blanke' (l. 249). Hogg also emphasised the importance of his title by changing the words 'powris of moseke' to read 'Powris of Moseke' throughout. 'The Powris of Moseke' is given in the present volume from the second, or *Midsummer Night Dreams*, volume of Hogg's 1822 *Poetical Works* (pp. 245–80) without emendation.

The Field of Waterloo (pp. 120–41)

From Hogg's letter to Scott of 16 November [1815] (*Letters*, i, 256) 'The Field of Waterloo' was written during November and December 1815, in the aftermath of the great battle of 18 June that had ended the Napoleonic Wars and in emulation of Scott's poem of the same name. Hogg's letter expressed an intention of dedicating 'The Field of Waterloo' to Scott, and in a subsequent letter of 24 November he included a draft dedication (*Letters*, i, 259). This was slightly revised and written at the start of Hogg's manuscript copy of his poem, a fragment of which survives in NLS, MS 582, fol. 182: the text of this fragment is printed in the present volume as 'Appendix 1: MS Fragment of "The Field of Waterloo. A Poem"'. In his letter to Scott of 24 November Hogg also outlined his publication plans for his new poem: 'My *Waterloo* is drawn out to a considerable length I intend either to publish it in a pamphlet as a thing of the day or put it into my new edition I am rather pleased with it' (*Letters*, i, 259). It seems that Hogg's poem was not published at that time, although in his letter of 17 December 1816[?] to Ebenezer Clarkson, the Selkirk doctor, Hogg mentions sending to Edinburgh 'for the only copy, extant by itself, of my "Tale of Waterloo"' (*Letters*, i, 287), which may imply that it was set up in type.

Towards the end of 1815 Hogg sent his manuscript to the Edinburgh publisher William Blackwood, who, from his letter to the London publisher John Murray of [20 December 1815], did not value it highly:

> I have a curious epistle from The Ettrick Shepherd to day enclosing me two sheets of "The Field of Waterloo a Poem by James Hogg. I'll cross it though it blast me. Hamlet" He says he wishes it printed forthwith and that you will lend it a helping hand. From the glance I have given it appears bitter bad, but as he says I may send the proofs to Mr Scott, I mean to consult him this afternoon about it. (John Murray Archive: NLS, Acc. 12604/1114)

In his subsequent letter of 22 December Blackwood reported, 'I call'd on Mr Scott yesterday by appointment to see what could be done with poor Hogg's lamentable production. He was rather averse to corresponding with the Shepherd himself, yet by means of Mr Wilson (Isle of Palms) and another friend of Hoggs I have got it knock'd on the head' (John Murray Archive: NLS, Acc. 12604/1114). Hogg was clearly extremely angry and hurt at the treatment his poem had met with in Edinburgh, and this may partly account for the fact that the dedication to Scott was dropped when 'The Field of Waterloo' was published subsequently in his *Poetical Works*. He wrote an angry letter to John Wilson on 2 January [1816], asking 'Who gave an ideot and a driveller like you a right to counterwork their designs to pick up manuscripts clandestinely and blab over them in taverns to your scum of acquaintance?' (*Letters*, I, 263). The first and only publication of 'The Field of Waterloo' in Hogg's lifetime was in the second volume of his 1822 *Poetical Works*.

The manuscript fragment in NLS, MS 582, fol. 182 appears to be the initial leaf of Hogg's fair-copy manuscript of 1815, with the title and dedication to Scott on one side and the opening lines of the poem on the verso, since the wording of the title and motto from Shakespeare's *Hamlet* agree with the details given in William Blackwood's letter to John Murray of [20 December 1815]. The dedication to Scott agrees with the draft in Hogg's letter to Scott of 24 November 1815, except for the substitution of 'converse higher' for 'converse bolder' in the fourth line.

Hogg's revisions for *Poetical Works* included giving the poem a new sub-title, 'and Death-Bed Prayer of a Soldier'. This raises interesting questions as to how far Hogg's poem of 1815 differed from the revised version he published in 1822, questions which cannot now be answered. Was the present ending of the poem, for instance, where the dead soldier's spirit hovers around his Border home unseen, to 'guard the mother and the child' (l. 726), part of the original, or was it added to adapt the work to the visionary *Midsummer Night Dreams*? Does the addition of the subtitle to the later version indicate that originally the poem concluded before the soldier's dying prayer or not? The thirty-five line opening of the poem on the verso of the manuscript fragment (see 'Appendix 1') when compared with the equivalent lines of the 1822 version (ll. 1–37) shows that Hogg certainly did revise his poem, but offers no clues to the solution of such questions.

'The Field of Waterloo' is given in the present volume from the second, or *Midsummer Night Dreams*, volume of Hogg's 1822 *Poetical Works* (pp. 281–323) without emendation.

Verses Addressed to the Right Honourable Lady Anne Scott of Buccleuch (pp. 142–47)

There is apparently no surviving manuscript of this poem, which was first published as the dedication to *The Brownie of Bodsbeck: And Other Tales*, 2 vols (Edinburgh: William Blackwood; London: John Murray, 1818), I, i–xii. At that time Hogg had recently settled at Altrive in Yarrow, a small farm granted to him rent-free by Charles, 4th Duke of Buccleuch. Although the poem's dating from Altrive is 1 April 1818, shortly before the May publication of his tale collection, Hogg seems to have written to his patron to ask permission to dedicate the work to his eldest daughter, Lady Anne Scott, towards the end of 1816. The Duke's reply of 20 December 1816 (NLS, MS 2245, fols 25–26) says, 'Lady Ann will be proud of the honour you intend her provided there is nothing profane or irreligious in the Tales'. The poem was quickly recognised as one of Hogg's most successful pieces, and was showcased as a 'very beautiful Poetical Dedication' in *Blackwood's Edinburgh Magazine*, 4 (October 1818), 74–76. Lockhart quoted from it approvingly to define the 'solemn, wrapped-up contemplative genius' of Wordsworth in *Peter's Letters to his Kinsfolk*, 3 vols (Edinburgh: William Blackwood; London: T. Cadell and W. Davies, 1819), II, 312. It was therefore natural that Hogg should have chosen to place the poem as the final item in the second volume of his 1822 *Poetical Works* (pp. 325–39).

An extract entitled 'Journey of the Soul', dated 7 November 1827, forms a presentation holograph for the actor Alexander Betty (NLS, MS 10,279, pp. 78–79). In 1832 Hogg published a third and revised version of the whole poem, including some additional lines, as the dedication to what was intended as the first volume of his collected prose works, in *Altrive Tales* (London: James Cochrane, 1832), pp. i–viii. For details of this final version published in Hogg's lifetime and an edited text see *Altrive Tales*, ed. by Gillian Hughes (S/SC, 2003), pp. 5–10, 191–94.

Most of the changes between the earlier version of the poem published in 1818 and the one published in 1822 consist of adjustments of spelling and punctuation, likely to be the result of a printer's adoption of his own house-style. Either the printer or author might have made the obvious correction of 'kind' to 'hind' (l. 7) or have decided that 'theme' was preferable to 'themes' (l. 10) and 'den' to 'dens' (l. 105). Other changes are plainly authorial: 'As minstrel must, and lady ought,' is reordered to read 'As lady must and minstrel ought,' (l. 108), while 'little wist' becomes 'never wist' (l. 218). In addition two lines (which would otherwise fall between ll. 164 and 165 in the present text) were deleted from the poem in *Poetical Works*. These describe the rapidly moving cloud with which the poet envisages his spirit travelling after death:

> That curls, and rolls, and fleets away
> Beyond the very springs of day,–

A further change from 'wild dark streamlet raves,' to the less appropriate 'wild dark streamlet waves,' (l. 89) appears to be a printer's error.

'Verses Addressed to the Right Honourable Lady Anne Scott of Buccleuch' is given in the present volume from the second, or *Midsummer Night Dreams*, volume of Hogg's 1822 *Poetical Works* (pp. 325–39) with the following emendation:

p. 144, l. 89 raves,] waves, 1822 [1818 raves,]

Hogg's Notes to The Pilgrims of the Sun (pp. 148–52)

No authorial notes were provided to *The Pilgrims of the Sun* on first publication in December 1814, and Hogg's notes were published on pp. 341–51 of the *Midsummer Night Dreams* volume of the 1822 *Poetical Works* for the first and only time during his life. Hogg's letter of 8 February 1822 to Archibald Constable, the publisher of *Poetical Works*, suggests that he was anxious to have all four volumes of a uniform length: 'I will make up each volume to the size of the Queen's Wake which must be the standard in size. The poetic Mirror will need some additions' (*Letters*, II, 136). *The Queen's Wake*, including Hogg's notes, takes up the whole of the first duodecimo volume of *Poetical Works* which is 381 pages long, The second volume is 351 pages long, the third 383 pages, and the fourth 359 pages, so that Hogg in fact failed to make each volume of equal extent. His second volume, however, would only have been 339 pages without the notes to *The Pilgrims of the Sun*. It would, of course, have been closer to the length of the first volume had Hogg written notes to the other poems in the volume as well, but had he done so he might then have felt obliged for the sake of consistency to add notes to all the poems in the other volumes of *Poetical Works*, making the third volume at least one folded sheet over the standard thickness.

Hogg's manuscript of his notes for *The Pilgrims of the Sun* survives as British Library, Add. MS 35,068, fols 110–11, and a transcript is included in the present volume as 'Appendix 2: Hogg's MS Notes to *The Pilgrims of the Sun*'. This manuscript seems to indicate that Hogg wrote his notes to accompany a copy of the first edition of *The Pilgrims of the Sun* for the printers of *Poetical Works*, since he references the quotations at the head of individual notes by naming the page number in the first edition on which the relevant passages occur. (The relevant lines to be copied were presumably marked for the printer on those pages.) The page references within the text of the notes (p. 148. l. 28 and p. 150, l. 6 in the present text) also relate to the first edition of *The Pilgrims of the Sun* rather than to *Poetical Works*. The occasional transcription errors in the quotations heading those notes (which have not been emended in the present volume) are probably the result of carelessness, since in no instance does a departure from the 1822 text restore a first edition reading.

In general the printed notes of 1822 follow Hogg's manuscript fairly closely. The customary tidying of spelling and punctuation has been performed by the printer. Other changes smooth Hogg's style and render it less colloquial, so that 'a great heiress' becomes 'an heiress' (p. 148, l. 25) and 'forgot' becomes 'forgotten' (p. 152, l. 6). Sometimes a change eliminates repetition, by removing, for instance, the phrase 'as is well known' in the manuscript's reading of 'The poem as is well known is founded on a traditional tale well known over all Scotland' (p. 148, ll. 17–18). Hogg's original 'hurry and confusion' was perhaps changed to 'hurry' (p. 150, l. 32) as being tautologous.

Occasionally, however, the printer has misread Hogg's hand, so that the seven lines of verse at the head of Note IV are referred to as 'these four lines' rather than 'these few lines' (p. 149, l. 37). He also substituted the standard spelling 'by' for 'be' in a speech of Northumbrian dialect (p. 151, l. 20). Hogg often gets proper names slightly out of kilter in his writing, and in this case the alert printer has cor-

rected a mistaken reference to 'Dr. Chambers' sublime astronomi-
cal sermons' to read 'Dr Chalmers' sublime astronomical sermons'
(p. 149, ll. 37–38).

A number of other differences between the manuscript and printed
text are more interesting since they suggest a degree of careful cen-
sorship, perhaps self-censorship by Hogg at the proof stage, in re-
sponse to misconceptions and adverse criticism of the first edition of
The Pilgrims of the Sun. These points are covered by the Editorial Notes,
while the inclusion of a transcription of Hogg's manuscript in 'Ap-
pendix 2' allows the reader of this edition to assess the full extent of
the variation between manuscript and printed text.

Hogg's 'Notes to the Pilgrims of the Sun' is given in the text of the
present volume from the second, or *Midsummer Night Dreams*, volume
of Hogg's 1822 *Poetical Works* (pp. 341–51). Page references to *The
Pilgrims of the Sun* within Hogg's notes have been silently emended so
that they refer to the relevant page in the present volume, and the
following emendations have also been made:

> p. 149, l. 37 these few lines] these four lines 1822 [MS these
> few lines]
> p. 150, l. 23 exist]   exsist 1822 [Editorial. Hogg's manuscript
> has 'subsist']
> p. 151, ll. 20–21 be a dead woife] by a dead woife [MS be a
> dead woife]

Editorial Notes

In the notes that follow references to poems are by page and line number, while references to prose items are by page number with a letter enclosed in brackets to indicate the relevant quarter of the page: (a) indicates the first quarter, (b) the second quarter, (c) the third quarter, and (d) the fourth quarter of the page. Where it seems useful to discuss the meaning of particular phrases, this is done in the Editorial Notes: single words are generally dealt with in the Glossary. Quotations from the Bible are from the King James version, the translation most familiar to Hogg and his contemporaries; in the case of the Psalms, however, reference is sometimes given to the metrical *Psalms of David* approved by the Church of Scotland, where this seems apposite. For references to plays by Shakespeare, the edition used has been *The Complete Works: Compact Edition*, ed. by Stanley Wells and Gary Taylor (Oxford: Clarendon Press, 1988). For references to other volumes of the Stirling/South Carolina Edition the editor's name is given after the title, with the abbreviation 'S/SC' and date of first publication following in parentheses. References to Sir Walter Scott's fiction are to the Edinburgh Edition of the Waverley Novels (EEWN). The National Library of Scotland is abbreviated to NLS. The notes are greatly indebted to the following standard works: *Oxford Dictionary of National Biography* (*Oxford DNB*) and *Oxford English Dictionary* (*OED*). Other works frequently referred to in the Editorial Notes are referred to by the following abbreviations:

Altrive Tales James Hogg, *Altrive Tales*, ed. by Gillian Hughes (S/SC, 2003)

Child *The English and Scottish Popular Ballads*, ed. by Francis James Child, 5 vols (Boston: Houghton Mifflin, 1882–98) (Ballads are referred to by number.)

Groome *Ordnance Gazetteer of Scotland: A Survey of Scottish Topography*, ed. by Francis H. Groome, 6 vols (Edinburgh: Jack, 1882–85) (Quotations from Groome in the Editorial Notes are from the entries for the places under discussion.)

Kinsley *The Poems and Songs of Robert Burns*, ed. by James Kinsley, 3 vols (Oxford: Clarendon Press, 1968) (Poems are referred to by number.)

Letters *The Collected Letters of James Hogg*, ed. by Gillian Hughes, Associate Editors Douglas S. Mack, Robin MacLachlan, and Elaine Petrie, 3 vols (S/SC, 2004–08)

Mador *Mador of the Moor*, ed. by James E. Barcus (S/SC, 2005)

Minstrelsy Walter Scott, *Minstrelsy of the Scottish Border*, 2nd edn, 3 vols (Edinburgh: Constable; London: Longman, 1803)

Mountain Bard James Hogg, *The Mountain Bard*, ed. by Suzanne Gilbert (S/SC, 2007)

Paradise Lost John Milton, *Paradise Lost*, ed. by Stephen Orgel and
  Jonathan Goldberg (Oxford: Oxford University Press, 2004)
Pilgrims James Hogg, *The Pilgrims of the Sun; A Poem* (London: John
  Murray; Edinburgh: William Blackwood, 1815)
Poetical Works *The Poetical Works of James Hogg*, 4 vols (Edinburgh: Con-
  stable; London: Hurst, Robinson & Co., 1822)
Queer Book James Hogg, *A Queer Book*, ed. by P. D. Garside (S/SC,
  1995; paperback, 2007)
SHW *Studies in Hogg and his World*
Winter Evening Tales James Hogg, *Winter Evening Tales*, ed. by Ian Duncan
  (S/SC, 2002)

To the Right Hon. Lord Byron

Hogg dedicated *The Pilgrims of the Sun* of 1815 to the celebrated poet George
Gordon, Lord Byron (1788–1824), who had helped to secure the prestigious
London publisher John Murray for the work. Hogg had first proposed to
dedicate his new poem to Byron in a letter to him of 14 August 1814 (*Letters*, I,
195). On 28 October 1814 he told Byron, 'As *The Pilgrims of the Sun* is now all
through my hands save three sheets the title page is likely to be called for by
the time I can have an answer from you by return of post', and this letter
included a draft version of the dedicatory poem published in the first edition
as well as an alternative verse dedication to Byron's bride should Byron be
married by the time Hogg's poem was published (*Letters*, I, 215–16). Since
Byron did not marry Miss Milbanke until January 1815 and *Pilgrims* was pub-
lished in Edinburgh on 12 December 1814, the poem was dedicated to Byron
himself. The published dedication, apart from the punctuation added by the
printer of *Pilgrims*, differs from Hogg's draft only in the penultimate line where
the draft's 'In thy inspiring influence to sing' was replaced by 'With thee a wild
aërial strain to sing'. Since Byron did not apparently reply to Hogg's letter of
28 October 1814 before the poem was published (see *Letters*, I, 217), Hogg
himself was almost certainly responsible for this alteration. The dedication
was published only once more in Hogg's lifetime, preceding the Contents
page of the second volume of *Poetical Works* of 1822, the copy-text for this
volume of *Midsummer Night Dreams and Related Poems*. Its placement in *Poetical
Works* parallels that of the similar dedication to John Grieve of *Mador of the
Moor* in the fourth volume, where the lead poem is followed by a more miscel-
laneous selection of shorter poems separated from it by appropriate sub-
headings. Although it seems probable, therefore, it is not certain that in 1822
Hogg intended to dedicate the whole volume rather than simply the lead
poem to Byron.

1, l. 1 crabbed state-creed Byron had a seat in the House of Lords, and before
  his departure from England for the continent in 1816 was intimate at the
  great Whig political bases of Holland, Melbourne, and Devonshire Houses.
1, l. 2 virtues high presumably an ironical allusion to Byron's many and
  widely-publicised love-affairs.
1, l. 9 round Shepherd's head thy charmed mantle fling just as the Ettrick
  Shepherd was painted wearing a shepherd's plaid so Lord Byron was painted
  by Thomas Phillips swathed in a cloak. John Murray had recently given

Hogg an engraving of the Byron portrait—see Hogg's letter to Byron of 18 October 1814 (*Letters*, I, 209–10) and also Gillian Hughes, '"Native Energy": Byron and Hogg as Scottish Poets', *The Byron Journal*, 34 no. 2 (2006), 133–42.

The Pilgrims of the Sun

The Pilgrims of the Sun was composed immediately after the completion of *Mador of the Moor*, probably between mid-February and late July 1814, and Hogg told Eliza Izett on 26 October that year that it had taken him only 'about three weeks' to write (*Letters*, I, 211). After following a difficult and complex path to publication (outlined in the 'Essay on the Genesis of the Texts'), it was published by William Blackwood in Edinburgh in December 1814 and by John Murray in London in January 1815. Like several other poems in *Midsummer Night Dreams*, *The Pilgrims of the Sun* seems to be prefigured in the third canto of *Mador of the Moor*, where Hogg describes the bias of his muse towards visionary subjects:

> Cease, thou wild Muse, thy vague unbodied lay!
>   What boots these wanderings from thy onward tale?
> I know thee well! when once thou fliest astray,
>   To lure thee back no soothing can avail.
> Thou lovest amid the burning stars to sail,
> Or sing with sea-maids down the coral deep;
>   The groves of visionary worlds to hail,
> In moonlight dells thy fairy rites to keep,
> Or through the wilderness on booming pinion sweep.
>   (*Mador*, p. 52, ll. 46–54)

Written after the spectacular success of *The Queen's Wake* (1813) Hogg's four-part poem is partly an extension of the theme of 'Kilmeny', where a pure maiden is taken from earth to experience a spiritual world, and partly the newly-confident poet's excursion into the poetic realms of Scott, Milton, Pope, and Dryden.

PART FIRST

3, l. 3 Yarrowdale the valley of the river Yarrow, extending south-west approximately twenty miles from Bowhill near Selkirk, the terrain changing from woods to high rolling hills.

3, l. 4 green coats kilted to the knee a ballad phrase, indicating activity, exertion, and enterprise.

3, l. 10 Ettrick's green and wizard shaw the valley of the river Ettrick, roughly parallel to Yarrow, and containing farms, hills, and ruins of old Border towers and castles. One of these, Aikwood, is associated with the wizard Michael Scott, subject of Hogg's later prose-fiction romance *The Three Perils of Man* (1822) and also featured in Scott's poem *The Lay of the Last Minstrel* (1805).

3, l. 12 Carelha' Hogg's note identifies this as Carterhaugh, the setting for the traditional ballad of 'Tam Lin' (Child, no. 39). Like Hogg's Mary Lee, the Janet of the ballad also wins and marries a fairy lover. The ballad is also a source for Hogg's fairy drama 'The Haunted Glen' in the *Midsummer Night Dreams* collection—see headnote to 'The Haunted Glen'. In his introduction to 'The Young Tamlane' Scott wrote of Carterhaugh as 'a plain, at the

conflux of the Ettrick and Yarrow, in Selkirkshire, about a mile above Sel-
kirk, and two miles below Newark Castle [...]. The peasants point out, upon
the plain, those electrical rings, which vulgar credulity supposes to be traces
of the fairy revels [...]. In no part of Scotland, indeed, has the belief in fairies
maintained its ground with more pertinacity than in Selkirkshire. The most
sceptical among the lower ranks only venture to assert, that their appear-
ances, and mischievous exploits, have ceased, or at least become infrequent,
since the light of the Gospel was diffused in its purity'—see *Minstrelsy*, II,
243–44.

3, ll. 17–20 The dogs [...] hand of Mary Lee Hogg refers to a virgin's immu-
nity from harm in poems, for instance, like 'Ane Rychte Gude and Preytious
Ballande'—see *Queer Book*, pp. 125–35. The lines also recall the animals gath-
ering harmlessly in a ring around Kilmeny—see *The Queen's Wake*, ed. by
Douglas S. Mack (S/SC, 2004), p. 99.

4, l. 38 Nature's plan a poetic commonplace, also used by James Beattie in
Book 2 of *The Minstrel; or, The Progress of Genius*. In the course of his self-
education Edwin 'mindful of the aids that life requires' and 'the services
man owes to man', 'meditates new arts on Nature's plan'—see *The Minstrel;
or, The Progress of Genius. A Poem, in Two Books*, 6th edn (London: Edward and
Charles Dilly; Edinburgh: W. Creech, 1779), p. 61.

4, l. 46 Blackandro's summit a wooded hill, just north of Bowhill in Selkirkshire.

4, l. 47 Bowhill the seat of the Dukes of Buccleuch. The modern house, built
between 1750 and 1850, is four miles west of Selkirk at the junction of the
Ettrick and Yarrow. Scott's *The Lay of the Last Minstrel* (1805) is performed by
the Minstrel at Newark, an older and ruinous Buccleuch residence a little
up-river from Bowhill.

4, l. 48 hymn [...] to the Virgin for an account of Hogg's sympathy with pre-
Reformation devotion to the Virgin Mary in *The Pilgrims of the Sun* see
Douglas S. Mack, 'Hogg and the Blessed Virgin Mary', *SHW*, 3 (1992), 68–
75.

4, l. 55 Heaven in pity earnest sent Hogg's use of the word earnest creates an
analogy between the foretaste of an afterlife divinely granted to Mary Lee
in her vision and the arrals, or earnest-money, given by an employer to a
servant on ratifying their contract.

4, l. 59 The third night of the waning moon folk belief associated the waning
moon with diminished energy. Trees offered less resistance to being cut
down under a waning moon, and business affairs and marriages were thought
to have a greater likelihood of success if they coincided with a waxing
moon. Hogg subsequently explains that on this night 'the spirits were free;
| That revels of fairies were held on the lea' (see Part Fourth, ll. 21–22).

5, l. 67 like the lily's bloom in paintings of the Annunciation, the visit of the
angel Gabriel to the Virgin Mary, a lily was often included as the symbol of
her purity.

5, l. 95 the ruby star presumably the unnamed star glows red in the light of
the setting sun.

5, l. 96 Eildon hills near the river Tweed between Melrose and Bowden in
Roxburghshire, according to legend magically cleft in three by the wizard
Michael Scott, a legend enacted in Hogg's *The Three Perils of Man* (1822). The
wizard was traditionally supposed to have been entombed at Melrose Ab-
bey. The Eildon Hills are also one of the places in Britain where King

Arthur and his knights lie asleep, waiting for their final call to battle, and associated with Thomas the Rhymer who delivered his prophecies under the Eildon Tree and was also a visitant of fairyland.

6, l. 103 she thought she saw her very form an early and clear signal that Mary Lee's translation is not a bodily one, like that of Kilmeny.

6, ll. 105–06 As ever you saw [...] yielding wind perhaps these lines were reworked by Hogg from a ballad original–compare the old Covenanter Nanny's 'As ever ye saw the rain down fa', | Or yet the arrow gae from the bow' in *The Brownie of Bodsbeck; and Other Tales*, 2 vols (Edinburgh: William Blackwood; London: John Murray, 1818), I, 99.

6, l. 108 the gloaming star Venus, named later as the Evening and the Morning star.

6, l. 110 the night's grey canopy Socia in Dryden's *Amphitryon*, III. 1. 50–51 refers to 'the dusky Canopy of Night inveloping the Hemisphere'–see *The Works of John Dryden: Volume XV. Plays*, ed. by Earl Miner, George R. Guffey, and Franklin B. Zimmerman (Berkeley and Los Angeles: University of Berkeley Press, 1976), p. 266. In Part Third of *The Pilgrims of the Sun* Hogg names Dryden as a poetic model, while Walter Scott had published an eighteen-volume edition of the works of Dryden in 1808.

6, l. 115 a saffron cloud Hogg also uses the phrase in 'The Russiadde', where Dame Venus promises Russ that she will take him to 'Sail on yon saffron cloud sublime'–see *Poetical Works*, III, 297–359 (p. 326).

6, l. 134 the gilded moon a phrase also used by Hogg in 'Mess John'–see *Mountain Bard*, p. 58 (l. 157, 1807 version).

6, l. 136 the maidens of the main one of whom is the subject of 'The Mermaid' in the *Midsummer Night Dreams* collection.

7, l. 145 Queen of Night the moon, contrasted to the sun, the abode of the 'God of Day'. The moon as Queen of Night, or Queen of Heaven, was traditionally associated with Diana the virgin huntress, and in Christian times with the Virgin Mary. This poetic commonplace was used by many writers from the seventeenth century onwards. Hogg's picture of the moon arising from the sea was also perhaps influenced by another title for the moon as virgin goddess, the Queen of Tides.

7, l. 153 streamers of the norland way the *aurora borealis*, or northern lights, caused by electrically-charged solar particles.

7, l. 155 the wraith of the waning moon the reflection of the waning moon on the water is contrasted with the 'moulded orb' Mary sees on high, as she herself is a human reflection of the Virgin Mary.

8, l. 178 Cheviot Cheviot Hill is the first in a range extending 25 miles southwest through the Borders to Peel Fell. It is the highest summit of the range and situated in Northumberland, 7 miles south-west of Wooler (Groome).

8, l. 187 chambers of the sun a phrase probably deriving ultimately from Psalm 104. 2–3, where God is 'clothed [...] in state' with light, and 'Who of his chambers doth the beams | within the waters lay'. William Blake refers to 'chambers of the East' and 'chambers of the sun' in his poem 'To the Muses', first published in his *Poetical Sketches* of 1783–see *The Poems of William Blake*, ed. by W. H. Stevenson and David V. Erdman (London: Longman, 1971 repr. 1980), p. 13.

8, l. 190 God of Day see *Mador*, p. 18 (Canto First, l. 130) for Hogg's use of this phrase elsewhere. His belief in the instinctive association between the godhead and the sun is also expressed in his epic *Queen Hynde* of 1824—see *Queen Hynde*, ed. by Suzanne Gilbert and Douglas S. Mack (S/SC, 1998), pp. 90–91, 174 (Book Third, ll. 1362–1407 and Book Fifth, l. 2137). See also Mary's mistaken assessment of Cela as 'heathen-born' because of his bowing to the sun (Part First, ll. 239–42). In his manuscript notes to *The Pilgrims of the Sun* Hogg had originally written, 'But it is an idea of which I never can entirely divest myself in all my contemplations of the glories of nature'—see 'Appendix 2', p. 156. The sun as God of Day in the present context is a symbolic counterpart to the Queen of Night.

8, l. 199 Harlaw cairn Cairn Hill in the Pentlands rises from Harlaw Muir.

9, l. 233 Seraph and cherubim's abode the two highest of the nine orders of angels. Milton refers to 'The great seraphic lords and cherubim | In close recess and secret conclave sat | A thousand demigods on golden seats'—see *Paradise Lost*, Book I, ll. 794–96 (p. 29).

10, l. 252 no attractive influence came Mary and Cela are outside the earth's gravitational field. See Hogg's Note III for his account of the outrage caused by this passage to one of his friends, reflected in the offence given by this 'error' to the 'mass-men' subsequently (p. 149).

11, ll. 297–98 my hill-harp [...] hang it on its ancient tree an allusion to Hogg's previous poetic persona of the native minstrel or bard in *The Mountain Bard* (1807), and more recently in *The Queen's Wake* (1813), where in the opening lines Hogg rejoices, 'I've found my Mountain Lyre again'—see *The Queen's Wake*, ed. by Douglas S. Mack (S/SC, 2004), p. 7. There is an obvious allusion to the blind minstrel Ossian, as well as to Scott's *The Lay of the Last Minstrel* of 1805.

11, ll. 301–02 holy harp of Judah's land [...] hung the willow boughs upon the harp also signifies the Old Testament King David, often portrayed with a harp, and traditionally the author of the Book of Psalms. In Psalm 137. 2 the exiled Israelites abandon their music and hang their 'harps upon the willows'.

11, l. 304 cedar groves of Lebanon a Biblical expression also employed, for instance, in Psalm 104. 16: '[...] the cedars that do stand | In Lebanon'.

11, l. 307 Israel's King King David, who was herding his father's sheep when anointed by the prophet Samuel as Saul's successor as King of Israel—see I Samuel 16. 11–13. The Ettrick Shepherd identifies with David as both minstrel and shepherd.

11, l. 312 Zion's holy hill compare Psalm 2. 6, 'And over Sion, my holy hill, | I have him King anointed'.

12, l. 315 On Kedar hills a warlike middle-eastern tribe—see Psalm 120. 5, where the psalmist laments 'That I in tabernacles dwell | to Kedar that belong'.

12, l. 316 Bethlehem's plain by night the shepherds were the first to be informed of the birth of Jesus, by a host of angels who appeared to them while they were out at night with their flocks—see Luke 2. 8–14.

12, l. 319 mountain lyre [...] wandering melody the harp of the Ettrick Shepherd concludes the list of notable shepherds. The closing lines of 'Part First' are reminiscent of the closing lines of *The Queen's Wake*, 'Where oft thy erring numbers born | Have taught the wandering winds to sing'—see *The Queen's Wake*, ed. by Douglas S. Mack (S/SC, 2004), p. 173 (Conclusion, ll. 392–93).

PART SECOND

12, l. 9 harp of Salem perhaps refering to the harp of King David, since Salem is a Hebrew word for 'peace' and through his playing David soothed the madness of King Saul—see I Samuel 16. 19–23.

12, l. 14 harp of David the old Testament King David was the reputed author of the Psalms, his harp being likened at the end of Part First to the hill-harp of James Hogg.

12, l. 16 Cela suggesting 'celestial'. The name may be another allusion to the psalms, since 'Selah', indicating perhaps some musical or liturgical direction, appears frequently there as well as three times in the prayer in Habbakuk 3. Alternatively, Shelah (meaning 'request') was the third son of Judah—see Genesis 38. 5, and O. Odelain and R. Séguineau, *Dictionary of Proper Names and Places in the Bible*, trans. by Matthew J. O'Connell (London: Robert Hale, 1982), p. 341.

13, l. 31 The motioned universe the idea of constant motion is borrowed from the Ptolemaic cosmos, though Hogg's is neither earth-centred nor human-centred.

13, l. 40 Or nigh, or distant, it was all the same Hogg suspends the laws of optics as well as gravity.

13, l. 59 pendent by some ray or viewless cord recalling Satan's first view of earth in Milton's *Paradise Lost*, Book II, ll. 1051–52: 'And fast by hanging in a golden chain | This pendent world' (p. 60).

14, l. 95 Tweed one of two major rivers in the Borders region (the other being the Teviot). It flows irregularly from southwest to northeast and enters the sea at Berwick. 'The Tweed is, for a considerable part of its course, the dividing line between the northern and southern parts of Britain, between Scotland and England. The valley through which it flows, and the glens watered by its tributary streams, form the main area of the Border District'—see John Veitch, *The History and Poetry of the Scottish Border*, 2 vols (Edinburgh: Blackwood, 1893), I, 2. Robert Chambers, in recalling a rhyme comparing the Tweed to the Till, characterises it as 'a broad, shallow, clear, and rapid river' by comparison to its English tributary—see *Popular Rhymes of Scotland* (Edinburgh: William Hunter, 1826), pp. 34–35.

14, l. 104 Caledonian mountains John Veitch in *The History and Poetry of the Scottish Border*, 2 vols (Edinburgh: Blackwood, 1893) comments that 'any one who views the region from one of its higher hills will be struck with the predominating mountainous appearance of the country, and will almost wonder how it can support the population it does. There are aspects of it thus seen which may even tempt one to put the question as to how man has come to secure a footing amid its wilds at all. Its most prominent feature is the great backbone of hills, which stretches from Loch Ryan on the south-west to St Abb's Head on the north-east, cut across now and again by a water-course, but still fairly continuous from sea to sea. These occupy by themselves and their offshoots the greater part of the region. In Tweeddale and in Galloway they rise to a height of upwards of 2700 feet, and for long miles of country they are more than 2000 feet above sea-level' (I, 1–2).

15, l. 106 the lone Saint Mary St Mary's Loch, a deep lake, seven-and-a-half miles in circumference, in the Yarrow valley. Hogg's poem 'St. Mary of the Lows' opens with an address to 'lone St. Mary of the waves'—see *Queer Book*,

p. 153.

15, l. 137 yon cloudy spot a phrase used by Milton in describing Raphael's flight down to Paradise in *Paradise Lost*, Book V, l. 266 (p. 122).

16, l. 150 all these fair worlds inhabited Robert Burton, citing Kepler, confronts the same dilemma: 'But who shall dwell in these vast bodies, Earths, Worlds, *if they be inhabited? rationall creatures*, as *Kepler* demands? *Or have they soules to be saved? Or doe they inhabit a better part of the World than wee doe? Are we or they Lords of the world? And how are all things made for man?*'—*The Anatomy of Melancholy*, ed. by Nicolas K. Kiessling, Thomas C. Faulkner, and Rhonda L. Blair, 6 vols (Oxford: Clarendon Press, 1989–2000), II, 53.

16, l. 176 the earthly pilgrim the pilgrim as a journeyer to a sacred place is an emblem of the Christian's passage to heaven in Bunyan's allegory, *The Pilgrim's Progress*, published in 1684. The idea of life as a state of passage to a goal derives in part from Hebrews 11. 13 where those who have died in the faith had 'confessed that they were strangers and pilgrims on the earth'.

17, l. 199 After a thousand years' progression Hogg posits a system of spiritual evolution, but clearly within limits since in Part Third there appears to be a hell where atheists suffer 'eternal grief' (l. 394).

18, ll. 224–25 men of all creeds, | Features, and hues compare Hogg's plea for mutual toleration between Presbyterian and Episcopalian in 'Verses Addressed to the Right Honourable Lady Anne Scott of Buccleuch', that the difference of creed is small and that 'As flowers which vary in their dyes, | We all shall bloom in Paradise' (ll. 79–80).

18, l. 253 all were in progression for a discussion of Hogg's order of beings see Richard D. Jackson, 'James Hogg's *The Pilgrims of the Sun* and the Great Chain of Being', *SHW*, 18 (2007), 65–76.

19, l. 270 Leaning upon their harps the heavenly assembly and concert perhaps derive from Milton's *Paradise Lost*, Book III, ll. 344–415 (pp. 71–73).

19, l. 283 the polar wain the seven bright stars of the Great Bear, or Charles's Wain constellation, include the polar star. For another use of this expression by Hogg see *Queen Hynde*, ed. by Suzanne Gilbert and Douglas S. Mack (S/SC, 1998), p. 79 (Book Third, l. 885).

19, l. 299 the missioners of heaven the mechanism for keeping order in the universe of an active, interventionist God. Guardian angels or spirits are alluded to in other poems in *Midsummer Night Dreams*, such as 'The Haunted Glen' and 'The Field of Waterloo'.

21, ll. 359–61 "O! holy! holy! holy! [...] evermore shall be compare Revelation 4, another source for Hogg's description of the heavenly assembly. In verse 8 four angels chant 'Holy, holy, holy, Lord God Almighty, which was, and is, and is to come'.

21, l. 378 The ways of God with man Milton's objective in *Paradise Lost* was to 'assert eternal providence, | And justify the ways of God to men'—see Book I, ll. 25–26 (p. 4).

22, l. 396 halo of bright golden air the sun's corona, the halo of radiating white light that can be seen during a total eclipse.

22, l. 402 that mysterious chain see note to p. 13, l. 59 above.

22, l. 413 roaming meteor see also 'Verses to the Comet of 1811', and notes to that poem, for a discussion of traditional and contemporary views of comets that were available to Hogg. Hogg's own note V is particularly addressed to what he terms the critical reception of this passage on its appearance in the first edition of *The Pilgrims of the Sun* (1815).

23, l. 426 the downfall of a sentenced world the end of the world, prefiguring the Last Judgement, is signalled in the Bible by the fall of stars—see Revelation 8. 10 and 9. 1.

23, l. 430 the golden cord this apocalyptic passage may contain an allusion to the time before judgment, 'Or ever the silver cord be loosed, or the golden bowl be broken', in Ecclesiastes 12. 6.

23, l. 443 The realms of night when Satan leaves the gate of hell in *Paradise Lost* he confronts 'The secrets of the hoary deep, a dark | Illimitable ocean without bound, | Without dimension, where length, breadth and heighth,| And time and place are lost'—see Book II, ll. 891–94 (p. 56).

24, l. 462 Showering thin flame, and shining vapour forth Sara Schechner Genuth explains in *Comets, Popular Culture, and the Birth of Modern Cosmology* (Princeton, NJ: Princeton University Press, 1997) that Newton and Halley had reformulated comet lore in terms of natural philosophy, and strengthened the belief that comets were the agents of cosmological circulation, reinforcing the sun and replenishing the humidity necessary for vegetation. Kant and Buffon also believed that comets 'could stoke the solar fires'. William Herschel (1738–1822) believed that comets travelled from sun to sun picking up new matter as they did so, until they grew to the size of planets. Pierre-Simon Laplace (1749–1827) viewed comets as outsiders to the solar system, formed from a random accumulation of diverse matter (pp. 185–87, 210).

24, l. 478 like two swans perhaps an image suggesting the coming union of the pair. The narrator of Spenser's 'Prothalamion' notes 'two Swannes of goodly hewe, | Come softly swimming downe along the Lee; | Two fairer Birds I yet did neuer see'—see *Spenser: Poetical Works*, ed. by J. C. Smith and E. de Selincourt (London: Oxford University Press, 1912 repr. 1965), p. 601 (ll. 37–39).

24, l. 485 Far other scenes a phrase occuring in Wordsworth's address to Coleridge in the second book of *The Prelude* (l. 467)—see *William Wordsworth*, ed. by Stephen Gill (Oxford: Oxford University Press, 1984), p. 404. It is also used by Coleridge in 'Frost at Midnight' (l. 51)—see *The Collected Works of Samuel Taylor Coleridge: Poetical Works I*, ed. by J. C. Mays (Princeton, NJ: Princeton University Press, 2001), p. 455. Hogg visited the Lake District in September 1814.

PART THIRD

24, l. 1 IMPERIAL England according to Timothy Parsons 'In 1815, the overseas British Empire consisted of the remaining North American colonies (which would eventually become Canada), India, the Cape Colony in southern Africa, the New South Wales territory in Australia, and a handful of naval bases scattered throughout the globe'—see *The British Imperial Century, 1815–1914* (Oxford: Rowman & Littlefield, 1999), p. 4.

24, l. 3 Peruvia's shore despite Hogg's later definition of the imperial harp as that of Dryden and Pope this image irresistibly recalls Samuel Johnson, an admired writer whose influence on Hogg is regrettably underestimated because of his notorious attacks on the Scots. In the opening lines of *The Vanity of Human Wishes* observation is to 'Survey Mankind, from *China* to *Peru*'—see *The Poems of Samuel Johnson*, ed. by David Nichol Smith and Edward L. McAdam (Oxford: Clarendon Press, 1974), p. 115.

25, l. 8 Well may'st thou lend what erst was not thine own Hogg's empire appears to be a two-way cultural traffic, reflecting the major part played by Scots in both the British empire and London cultural life. The Manchester novelist Elizabeth Gaskell makes a similar point about the drain of talent to London in a humorous fashion in *Wives and Daughters*. Miss Browning considers London 'a pickpocket and a robber dressed up in the spoils of honest folk'—see *Wives and Daughters*, ed. by Angus Easson (Oxford: Oxford University Press, 1987), p. 476.

25, l. 10 Dryden's twang, and Pope's malicious knell John Dryden (1631–1700) and Alexander Pope (1688–1744) were both composers of celebrated poetic epics as well as satirists: Dryden's verse translation of Virgil's *Aeneid* and Pope's translation of Homer's *Iliad* into heroic couplets are probably what Hogg has in mind here.

25, l. 14 crabbe that grovels on the sandy shore a reference to the poet George Crabbe (1754–1832), who had published *The Parish Register* (1807), *The Borough* (1810), and *Tales* (1812). Hogg may have found Crabbe's realism depressingly unrelieved, since in his letter to John Murray of 21 January 1815 Hogg remarks that *The Pilgrims of the Sun* is 'as far superior to any thing in the *Wake* as Milton is above Mr. Crabbe' (*Letters*, I, 234). There is no evidence of any personal quarrel.

25, l. 18 Come to the silent moorland dale the imperial harp, in keeping with Hogg's earlier references, is taken back to Scotland from south-eastern England, becoming less strident when 'swept by the winds, and mellowed by the dew'.

25, l. 31 wicked worlds the phrase also occurs in 'The Legend of S. Calidore or Of Courtesie' in Book 6 of Edmund Spenser's *The Faerie Queen*—see *Spenser: Poetical Works*, ed. by J. C. Smith and E. de Selincourt (London: Oxford University Press, 1912 repr. 1965), p. 336 (ll. 19–22):

> Reuele to me the sacred noursery
> Of vertue, which with you doth there remaine,
> Where it in siluer bowre does hidden ly
> From view of men, and wicked worlds disdaine.

Hogg was 'fond of the Spenserian measure' and his recently-composed *Mador of the Moor* had been intended 'to give the world a new specimen of this stanza in its proper harmony'—see *Altrive Tales*, p. 35.

25, l. 36 long and still the night compare Hogg's preference in his letter to Margaret Phillips of 20 August 1819 for a November wedding, 'when the nights are long and cold. I would not venture on it just now on any account' (*Letters*, I, 414).

26, l. 54 love can every power of earth controul *amor vincit omnia* ('Love conquers all') is a popular tag, familiar from Virgil, *Eclogues*, X, 69–see Virgil, *Eclogues, Georgics, Aeneid* I–VI, ed. by H. Rushton Fairclough (London: William Heineman, 1935 repr. 1986), pp. 74–75.

26, l. 65 the dreary bourn of death compare *Hamlet*, III. 1. 81–82: 'The undiscovered country from whose bourn | No traveller returns'.

27, l. 88 nurseries of life the passage from Book 6 of Spenser's *The Fairy Queen* which refers to 'wicked worlds' also mentions 'the sacred noursery | Of vertue'—see note to 25, l. 31.

27, l. 92 Souls, thick as blossoms of the vernal field a recollection perhaps of Milton's 'Thick as autumnal leaves that strew the brooks | In Vallombrosa' in *Paradise Lost*, Book I, ll. 302–03 (p. 13).

27, l. 102 the garden of the God of heaven recalling Eden, where God went 'walking in the garden in the cool of the day' (see Genesis 3. 8) and thus the Fall of Man.

27, l. 104 The tree [...] immortal fruit recalling both the tree of the Knowledge of Good and Evil in Eden, and the cross on which Jesus was crucified, obviously central to Milton's *Paradise Lost*.

27, l. 105 she, all selfish a marked contrast to the high value placed on perpetual virginity in 'Kilmeny' in *The Queen's Wake*.

27, l. 108 She sinks into the dust a nameless thing Hogg seems to echo Scott's 'The wretch, concentered all in self [...] doubly dying, shall go down | To the vile dust, from whence he sprung, | Unwept, unhonoured, and unsung'—see *The Lay of the Last Minstrel. A Poem* (Edinburgh: Archibald Constable; London: Longman, Hurst, Rees, and Orme, 1805), p. 162 (Canto VI, ll. 12–15).

28, l. 139 Beauty with wisdom shall have heritage perhaps recalling the 'goodly heritage' promised in Psalm 16. 6 to those who put their trust in God.

28, ll. 145–46 either perpetual blessings [...] endless woe Calvinist theology insisted that the soul's future fate was determined at the moment of its separation from the body by death, as William Blackwood subsequently pointed out in his letter to Hogg of 17 September 1831 (NLS, MS 30,312, p. 225), objecting to Hogg's 'On the Separate Existence of the Soul': 'it is directly in the teeth of revelation to permit the soul to exist separately for one moment without at once having its eternal state fixed'. Praying for the dead was therefore wrong, and when a minister recommended that prayers be said for a vanished child he added 'if she is dead, God will forgive our sin in praying for the dead, as we do it through ignorance'—see *The Queen's Wake*, ed. by Douglas S. Mack (S/SC, 2004), p. 186.

28, l. 148 the Evening and the Morning Star Venus, the planet named after the goddess of love.

28, l. 150 old Lindeen Lindean church, disused since 1586, was near the confluence of Ettrick Water with the Tweed about 2 miles north-east of Selkirk. The body of William Douglas, knight of Liddesdale, lay there the night after his assassination in 1353 (Groome). It is also the place where Mary's mother inters her body during this spiritual journey.

28, ll. 155–56 yon gloomy sphere [...] crimson in 'Palamon and Arcite; or, The Knight's Tale' Dryden also uses the phrase 'the gloomy sphere'—see *The Poems and Fables of John Dryden*, ed. by James Kinsley (London: Oxford University Press, 1962 repr. 1969), p. 582 (Book III, l. 218). Here Hogg refers to the planet Mars, named after the god of war because of its reddish tinge.

29, l. 163 Like simple babes, the land of peace to win recalling the instruction 'As newborn babes, desire the sincere milk of the word' in I Peter 2. 2. Subsequently Cela insists that the spirits of this world must 'beg the bosom of a child again'.

29, l. 184 shoally darkness Ian Duncan suggests that the margin between night and day is likened to the margin between land and water, parallel perhaps to the 'bank and shoal of time' in *Macbeth*, I. 7. 6. Patches of faint gloaming light could be seen as shallows, particularly in the light of Hogg's earlier use of the phrase 'the steeps of night' (Part Second, l. 439).

29, l. 194 the wind our charioteer compare 'Verses Addressed to the Right Honourable Lady Anne Scott of Buccleuch', 'The breeze of heaven my charioteer' (l. 168).

30, l. 214 pierced the bosom of the hideous night Shakespeare uses the expression 'hideous night' in Sonnet 12 (l. 2), and Edward Young also has 'hideous *Night*' in *The Consolation* (London: G. Hawkins, 1745), p. 78. See also Milton's association of 'Chaos and old Night' and reference to 'sable-vested Night, eldest of things' in *Paradise Lost*, Book I, l. 543 and Book II, l. 962 (pp. 21, 58).

30, l. 223 pilgrim birds migrating birds from Northern Europe.

30, l. 230 Albyn's coast Albany, from a celtic word for rock or cliff, is an ancient name for the North of Scotland, and surviving in place-names such as Breadalbane in western Perthshire.

30, l. 235 the bloody sun compare 'The bloody sun at noon, | Right up above the mast did stand, | No bigger than the moon', in Samuel Taylor Coleridge, 'The Rime of the Ancient Mariner', Part II, ll. 112–14—see *The Collected Works of Samuel Taylor Coleridge: Poetical Works I*, ed. by J. C. Mays (Princeton, NJ: Princeton University Press, 2001), p. 380.

31, l. 242 culture probably agriculture, in view of the 'scathed soil'.

31, l. 250 A fiend, that in Tartarian gulf was tossed the infernal regions of classical mythology were called Tartarus. The fiend is Napoleon, subsequently characterised again as a 'wolfish fiend, from hell that thither came'.

31, l. 256 The scourge of God alluding to the idea frequently expressed in the Old Testament that the victories of Israel's enemies are permitted by God as a punishment for his people's sins. Christopher Marlowe's Tamburlaine refers to himself as 'the scourge and terrour of the world'—see *Tamburlaine Part II*, I. 3. 60, in *The Complete Works of Christopher Marlowe*, ed. by Fredson Bowers, 2nd edn, 2 vols (Cambridge: Cambridge University Press, 1981), I, 161.

31, l. 258 stars in courses fight upon his side see Judges 5. 20, where Deborah in celebration of Jael rejoices that 'the stars in their courses fought against Sisera'.

31, ll. 259–60 "On yon high mountain [...] the times that are to be an equivalent passage to the one where Kilmeny in the Land of Thought is taken to 'ane mountyn greine, | To see quhat mortyl nevir had seine', and witnesses the future fate of Mary, Queen of Scots, and the Napoleonic Wars—see *The Queen's Wake*, ed. by Douglas S. Mack (S/SC, 2004), pp. 96–98.

31, l. 261 deeds of weir a favourite Hogg phrase, also used in his song 'To the Ancient Banner of Buccleuch' written when Hogg was both celebrating the martial past of the Buccleuch family and the end of the Napoleonic wars—see his letter to Scott of 24 November [1815] in *Letters*, I, 258–59.

31, l. 262 first performed by warrior spirits here Hogg's assertion elsewhere that the inhabitants of the planets Mary and Cela visit are in a state of spiritual progression after death seems to be contradicted by the fact that here their actions are prophetic of the future on earth.

31, l. 263 one eternal chain compare Hogg's description elsewhere of a pure maiden forming 'That link of the eternal chain, | Which earth unto the heavens combined'—see *Queen Hynde*, ed. by Suzanne Gilbert and Douglas

S. Mack (S/SC, 1998), p. 15 (Book First, ll. 413–14).

32, l. 287 Long yet the time, ere wasting war shall cease Hogg seems to have cherished the hope at first that the Napoleonic Wars constituted a war to end wars, so far as Europe was concerned. See *A Series of Lay Sermons*, ed. by Gillian Hughes with Douglas S. Mack (S/SC, 1997), p. 41: 'After the campaigns of Buonaparte, and the slaughter of so many millions among the most civilised nations on the face of the earth, and which ended so completely in smoke, I really thought there would never be any more wars in Europe, but that all would be settled by arbitration'.

32, l. 304 'Tis the high right of nations to decree a statement favouring the self-determination of peoples.

33, ll. 315–16 Those triple minds [...] Are called Silesians Silesia is a province in the east of Germany, and Silesian troops had been a notable force during the wars of Frederick the Great of Prussia, between 1740 and 1745. The army of Silesia in 1813 numbered approximately 57,00 Prussian and Russian troops commanded by Gebhard Leberecht Blücher (1742–1819)– see Antony Brett-James, *Europe Against Napoleon: The Leipzig Campaign, 1813 from Eyewitness Accounts* (London: Macmillan, 1970), pp. 41–55.

33, l. 323 What is the soldier but an abject fool Hogg also expresses anti-militaristic sentiments in 'Sermon IV. Soldiers', in *A Series of Lay Sermons*, ed. by Gillian Hughes with Douglas S. Mack (S/SC, 1997), pp. 40–47.

33, l. 341 a watery world of sea and shore each occupation seems to have its planet. As the lovers have Venus and the soldiers Mars, it might be supposed that Neptune is intended here, but in fact this planet was not discovered until 1846.

34, l. 349 One mighty hill Parnassus, a mountain near Delphi with two summits, one of which was dedicated to Apollo and the nine Muses and was regarded as the seat of poetry and music.

34, l. 353 a world accursed that of lawyers, since the words 'deeds, respondents, and replies' form part of the jargon of the legal profession.

34, l. 364 bedesmen discontent Hogg contrasts the actual materialism of priests with their reputed spirituality, particularly in eating and money-getting. These are testaments, or witnesses, against them.

34, ll. 366–67 snarling critics [...] circumvent the poor Hogg also attacks critics in 'Sermon X. Reviewers' in *A Series of Lay Sermons*, ed. by Gillian Hughes with Douglas S. Mack (S/SC, 1997), pp. 99–107. His chief criticism there, however, is rather that writers are pre-judged on political or party grounds than that they are judged by wealth or social status.

34, l. 368 knowing patriots perhaps recalling Johnson's famous dictum that 'Patriotism is the last refuge of a scoundrel'–see James Boswell, *Life of Johnson*, ed. by R. W. Chapman, rev. J. D. Fleeman, 3rd edn (London: Oxford University Press, 1970, repr. 1989), p. 615.

35, l. 394 their eternal grief atheists seem to be excepted from the spiritual progression posited by Hogg, and to languish in the traditional hellfire.

35, l. 415 Phillip plain Philiphaugh, to the west of Selkirk close to the confluence of the Ettrick and the Yarrow, and scene of the Covenanting victory over the Royalist forces of the Marquis of Montrose on 13 September 1645 that ended Montrose's succession of splendid military victories. Hogg later focused on this battle in 'Wat Pringle o' the Yair'–see *Tales of the Wars of Montrose*, ed. by Gillian Hughes (S/SC, 1996), pp. 191–222.

36, l. 427 something were unmeet Mary's body is no longer at her bower to be reanimated.

36, l. 449 yon hoary pile the church of Lindean.

37, l. 482 my ancient harp again the hill-harp of Part First—see note to p. 11, ll. 297–98.

PART FOURTH

37, l. 8 The river-lark probably the common sandpiper, whose plaintive call can often be heard at night by rivers in Scotland. The word 'lark' is often used in the old regional names for several wading birds, and 'sand lark' in Scotland for the sandpiper (information from David Shirt). Hogg refers to the sandpiper as 'the sand-lark' in 'Ane Waefu' Scots Pastoral'—see *Contributions to Annuals and Gift-Books*, ed. by Janette Currie and Gillian Hughes (S/ SC, 2006), p. 29 (l. 41).

38, l. 30 the old borough town Selkirk, on the banks of the Ettrick, originating in a monastic settlement dating back at least to 1126—see T. Craig-Brown, *The History of Selkirkshire*, 2 vols (Edinburgh: David Douglas, 1886), II, 2.

38, l. 31 thrice the bedesman renewed the host the host is the consecrated bread of the Eucharist, or Mass. It seems surprising that the priest would perform mass three times overnight, but this may be part of a ritual designed to secure the return of a missing person. In a similar situation in 'The Hunt of Eildon' holy men suggest to the King 'that prayers should be offered up' for two missing children 'in seven times seven holy chapels and cells at the same instant of time, and the like number of masses said, with all due solemnity; and that then it would be out of the power of all the spirits of the infernal regions [...] to detain the children longer'—see *The Brownie of Bodsbeck; And Other Tales*, 2 vols (Edinburgh: William Blackwood; London: John Murray, 1818), II, 229–346 (pp. 299–300).

39, l. 68 seraph Hope both the hope of bodily recovery and the hope of the resurrection in Christ.

39, ll. 80–81 Between her breasts [...] begirt her head presumably attempts to determine whether life is still extant in a body, like putting a feather or holding a mirror to the lips for evidence of breathing. Faye Getz remarks, 'the boundary between the living and the dead was further obscured by the difficulty medieval people had in determining whether life had actually left a body irretrievably, in the modern sense. One chronicler remarked that revival of the dead after a couple of days was not unusual in England, but that after seven days it was very surprising'—see *Medicine in the English Middle Ages* (Princeton, NJ: Princeton University Press, 1998), p. 92. Robert S. Gottfried cites a method given by Gilbertus Anglicus, 'Place a little vessel full of water on her breast; if it moves, she is alive, but if not, she is dead'—see *Doctors and Medicine in Medieval England 1340–1530* (Princeton, NJ: Princeton University Press, 1986), p. 194.

39, l. 83 another moon Mary disappeared on 'the third night of the waning moon' (Part First, l. 59), three days into the second half of the twenty-nine day lunation, so that an interval of about ten days is probably implied here since the lunar cycle is counted from new moon to new moon.

39, l. 84 the lykewake maidens an unbroken vigil beside the coffin until the funeral, based on the belief that a corpse must never be left alone. Young virgins kept this watch over the body of one of their own.

40, l. 87 gentle shivering of the chin a phrase also cited by Hogg in *The Queen's Wake* and deriving from the traditional ballad 'The Mother's Malison, or, Clyde's Water'—see *The Queen's Wake*, ed. by Douglas S. Mack (S/SC, 2004), pp. 39, 412. Hogg indicates in his Note I to the poem (see p. 148) that this movement was simultaneous with the point in Mary Lee's vision where she became insensible after hearing the angels' song of praise to God.

40, l. 123 To cut the rings and fingers away in his Note I Hogg describes the subject-matter of *The Pilgrims of the Sun* as 'founded on a traditional tale well known over all Scotland, and affirmed to have happened, not only at old Lindeen, but in some lonely and eiry churchyard here and there over the whole country' (p. 148). One reviewer of Hogg's poem located the legend to 'the church of St. Giles, Cripplegate' in London—see *The Pilgrims of the Sun* in the *New Monthly Magazine*, 3 (February 1815), 54. The episode of the cutting away of a ring-finger reawakening a supposed corpse appears to have European currency. A similar case, reported on the authority of 'Father *Le Clerc*, formerly Principal of the College of *Lewis* the Great', is given in Jacques Bénigne Winslow (1669–1760), *The Uncertainty of the Signs of Death, and the Danger of Precipitate Interments and Dissections, Demonstrated [...]*, trans. by T. T. Bruhier d'Ablaincourt (London: M. Cooper, 1746), p. 7:

> [...] the Sister of his Father's first Wife being interr'd with a Ring on her Finger in the publick Church-Yard of *Orleans*, next Night a Domestick, induced by the Hopes of Gain, uncovered and opened the Coffin, but finding that he could not pull the Ring off the Finger, began to cut the latter; the violent Agitation produced in the Nerves by the Wound, rouzed the Woman, whose hideous Shrieks, extorted by the Pain, not only struck Terror into the sacrilegious Robber, but also put him to Flight without his intended Booty; the Woman in the mean time disengaged herself, as well as possible, from her Shroud, returned home, and lived with her Husband ten Years, during which Time she furnished him with an Heir and Representative of his Family.

41, l. 157 The dead-rose waved upon her breast perhaps simply flowers strewed on a corpse, but the reference by Mary's mother subsequently to 'The grave-rose that my own hands made' (Part Fourth, l. 230) perhaps implies a rose or rosette of ribbons adorning the shroud. A third possibility is a rose that has been deliberately smashed or broken to indicate death. Christopher Daniell, in *Death and Burial in Medieval England 1066–1550* (London: Routledge, 1997) notes the 'continuation of the practice of bending, folding or breaking objects throughout the Middle Ages to signify death' (p. 151). Hogg also writes 'The dead rose rustles on the breast' in 'Elen of Reigh', and refers to 'The dead rose and funereal wreath | Above the breast of virgin snow' in 'St. Mary of the Lows'—see *Queer Book*, pp. 50, 155.

41, l. 160 'Twas late, late on a Sabbath night a formulaic phrase used by Hogg elsewhere. See for instance 'Lete, lete in the glomyn, Kilmeny came heme' in *The Queen's Wake*, ed. by Douglas S. Mack (S/SC, 2004), p. 92, and also the opening line of 'The Pedlar' ('Twas late, late, late on a Saturday's night') in *Mountain Bard*, p. 26 (1807 version).

41, l. 161 the hour of the ghost traditionally ghosts would appear at midnight and vanish at cock-crow in the morning.

42, l. 169 Each hair had life, and stood upright the ghost of Hamlet's father expects the hair of his listeners to 'stand on end | Like quills upon the fretful porcupine'—see *Hamlet*, I. 5. 19–20.

43, l. 226 *my* glass is run an hour-glass filled with sand was used as a measurement of time, and an emblem of the shortness of human life.

44, ll. 258–59 I pledge no word [...] | The virgin's tale I have told to you a narrative disclaimer comparable to the emphasis in Hogg's notes to the poem that this is the report of a vision and not a relation of historical events. Compare, for instance, Scott's declaration, 'I cannot tell how the truth may be; | I say the tale as 'twas said to me' in Canto II of *The Lay of the Last Minstrel. A Poem* (Edinburgh: Archibald Constable; London: Longman, Hurst, Rees, and Orme, 1805), p. 51 (ll. 262–63). For a detailed examination of the ways in which Hogg balances credulity and disbelief elsewhere see Jill Rubenstein, 'Varieties of Explanation in *The Shepherd's Calendar*', *SHW*, 4 (1993), 1–11.

44, l. 260 vouched, by age and worth compare Hogg's defence of his portrait of Claverhouse and the Royalists in *The Brownie of Bodsbeck* to Scott: 'I had it frae them whom I was most bound to honour and believe'—see *Anecdotes of Scott*, ed. by Jill Rubenstein (S/SC, 1999), p. 51.

45, l. 280 Her blood yet runs in Minstrel veins as Hogg's narrative goes on to relate, Mary marries Hugo the Harper, a counterpart to Hogg the hill-harper of Part First of *Pilgrims of the Sun*. It is implied that James Hogg is the descendant of Mary Lee and Hugo. After his marriage Hugo becomes a shepherd.

45, l. 290 rose of paradise flowers that grew in the mythical Garden of Eden, but perhaps also referring to some native Scottish wild-flower. Jock Allanson in 'Mary Burnet' understands that the girl he sees at Moffat hiring-fair is looking for a place because 'she had the badge of servitude in her bosom, a little rose of Paradise, without the leaves, so that Allanson knew she was to hire'—see *The Shepherd's Calendar*, ed. by Douglas S. Mack (S/SC, 1995), pp. 200–22 (p. 210).

46, l. 336 every heart, as he desired Hugo's power over his audience and positive reception compared to the abject situation of the Bard of Ettrick mark an increase of confidence on Hogg's part since the publication of *The Queen's Wake* in 1813.

46, l. 341 Hugo of Norroway Hogg seems to have associated northern Europe with the fairies and with witchcraft. The Witch of Fife flies through Norway to Lapland to meet 'warlock men and the weerd wemyng, | And the fays of the wood and the steep', together with mermaids and phantom hunters—see *The Queen's Wake*, ed. by Douglas S. Mack (S/SC, 2004), p. 44. In a letter to Byron of 14 August 1814 Hogg wrote, 'I have been thinking my lord that Norway would be a fine scene for romance, nay I am sure of it if the names of the country are as appropriate as the shores, seas mountains and primitive inhabitants are. I wish you would make the tour of it and take me with you'—see *Letters*, I, 194–95.

46, l. 345 Melrose fane Melrose Abbey, founded by David I of Scotland in 1136 and subsequently burned by the English under Richard II in 1385. The surviving ruins (including the Perpendicular-style choir) largely post-date this period. Scott famously described these ruins in some detail urging the reader to 'visit it by the pale moon-light'—see the opening of Canto II of

The Lay of the Last Minstrel. A Poem (Edinburgh: Archibald Constable; London: Longman, Hurst, Rees, and Orme, 1805), p. 35 (l. 2).

48, l. 403 The flower of the Forest most obviously the choicest girl in the Ettrick Forest district, but perhaps too with an allusion to the celebrated song of 'The Flowers of the Forest', which alludes to the heavy casualties of that district in the battle of Flodden in 1513 with its lament that 'The Flowers of the Forest | Are a' wede away'.

48, ll. 416–17 The first [...] The shepherd's rich and peaceful art in his essay on the 'Statistics of Selkirkshire' Hogg dates the change in Ettrick Forest from a hunting preserve to a pastoral country to the time of James IV of Scotland (1473–1513, ruled from 1488), who was killed at the battle of Flodden–see 'Statistics of Selkirkshire', *Prize Essays and Transactions of the Highland Society of Scotland*, new series, 3 (1832), 281–306 :

> The forest of Ettrick continued a hunting station of the kings of Scotland from the days of Alexander the Third to those of Queen Mary Stuart, who was the last sovereign that visited it [...] But by some means or other, the Douglasses and other feudal lords had taken the whole of the revenues into their hands, for the space of 200 years. In 1503, however, James the Fourth resumed his royal rights over the district, took it all again into his own hands, stocked it with 20,000 sheep [...] and thus began the first attempt at improvement in Selkirkshire, by a brave and beloved sovereign, whose temerity afterwards cost the natives so dear. (pp. 290–91)

Hogg goes on to state that the black-faced sheep common to the district in his own youth were 'all from the king's breed'.

48, l. 437 his body was lost Hugo's ascent as a spirit further identifies him with Cela, while the 'fairy rose' emphasises his affinity with the fairy lovers of 'Tam Lin' and 'The Haunted Glen'.

49, ll. 465–66 A lovely form [...] Round green Bowhill Hogg's patron, Harriet, Duchess of Buccleuch, who as Hogg's note VII records (pp. 151–52), died as *The Pilgrims of the Sun* was in the course of publication, on 24 August 1815. Hogg gives an account of her in *Altrive Tales*, pp. 53–54, and besides this tribute wrote another poem on her death which he presented to her widower and published in the Edinburgh newspapers–see Gillian Hughes, 'Hogg's Poetic Responses to the Unexpected Death of his Patron', *SHW*, 12 (2001), 80–89.

Connel of Dee

According to Hogg's 'Memoir of the Author's Life' 'Connel of Dee' was the first of the *Midsummer Night Dreams* poems to be written and was composed immediately after Hogg had finished writing *Mador of the Moor* in the early spring of 1814–see *Altrive Tales*, p. 35. It was not published, however, until the appearance of Hogg's collection of *Winter Evening Tales* in 1820, when it formed part of the section subtitled 'Country Dreams and Apparitions'–see *Winter Evening Tales*, pp. 410–25, 582. It was only republished once in Hogg's lifetime subsequently, in the second, or *Midsummer Night Dreams* volume of the 1822 *Poetical Works*–for further details see the entry for 'Connel of Dee' in the 'Note on the Texts'.

Duncan comments on the poem's 'combination of Hogg's "ancient style" and Gothic psychosexual fantasy' (*Winter Evening Tales*, p. 582), and points to Kate McGrail's argument that it represents a reworking of Dunbar's 'Tretis of the Tua Mariit Wemen and the Wedo'—see also 'Re-Making the Fire: James Hogg and the Makars', *SHW*, 7 (1996), 26–36 (pp. 30–32). The hellish vision of this poem, as Douglas Mack has indicated, is a match to and counterpart of, the heavenly vision of *The Pilgrims of the Sun*. The notes which follow are indebted to Ian Duncan's notes to 'Connel of Dee' in *Winter Evening Tales*.

51, l. 26 the bodyng Benshee the banshee is a Celtic death spirit, the name meaning 'Woman of the Hill', resembling a woman with long white hair and eyes red from constant weeping. Her wailing predicts the death of a member of the particular family to which the banshee attends.

54, l. 111 O Connel, dear Connel, be patient a while Hogg's humorous moralising address to the chief character of his poem may be modelled on Burns's similar ones in 'Tam o' Shanter' (Kinsley, no. 321). This was Hogg's favourite poem—see *Altrive Tales*, p. 18.

54, l. 125 balms of Arabia resinous gums or fragrant oils, though the murderous atmosphere concealed under the perfumes may also recall Lady Macbeth's 'All the perfumes of Arabia will not sweeten this little hand'—see *Macbeth*, v. 1. 48–49.

55, l. 141 the clear springing well Deeside waters were thought to be particularly salubrious. Robert Smith in *Valley of the Dee* (Aberdeen: Keith Murray, 1989), notes, 'In 1760, an old woman suffering from scrofula drank from a spring near Pannanich and bathed her sores in its waters. The "King's Evil", as the disease was called, disappeared—and Pannanich became the Lourdes of Deeside'. Smith also notes that the wells there are rich in iron, and that bath-houses were built there, sparking off a health-boom and bringing many visitors to Deeside. Byron's mother brought him there in 1795–96 to recuperate from scarlet fever (p. 42).

55, l. 145 The laverock the male lark was a symbol of love and poetry, because of his habit of singing high in the sky to the female on her nest. Hogg, in a letter to an unknown correspondent of 27 October 1833, wrote, 'The laverock (or skylark) has always been a peculiar favourite of mine, for he was, like myself, an inmate of the wilds, and the companion of my boyhood' (*Letters*, III, 182).

55, l. 151 blue bonnet part of the traditional dress of the male Scottish lowlander, and produced in great quantities in Dundee. The blue bonnet was the usual wear of agricultural labourers, servants, and soldiers, while merchants, professional men, and kirk elders might wear black. For instance Burns in 'The Holy Fair' writes of the church collection, 'A greedy glowr *Black-bonnet* throws, | An' we maun draw our tippence' (Kinsley, no. 70, ll. 66–67).

56, l. 180 eynied of him to make game although socially confident Hogg sometimes resented the ridicule drawn in Edinburgh by his unfashionable clothes and country manners—see, for instance, his letter to Timothy Tickler of 3 August 1818, in *Letters*, I, 367.

57, l. 219 kill her, at least, for her heinous offence the narrator's apparent justification of murder as a due punishment for infidelity is undercut by the irony and humour of 'at least' here.

57, l. 242 I have had some fair husbands ere now usually women are the victims in the Bluebeard story. Hogg may have known the ballad 'May

Colven' (Child, no. 4, 'Lady Isabel and the Elf-Knight') where the false Sir John carries the heroine to the coast and tells her to take off her costly dress before he throws her from a rock into the sea as he has done seven previous ladies. She asks him to turn his back while she undresses, and then when he is off-guard drowns him instead.

58, l. 258 A pair of dread shears Perrault's Bluebeard butchered his wives with a cutlass, a male implement. Shears perhaps suggest the female figure of Atropos, the eldest of the three Fates and the one who severs the thread of human life. The decapitation may also suggest fears of castration.

60, l. 329 He rainbowed the hawthorn spanned like a rainbow, presumably in jumping over a hawthorn shrub.

60, l. 329 needled the brake Hogg uses a similar image for a person alternately passing over and under an obstacle in 'The Witch of Fife', 'Quhan we culdna speil the brow of the wavis, | We needilit them throu belowe'—see *The Queen's Wake*, ed. by Douglas S. Mack (S/SC, 2004), p. 43.

60, l. 338 From *traps* of the wicked Ian Duncan points out that Psalms 140 and 141 are prayers for an escape from the snares of the wicked—see *Winter Evening Tales*, p. 582.

61, l. 359 O could he get over, how safe he might be running water formed a powerful barrier against evil. Burns, in a note to 'Tam o' Shanter', states, 'It is a well known fact that witches, or any evil spirits, have no power to follow a poor wight any farther than the middle of the next running stream' (Kinsley, no. 321).

61, l. 373 he had been sinning, and misery condign the suffering merited by crimes in this religious context probably implies damnation.

63, l. 430 the Cluny, or Gairn tributaries of the river Dee, as Ian Duncan indicates—see *Winter Evening Tales*, p. 582. The Clunie meets the Dee at Braemar, and the Gairn close to Ballater.

63, l. 450 his bowels about on the tide two lines from the poem in *Winter Evening Tales* have been cut here, presumably censored:

> One snapt him on place he no longer would bide.
> It was more than a dead man could bear!
>
> (*Winter Evening Tales*, p. 423)

64, l. 462 It was but a night, and a midsummer night the few hours of one of the shortest nights of the year, during which in reality Connel's vision occurred, contrast with the months that his marriage appeared to him to occupy. The celebration of Midsummer Day (24 June, dedicated to John the Baptist) was associated with the summer solstice before the change from the Julian to Gregorian calendar moved the shortest day of the year forward to 21 June. As Douglas Mack noted (*Winter Evening Tales*, p. 582) Midsummer Night is 'devoted to lovers, and is also a night (like Halloween) when spirits and supernatural beings are abroad', both important aspects of Shakespeare's *A Midsummer Night's Dream*, a play which must have influenced Hogg's choice of the title *Midsummer Night Dreams* for his own poetry collection.

65, l. 516 At kirk or at market the occasions when in rural areas large numbers of people would assemble. Hogg also uses this commonplace phrase in 'Storms', saying that the none of the shepherds who were popularly supposed to have raised the devil and thus been responsible for the devastations of the storm 'durst well show their faces at either kirk or mar-

ket for a whole year, and more'—see *The Shepherd's Calendar*, ed. by Douglas
S. Mack (S/SC, 1995), pp. 1–21 (p. 19).

65, l. 521 the fair in *Hood in Scotland* (Dundee, 1885) Alexander Elliot quotes
from an unfinished rhyming guide to Dundee by Thomas Hood, 'Some
large markets for cattle, or fairs, are held here, | On a moor near the town,
about thrice in a year', going on to describe the tents made up of blanket-
draped poles and the smoking, drinking, and quarelling that accompanied
the trading (pp. 70–71). Ian McCraw states that the most popular of the
Dundee fairs 'in terms of attendance both of customers and traders, were
undoubtedly the First or Lady Mary [held on 15 August] and Stobb's [held
in July], both held in the summer months. There is little to suggest that the
others ever enjoyed any significant degree of success'—see Ian McCraw, *The
Fairs of Dundee* (Dundee: Abertay Historical Society, 1994), p. 37. Connel
probably attended one of these.

Superstition

In his Notes in the *Midsummer Night Dreams* volume of his 1822 *Poetical Works*,
Hogg refers to 'Superstition' as one of a group of three poems forming part of
his *Midsummer Night Dreams* collection as conceived in 1814 (p. 148), despite his
statement elsewhere that it was composed during his visit to John Wilson at
Elleray in the Lake District in September 1814 after his original plan had been
abandoned—for details see 'Note on the Texts'. It was, however, first published
with *The Pilgrims of the Sun*, and certainly acts as a summary of many of the
themes running through not only that poem but through the *Midsummer Night
Dreams* collection as a whole. Hogg's declaration of 'visions that have been' and
'visions yet to be' as his subject-matter asserts his position as the 'king o' the
mountain and fairy school' (*Anecdotes of Scott*, ed. by Jill Rubenstein (S/SC,
1999), p. 9), while the line 'Be mine the faith diverging to extremes' formulates
the essential doubleness that many critics have detected in James Hogg. Here,
as so often in his work, Hogg juxtaposes a powerful depiction of the tradi-
tional life-style and superstitions of his upbringing with a dryer and conse-
quently less effective modern interpretation, chiefly given voice here in the
slightly jarring facetiousness of stanzas 21 and 22 where enchantment is re-
duced to flirtatiousness and witchcraft to malicious gossip. 'Superstition' (like
The Pilgrims of the Sun) also reveals the influence of a classic English poetic
tradition, particularly in its allusions to Thomas Gray's celebrated 'Elegy Writ-
ten in a Country Church-Yard'.

67, l. 1 Caledonia's glens Caledonia is the ancient Roman name for Scotland.
67, l. 6 Far from the busy world's unceasing stir echoing 'Far from the madding
crowd's ignoble strife', in Gray's 'Elegy Written in a Country Church-Yard'—
see *Thomas Gray and William Collins: Poetical Works*, ed. by Roger Lonsdale
(Oxford: Oxford University Press, 1977), p. 37 (l. 73). Hogg in this poem
also traces the 'annals of the poor', but emphasises their imaginative rich-
ness rather than their simplicity.
67, l. 9 loose garb [...] Corruption's harbinger loose clothing was often the
clothing of the radical as well as of the sexually immoral in the nineteenth
century. Hogg may be associating the sceptic with the sans culotte of the
French Revolution.
67, ll. 26–27 The converse here [...] wing sublime as in 'Kilmeny', Hogg

attempts to reconcile the traditional beliefs about fairies and other super-natural beings with orthodox Christianity.

67, l. 29 those I loved and honoured to the last probably an indirect allusion to the death of Hogg's mother, Margaret Laidlaw, in June or July 1813 (*Letters*, I, 150). Her knowledge of folk tradition is shown in her role as an informant for Scott's *Minstrelsy of the Scottish Border* (1802–03), and by Hogg's poem on her death 'A Last Adieu', *Blackwood's Edinburgh Magazine*, 1 (May 1817), 169. Hogg's maternal grandfather, William Laidlaw, died on 17 September 1778 (Ettrick OPR), when Hogg was less than eight years of age. Hogg later wrote that he remembered him 'very well' and gave an account of his grandfather's athletic prowess and past dealings with the fairies: 'He was the last man of this wild region, who heard, saw, and conversed with the fairies; and that not once or twice, but at sundry times and seasons'—see 'Odd Characters', in *The Shepherd's Calendar*, ed. by Douglas S. Mack (S/SC, 1995), pp. 103–17 (pp. 111, 107).

68, l. 37 the brown and careless boy probably an implicit reference to Hogg's own childhood.

68, ll. 43–44 form of cerement or of bier | Within the cottage fire tracing pictures in the fire as omens of future events is a common superstition. Cowper in *The Task* describes tracing pictures in the fire on a winter evening and observing the gatherings of soot on the grate, 'foreboding, in the view | Of superstition, prophesying still, | Though still deceiv'd, some stranger's near approach'—see *Cowper: Poetical Works*, ed. by H. S. Milford rev. Norma Russell (London: Oxford University Press, 1967), p. 189 (Book IV, ll. 293–95).

68, l. 54 That hour with danger fraught the best times for sighting fairies are at twilight and at midnight under a full moon, and the most likely days Halloween (31 October), May Day (1 May), Midsummer Eve (23 June), Lady Day (25 March), and Christmas.

68, l. 55 ancient cemetery such as that of the ruined St Mary's church in Yarrow, described by Hogg in 'St. Mary of the Lows'—see *Queer Book*, pp. 153–56.

68, l. 57 wandering pedlar one such legend formed the basis of Hogg's poem, 'The Pedlar'—see *Mountain Bard*, pp. 26–36 (1807 version).

68, l. 59 grave of suicide such a grave was the subject of a letter communicated by Hogg to *Blackwood's Edinburgh Magazine* for August 1823, and forming part of his subsequent best-known work of fiction published the following year—see *The Private Memoirs and Confessions of a Justified Sinner*, ed. by P. D. Garside (S/SC, 2001), pp. xliv, lx–lxi.

68, ll. 64–66 many a wild, heart-thrilling Scottish bard [...] sleeps 'neath some little mound echoing Gray's supposition that 'in this neglected spot is laid | Some heart once pregnant with celestial fire' that might in other circumstances have 'wak'd to extasy the living lyre'. Gray's 'mute inglorious Milton' may also be relevant to Hogg's *Midsummer Night Dreams* collection, which in effect places local traditions as equally worthy of attention with Milton, Dryden, Pope, and Shakespeare. See 'Elegy Written in a Country Church-Yard', in *Thomas Gray and William Collins: Poetical Works*, ed. by Roger Lonsdale (Oxford: Oxford University Press, 1977), p. 36 (ll. 45–48, 59).

69, l. 68 Mary's silent flood St Mary's loch in the Yarrow valley.

69, l. 69 glen of dark Buccleuch the glen of the Rankle Burn in Ettrick valley, and formerly a separate parish before being united to that of Ettrick. The head of the Scott family hence derives his title of Duke of Buccleuch, and as one of the largest landowners in Scotland contrasts with the unnamed Scottish bard perhaps buried there. Hogg subsequently cited a conversation with Scott about the characterisation of an ancient Sir Walter Scott of Buccleuch in Hogg's novel, *The Three Perils of Man*, responding to Scott's remark that the character had been made too selfish with the reply, 'Oo ay but ye ken they were a' a little gi'en that gate else how could they hae gotten haud o' a' the south o' Scotland nae body kens how?'—see *Anecdotes of Scott*, ed. by Jill Rubenstein (S/SC, 1999), p. 48.

69, l. 72 yeaning ewe presumably one accompanied by its lamb (rather than giving birth). The lamb would probably be born in early February and be kept with its mother until the following autumn.

69, l. 74 The marble fount-stone, and the rood so grey at the time of his first significant meeting with Scott, probably in the early autumn of 1802, Hogg and he as members of a party of five made an expedition to Rankleburn, where

> [...] there was a remaining tradition in the country that there was a font-stone of blue marble, out of which the ancient heirs of Buccleuch were baptized, covered up among the ruins of the old church. Mr. Scott was curious to see if we could discover it, but on going among the ruins where the altar was known to have been, we found the rubbish at that spot dug out to the foundation, we knew not by whom, but it was manifest that the font had either been taken away, or that there was none there.

Scott decided that a metal pot discovered by the party was 'an ancient consecrated helmet' until Laidlaw's discovery of a scraping of tar inside revealed it to be a tar-pot, used in marking sheep. The same incident is alluded to in Hogg's poem, 'Lines to Sir Walter Scott, Bart.' (*Anecdotes of Scott*, ed. by Jill Rubenstein (S/SC, 1999), pp. 39–40, 33–36).

69, ll. 89–90 the forgotten names [...] many a warrior wight, and nameless bard compare 'Perhaps in this neglected spot is laid | Some heart once pregnant with celestial fire, | Hands, that the rod of empire might have sway'd', in 'Elegy Written in a Country Church-Yard', *Thomas Gray and William Collins: Poetical Works*, ed. by Roger Lonsdale (Oxford: Oxford University Press, 1977), p. 36 (ll. 45–47).

69, l. 91 holiness of frame perhaps alluding to the poet's art of composition, which coexisted more harmoniously in the visionary world whose passing Hogg mourns.

69, l. 100 linger in the wild Hogg had written in 1813, 'The fairies have now totally disappeared, and it is a pity they should; for they seem to have been the most delightful little spirits that ever haunted the Scottish dells. There are only very few now remaining alive who have ever seen them; and when they did, it was on Hallow-evenings while they were young, when the gospel was not very rife in this country'—see *The Queen's Wake*, ed. by Douglas S. Mack (S/SC, 2004), p. 182.

70, l. 114 An evil eye witchcraft was clearly longer in vanishing than the fairies. Hogg stated in 1813, 'Never, in the most superstitious ages, was the existence of witches, or the influence of their diabolical power, more firmly believed in, than by the inhabitants of Ettrick Forest at the present day'—

see *The Queen's Wake*, ed. by Douglas S. Mack (S/SC, 2004), p. 182.

70, l. 117 the eldron crone most accused or pretended witches were poor old women. Not surprisingly, the physical traits attributed to the witch included many of the marks of old age, including missing or broken teeth, sunken cheeks, and a hairy lip.

70, l. 118 O! I have seen the door most closely barred this counter-spell was designed to identify the person causing a cattle infection commonly thought to be the result of witchcraft. Hogg wrote, 'I am not so thoroughly initiated into this mystery as to describe it minutely; but, in the first place, a fire is set on, and surrounded with green turfs, in which a great number of pins are stuck. A certain portion of the milk of each cow, so infected, is then hung on in a pot, with a horse's shoe, and a black dish, with its mouth downward, placed in it. The doors are then carefully shut, and the milk continues to boil; and the first person that comes to that house afterwards, is always blamed for the mischief' (*Mountain Bard*, p. 33).

70, l. 126 cut above the breath Hogg relates how a miller, suspecting that a woman was a witch, 'enticing her into the kiln one Sabbath evening [...] seized her forcibly, and cut the shape of the cross on her forehead: This they call, *scoring aboon the breath*, which overthrows their power of doing them any further mischief' (*Mountain Bard*, p. 36). An assault of this description was reported as follows in the *Edinburgh Evening Courant* of 3 September 1814:

> Lately, in the upper end of Peebleshire, a young man, a shepherd, being dissatisfied with the quantity of milk which some of his cows yielded, shrewdly suspected they were bewitched by an old woman who lived about 15 miles from the spot, whose great age excited the boor's suspicions. *Scoring aboon the breath* being the only remedy prescribed by the superstition which yet remains in that part of the country, for an evil of such a desperate nature, the owner of the cattle determined to try the cure, set out for the residence of the supposed delinquent, and finding the poor old woman at home, cut her severely on the brow. The fellow was immediately brought before the justices, who very properly inflicted on him a heavy pecuniary penalty, and dismissed him with a suitable admonition.

70, l. 131 she is forced to carry neighbour cats were commonly viewed as witches' familiars, and witches could also change themselves into the form of various animals, including cats, but no contemporary source has been found for the belief that cats were used to carry witches on their backs.

71, l. 140 moon's distempered beams the moon was the traditional cause of madness (lunacy), and was also sometimes believed to cause blindness or facial mutilation.

71, l. 141 thy matrons gallopped through the heaven for the power of flight as an attribute of witches see 'The Witch of Fife' in *The Queen's Wake*, ed. by Douglas S. Mack (S/SC, 2004), pp. 40–48.

71, l. 144 hills in twain were riven the Eildon hills were supposed to have been one hill originally until divided into three by the demonic agents of the wizard Master Michael Scott. The incident features in Hogg's *The Three Perils of Man* (1822).

71, l. 148 gleesome demon in the church-aisle raised like the 'towzie tyke, black, grim, and large' playing the bagpipes in Alloway kirk in Burns's 'Tam o' Shanter' (Kinsley, no. 321, l. 121).

71, l. 153 swear them at the stake until the witchcraft laws were repealed in 1736 several thousand witches were burnt at the stake in Scotland. Witches could be anonymously accused and were almost always found guilty, as trials were tainted by corrupted evidence as well as superstition and witches could be tortured to extract a confession. Suspects were sometimes tested by a water ordeal (the innocent drowned, the guilty floated) or examined for a witch mark.

71, l. 159 Even from dry bones the drops of blood have sprung as in Hogg's ballad 'The Pedlar' where the guilty miller years after the murder is tricked into handling 'a bane o' the pedlar's heel'—see *Mountain Bard*, pp. 30–31 (1807 version). The belief that a murdered person's corpse would bleed at the touch of the murderer was used as an ordeal to determine guilt or innocence.

71, l. 160 Inquisitor superstition is likened to an official with the charge to question or investigate, thus challenging the Enlightenment view of it as useless and barbaric.

71, l. 169 In heaven were registered their days below superstition and Calvinism united to favour the idea of fate or destiny, while a knowledge of one's appointed end precluded fear.

72, l. 181 our king probably the generic figure of a Stuart king of Scotland, like the one of Hogg's tale 'The Hunt of Eildon' whose duty as monarch includes enquiry into 'diablery and exorcism' and who had 'sworn to rid the country of witches'—see *The Brownie of Bodsbeck: And Other Tales*, 2 vols (Edinburgh: William Blackwood; London: John Murray, 1818), II, 229–346 (pp. 290, 329). Douglas Mack points out that Hogg wrote elsewhere that 'fairies, brownies, and witches, were at the rifest in Scotland' in the reign of James IV—see *The Queen's Wake*, ed. by Douglas S. Mack (S/SC, 2004), p. 414. Hogg may also have James VI of Scotland in mind here, who published his *Daemonologie* in 1597 to inform his subjects about the extent and wickedness of witchcraft.

72, l. 184 the mark of hell a mole or other patch of skin that was impervious to pain on the body of a supposed witch and supposedly made by the devil. The discovery of this was a feature of the investigation into a group of witches who, in 1590, were accused of having raised a storm with the intention of wrecking the ship in which James VI was returning from his wedding to Anne of Denmark—see Barbara Bloedé, 'The Witchcraft Tradition in Hogg's Tales and Verse', *SHW*, 1 (1990), 91–102 (pp. 96–97).

72, l. 189 Stuarts back again the Stuart monarchy ended in 1689 in Scotland, when William of Orange became king.

72, l. 202 Saint Valentine's or Hallow Day times when country girls would practise various rites of divination to find out about their sweethearts and future husbands. Burns describes some of these in notes to his poem 'Halloween' (Kinsley, no. 73).

72, l. 207 'Twas sin to counteract what Providence ordained again Hogg laments a lost conflation of heathen and Christian beliefs, here Fate and Predestination.

73, l. 210 thy plastic finger Hogg is fascinated by the relation between the creative power of superstition and the visual or auditory impressions of natural phenomena.

73, l. 218 The bard of fancy Hogg himself.

73, l. 222 Norway Hogg associates northern Europe with creative power, and with witches—see note to p. 46, l. 341 on Hugo of Norroway in *The Pilgrims of the Sun*.

73, l. 224 The tuneful sea maid the subject of 'The Mermaid', in *Midsummer Night Dreams*.

73, l. 226 where the Tana rolls a river in the Finmark region of northern Norway, which empties into the Barents Sea.

The Gyre Caryl

'The Gyre Caryl' had previously appeared under the title of 'The Harper's Song' in *Mador of the Moor* (Edinburgh: William Blackwood; London: John Murray, 1816), pp. 29–37, and its theme is similar to that of 'Superstition', the preceding item in *Midsummer Night Dreams*, the disenchantment of the world. *Mador of the Moor* was written immediately before Hogg began his original *Midsummer Night Dreams* collection, though published after *The Pilgrims of the Sun* and 'Superstition', and provides ample indication that Hogg's mind was turning increasingly to the visionary theme. At one point, indeed, he rebukes his Muse for wandering from the subject, because she loves 'amid the burning stars to sail' (as in 'Verses to the Comet of 1811'), 'Or sing with sea-maids' (as in 'The Mermaid'), 'The groves of visionary worlds to hail' (as in *The Pilgrims of the Sun*), and in 'moonlight dells thy fairy rites to keep' (as in 'The Haunted Glen')—see *Mador*, p. 52. Hogg had reused two lines of the inset 'The Song of the Fairies' from 'The Harper's Song' in 'The Haunted Glen' in his *Dramatic Tales* of 1817 (see note to 76, ll. 81–82). It was natural enough, then, that when he came to reconstitute the *Midsummer Night Dreams* collection aborted in 1814 he should have decided that 'The Gyre Caryl' belonged there. It is a lament for the loss of the fairies from Scotland, at the birth of religious grace, and appropriately written in the 'ancient stile' that Hogg used both to indicate a medieval, pre-Reformation Scotland, and the liberation of his imagination into freer verse-forms and subject matter. A later version, substantially revised for an Annuals context and entitled 'Superstition and Grace' was produced by Hogg for *The Bijou* for 1828, and included in Hogg's 1832 ballad collection of *A Queer Book*—for further information on these later versions see *Queer Book*, ed. by P. D. Garside (S/SC, 2007), pp. 263–64. (The notes which follow are greatly indebted to Peter Garside's work on 'Superstition and Grace' and to James E. Barcus's notes to 'The Harper's Song' in *Mador of the Moor*.)

What Garside refers to as 'the more arcane chants' in this poem are difficult, since at several points these seem to defy rational and coherent explanation, and perhaps were intended to do so. The fairy songs are distinguished from the 'ancient stile' narrative passages in which they are set by being even wilder and more archaic. At times they recall to the modern reader the nonsense verse of later writers such as Lewis Carroll or Edward Lear where words are used as suggestions, to evoke a mood, rather than precisely, to evoke a fixed meaning. If 'The Song of the Fairies' is chanted aloud it goes with a swing and gives an impression of great energy, replicating the glancing movement of the fairies themselves, and similarly its movement of ideas and images are glancing and associative rather than set and logical.

74 title The Gyre Caryl a supernatural being, but usually envisaged as female, the *Gyre Carline*. She was believed to be 'the mother of glamour, and near a-kin to Satan himself. She is believed to preside over the "*Hallowmass Rades*;" and mothers frequently frighten their children by threatening to give them to *M'Neven*, or the *Gyre Carline*. She is described as wearing a long gray mantle, and carrying a wand, which, like the miraculous rod of Moses, could convert water into rocks, and sea into solid land'—see R. H. Cromek, *Remains of Nithsdale and Galloway Song* (London: Cadell and Davies, 1810), p. 292. Just as in Hogg's poem the benevolent male spirit may recall this threatening female one, so the heavenly baby may recall the infants stolen by the fairies, which, like Kilmeny in *The Queen's Wake*, are benefited by their stay among them. Robert Chambers relates that 'The fairies [...] were in the habit of frequently stealing away children [...]. These adopted children, perhaps, remained amongst them only in the quality of friends, platonic lovers, or servants; and were permitted, after a few years of probation, to return to earth, in a fitter condition than formerly to enjoy its blessings'— see *The Popular Rhymes of Scotland* (Edinburgh: William Hunter, 1826), pp. 260–62.

74, l. 2 *Lemedon! lemedon! ayden lillelu!* according to David C. Fowler the function of such lines, which do not advance the narrative, is to allow an oral performer room for improvisation—see *A Literary History of the Popular Ballad* (Durham, North Carolina: Duke University Press, 1968), p. 10. Hogg's employment of it here places his work with the ballad and with early English carols, and reinforces the effect of his 'ancient stile'. A refrain with the word 'lillelu' is also used in 'The Song of the Fairies', linking the two sections of the poem, narrative and arcane chant.

74, l. 4 *Gillan of Allanhu* the meaning of this phrase, its pattern vaguely suggesting a personal identity (as in 'Scott of Abbotsford'), is unknown. Barcus suggests that it is 'perhaps an echo of "Roderigh Vich Alpine dhu, ho! iero!", the chorus in the 'Boat Song' in Canto II of *The Lady of the Lake*' (*Mador*, p. 114).

74, l. 8 the Lammer Law Lammer Law is the highest peak in the Lammermuir Hills, four miles south of Gifford in the south-east of Scotland (*Queer Book*, p. 263; *Mador*, p. 114).

74, l. 30 they sang ane hyme 'Faeries are passionately fond of music [...]. Faerie melodies are known to be beautiful and plaintive yet wild and capricious and they have a fatal charm for mortal ears. [...] Faeries play a variety of musical instruments; fiddles, harps, tambourines, cymbals and the jew's harp'—see Brian Froud and Alan Lee, *Faeries* (New York: Harry N. Abrams, 1978), pp. [12]–[13].

75, l. 45 AYDEN! AYDEN! LILLELU a similar refrain to the one at the start of the narrative section of 'The Gyre Caryl' begins the chant entitled 'The Song of the Fairies'. The word 'ayden' recalls the word 'ay' or always and the archaism 'good den' for 'good day'.

75, l. 48 No ane the first stanza emphasises the fairies' dissimilarity to humankind by listing what they do not have or do not, or cannot, do.

75, l. 56 The moone-rak speile the second stanza emphasises the fairies' movement, the 'moone-rak' suggesting both the clouds that drift across the moon and a framework for climbing, their motions being connected both with domesticity (through images of spinning), and with the countryside. There is perhaps an allusion to the Puck of Shakespeare's *Midsummer Night's*

Dream, who can both pull a gossip's stool away and put a girdle round about the earth in forty minutes.

75, l. 57 Warre the rowan, warre the steile supernatural agency may be kept at bay by the wood or berries of the rowan tree and by iron.

75, l. 68 Laplin's tyrling dryfte another instance of Hogg's association of fairies and supernatural beings with northern Europe—see also notes to p. 46, l. 341 for *The Pilgrims of the Sun* and to p. 73, l. 222 for 'Superstition'. Hogg's witch of Fife flies north to meet the fairies in Lapland—see *The Queen's Wake*, ed. by Douglas S. Mack (S/SC, 2004), p. 43.

75, ll. 71–72 hune! hune! | And ante-tune another refrain, apparently meaningless, though 'hune' suggests both tune and a singing note, while ante-tune might imply either a prelude or even perhaps counterpoint. There is an older and very rare Scots word 'antetewme', meaning 'the text of a sermon' (information from Maggie Scott).

76, l. 74 Leider [...] Dye Leader Water rises on the southern slope of Lammer Law and empties into the Tweed, while Dye Water rises south of Lammer Law and eventually falls into the Whitadder.

76, ll. 81–82 For the bairnis sleipe […] blest and pure the same lines occur in modernised form in Hogg's fairy drama 'The Haunted Glen', Scene I, ll. 194–95. From their first appearance in *Mador of the Moor* (see *Mador*, p. 25) they were modernised to form the opening lines of the fairies' song to Lu at the conclusion of Scene I of 'The Haunted Glen' in *Dramatic Tales*, 2 vols (Edinburgh: John Ballantyne; London: Longmans, 1817), II, 203–04.

76, ll. 85–87 Scho comis owr-nychte [...] Scho swawis withe the dewe until the baby is named, near the end of the poem, she appears to retain something of her fairy nature, appearing in the evening and disappearing again at the start of the day. The fairies' song anticipates the time when she, like humankind, will sleep at night and wake by day.

76, l. 89 The deide shall ake the dawning day symbolises the end of time and the resurrection of the dead. 'Superstition and Grace' has 'quake' as a replacement for 'ake' (*Queer Book*, p. 190).

76, l. 95 Hyde! hyde the coming of the sacred baby banishes all evil spirits, perhaps recalling the similar superstition about Christmas, the time of the birth of Christ. In *Hamlet*, I. 1. 139–45 so 'hallowed and so gracious is the time' that the 'bird of dawning singeth all night long' and no spirit can walk abroad. The fairies, however, are not restricted to such banishments from daylight, being, as Oberon has it, 'spirits of another sort'—see *A Midsummer Night's Dream*, III. 3. 389.

76, l. 109 Pace! pace from 'pax', Latin for 'peace'. The fairies were sometimes called 'folk of peace', and this stanza continues the theme of the banishment (which does not apply to the fairies) of all evil spirits by the sacred baby.

76, l. 112 The kelpye a water demon, usually in the form of a horse. The narrator and the hero of Hogg's prose tale 'Duncan Campbell' as children 'were a little jealous of the water-kelpies, and always kept aloof from the frightsome pools'—see *The Spy*, ed. by Gillian Hughes (S/SC, 2000), p. 491. In *The Mountain Bard* Hogg relates legends about the water-cow of St Mary's Loch in Yarrow, which 'possessed the rare slight of turning herself into whatever shape she pleased, and was likewise desirous of getting as many dragged into the lake as possible' (*Mountain Bard*, p. 66).

77, l. 114 Gil-Moules a devil-figure, also referred to in Hogg's play 'All-Hallow-Eve', *Dramatic Tales*, 2 vols (Edinburgh: John Ballantyne: London: Longmans, 1817), I, 1–134 (p. 56). In Hogg's poem 'Jocke Taittis Expeditoune till Hell' Gil-Moules is termed 'the shepherdis deille' (*Queer Book*, p. 138).

77, l. 116 the mer-mayde for further information on mermaids see 'The Mermaid' and notes.

77, l. 120 ouir last aduc although they are not banished by the appearance of the sacred baby, her naming as Grace means that the fairies no longer belong in Scotland.

77, l. 125 the spyritis King fairies were generally supposed to occupy a middle ground between human and spirit nature, possessing magic powers but being dependent on mankind for many things, particularly in relation to childbirth. British fairies were generally regarded as being ruled by monarchs—see, for instance, Hogg's 'Invocation to the Queen of the Fairies', in *Contributions to Annuals and Gift-Books*, ed. by Janette Currie and Gillian Hughes (S/SC, 2006), pp. 3–6. The phrase may imply, however, that God is the overlord of the fairies as he is of humankind.

77, l. 130 quhair the nychte-wynd neuir blewe Hogg's 'Kilmeny' had also been to the land where 'the wynd nevir blue'—see *The Queen's Wake*, ed. by Douglas S. Mack (S/SC, 2004), p. 93. 'The Mermaid' also inhabits a region where 'the winds o' heaven never blew' (l. 7).

77, l. 147 the bairne of Hevenly Truthe after her christening as Grace, the baby is no longer characterised as 'the bairne of the Spyritis King' but related to earth and to the Christian scheme of redemption.

78, l. 156 eiless ouphen trayne the coming of Grace banishes not only wicked but also harmless spirits. Elves were known to torment or lead travellers astray and to cause pain to birds and animals, but presumably as they have no souls they cannot be guilty.

78, l. 161 emerant isle of the se Britain, referred to as the 'queen isle of the sea' in 'Superstition and Grace'—see Peter Garside's note in *Queer Book*, p. 264.

The Haunted Glen

'The Haunted Glen' appears to have been composed as Hogg's *Dramatic Tales* was being printed, since in his 'Memoir of the Author's Life' Hogg declared that 'the fragment of "The Haunted Glen" was written off-hand, to make the second volume of an equal extent with the first' (*Altrive Tales*, p. 42). It was first published in *Dramatic Tales*, 2 vols (Edinburgh: John Ballantyne; London: Longmans, 1817), II, 189–271, with a somewhat disingenuous end-note apologising for the fact that it was incomplete by stating that its 'great length' 'rendered its full insertion here inconvenient'. As published in 1817 'The Haunted Glen' alternates poetic scenes concerning the fairy prince Lu and his desire to win Lula as a mate with comic scenes about a local family of cottars, Eps and Cairney and their uncouth son, Simon, who wants Lula himself. Hogg's note stated that 'it is founded on the old romance of Tam Lane, and from that the issue may be divined' (p. 271). In Hogg's fairy drama Lu is near the end of a process of transformation from a human to a fairy. While the fairies are interested in Lula as the pure virgin who, by crowning Lu, will complete this transformation, he is in love with her and tempted to resume his full humanity in order to become her lover. Hogg therefore implies that if his drama had been completed, Lula would have managed to rescue Lu from the fairies and that the two would have married, since in the ballad 'Tam Lin' (Child, no. 39) Janet rescues her fairy lover from the fairies to be a father to her unborn child. Hogg's other literary model for 'The Haunted Glen' is, of course, Shakespeare's *A Midsummer Night's Dream*, with its human lovers, fairy court, and rude mechanicals.

When Hogg revised 'The Haunted Glen' for the second, or *Midsummer Night Dreams* volume, of his 1822 *Poetical Works* he omitted the comic scenes, shortening his unfinished play and placing the emphasis more firmly on the fairies and their relationship to human existence.

79–80, ll. 10–12 whither away [...] much to do ere the break of day a passage emphasising the pervasive debt of 'The Haunted Glen' to Shakespeare's fairy play. Puck or Robin Goodfellow first appears in *A Midsummer Night's Dream* accosting another fairy, 'How now, spirit, whither wander you?' (II. 1. 1). He is subsequently given various tasks by Oberon to be performed 'ere the first cock crow' (II. 1. 267), and later urged to 'haste, make no delay; | We may effect this business yet ere day' (III. 2. 395–96). At the end of the play Oberon instructs the fairies who are to bless the lovers' bride-beds to 'Trip away, make no stay, | Meet me all by break of day' (V. 2. 51–52).

81, l. 59 I cannot hurt where sin is not similar rules appear to govern malevolent spirits elsewhere in Hogg's work. Master Michael Scott and the devil, for instance, cannot turn Border warriors into cattle before they have indulged in drunken fornication—see *The Three Perils of Man*, 3 vols (London: Longman, 1822), III, 138–39.

81, l. 76 Lu of Kyle Kyle was an ancient castle in Auchinleck parish, Ayrshire (Groome).

82, l. 104 over brake, over thorn compare *A Midsummer Night's Dream*, II. 1. 2–3 ('Over hill, over dale, | Thorough bush, thorough brier').

82, l. 111 Ara Lu! Ora Lu a refrain which is presumably in praise of Prince Lu, as it includes his name and a word derived from the Latin 'oratio' meaning a speech.

83, l. 120 Our new names reminiscent of Peaseblossom, Cobweb, Mote, and Mustard-seed, the fairies who attend on Bottom the weaver in *A Midsummer Night's Dream*, III. 1. 149–88. The name of Philany, the fairy who guards birds, may echo the word 'Philomel' for a nightingale, used by Shakespeare in the fairies' lullaby for Titania at II. 2. 13.

84, ll. 194–95 The baby's rest [...] blest and pure lines previously used by Hogg in 'The Gyre Caryl' (ll. 81–82).

85, l. 202 The lamb beside the fox shall stray recalling the gathering of wild and tame animals, 'the tod, and the lam' to hear Kilmeny sing her 'hymis of other worildis'—see *The Queen's Wake*, ed. by Douglas S. Mack (S/SC, 2004), p. 99. The ultimate source, as Douglas Mack indicates, is Isaiah 11. 6–9 and Isaiah 65. 17–18, 25 (p. lxxxiii).

85, l. 12 seven years' penance seven is a number associated with the fairies. In the ballad 'Tam Lin' (Child, no. 39), for example, the fairies pay a tithe to hell every seven years.

86, l. 56 The Queen of heaven compare the title of 'Queen of Night' given by Hogg to the moon in *The Pilgrims of the Sun*, Part First, l. 145.

87, l. 79 the blood of my white steed the horse, the hound, and the lady are traditional associates of the knight in ballads. In 'The Twa Corbies' (Child, no. 26, 'The Three Ravens') the knight's death is signalled by his horse. Hogg's poem 'Sir David Graeme' is based upon this ballad (see *Mountain Bard*, pp. 21–26, 403–05).

88, l. 121 these simple cottagers a reference to Eps, Cairny, and Simon in the version of 'The Haunted Glen' in *Dramatic Tales*.

89, l. 165 struck to earth Master Michael Scott fells his steward Gourlay in the same way, simply by a gesture and without touching his person—see *The Three Perils of Man*, 3 vols (London: Longman, 1822), II, 26.

91, l. 35 "The sun shone through my thin bodye echoing the appearance of the ghost in Hogg's 'The Pedlar', where 'the moon shone throw his thin bodye' (*Mountain Bard*, p. 29).

93–94, ll. 137–38 A clown [...] open to the gin in the *Dramatic Tales* version of 'The Haunted Glen' Simon, encouraged by Cairney, had planned to sneak into Lula's cottage and rape her.

94, l. 176 Leven side perhaps on the shores of Loch Leven, a lake in southeast Kinrosshire with a castle on an island in which Mary, Queen of Scots was imprisoned in 1567–68.

95, l. 186 "Love is Heaven, and Heaven is Love see Scott's *The Lay of the Last Minstrel. A Poem* (Edinburgh: Archibald Constable; London: Longman, Hurst, Rees, and Orme, 1805), p. 66 (Canto III, l. 17).

95, ll. 193–210 Never, gentle spirits [...] Never!–Never these lines were subsequently reworked by Hogg in his 'Fairy Songs', an intended contribution to the annual *The Musical Bijou*—for details see the entry for 'The Haunted Glen' in 'Note on the Texts'.

95, l. 201 Dawn of truth that shine shall ever the Last Judgement, when the future of the spirits, not being human, is unclear.

95, l. 207 Over rock, and over river another reminiscence of *A Midsummer Night's Dream*, II. 1. 2–3 ('Over hill, over dale, | Thorough bush, thorough brier').

96, l. 10 Then my sport will all be done compare the relish of that 'lob of spirits', Puck, in mischief in *A Midsummer Night's Dream*, III. 2. 353–54: 'so far am I glad it so did sort | As this their jangling I esteem a sport'.

97, l. 58 By rite divine traditionally fairies have no power to take children that have been baptised. See, for example, the anxiety of Kincraigy's wife in Hogg's *Mador of the Moor* that the 'malignant elves' were on the watch for Ila Moore's 'unchristen'd' babe (*Mador*, p. 56).

98, l. 80 It is not yet the wane of the moon Mary Lee of *The Pilgrims of the Sun* disappeared on the 'third night of the waning moon' (Part First, l. 59), which as Hogg explains subsequently is the night when 'the spirits were free; | That revels of fairies were held on the lea' (Part Fourth, ll. 21–22).

98, ll. 90–92 two eyes of lead [...] heart of stone the angry Queen of the Fairies tells the rescued Tam Lin that if she had known what was intended she would have 'taen out thy twa grey een, | Put in twa een o' tree', and 'tane out your heart o' flesh, | Put in a heart o' stane'—see the version of the ballad, 'The Young Tamlane' in *Minstrelsy*, II, 245–59 (p. 258).

98–99, ll. 105–29 Then hie [...] end shall be these lines were subsequently reworked by Hogg in his 'Fairy Songs', an intended contribution to the annual *The Musical Bijou*—for details see the entry for 'The Haunted Glen' in 'Note on the Texts'.

99, l. 129 little we know what the end shall be perhaps a reference to the fading of the fairies at the Last Judgement, but possibly too an allusion to the tithe to hell paid every seven years by the fairies.

99–100, ll. 130–59 O weel befa' […] smiles in yonder glen these lines were subsequently published by Hogg, with various modifications, as a separate song—for details see the entry for 'The Haunted Glen' in the 'Note on the Texts'.

99, l. 132 the bonnie May in a footnote to *Mador of the Moor* Hogg explains, 'A May, in old Scottish ballads and romances, denotes a young lady, or a maiden somewhat above the lower class' (*Mador*, p. 33).

The Mermaid

'The Mermaid' continues the theme of love between supernatural being and mortal that was explored in 'The Haunted Glen', the previous item in the *Midsummer Night Dreams* volume of Hogg's 1822 *Poetical Works*. Hogg revised a poem he had contributed to Constable's *Edinburgh Magazine* in 1819—for further details see 'Note on the Texts'. Hogg also refers to the fatal love of a young man for a beautiful mermaid in 'The Renowned Adventures of Basil Lee'—see *Winter Evening Tales*, pp. 52–53.

> They told me of one that fell in love with a young man, named Alexander M'Leod, who often met her upon the shore, at a certain place which they showed me, and had amorous dalliance with her; but he soon fell sick and died, and when she came to the shore, and could no more find him, she cried one while, and sung another, in the most plaintive strains that ever were heard. [...]
>
> M'Leod, when on his death-bed, told his friends of all that had passed between them, and grievously regretted having met with her.

Hogg had previously encountered the theme in the ballad 'The Mermaid of Galloway' in R. H. Cromek's *Remains of Nithsdale and Galloway Song* (London: Cadell and Davies, 1810), pp. 229–48. Many of the ballads in that collection were the work of Hogg's friend Allan Cunningham, and in a letter to James Cunningham written in the summer of 1811 (*Letters*, I, 114) Hogg had humorously referred to Allan's bride as 'the beauteous mermaid of Galloway'. In this ballad young Cowehill, engaged to be married, is nevertheless seduced by a beautiful mermaid. She casts a spell on him by binding his head with her hair, throws his rich clothes and bridal ring into the sea, and carries him over the water. He appears to his bride in her sleep, and advises her to choose another bridegroom as 'My bride is the yellow water lilie, | Its leaves my brydal sheet' (p. 246). A note to the ballad includes the following explanation:

> Her beauty was such that man could not behold her face, but his heart was fired with unquenchable love. 'Her long hair of burning gold,' through the wiling links of which appeared her white bosom and shoulders, were her favourite care; and she is always represented by tradition with one hand shedding her locks, and with the other combing them.
>
> Tradition tells, that this world is an outer husk or shell, which encloses a kernel of most rare abode, where dwell the Mermaids of popular belief. According to Lowland mythology, they are a race of goddesses, corrupted with earthly passions—their visits to the world, 'though few

and far between,' are spoken of and remembered with awe–their affections were bestowed on men of exalted virtue and rare endowments of person and parts' (p. 230)

101, l. 7 Where the winds o' heaven never blew compare the fairy world visited by Kilmeny where 'the rayne nevir fell, and the wynd nevir blue'– see *The Queen's Wake*, ed. by Douglas S. Mack (S/SC, 2004), p. 93.

101, l. 23 Maid of the Mountain Lake mermaids in Hogg's *Midsummer Night Dreams* collection have previously been associated with the sea. In *The Pilgrims of the Sun* (Part First, l. 136) he mentions 'maidens of the main', in 'Superstition' (l. 224) he mentions the 'tuneful sea maid', and in 'The Gyre Caryl' (l. 116) 'the mer-mayde mootes in the saifrone se'. Here, however, the mermaid's home is clearly an inland fresh-water lake.

102, ll. 37–38 the burning beal | Upon the mountain's brow perhaps alluding to the practice of burning heather on pasture land so as to improve the quality of the shoots as food for sheep. Hogg noted that 'I have heard Mr Laidlaw of Blackhouse aver, that rather than miss a year's burning, he would lose L. 50.'–see James Hogg, *The Shepherd's Guide* (Edinburgh: Archibald Constable; London: John Murray, 1807), p. 50.

102, l. 41 "O mother, mother, make my bed echoing the ballad of 'Lord Randal' (Child, no. 12).

103, l. 82 Hope lingers o'er thy slumber in the prospect of resurrection promised to Christians.

103, l. 94 Their long last farewell the departure of the fairies from a modernised country, a theme of the *Midsummer Night Dreams* collection, is the subject of 'The Fairy's Farewell' of Richard Corbet (1582–1635).

Verses to the Comet of 1811

The comet of 1811, which Hogg's poem commemorates, was a focus of study in a golden age of British astronomy. It was visible by telescope from March 1811 to August 1812 and with the naked eye from April 1811 to January 1812, one of the longest periods ever recorded for such visibility. It also had the largest coma, or head, ever recorded, with a visible diameter larger than that of the sun–see Roberta J. M. Olson and Jay M. Pasachoff, *Fire in the Sky: Comets and Meteors, the Decisive Centuries, in British Art and Science* (Cambridge: Cambridge University Press, 1998), p. 128.

Comets and meteors appear frequently in early nineteenth-century caricatures, artists both ridiculing and adapting ancient superstitions about them for their own use. Napoleon adopted the comet as his personal guide, and the 1769 comet is often termed 'Napoleon's Comet'. His pretension was mocked by James Gillray's parodic 'The Grand Coronation Procession of Napoleon the First, Emperor of France, from the Church of Notre-Dame, Dec. 2nd, 1804' in which the procession is led by a banner depicting a huge comet inscribed 'N' above a scorched earth. The 1811 comet inspired a number of political caricatures on both foreign and domestic public affairs and was the focus of a comet mania. There was even a commemorative silver beer tankard ornamented with the 1811 comet–for further information see *Fire in the Sky*, pp. 143–44, 149–54. Pushkin alludes to 1811 champagne as 'wine of the Comet'–see *Eugene Onegin: A Novel in Verse*, trans. by Charles Johnston (London: Penguin, 2003), p. 14.

In the context of the *Midsummer Night Dreams* volume of Hogg's 1822 *Poetical Works* 'Verses to the Comet of 1811' (like 'The Mermaid') forms part of a group of 'otherworldly' poems previously contributed to the Constable firm's *Edinburgh Magazine*, and seems naturally to find a permanent home in a collected edition also produced by William Blackwood's chief Edinburgh publishing rival. By his inclusion of recent items from the *Edinburgh Magazine* Hogg is signalling that the poet of 'the mountain and fairy school' is now a Constable rather than a Blackwood author. The poem connects with another item in the volume in which comets are described as, like the poet himself, 'Ranging through Nature on erratic wing', as the volume dedication puts it. A comet is described in Part Second, ll. 405–73 of *The Pilgrims of the Sun* in terms of 'the downfall of a sentenced world' (l. 426) which for all its force and wildness God can lead 'unhurtful through the spheres' (l. 466). Similar spiritual and unearthly journeys feature in 'Superstition', which Hogg noted as able to flee across 'the heaven upon the meteor' (l. 215), and in 'Verses Addressed to the Right Honourable Lady Anne Scott of Buccleuch', where Hogg hopes after death to travel to supernatural worlds by means of a cloud, '[t]he soul's own energy my guide' (l. 169). Hogg seems to have viewed the comet, with its erratic yet impressive motions, as resembling his own poetic Muse.

105, l. 8 Dread traveller of immensity! although by the end of the eighteenth century comets were widely regarded as barges that transported life-sustaining materials to the earth and fuel to the sun, this coincided with the traditional understanding that they were harbingers of radical change or even tools of divine displeasure. Comet theories came to be considered dangerous because of their association with political dissension and religious scepticism: 'In the charged political atmosphere of eighteenth-century England, in which religion and politics were tightly enmeshed, adventist expectations of the arrival of comets that were to reform the natural and political worlds seemed only too apt–once again–to fuel religious enthusiasm and justify rebellions as the fulfillment of biblical prophecy'–see Sara Schechner Genuth, *Comets, Popular Culture, and the Birth of Modern Cosmology* (Princeton, NJ: Princeton University Press, 1997), p. 177.

105, l. 12 pennon of the King of Heaven linking the comet with God rather than any earthly ruler, such as Napoleon.

105, l. 18 plains of Bethlehem comets were associated with the Star of Bethlehem that announced the birth of Jesus as early as the eighth century, while a sixteenth-century illustration of the Book of Revelation linked comets with the Apocalypse–see Sara Schechner Genuth, *Comets, Popular Culture, and the Birth of Modern Cosmology* (Princeton, NJ: Princeton University Press, 1997), pp. 38–44.

105, l. 28 the wain Charles's Wain, the constellation also known as the Plough.

106, l. 33 Oh! on thy rapid prow to glide compare 'Verses Addressed to the Right Honourable Lady Anne Scott of Buccleuch', ll. 163–72.

106, l. 40 other moons and planets roll compare the heliocentric universe explored by Mary Lee in *The Pilgrims of the Sun*, where different planets represent stages in a process of perfection and God dwells in the sun.

106, l. 43 Eccentric as thy course the poet's creative energies, like the natural energy of the comet, lead him to wander out of a regular course. He is likened to a 'meteor of the wild' in *Queen Hynde*, ed. by Suzanne Gilbert and Douglas S. Mack (S/SC, 1998), p. 31 (Book First, ll. 1088–97).

The Powris of Moseke

'The Powris of Moseke, Ane Rychte Plesant Ballaunt' was published in Constable's *Edinburgh Magazine* not long before the preparation of the 1822 *Poetical Works* (for further details see the entry for 'The Powris of Moseke' in 'Note on the Texts'), and therefore falls into the same category as 'The Mermaid' and 'Verses to the Comet of 1811'. With its emphasis on grotesque fantasy, however, it also forms a natural companion piece to 'Connel of Dee'. Shakespeare's *Midsummer Night's Dream* famously described the 'lunatic, the lover, and the poet' as 'of imagination all compact' (v. 1. 7–8), and the blind minstrel of this poem perhaps represents the poet as Connel does the lover. Hogg's title appears to allude to Dryden's famous poem, 'Alexander's Feast; or The Power of Musique: An Ode, in Honour of St. Cecelia's Day'—see *The Poems and Fables of John Dryden*, ed. by James Kinsley (London: Oxford University Press, 1962, repr. 1969), pp. 504–09. Hogg may have encountered Dryden's poem in Scott's eighteen-volume edition of *The Works of John Dryden*, published in 1808. St Cecelia is both the patron saint of the blind and of musicians, and an angel is supposed to have fallen in love with her for her musical skill. Dryden alludes to this in stating that by her music she 'drew an Angel down' (l. 170). Hogg's comic minstrel parodies the saint's legend when he believes that by his music he attracts firstly the fairies and then the devil himself. The poem illustrates Hogg's fascination with the human ability for self-deception, paralleling other episodes in his work where a narrator tells what he believes to be a fantastic truth that is nevertheless easily resolved into natural and even humdrum events by the reader. Ensign Odogherty in 'The Renowned Adventures of Basil Lee', for example, relates that he took his breeches off to avoid wetting them in wading across a non-existent river—see *Winter Evening Tales*, pp. 37–40.

Like 'The Gyre Caryl' this poem is written in what Hogg referred to as his 'ancient stile', accurately described by Peter Garside as 'a combination of ballad phraseology, the rhetoric of the late medieval Scottish "makars", such as Robert Henryson, and more modern idiomatic expression', which provided a sense of freedom for Hogg, its 'extended linguistic range and spontaneous rhythmic effects' allowing an escape from both tired English lyricism and the Anglo-Scots of modern Scottish poetry into something like modern 'magic realism' (*Queer Book*, pp. xv–xvi). There is a brief note on this at the head of the Glossary to the present volume, and many initial difficulties in reading the poem are also resolved if it is read aloud.

107, l. 1 Bowman Lawe no precise location for the poem has been identified. Other topographical references are to the 'Bowman Lynne' and 'Bowman brae', and the allusion may be to the expression 'to draw a longbow' meaning to exaggerate or tell a tall tale. Hogg would be familiar with the tales told about wonderful longbow exploits from the Robin Hood stories and ballads. The Bowman of Rayne in Aberdeenshire is a tabular rock, formerly used for archery practise, and does not appear to fit the circumstances of Hogg's poem (Groome).

107, l. 6 noe yung hillis were borne Horace in his *Ars Poetica* mocks the boastful poet who begins his own epic in the same words as the *Odyssey*, saying 'quid dignum tanto feret hic promissor hiatu? | parturient montes, nascetur ridiculus mus' ('What will this boaster produce in keeping with such mouthing? Mountains will labour to give birth to a ridiculous mouse')– see *Satires, Epistles and Ars Poetica*, ed. by H. Rushton Fairclough, Loeb Classical Library (London: William Heineman, 1926 repr. 1970), pp. 462–63 (ll. 138–39).

107, l. 12 Queen's foreste the royal hunting forests of Scotland included Hogg's native district of Ettrick Forest, which may be the generalised setting of the poem. The reference to a Queen rather than a King probably implies that the events described take place during the time of Mary, Queen of Scots (1542–87), a period which Hogg treated elsewhere as a junction between an older Scotland of superstition and legend and its modern post-Enlightenment equivalent–see *The Queen's Wake*, ed. by Douglas S. Mack (S/SC, 2004), pp. xxxviii–xlviii.

107, l. 13 the deuill Hogg comically compares his mischievous half-starved child to a great enchanter such as Merlin, supposedly also fathered by the devil. His role in the poem as a comic bridge between the human and otherworldly is reinforced by the absurdly sinister alternative paternities of an elfin man and a water-kelpy. For the water-kelpy see the note to p. 76, l. 112.

107, l. 27 I won these notis frae the fairye folke 'Faeries are passionately fond of music [...]. Faerie melodies are known to be beautiful and plaintive yet wild and capricious and they have a fatal charm for mortal ears. [...] Faeries play a variety of musical instruments; fiddles, harps, tambourines, cymbals and the jew's harp'–see Brian Froud and Alan Lee, *Faeries* (New York: Harry N. Abrams, 1978), pp. [12]–[13].

108, l. 45 "Lende me thine eire perhaps a comic echo of Mark Anthony's 'Friends, Romans, countrymen, lend me your ears' in Shakespeare's *Julius Caesar*, III. 2. 74.

108, l. 49 stokel horne the stockhorn, or stock-and-horn is an obsolete Scottish wind instrument. 'The stock is either a wooden tube, bored with finger-holes, or the thigh bone of a sheep, similarly treated, the horn is a part of that of a cow, fixed to the end of the stock, at the other end of which is a mouth-piece with a reed'–see *The Oxford Companion to Music*, ed. by Percy A. Scholes, rev. by John Owen Ward, 10th edn (Oxford: Oxford University Press, 1970, repr. 1989), p. 984. The gold-chased instrument of the minstrel is essentially a primitive clarinet, an emblem of Hogg's poem as a playful and knowing version of ancient traditions.

111, l. 162 Like chrystal spleetis perhaps deriving from 'split brilliant' which, according to the *OED*, is a brilliant, the foundation squares of which are divided horizontally into two triangular facets. The swords glitter like crystals cut in similar fashion to these diamonds.

112, l. 177 "For ae glance of the bonnie damis recalling the narrator's willingness to give his plush breeks 'For ae blink o' the bonie burdies!' if the capering witches in the Alloway kirk of Burns's 'Tam o' Shanter' had been attractive teenagers instead of old women (Kinsley, no. 321).

112, l. 201 "Liloo–liloo probably an onomatopoeic representation of the notes of the stockhorn.

113, l. 209 Saint Bothan a saint associated with place-names in Shetland and elsewhere in Scotland, and giving his name to parishes in Berwickshire and East Lothian. Bothanus, Bishop of Dunblane was commemorated on 18

January—see David Hugh Farmer, *The Oxford Dictionary of Saints* (Oxford: Clarendon Press, 1978), p. 32.

113–14, ll. 241–48 "His fingeris [...] coolyng them in the wynde an evocation of the folklore devil comparable to the portrait in *The Three Perils of Man*, and probably composed at much the same time. Both look affectionately towards Hogg's favourite poem, Burns's 'Tam o' Shanter' (Kinsley, no. 321).

114, l. 271 ane braif corante a dance characterised by a running or gliding step, mentioned, for instance, in Shakespeare's *Henry V*, III. 5. 33.

116, l. 345 the Bulle of Norrowaye a traditional Lowland Scottish tale about an enchanted knight in the form of a black bull who carries off the heroine, a tale which may be conveniently read in *A Forgotten Heritage: Original Folktales of Lowland Scotland*, ed. by Hannah Aitken (Edinburgh: Scottish Academic Press, 1973), pp. 82–87. John Leyden refers to it in 'The Cout of Keeldar', 'To wilder measures next they turn: | "The Black Black Bull of Noroway!"'— see *Minstrelsy*, II, 389–406 (p. 399). Queen Hynde's dream of being threatened by the creature presages the invasion and attempt at a forced marriage by King Eric of Norway—see James Hogg, *Queen Hynde*, ed. by Suzanne Gilbert and Douglas S. Mack (S/SC, 1998), pp. 11–18, 250. For further information see Elaine Petrie, '*Queen Hynde* and the Black Bull of Norroway', in *Papers Given at the Second James Hogg Society Conference (Edinburgh, 1985)*, ed. by Gillian Hughes (Aberdeen: Association for Scottish Literary Studies, 1988), pp. 128–43.

117, l. 362 nouther to houlde nor bynde ungovernable, beyond control.

117, l. 377 Saint Fillanis sholder-bone Saint Fillan was an early eighth-century abbot of Irish extraction, and associated both with Pittenweem in Fife (where he lived firstly as a solitary and then as an abbot) and with Strathfillan, where he was buried. In the pool of Strathfillan the insane were dipped and then left tied up overnight in the saint's chapel: if freed by morning they were considered to be cured. This treatment apparently persisted into the beginning of the nineteenth century. Fillan's feast day is either 9 or 19 January. His cult was sufficiently important in medieval times for King Robert I (the Bruce) to take his arm relic to the battle of Bannockburn and to attribute his victory to the intercession of the saint—see David Hugh Farmer, *The Oxford Dictionary of Saints* (Oxford: Clarendon Press, 1978), p. 149. This, like the earlier mention of St Bothan, implies a pre-Reformation setting for Hogg's poem.

121 MORALITAS Hogg's use of this device recalls the *Moral Fables* of Robert Henryson, adding to the medieval feel of 'The Powris of Moseke'. In his letter to John Macrone of 12 May 1833 (*Letters*, III, 156) Hogg subsequently adapted the second stanza of this comic moral to refer to an alcoholic employee, changing the initial line to 'One single glass will set him on'.

The Field of Waterloo

'The Field of Waterloo' was written during November and December 1815, in the aftermath of the great battle of 18 June 1815. The final ending of a twenty-year-long European conflict with France sparked an explosion of celebrations in Scotland in which Hogg participated in various ways—see Gillian Hughes, 'James Hogg, and Edinburgh's Triumph over Napoleon', *Scottish Studies Review*,

4 no. 1 (Spring 2003), 98–111. Elizabeth Grant remembered how in 1816, 'Everything new was "Waterloo," not unreasonably, it had been such a victory, such an event, after so many years of exhausting suffering; and as a surname to hats, coats, trousers, instruments, furniture, it was very well [...]'–see *Memoirs of a Highland Lady*, ed. by Lady Strachey (London: John Murray, 1898), p. 278. Naturally enough, the battle was also the subject of a large number of commemorative poems: of these Hogg was certainly aware of Walter Scott's *The Field of Waterloo*, published in October 1815, before his own poem was written (see 'Note on the Texts'), and he subsequently owned a copy of Henry Davidson's *Waterloo. A Poem, with Notes* (1816), which was a gift from its London publisher, John Murray (*Letters*, I, 287–88). Hogg's letter to John Scott of 28 February 1816 (Letters, I, 268) thanks him for the gift of a copy of his *Paris Revisited in 1815 by Way of Brussels, including a Walk over the Field of Battle at Waterloo* (London: Longman and Co., 1816). The battle, indeed, continued to be a focus of interest for creative writers throughout the nineteenth century and almost to the First World War, from Thackeray's *Vanity Fair* (1847–48) to Thomas Hardy's *The Dynasts* (1904–08).

Herbert F. Tucker comments sardonically that works with an Edinburgh imprint 'made the victory that Britain and her allies had won under an Irish general an occasion for setting Scottish valor above all the rest'–see *Epic: Britain's Heroic Muse 1790–1910* (Oxford: Oxford University Press, 2008), p. 194. Hogg would certainly be aware of the heavy losses sustained by Scottish regiments in the battle, but while his poem celebrates a British victory it focuses specifically on the local as much as the national contribution. Hogg's dying soldier was born in Yarrow, and his spirit apparently returns to his native district at the end of the poem in response to the request made in his dying prayer that he might be allowed in death to guard the mother and the child who live there. This supernatural conclusion to 'The Field of Waterloo', clearly signalled in the poem's subtitle of 'and Death-Bed Prayer of a Soldier', also connects it with the visionary theme of the *Midsummer Night Dreams* volume of the 1822 *Poetical Works*.

123, l. 1 eventful day the battle of Waterloo took place on 18 June 1815.

123, l. 4 the plains of Belgium west away battles at Ligny and Quatre Bras preceded the decisive one at Waterloo. On 18 June the British were deployed in a defensive position across the road to Brussels just south of the Forest of Soignes.

123, l. 8 that lurid sky there had been a thunderstorm in the afternoon and evening of 17 June.

123, l. 10 blood on the heaven, and blood on the earth the first of a number of lines recalling the imagery of the biblical book of Revelation, where the coming of Christ's kingdom is preceded by universal tribulation. The moon for instance is turned to blood (Revelation 6. 12), hail and fire mingled with blood are cast upon the earth (8. 7) and a third part of the sea also becomes blood (8. 8). Hogg, like many of his contemporaries, was led by the unprecedented scale of the Napoleonic Wars, to view the conflict in apocalyptic terms: the biblical conflict precedes lasting peace, and Hogg thought that after 'the campaigns of Buonaparte, and the slaughter of so many millions among the most civilised nations on the face of the earth, and which ended so completely in smoke [...] there would never be any more wars in Europe, but that all would be settled by arbitration [...]'–see *A Series* *of Lay Sermons*, ed. by Gillian Hughes with Douglas S. Mack (S/SC, 1997), p. 41.

123, l. 12 the Tyrant prostrate after his escape from Elba Napoleon returned to France on 1 March and entered Paris on 20 March 1814, the same day that Louis XVIII fled to Ghent. After Waterloo he was effectively imprisoned on St Helena.

123, l. 14 rolling to the southward having driven off a series of French cavalry charges the British pursued the surviving horsemen in a running battle. That night, after the battle was won, the Prussian cavalry took over the task of chasing those French soldiers who chose to flee rather than surrender.

123, l. 18 Who of his deadly wound not knew in his discussion of motivation at Waterloo John Keegan argues, 'It was the receipt of wounds, not the infliction of death, which demonstrated an officer's courage; that demonstration was reinforced by his refusal to leave his post even when wounded, or by his insistence on returning as soon as his wounds had been dressed'—see *The Face of Battle* (London: Jonathan Cape, 1976), p. 189.

123, l. 23 the tartans the soldier is apparently a member of the cavalry regiment of the Scots Greys.

123, l. 24 tall mould, and Doric tongue Lowland Scots, often compared to the rustic or provincial dialect of Doris or Doria in ancient Greece. In describing Douglas's forces in *The Three Perils of Man* Hogg makes a similar point about the obvious distinction between Highland and Lowland Scots:

> The one rank was made up of Mar Highlanders; men short of stature, with red locks, high cheek bones, and looks that indicated a ferocity of nature; the other was composed of Lowlanders from the dales of the south and the west; men clothed in grey, with sedate looks, strong athletic frames, and faces of blunt and honest bravery. Musgrave weened himself passing between the ranks of two different nations, instead of the vassals of one Scottish nobleman. (*The Three Perils of Man*, 3 vols (London: Longmans, 1822), I, 148)

123, l. 28 Douglas fought the family of Douglas was a leading one in the Scottish Borders in medieval times. Hogg's novel *The Three Perils of Man* (1822) partly charts the rise of the Scott clan at the expense of the Douglas family. Hogg may intend a specific reference here to Sir James Douglas (*c.* 1268–1330), known as 'the Good' for his support of King Robert I, and his attempt to fulfill Robert's dying wish that his embalmed heart should be taken to the Holy Land.

123, l. 30 Elliots [...] Scotts as the context implies, these are the names of two large clans or common surnames in the Scottish Borders.

123, l. 31 That Border land usefully defined by John Veitch as 'that district of hill and valley through which flow the streams of the Liddel, the Teviot, the Ettrick, the Yarrow, and the Tweed—thus nursed in far back times of Scottish history, down to the Union of the Crowns, a people remarkable for personal courage and warlike spirit, for a proud feeling of independence, a stern strong individualism of character'—see *The History and Poetry of the Scottish Border*, 2 vols (Edinburgh: Blackwood, 1893), II, 71.

124, l. 41 God's own blessed and holy day Sunday, or the Sabbath—see Genesis 2. 3: 'And God blessed the seventh day, and sanctified it: because that in it he had rested from all his work which God created and made'.

124, l. 46 scorn cast from a maiden's eye since it is revealed subsequently that the soldier has a lover and a child, it is possible that he was scorned for having fathered a child out of wedlock and fled the scene by enlisting. Alternatively, he met with a more amenable maiden subsequently during a return to Scotland.

124, l. 49 Gallia's troops Gaul was a Roman province comprising France and upper Italy, so that in this context the French army is indicated.

124, l. 49 at break of morn the battle actually began at about eleven in the morning.

124, l. 58 the red and rueful scene the British survivors were too exhausted to begin evacuation of the wounded until the following morning. Keegan describes the scene as follows in *The Face of Battle* (London: Jonathan Cape, 1976), p. 197:

> Within a space of about two square miles of open, waterless, treeless and almost uninhabited countryside, which had been covered at early morning by standing crops, lay by nightfall the bodies of forty thousand human beings and ten thousand horses, many of them alive and suffering dreadfully. The French, who might have helped in their relief, had fled; many of the Prussians were hot on their heels; those British who were left contemplated the spectacle and closed their eyes.

124, l. 67 All tongues and languages Wellington's army consisted of German and Dutch-Belgian soldiers in addition to the British ones, while the Prussians advanced from the east at about 4 p. m. that afternoon.

125, l. 78 flies inglorious from the strife Napoleon fled the battlefield, along with the disordered remnants of the French Imperial Guard.

125, l. 85 Soldiers they were, or late had been the Russian and Prussian seem not to have fought at Waterloo themselves, but to have acted only as messengers after the battle.

125, l. 88 from Wolga's stormy side a Russian, since the river Volga flows through that country into the Caspian Sea.

125, l. 94 Wallace fought and Douglas reaved Sir William Wallace (1270–1305), the epitome of the disinterested Scottish patriot, and victor of the battle of Stirling in 1297. James Douglas (*c.* 1286–1330) assisted Robert I by engaging in a brilliant guerilla campaign in the south-west of Scotland. The Scottish Wars of Independence, as a struggle for national self-determination, form a parallel with the attempt to free Europe from French dominance under Napoleon. Hogg's poem 'Wallace' was written in this context and published in *Poetical Works*, IV, 141–60: for background information see Gillian Hughes, 'Hogg, Wallace, and Waterloo', *SHW*, 18 (2007), 24–33.

126, ll. 113–14 since human guilt | Provoked to war perhaps a reference to the Biblical story of Cain's murder of his brother Abel, part of the consequences of the Fall—see Genesis 4. 8.

126, l. 121 Bannockburn a decisive Scottish victory against the English in the Wars of Independence, fought on 23 and 24 June 1314.

126, l. 122 The bold Silesian the army of Silesia consisted in 1813 of approximately fifty-seven thousand Prussian and Russian troops, commanded by Blücher (1742–1819), who tried hard to minimise the mutual mistrust of the Prussian and Russian officers—see Antony Brett-James, *Europe Against Napoleon: The Leipzig Campaign, 1813 from Eyewitness Accounts* (London:

Macmillan, 1970), pp. 41–55. Hogg refers to Silesian warriors in *The Pilgrims of the Sun*, Part Third, ll. 315–16.

126, l. 123 Leipsic's bloody fight an extremely brutal battle lasting three days (16–18 October 1813), which resulted in a hasty French retreat towards the Rhine. Thousands were killed, both military and civilians.

126, l. 125 Borodina Napoleon's army crossed the Niemen and entered Russia on 24 June 1812, heading for Vilna. The Russians retreated to Drissa and then Smolensk. Napoleon took Smolensk on 17 August and the Russians continued their retreat to Borodino, within seventy miles of Moscow. The savage battle of Borodino of 7 September 1812 in fact ended inconclusively, but some seventy thousand soldiers were killed as well as ten French generals.

127, l. 152 things half known, and half forgot most of the participants on both sides had a very limited and incomplete sense of the battle, which took place on wet uneven ground amidst confusion, deafening noise, and dense smoke. Wellington wrote in a famous letter to J. W. Croker a few weeks after Waterloo, 'The history of a battle is not unlike the history of a ball. Some individuals may recollect all the little events of which the great result is the battle won or lost; but no individual can recollect the order in which, or the exact moment at which, they occurred, which makes all the difference as to their value or importance'—see *The Dispatches of Field Marshal the Duke of Wellington*, ed. John Gurwood, 8 vols (London: Parker, Furnivall and Parker, 1844–47), VIII, 231–32.

127, l. 164 our Scottish files the 92nd Regiment of Gordon Highlanders, and the 42nd Royal Highland Regiment, with other Scottish forces, were particularly distinguished in the action at Waterloo. The pipers of the 71st Regiment repeatedly played 'Hey Johnnie Cope', and the cavalry of the Scots Greys fought heroically and suffered proportionate losses. Hogg's song, 'The Highland Watch', later entitled 'The Forty-Second's Welcome to Scotland' was written for the return of the 42nd Regiment to Scotland after Waterloo—see *Songs by the Ettrick Shepherd* (Edinburgh: William Blackwood; London: T. Cadell, 1831), p. 218.

127, l. 177 Wove by some shepherd of the dale such as James Hogg himself perhaps. His description of future local tale-telling events concerning Waterloo is not dissimilar to that in the 'Borodino' of Mikhail Lermontov (1814–1841), in which an aged veteran relates his personal experiences of the famous battle in response to questioning by youngsters.

127, l. 185 Begging again to hear the song the soldier's heroic exploits will take on the same legendary appeal as that of traditional heroic ballads. In no. 20 of *The Spy* a group of boys listening to an old woman chanting ballads behave similarly: 'How I have seen their eyes kindle and glow, when they heard the feats of Old Maitland's three Sons, Robin Hood and the Three Giants, or the battle of Chevy-Chace! and instead of being wearied by the length of them, they would beg as a particular favour to hear some favourite parts a second time. I have even heard some of them cry, because she refused to begin and sing one of them all over again'—see *The Spy*, ed. by Gillian Hughes (S/SC, 2000), p. 207.

128, ll. 192–94 fondly dwell [...] on this day's list of fame perhaps recalling the St Crispin's Day speech in Shakespeare's *Henry V*, IV. 3. 40–67.

128, l. 197 Wellesley Arthur Wellesley, 1st Duke of Wellington (1769–1852) was commissioned commander of the British and Hanoverian forces in Europe in March 1815. After Waterloo, at his suggestion, all who fought there received a special medal. Wellington entered politics on the conservative side after the Napoleonic Wars and incurred considerable opprobrium for his opposition to Parliamentary Reform. On his death, however, he was buried with full ceremony in St Paul's Cathedral as the national hero of Waterloo.

128, l. 198 the gallant Picton General Sir Thomas Picton had been wounded at Quatre Bras on 16 June but concealed the extent of his injury and died at Waterloo fighting at the head of his division.

128, l. 200 Ponsonby Sir William Ponsonby, the brigade commander of the Scots Greys, was killed at Waterloo 'because of a false economy. He had left his best charger, worth far more than the government compensation fund would pay if it were killed, behind the lines and chosen to ride instead an inferior hack. The French Lancers caught him struggling to safety over heavy ground, easily rode him down, and speared him to death'—see John Keegan, *The Face of Battle* (London: Jonathan Cape, 1976), p. 150.

128, l. 219 droich of three a droich is a dwarf: in other words the soldier is a lesser man than either Ponsonby or the unnamed 'Border Chief' of the party.

128, ll. 225–26 wolf [...] eagle [...] harper probably the wolf is the fleeing Napoleon and the eagle the French army. The identity of the harper is unclear.

128, l. 227 an angel grim Napoleon, envisaged as a permitted scourge of God, along the lines of the 'angel of the bottomless pit' in Revelation 9. 11.

129, ll. 229–30 On such an eve [...] Thou shalt remember in Hogg's *The Three Perils of Woman* too the person who is warned of forthcoming personal disaster (Cherry in that case) forgets the omen only to remember it when it has been fulfilled—see *The Three Perils of Woman*, ed. by David Groves, Antony Hasler, and Douglas S. Mack (S/SC, 1995), p. 166.

129, l. 243 Moscow's flame the Russian general Kutuzov withdrew his army and evacuated Moscow. Napoleon entered the almost deserted city on 14 September 1812. The Governor, Count Rostopchin, had ordered armouries and markets to be burned, and two days later the entire city was in flames.

129, l. 254 Thousands of hopeless journeyers the civilian refugees from Moscow. Hogg had himself supported a Forum Society debate held at Edinburgh's George Street Assembly Rooms on 29 January 1813 the proceeds of which were to go 'for RELIEF of the RUSSIANS SUFFERERS in the war with France'—see an advertisement in the *Edinburgh Evening Courant* of 23 January 1813, and Hogg, *Letters*, I, 131.

130, l. 272 Kaluga's northmost dreary waste as winter threatened supplies became exhausted and stretched lines of communication frayed, so Napoleon withdrew his army from the ruins of Moscow on 19 October 1812, and moved southwest hoping for warmer weather and supplies in the Ukraine. Worried about Russian resistance, however, he stopped short of Kaluga and continued the retreat westwards.

130, l. 290 From Moscow's gate to Niemen's flood the last of Napoleon's soldiers crossed back over the Niemen on 14 December, finally leaving Russia and Lithuania after the disastrous retreat of 550 miles from Moscow.

131, ll. 310–14 monster's head [...] severed tail Napoleon and his forces are likened to 'the dragon, that old serpent, which is the Devil and Satan' (Revelation 20. 2). St Patrick is often depicted treading on a snake, since he is supposed to have driven all snakes out of Ireland.

131, l. 311 The Germans joined as the Russians advanced Prussia changed sides and signed a treaty of alliance with Russia at the end of February 1813, formally declaring war on France.

131, l. 317 *our* brave Bulow General Friedrich Wilhelm Bülow von Dennewitz, who led the body of Prussian troops which first came to the aid of Wellington at Waterloo.

131, l. 331 She only fought to turn and flee when Napoleon crossed the Russian border on 24 June the Russian army retreated eastward until after the French left Moscow, and even then only pursued from a distance until the two armies engaged at Viazma in early November.

131, l. 334 Prussia's boast the Prussian soldier has spoken of his country's achievement in ll. 315–19.

132, l. 347 Where green Mount Benger Yarrow valley. Hogg himself farmed at Mount Benger between 1821 and 1830.

132, l. 368 yeaning ewe this would normally signify a ewe giving birth to a lamb, but here (as in 'Superstition') Hogg appears to mean a ewe accompanied by her suckling lamb.

132, ll. 377–78 Encircled [...] sovereignty unfurled Hogg employs two images of the British isles, that of a small sea-protected entity, and that of an imperial world-power based on naval dominance. According to Timothy Parsons 'In 1815, the overseas British Empire consisted of the remaining North American colonies (which would eventually become Canada), India, the Cape Colony in southern Africa, the New South Wales territory in Australia, and a handful of naval bases scattered throughout the globe'—see *The British Imperial Century, 1815–1914* (Oxford: Rowman & Littlefield, 1999), p. 4.

133, l. 393 At friendship's and at honour's call Britain went to war with France in February 1793 to combat French aggression in the Low Countries. Although a French invasion of Britain was sporadically expected it never took place and fighting was confined to mainland Europe.

133, l. 406 the sand of life as in an hour-glass, where the gradual fall of sand from an upper to a lower chamber marks the expiry of the given period of time.

133, ll. 412–13 a stoic cool, | Of Voltaire's and of Frederick's school Frederick the Great, King of Prussia from 1740 to 1786, exemplified enlightened government. He supported religious toleration, judicial reform, overseas trade, and admired and promoted French culture. In 1750 he invited Voltaire to visit Prussia, but in 1753 the two men quarrelled and Voltaire fled to Geneva.

134, l. 426 the love of freedom the Prussian appears to view all kingship as tyranny, admiring the original role played by Napoleon as the liberator of the French Revolution before his coronation as Emperor. Such admiration was not unusual for German liberals. Beethoven had originally intended, for instance, to dedicate his third symphony ('Eroica') to Napoleon, before his angry disillusionment when Napoleon declared himself Emperor of

France.

134, ll. 434–37 O he might conquer [...] soul of man! a version of these lines had previously formed part of Hogg's patriotic 'Verses Recited by the Author, in a Party of his Countrymen, on the Day that the News arrived of our final Victory over the French', which was first published in the *Edinburgh Evening Courant* of 11 April 1814. It marked the arrival in Edinburgh of the news of the taking of Paris by the Allies: despite the title this was not a final victory, since Napoleon escaped from his exile on Elba to fight again at Waterloo. The passage then read:

> O he might conquer queens an' kings,
>> They're nought but specks in Nature's plan;
> But fool is he the yoke that flings
>> O'er the unshakled soul of man.

Hogg subsequently revised his poem for publication in *Blackwood's Edinburgh Magazine*, 1 (April 1817), 72, where the lines appear in the form they do in 'The Field of Waterloo', apart from minor variations in punctuation that are attributable to the preferences of the different printers. For further details of the magazine poem see *Contributions to Blackwood's Edinburgh Magazine Volume 1: 1817–1828*, ed. by Thomas C. Richardson (S/SC, 2008), pp. 393–95. Clearly Hogg's sentiments coincided in some respects with those of his mythical Prussian.

134, ll. 448–49 God, the Russian's guard and guide, | And Alexander Alexander I, Tsar of Russia from 1801 to 1825, was the sponsor of the Holy Alliance between Austria, Prussia, and Russia after the fall of Napoleon in 1815. The rulers of these countries undertook to base their relations upon the Christian religion. In effect it became a reactionary influence maintaining autocratic rule. Those younger aristocrats who had fought with Russia's peasant army, known as the men of 1812, wanted a more open and democratic society and this eventually led to the Decembrist uprising of 1825.

135, l. 467 conquered like the rest the final foe is death, which came into the world through the Fall and is overcome by the sacrifice of Christ—see I Corinthians 15. 21–22.

136, l. 505 To brave the eye of the frigid zone Napoleon's Continental System, the maritime blockade designed to eliminate British trade with Europe, placed Russia at a significant economic disadvantage. Czar Alexander refused to accede to Napoleon's demand that he should confiscate the cargoes of neutral ships in the Baltic and signed an alliance with Sweden in March 1812. Napoleon had begun to assemble the vast forces of the Grand Army in Poland and Russia as early as January. He and his wife Marie-Louise spent two weeks in Dresden being entertained in grand style by German princes, the Empress of Austria, and the King of Prussia. On 29 May 1812 he left Dresden to join his forces.

136, l. 521 Russian eagles the symbol of imperial Russia was a double-headed eagle. The Russian army fled in the face of Napoleon's march from June 1812 on Moscow.

136, l. 524 Iberia spurned the yoke the resistance of Spain and Portugal to French blockade and occupation in the Peninsular campaign of 1808–09.

136, l. 525 the seals were broke in the biblical book of Revelation there is a book with seven seals, the breaking of which heralds God's judgement on an evil world and the apocalypse—see in particular Revelation 5–8.

136, l. 526 the city of sacred fame Moscow was the symbolic centre of Holy Russia. Orlando Figes explains, 'The union of Moscow and Orthodoxy was cemented in the churches and the monasteries, with their icons and their frescoes, which remain the glory of medieval Russian art. According to folklore, Moscow boasted "forty times forty" churches. The actual number was a little over 200 (until the fires of 1812), but Napoleon, it seems, was sufficiently impressed by his hilltop view of the city's golden domes to repeat the mythic figure in a letter [...]'–see *Natasha's Dance: A Cultural History of Russia* (London: Allen Lane, 2002), p. 152.

136, l. 529 the cup of the Amorite in Genesis 15. 16 God predicts to Abraham the subsequent captivity of the children of Israel but promises that Abraham's descendants will administer divine justice to the Amorites when their iniquity is full.

136, l. 533 the stars in their courses fought thy foe echoing Judges 5. 20, where Deborah in celebration of Jael rejoices that 'the stars in their courses fought against Sisera'.

137, l. 542 The storm descended snow began to fall three weeks after the burning of Moscow in September 1812, the winter having come early and unexpectedly. Short of supplies and exposed to an unusually severe winter the French were then obliged to retreat.

137, l. 547 the Elbe the river Elbe rises in Czechoslovakia and flows through northern Germany near Leipzig, emptying into the North Sea above Hamburg.

137, l. 548 the Saale the river Saale rises in Bavaria and flows north-west through Germany to join the Elbe at Barby.

137, l. 551 the hearts of the nations combine a reference to the alliance against Napoleon of Prussia and Russia (see note to p. 131, l. 311), but perhaps echoing the prophecy against the Egyptians, oppressors of Israel, in Ezekiel 32. 9: 'I will also vex the hearts of many people, when I shall bring thy destruction among the nations'.

137, l. 554 the friendship and hands of the north on 25 June 1807 Alexander of Russia and Napoleon met on a raft in the river Niemen at Tilsit to cement an alliance, which declined in subsequent years because of the imposition of Napoleon's Continental System, regarded by the Russians as an economic threat. Furthermore, Napoleon in December 1810 annexed Oldenburg. This particularly angered Alexander since his sister was married to the heir of the Duchy of Oldenburg and the territory had been guaranteed by the Tilsit Alliance. By early 1811 France and Russia were on the brink of war.

137, l. 561 parted'st Jordan's tide God parted the river Jordan to allow the Ark and the Israelites to pass over as a sign to his people that he was with Joshua as he had been with Moses previously–see Joshua 3. 14–17.

137, l. 562 the Red Sea opened'st wide God parted the Red Sea to allow the Israelites to escape from the pursuing Egyptians–see Exodus 14. 21–29.

139, l. 616 the scenes of my infancy perhaps echoing the title of John Leyden's well-known poem, *Scenes of Infancy* (1803).

139, l. 622 So like the scenery of a fairy dream compare Scott's description of the scenery around Loch Katrine as being 'So wondrous wild, the whole might seem | The scenery of a fairy dream' in Canto I of *The Lady of the Lake; A Poem* (Edinburgh: John Ballantyne; London: Longman, Hurst, Rees, and Orme, 1810), p. 16.

139, l. 642 a guardian spirit, empowered by thee according to Veitch another theme of the Border ballads is 'the belief and expectancy on the part of the living of a return of the dead to earth. The Lowland Scot has always had a strong conviction that the grave formed no real break in the continuity of the essential life of man. He only passed from the visible to the invisible, and might naturally take an interest in the affairs and in the people of the world he had left. Hence the simple unastonished realism with which all the ballads referring to a return from the dead are strongly characterised'– see *The History and Poetry of the Scottish Border*, 2 vols (Edinburgh: Blackwood, 1893), II, 121–22.

140, ll. 653–54 bond [...] sealed and finished on the tree the sacrifice of Christ on the cross, seen as the fulfilment of God's covenant with man.

141, l. 703 We learned our comrade was no more the word comrade presumably suggests the Border friends of the soldier's youth rather than his fellow-soldiers, since the narrator appears to resemble Hogg himself.

141, l. 718 something seen animals and babies who have not yet learned to speak are supposed to be able to see or sense the presence of supernatural beings–see, for instance, the restlessness and terror of the horses as Gil-Martin approaches the stable-loft in *The Private Memoirs and Confessions of a Justified Sinner*, ed. by P. D. Garside (S/SC, 2001), p. 155. The belief is extremely ancient and occurs, for example, in the story of Balaam and his ass in Numbers 22. 21–35, where the animal sees the angel blocking the path but his rider does not.

Verses Addressed to the Right Honourable Lady Anne Scott of Buccleuch

Hogg's poem (as his footnote indicates) was originally the verse dedication to Lady Anne Scott of *The Brownie of Bodsbeck: And Other Tales* (1818). As a plea to a modern and genteel young lady for a sympathetic reading of supernatural and legendary tales it is also a fitting conclusion to the *Midsummer Night Dreams* volume of his 1822 *Poetical Works*. It may also perhaps signal a conclusion to a book of poems largely, though not exclusively, composed during Hogg's years of living in Edinburgh by authorship, a period that came to an end with his building of a new house at Altrive in Yarrow on the Buccleuch estates during 1818 and his subsequent marriage to Margaret Phillips in April 1820. The notes to the poem which follow are partly indebted to those for the later version of the poem in *Altrive Tales*, ed. by Gillian Hughes (S/SC, 2003).

142 Title Lady Anne Elizabeth Montagu Scott was the eldest daughter of Charles, 4th Duke of Buccleuch (1772–1819) and his Duchess, Harriet (1773–1814), and sister to the current Duke of Buccleuch. She was born in 1796 and died unmarried in 1844.

142, l. 10 theme of many a winter night a generic description for many of Hogg's tales, which sought to replicate in print the kind of stories told around the fire during the long winter evenings in the cottages and farmhouses of his childhood. In 1820 Hogg had published a collection entitled *Winter Evening Tales*. These traditions included 'fairy tales of ancient time', in keeping with the *Midsummer Night Dreams* title also.

142, l. 13 other living name is none the Duke of Buccleuch was the head of the Scott clan and a major landowner in Ettrick Forest. In his account of his 1802 Highland journey Hogg had termed Henry, 3rd Duke of Buccleuch 'the father and benefactor of his country. His name is never mentioned but with respect: His health is the first toast at all convivial meetings [...]'—see 'A Journey Through the Highlands of Scotland, in the Months of July and August 1802', *Scots Magazine*, 64 (October 1802), 813–18 (p. 815).

143, ll. 35–44 The heart unaltered [...] glow for ever Hogg cited these lines in writing to another benefactor many years later—see his letter to Sir Robert Peel of 25 April 1835 (*Letters*, III, 266).

143, l. 38 where once an angel trode Lady Anne Scott's mother, Harriet, Duchess of Buccleuch, had been a warm friend and patron to Hogg, who had dedicated *The Forest Minstrel* (1810) to her. She had died unexpectedly, probably as a consequence of complications following childbirth, on 24 August 1814, and this is alluded to in the closing lines of *The Pilgrims of the Sun*. Her widower, in his letter to Hogg of 26 January 1815 (NLS, MS 2245, fols 13–14), granting him the little farm of Altrive in Yarrow, stated that in doing so he was performing 'an act that I know would have been most agreeable to her'. The Duchess had been the daughter of Viscount Sydney, and many years later Hogg named one of his daughters Harriet Sidney Hogg in memory of her.

143, l. 54 Our converse was with Heaven alone Hogg declared elsewhere that, because of their isolation and dependence on the weather, there was 'no class of men professing the Protestant faith, so truly devout as the shepherds of Scotland'—see *The Shepherd's Calendar*, ed. by Douglas S. Mack (S/SC, 1995), pp. 97–98.

144, l. 74 something that's without a name a benign adaptation perhaps of the 'deed without a name' in Shakespeare's *Macbeth*, IV. 1. 65.

144, l. 77 Our creeds may differ Hogg was a member of the established Church of Scotland, which was Presbyterian, whereas the Buccleuch family was Episcopalian.

144, l. 86 scenes where martyrs bled *The Brownie of Bodsbeck* is a local tale about the persecuted Covenanters, and Hogg also retails similar legends elsewhere—see, for example, *Mountain Bard*, pp. 53–67 ('Mess John').

144, l. 88 those most honoured and revered Hogg makes a similar apology for his partisanship towards the Covenanters in a reported conversation with Scott, 'It is the picture I hae been bred up in the belief o' sin' ever I was born and I had it frae them whom I was most bound to honour and believe'—see *Anecdotes of Scott*, ed. by Jill Rubenstein (S/SC, 1999), pp. 50–51. Hogg alludes in this speech to the commandment, 'Honour thy father and thy mother' in Exodus 20. 12.

144, l. 96 Thy fathers bled perhaps an allusion to Lady Anne's descent from James Scott, Duke of Monmouth and 1st Duke of Buccleuch (1649–1685), who was a natural son of Charles II and was executed after leading an unsuccessful rebellion against the Catholic James II and VII.

144, l. 102 fairy ring circles of darker green grass, in fact caused by extra nitrogen released by fungus, but traditionally supposed to mark the site of fairy dances.

144, l. 106 Carterhaugh the setting of the traditional ballad 'Tam Lin' (Child, no. 39), an influence on both *The Pilgrims of the Sun* and 'The Haunted Glen' in the *Midsummer Night Dreams* volume.

145, l. 113 fairies at the fall of even fairies feature in both 'The Gyre Caryl' and 'The Haunted Glen'. Their departure from Scotland is alluded to in 'Superstition', and a lingering belief in them informs 'The Powris of Moseke'.

145, l. 122 Bowhill the Duke of Buccleuch's mansion about four miles from Selkirk, situated near the right bank of the Yarrow and set in extensive grounds.

145, l. 124 Lover or sister Lady Anne Scott had five younger sisters: Charlotte (1799–1828), Isabella (1800–1829), Katherine (1803–1814), Margaret (1811–1846), and Harriet (1814–1870).

145, l. 148 That had not death impressed within unlike mankind fairies have not experienced the Fall and original sin and are therefore not subject to death.

146, l. 150 What Scotland had, and now has not a restatement of a major theme of this volume. Hogg relates of the fairies elsewhere that his own grandfather was one of the last Borderers to see and converse with the fairies—see 'General Anecdotes. Odd Characters', in *The Shepherd's Calendar*, ed. by Douglas S. Mack (S/SC, 1995), pp. 103–17 (pp. 107–11). Scott wrote in his notes to 'The Young Tamlane', 'In no part of Scotland, indeed, has the belief in fairies maintained its ground with more pertinacity than in Selkirkshire. The most sceptical among the lower ranks only venture to assert, that their appearances, and mischievous exploits, have ceased, or at least become infrequent, since the light of the Gospel was diffused in its purity' (*Minstrelsy*, II, 243–44).

146, l. 166 my travelling equipage visionary or out-of-body journeying is alluded to in *The Pilgrims of the Sun*, 'Connel of Dee', and 'Verses to the Comet of 1811'.

146, l. 180 short the time since it befell a line which is also present in the 1818 version of the poem.

146, l. 187 Newark Cairn a locality popularised by Scott's poem *The Lay of the Last Minstrel* (1805) in which the eponymous minstrel performs to the Duchess of Buccleuch and her ladies at Newark, and is granted a place of refuge and retirement in his old age. Bowhill is a little downriver from the ruinous border stronghold of Newark on Yarrow Water, which is backed by Newark Hill.

147, l. 192 The kelpie's cry a water demon, usually in the form of a horse—for further information see note to p. 76, l. 112.

147, l. 193 love and peace within Hogg is presumably recalling a visit paid to the Buccleuch home of Bowhill near Selkirk before the 1818 publication of the poem. During the first few years after taking possession of the farm of Altrive in the summer of 1815 Hogg dined occasionally with his landlord, Charles, 4th Duke, at Bowhill—for details see Gillian Hughes, *James Hogg: A Life* (Edinburgh: Edinburgh University Press, 2007), pp. 140–41.

147, l. 195 thy woodland harp the harp was a fashionable ladies' instrument during the Regency years as well as the traditional symbol of the bard or minstrel.

147, l. 207 flowers that spring where others grew Lady Anne is seen as the natural successor of her mother, Harriet, Duchess of Buccleuch, who was Hogg's patron.

147, l. 211 The mountain music the traditional legends and songs of Ettrick

Forest, also alluded to by Hogg in titles such as *The Mountain Bard* (1807) and *The Forest Minstrel* (1810). Hogg asserted to Scott on one occasion, 'I'm the king o' the mountain and fairy school' of poetry—see *Anecdotes of Scott*, ed. by Jill Rubenstein (S/SC, 1999), p. 9.

147, l. 213 A family's and a nation's ties the local bonds Hogg asserts between the people of Selkirkshire and the Buccleuch family form a model for ties between the nation and its rulers in poems such as 'To the Ancient Banner of the House of Buccleuch'—see *The Ettricke Garland; Being Two Excellent New Songs on the Lifting of the Banner of the House of Buccleuch, at the Great Foot-Ball Match on Carterhaugh, Dec. 4, 1815* (Edinburgh: Ballantyne, 1815).

147, end-date ALTRIVE LAKE, | *April* 1, 1818 the original date of the poem as it appeared in *The Brownie of Bodsbeck: And Other Tales* of 1818.

Hogg's Notes to *The Pilgrims of the Sun*

No authorial notes were provided to *The Pilgrims of the Sun* on first publication in December 1814, and Hogg's notes were first published on pp. 341–51 of the *Midsummer Night Dreams* volume of *The Poetical Works of James Hogg* of 1822. Hogg's motive for adding them was probably to increase the length of the second volume, making it closer to the standard set by the first volume, which contained *The Queen's Wake* and the notes to that poem. (For further details see 'Note on the Texts'.) His manuscript for these notes survives in British Library, Add. MS 35,068, fols 110–11—further details and a transcription are given in the present volume in 'Appendix 2: Hogg's MS Notes to *The Pilgrims of the Sun*'. Some of the changes made to Hogg's notes before publication are particularly interesting in that they reveal Hogg's anxieties about the reception of his poem, and these are discussed individually in the detailed notes below.

148(a) the late James Park, Esq. of Greenock James Park (1778?–1817) was the early friend of the novelist John Galt, and contributed to various periodicals including Hogg's *The Spy* of 1810–11. None of Hogg's letters to him appear to have survived. Hogg's acquaintance with Park and Galt probably dates back to 1803 at least—see Hans de Groot, 'When did Hogg meet John Galt?', *SHW*, 8 (1997), 75–76. Hogg gives a similar account in his 'Memoir of the Author's Life' (*Altrive Tales*, pp. 35–36):

> It happened that a gentleman, Mr. James Park of Greenock, on whose literary taste I had great reliance, came to Edinburgh for a few weeks about this time; and, as we had been intimate acquaintances and correspondents for a number of years, I gave him a perusal of all my recent pieces in manuscript. His approbation of the "Pilgrims of the Sun" was so decided, and so unqualified, that he prevailed upon me to give up my design of the Midsummer Night Dreams [...] and to publish the [...] poem as an entire work by itself. This advice of my inestimable and regretted friend, though given in sincerity of heart, I am convinced was wrong; but I had faith in every one that commended any of my works, and laughed at those who did otherwise, thinking, and asserting, that they had not sufficient discernment. Among other wild and visionary subjects, the "Pilgrims of the Sun" would have done very well, and might at least have been judged one of the best; but, as an entire poem by itself, it bears an impress of

extravagance, and affords no relief from the story of a visionary existence.

148(b) "Kilmeny" the Thirteenth Bard's song in *The Queen's Wake*. For an account of the reception of the first edition of 1813 see *The Queen's Wake*, ed. by Douglas S. Mack (S/SC, 2004), pp. xlviii–liii.

148(c) The poem is founded on a traditionary tale well known Hogg's manuscript reads, 'The poem as is well known is founded on a traditionary tale well known'. The first occurrence of 'well known' was presumably deleted to avoid repetition, but Hogg may have intended to indicate that the origin of his poem was well known and so was the traditionary tale itself.

148(c) over all Scotland for the European currency of this tale and its probable foundation in the difficulties of determining death see the notes to p. 39, ll. 80–81 and to p. 40, l. 123.

148(d) the soul's short oblivious state Hogg's manuscript reads, 'the soul's short oblivious state in the heavenly mansions'. He probably decided on reflection that these words might reinforce a misapprehension (i.e. that Mary Lee had been actually transported to another state of existence) that he is otherwise at pains to remove.

149(a) The extravagant and heterodox position on the first publication of *The Pilgrims of the Sun* there was clearly some ridicule of Hogg's having placed the throne of God in the sun. One reviewer enquired 'Ought not the author to have favored us with the average state of the thermometer at the centre of our system?'—see *Augustan Review*, 1 (May 1815), 30–32 (p. 32).

149(b) exhibited in the work; infinitude Hogg's manuscript reads 'exhibited in the work. But it is an idea of which I never can entirely divest myself in all my contemplations of the glories of nature. Infinitude'. In view of the calvinist religious orthodoxy of Edinburgh it was probably wise of Hogg to make it clear that his own views had nothing in common with pagan sun-worship.

149(b) A friend [...] himself a poet probably John Grieve (1781–1836), who had grown up in Ettrick though he later became a prosperous Edinburgh hatter. He had contributed songs to Hogg's *The Forest Minstrel* (1810). Since the friend's comment on Part First of *The Pilgrims of the Sun* had influenced lines in Part Fourth it seems likely that he was someone to whom Hogg had read the poem in instalments as he composed it. Both George Goldie's letter to Bernard Barton of 28 October 1813 (NLS, MS 1002, fols 85–86) and Hogg's 'Memoir of the Author's Life' (*Altrive Tales*, p. 28) indicate that while he was living in Edinburgh Hogg was in the habit of reading aloud his poems to Grieve as he composed them.

149(d) Dr Chalmers' sublime astronomical sermons Thomas Chalmers (1780–1847) was a popular Evangelical preacher and writer, greatly concerned with the pastoral care and social work undertaken by the Church of Scotland. In his popular *A Series of Discourses on the Christian Revelation, Viewed in Connection with the Modern Astronomy* (Glasgow: John Smith & Son, 1817) Chalmers tries to meet the challenges posed to the Christian believer by the discoveries made by the microscope and the telescope. He argues that 'we can assert with the highest probability, that yon planetary orbs are so many worlds, that they teem with life, and that the mighty Being who presides in high authority over this scene of grandeur and astonishment, has there planted the worshippers of his glory' (p. 32). He also comments that the universe at large 'would suffer as little, in its splendour and variety, by the destruction of our planet, as the verdure and sublime magnitude of a forest would suffer by the fall of a single leaf' (p. 50).

150 (a) copied into several miscellaneous works [...] loudly censured the lines describing the formation of a comet (Part Second, ll. 405–72) are quoted and highly praised in the *Eclectic Review*, new series, 3 (March 1815), 280–91 (pp. 286–88), while they are termed 'very sublime and very novel' in the *Salopian Magazine*, 1 (July 1815), 273–74.

150 (c) Burnlee no specific locality has been identified, but Hogg's phonetic rendering of the smith's speech perhaps suggests that somewhere in Northumberland is envisaged.

150 (d) the old song the source of Hogg's quotation has not been identified, though he uses a similar phrase in Book First of 'The Russiadde': 'It happened ill, it happened worse, | (Men's joys too often earn a curse!)'—see *Poetical Works*, III, 297–359 (p. 312).

151 (d) whose lamented death Harriet, Duchess of Buccleuch, died on 24 August 1814.

152 (a) not known to me till several years afterwards Hogg's manuscript reads 'not known to him for some years afterward'. In fact less than six months elapsed between Duchess Harriet's death on 24 August 1815 and Hogg's receipt of her widower's letter of 26 January 1815 (MS, 2245, fols 13–14), which, after referring to Hogg's having made a request for a farm in 1813 and granting him Altrive rent-free, continues, 'The object you had in view was never lost sight of by one who admired your genius, & was your sincere well wisher—She alas is now no more, but I feel additional pleasure in offering you this possession, as by doing so, I not only consult my own personal feelings of good will towards you, but perform an act that I know would have been most agreeable to her'.

Glossary

This Glossary sets out to provide a convenient guide to Scots, English, and other words in *Midsummer Night Dreams and Related Poems* which may be unfamiliar to some readers. For English words it is greatly indebted to the *Oxford English Dictionary*. For Scots words it is greatly indebted to *The Concise Scots Dictionary*, ed. by Mairi Robinson (Aberdeen: Aberdeen University Press, 1985) and to the *Dictionary of the Scots Language* at http://www.dsl.ac.uk, to which works the reader who wishes to undertake further study of Hogg's Scots is referred. The Glossary concentrates on single words, and guidance on phrases and idioms of more than one word will normally be found in the Editorial Notes.

It may be helpful in interpreting Hogg's mock-antique Scots to read the relevant passage aloud, since unusual orthography somtimes confuses straightforward sound. Words that appear unfamiliar primarily as a result of Hogg's spelling (such as 'mychtye' for 'mighty' or 'grasse' for 'grass') are not generally included in this glossary. It is also important to remember that 'quh-' stands for 'wh-' and '-it' for '-ed', while plurals can be given as '-is' rather than '-s'. Hogg also sometimes uses 'f' or 'u' for 'v', 'y' for 'i', 'ai' for 'a' and 'ei' for 'ee'.

abeigh: aside, apart, aloof
aboon: above
adamantine: invincible, hard as adamant
airel, ayril: wind-instrument like a flute
amain: with full force, exceedingly
amarynth: an imaginary flower reputed never to fade
anathema: curse, imprecation
anent: concerning, about; alongside
apocryphal: of dubious authenticity
asklent: aslant, astride
asphodel: a liliaceous flower, associated with the Elysian fields; the Scotch asphodel, *Tofielda pusella*, a native plant with white flower-spikes
assay: to attempt; to try, to put to the proof
asteer: astir
attour: across, down over, around
avaunt: begone
Aves: devotional recitations taken from Luke 1. 28, named from the opening words *Ave Maria* ('Hail Mary')

axiom: a well-established or self-evident proposition
aye: always; yes

babbled: subjected to incoherent and foolish talk
bairn: child
baldrick: a belt worn across the chest and shoulder
ban-dog: a ferocious dog, usually tied or chained up
bane: that which causes harm or ruin
bangit: jumped, rose hastily
bark: a small sailing-ship or rowing-boat
barkit: encrusted; scaly
barrit: barred, shut out, excluded, prohibited
barrow: tumulus, grave-mound, hillock
barrowe tramis: the shafts of a hand-barrow
basnet: a small globular steel headpiece with a visor
beal: bale, bonfire, beacon fire
beat: rough moorland; beaten track

beck: a bow, or nod of assent

bedesmen: men paid to pray for the souls of benefactors

bedight: arrayed, bedecked

begirt: surrounded, enclosed

begoud, begoude: began

behest: a command or injunction

behoves, behoved: to be incumbent upon, ought to

beik: bask, warm oneself

belay: beleaguer, surround

beldames: old women, hags, witches

bell: prime, the foremost part

belled: bubbled

ben: inwards, towards the inner part

bende: in a bent condition

benefice: an ecclesiastical living

Benshee: a female spirit, often connected with a particular family, whose wail forecasts death or disaster

bensil: force, rush, sudden movement

bested: hard pressed, beset by

bier: a moveable stand on which a corpse is placed or carried before burial

bittern: a bird resembling a heron, *Botaurus stellaris*, that has a booming cry

biz: to buzz, to bustle

blasted: curst; infected by the breath of a malevolent being

blever: blawart, blevet, the harebell

blewe: was carried by the wind

blink, blynke: glance

blithe: joyous, cheerful, glad, in good spirits

blows: blossoms

boardly: burly

bob: to move up and down with a slight jerk in dancing

boded: foreboded; proclaimed, announced beforehand, predicted

boding, bodyng: foretelling, portending

bombs, boombs: hums or buzzes, like a bee or beetle

bombying: bumping, boombing

booby: a stupid, heavy fellow; a dunce

boon: fortunate, prosperous

boonmost: highest, uppermost

bootless: unprofitable; to no purpose, without remedy

booyng: bellowing

bored, borit: made a hole with a cylindrical object

bosky: bushy

boun: set out, make ready

bourack: a little bower, or shady arbour; a cairn or mound

bourn: goal, destination; bound, domain

bower: a shady recess or arbour

brae: the slope of a river-bank or hillside

braif, braife: fine, splendid, illustrious

brake: a clump of bushes, a thicket

braken: brachiate, branched

brand: burning wood from a fire (often used figuratively)

bree: brow, forehead; eyebrow

breers: briers; thorny shrubs, especially the wild rose

breide: breed, stock, birth, extraction

brente: smooth, unwrinkled

brindled: tabby; marked with streaks

brooit: browed, faced, confronted

broz: oatmeal mixed with boiling milk or water

bruffit: bruffled, sweated, overheated

brukit: dirty, filthy

brullyit: broiled with rage

brume: broom, a shrub with yellow papilionaceous flowers

brymme: brim, edge, margin, brink

buckled: joined, as in marriage

bught: a sheepfold, an enclosure for milking sheep

bullered: boiled or bubbled up; gurgled

bummit: boomed, droned

burel hole: a bored hole, as in a woodwind instrument

burn: a brook, a stream

but and: and also

bydde: bid, ask, entreat, demand

byde: stay, remain

bygane: bygone, things of the past

bynde: tie up, tether, restrain
byzenit: monstrous

cadence: the close of a musical phrase
cairn: a heap of stones used as a boundary or grave marker
cake: oatcake
cantrips: magic spells or charms
carl, caryl: carle, man, old fellow; a peasant or working man
carol: a joyous song
carolling: singing in lively fashion
cerement: grave-clothes; shroud
certes: certainly, assuredly
cherk: croak, a harsh strident noise
cherubim: an order of angels excelling particularly in knowledge
chumpit: champed, chewed vigorously
chylder: children
claumb: climbed
clay: earth as the material of the body (see Genesis 2. 7)
clewe: clawed, scratched
clothe yardis: a measure for cloth; the length of a long-bow arrow
coats: a woman's or child's skirts or petticoats
coddye: cuddy, donkey
coil: noisy disturbance
condescendencies: legal statements of fact
condign: merited, especially merited by crimes; fitting, appropriate
coney: a rabbit
corante: a running dance, one with a running or gliding step
coronals: crowns, coronets
corse: body, corpse
corslet: a close-fitting piece of armour covering the body
cot: cottage
crap: crept
craw: crawfish, or crayfish
creukis: crooks, nooks, odd places
cronach: coronach, a dirge or funeral lament
crouchand: crouched, hump-backed
cuerlet: coverlet, counterpane

dam: female parent
damask: twilled linen fabric with designs reflecting the light from their surface; Damascus rose
dapper: trim, little and active
darn, dern: hide
deane: the deep, narrow, wooded vale of a rivulet
deaved: deafened, stunned
deivin: deafening, stunning
delle: a small, deep natural hollow
dern: dark, dismal, secret
dernis: derns, hides
dingillye: hollow and wooded, like a dingle
diske: dusk
dole, dool: grief, sorrow, distress, mourning
dome: house, home, house of God
doned: donned, put on clothes
doom: fate, final lot or judgement
Doric: Scots, by analogy with the rustic language of Dorian Greeks
dought: could, was able to
doughtna: could not, was unable to
doure: stern, severe, sullen
dowie, dowy: sad, dull, dismal
dowle: perhaps from *doolie*, a hobgoblin
dreide: dread, extreme fear or awe
droich, droiche: a dwarf, someone of stunted growth
drumble: mud raised when water is impure
dryfte: falling snow driven by the wind
dud: coarse piece of cloth; dishcloth or rough towel
dule: grief, distress
dun: dusky, murky; of a dull brown colour
dyng: ding, knock, strike

earnest: a foretaste or pledge of what is to come
earthed: buried, committed to earth
ee, eyne: eyes
ee-bree: eyebrow
e'en: even, evening

eidently: assiduously, diligently

eild: old age

eiless: ill-less, harmless, having no evil intentions

eirie, eiry, eirye: eerie, ghostly, strange, fearful of the supernatural

eirysome: wierd, gloomy, fear-inspiring

eithlye: easily

eldritch: weird, ghostly, unearthly

eldron: old

emerant: emerald

emmets: ants

empyreal: celestial

enow: enough

ergh: reluctant, afraid to, timorous

erlisch: elf-like; weird, ghastly

erst: at first, in the first place

everilke: every, each

eynied, eynit: presumed, thought fit

fain: glad, gladly, willingly; well-pleased

fallis: falls, cadences

fane: temple

fauldyng out: bending from, layering, doubling up

fays: fairies

fell: fierce, cruel, savage, ruthless

feres: companions, mates, comrades; dwarves

ferlies: wonders, marvels, curiosities

filch: steal, carry off furtively

flapperit: flappered, fluttered noisily

flauchtit: woven, linked, intertwined

flawmand: flawmont, a history or narrative

fleece: woolly covering of a sheep; base of a feather

fleech: coax, flatter, entreat

fleyit: frightened, scared, put to flight

flurred: flurried, agitated into sudden or gusty showers

flycherynge: flickering, wavering, unsteady

foray: a raid, a predatory incursion

forespent: spent previously

foreworne: utterly tired

fount-stone: a stone receptacle for the water used in baptism

frehynde: from behind, out of

frith: an arm of the sea; estuary of a river

front: forehead; expression of the countenance

froward: refractory, perverse, ungovernable

fuming: transient, unsubstantial

furs: furrows

gaire: a strip or patch of green grass on a hillside

gaire: a gore or triangle of cloth; something striped

gairies: vagaries, fancies

gaiste, gaistis: ghost, ghosts

gaitis: goats

gallows: roars

gallwood: bare spots in coppices or fields; wood with excrescences, especially those produced by insects

gamesome: frolicsome, sportive

gapit: stared open-mouthed

gar: make, cause, compel

gastrously: in a horrifying or unearthly manner

gazoon: a wedge-shape

ged: a pike

geire: goods or stuff

genius: spirit

gerse: grass

getis: progeny, offspring, children

ghaste, ghastis: ghost, ghosts

gillour: abundance, plenty

gin: if, whether

gin: snare, trap

glass: a sand-glass for measuring time

gleide, gleides: glimmers, sparkles of light

glisk: glimpse, glance

gloaming, gloamyng: twilight; dusk

glyming, glymit: squinted, squinting; glancing sidelong

gor-cock: male of the red grouse

gossamer: filmy substance composed of cobwebs, floating in the air or spread over a grassy surface

goud, gouden: gold, golden
gowan, gowin: daisy
gowd, gowden: gold, golden
gowlin: howling, weeping noisily
gowlit: howled, or wept noisily
graif: a grave
grainit: groaned
grenit: desired ardently, yearned, longed to
grevit: grieved
guddled: tickled; disordered
guerdon: recompense, reward
gushet: ornamental pattern; scales protecting a joint
gyis: gyses, guys, odd-looking persons or shapes; masqueraders
gyre carle: a supernatural being; an ogre or hobgoblin
gysand: dried up, withered, shriveled; guising, masquerading
gyzenit: parched, shrivelled

haffat: the temples; side of the face
hale: whole, free from disease or injury, sound
halesom: wholesome, salutary, sound of health
hallen: an inner wall or partition between the door and fireplace of a cottage
hammis: hams, thighs and buttocks, hindquarters
harbinger: a forerunner
hark: whisper, listen
hart, hartis: male deer
haw: the fruit of the hawthorn
heath-cock: the male of the black or red grouse
heath-fowl: birds which live on heath, especially grouse
heezit: lifted up, raised, hoisted
helm: that by which affairs are guided; the top or crown of something
herkenyng: hearkening, listening
hind: a farm-servant
hind, hyndis: female deer
hinny: honey, sweetness
hoary: grey-haired with age

hofe: hoof
holme, holms: flat ground by a stream or river, water meadow
holt: a copse; a wooded hill
horse-mussel: a large and coarse kind of mussel of the genus *Modiola*; a freshwater mussel
host: the wafer consecrated in the mass as the body of Christ
houf: favourite haunt, refuge
houlat: owl
houlit: howled
howe: a hollow; a basin-shaped piece of ground
humoursome: humorous, witty

igneous: fiery
ilkane: each or every one
ineffable: inexpressible, unutterable
intermundane: situated between different worlds
isle: aisle, a lateral division of a church

keikes: keeks, peeps, glances
kelpie, kelpy: a water demon, usually in the form of a horse, which haunts rivers and lochs and lures the unwary to their deaths
kemb: comb
kenne: to know, to be acquainted with
kilted, kiltit: tucked up
kine, kyne: cows, cattle
kirne-mylke: buttermilk, or curds made from buttermilk
klaiver: clover
knell: solemn ringing sound
knellit: knelled, rung, reverberated
kythe, kythed, kything: appear, show, become manifest

laigh: low
lair: resting-place
laith: loath, reluctant, unwilling
laithly: loathsome, hideous, repulsive
lak: lack, want, deficiency
lambent: softly radiant
lampreys: fish resembling eels
lane: alone, by (him or her) self

lapperit: clotted, smeared; lapped, wrapped around

lattice: a structure of strips of wood or metal crossed together; a window furnished with a lattice

laueroke, laverock: skylark

lawn: piece of fine linen resembling cambric

le, lee: lea, untilled ground, pasture

leal: faithful, dutiful, honest; pure, chaste

leech: a physician

leifu: lovely, amiable

leme: radiance, gleam of light

lene: alone, by (him or her) self

les: lies; something said in error with no intent to deceive

leuer: gleam, a faint ray

leveller: something which reduces all men to an equality

leveret: a young hare

levin: a flash of lightning; any bright light or flame

libbert: possibly *liberty*, an area of land, a district

lift: sky, the heavens

limber: pliant, supple, limp

links: windings, especially of a stream or river; undulating ground

linn, lynne: ravine

lirk: crease, wrinkle

lists: enclosures, spaces enclosed by pallisades

liths: joints, limbs

loan: a green or milking-ground

lo'e: love

lubber: a clumsy person; a lout

lufe: the palm of the hand

lug, lugs, luggis: ear, ears

luias: alleluias, hymns of praise

lustres: bright lights; chandeliers

lyfte: lift, sky, the heavens

lykewake: the watch kept at night over a dead body

lyng: ling, rush forward speedily

lynkis: undulating ground; windings, especially of a stream or river

mailed: clothed as with mail; armoured

mailen: land held on a lease, a tenant farm

maine: sea, ocean

marled: spotted, streaked

mart: an animal killed for meat

mass-men: priests

meed, meide: reward, desert, recompense

meer: moor, a tract of rough uncultivated ground

meet, meite: decorous, becoming, proper

meite: meat, food in general

mene: moan, complaint

mene: maun, must, is compelled to

meridian: mid-day, the period of greatest power and splendour

merle, merlinis: blackbird, the blackbird's

merlit: variegated, streaked, mottled

middis: middle, midriff

mien: a person's air, bearing, or manner

mirkness: darkness

misleered: ill-bred, unmannerly, rude

mochte: might

mools: mould, soil, clods of earth

moone-rak: moon-rack, clouds partially obscuring the moon

mootes: mutters; moults, crumbles away, decays slowly

mot: may, must

mouis: mouths

mouser: a cat

muckil: great, large

mudwart: pondweed; the plant *limosella aquatica*

nelit: kneeled

nemit: named

nether: lower, under

nurice: nourish, nurse

omniferous: possibly *omnifarious*, of all kind and forms

ordinal: notes according to a series or order

orisons: prayers

ostensible: presentable, open to view

ouchtis: ought, anything

ouphen: elfin

ousen: oxen

outower: over the top of, across

pace: peace; to walk with a measured or regular step

pales: boundaries, limits

pavilion: tent or canopy

peel: small square fortified tower

pile: mass of masonry

plastic: modelling, capable of shaping

powe: poll, the crown of the head

pule: to whine

pyat: magpie

quhat: what

quhille: until

quhite: white

quidderyng: shaking, darting about; quivering

racks: clouds or mist driven by the wind

raeis: roe-deer

raif, rave: rived, rended, tore apart

raike: to range over or wander through

rail: a bird of the genus *rallidæ*, land-rail or water-rail

raile: a garment, especially a woman's short-sleeved bodice

ram-race: a run to gather impetus for a leap

rankyng: in rows

raschit: rushed violently or hastily

rathly: rapidly, early

raves: dashes, rushes, roars

rayre: roar

reave: steal, rob, pillage

redbreiste: the robin

reek: vapour, steam, or smoke

reile: reel, a rotating device on which thread is wound when spinning

relay: relief, a set of persons appointed to relieve others; a supply of fresh hounds or runners on a trail

remeide: remedy, redress

requiem: a musical setting of a mass for the dead

respondents: defendants in lawsuits

reuth: ruth; remorse, regret, contrition

rhattyng: perhaps onomatopoeic as in rat-a-tat

riddle: a coarse-meshed sieve

rife: plentiful, abundant

rime: a frosty haze or mist

river-lark: [see note to p. 37, l. 8]

rok: rock, distaff used in spinning

rone: thicket of brushwood or thorns

rood: cross or crucifix

roryng: roaring, resounding, reverberating

routh: plenty, abundance

rowte, rowtis, rowtyng: bellow, bellows, bellowing

rugged: pulled vigorously, tugged

ryvyng: riving, tearing apart, rending

Sadducee: a member of a sect that denies the resurrection of the dead and the existence of angels and spirits

saturnine: affected by the planet Saturn; cold, gloomy, sluggish

saur: savour; an evil smell or taste

say: remark, speech

saynit: sained, protected against harm by making the sign of the cross

scathe: harm, injury

schaw: a small wood, a thicket

scho: she

sellible: fortunate, happy, blessed

sen: since

seraph: a member of the highest of the nine orders of angels, distinguished for the fervour of their love

sere: dry, withered

seye: essay, attempt, try, test

seymar: a woman's loose, light robe; a chemise

shaw: a thicket, a small copse or grove

sheen, sheine: bright, shining

shill: shrill

shoally: [see note to p. 29, l. 184]

siller: silver, money

sinks: flat, low-lying lands where water collects and forms bogs or marshes

skaddaw, skaddow: shadow

skiffs: small, light boats

slid: slippery, smooth

snood: a ribbon bound round thc brow and tied at the back of the hair, symbolic of virginity

snouke: sniff, smell, scent out

sough: a rushing, murmuring sound

speal: splinter, chip

speile, spiele: ascend, climb, clamber up

spring: a quick, lively dance-tune

stark: strong, vigorous

sternis: stars

stoattit: bounced, rebounded

stocke: tree-stump, log, or stem

stokel horne: stock-and-horn, an old wind instrument resembling a clarinet

stouin: stown, stolen

stounds: pangs; an intermittent ache

stour: swirl or spray of dust, dust-cloud

streekit: stretched

stroamyng: wandering idly about; walking with long strides

strummit: strummed, played carelessly (usually on a stringed instrument)

sturt: disquiet, trouble, contention

stycke: stick, gore, stab

stymit: blinked, peered, attempted to see

subjacent: situated underneath, underlying

swathed: wrapped up, enveloped

swawis: swaws, sways, ripples

swoof, swoofit: rustling or swishing like the wind

symphony: voices in concert, harmony of sound

syne: thereupon, next, directly afterwards

tabernacle: a temporary dwelling-place

taeis: toes

tarn: a small mountain lake without significant tributaries

tedderstakis: tethering-stakes, upright posts to which an animal can be tied

thoche: though

thochtis: thought

thole: endure

thraldom: bondage, servitude

thrall: bondagc, captivity

thrawe: twist, distort, writhe

timbrel: a hand-held percussion instrument such as a tambourine

tint: lost

tithes: the tenth part of agricultural produce as a due for the support of the priesthood

tod: a fox

toome: empty, vacant

toutit: trumpeted, made a noise like a horn

traissel: trampled or trodden area

travail: the labour of childbirth; labour, work, or exertion

trowed, trowit: believed, accepted as true

truff: turf, surface of peat

tyrling: swirling, spinning, rotating

umbered: shadowed, darkened

unchancie: inauspicious, unlucky, ill-omened

unmeet: unbecoming, improper

unweeting: unconscious, unknowing, unheeding

vele: viol, a stringed instrument played with a bow

venal: subject to mercenary or corrupt influences

vermilion: scarlet, bright red

vernal: flourishing, spring-like

vest: vestment, garment

wae, waefu: woeful, sorrowful

waesome, waesum: woeful, sorrowful

waik: to stay up overnight for pleasure or revelry; to enjoy or make a midnight serenade or concert

wain: cart or waggon; *Charles's Wain,* the constellation of the Great Bear

wanyirdlye: unearthly

wassail: to carouse or revel

wat: know

water-kelpie: water-horse; a water de-
mon which haunts rivers and lochs
and lures the unwary to their
deaths

weeds: garments, clothing

ween, weened, weenit: surmise, guess,
imagine, believe

weir: war, warfare

weird: one pretending to foresee or
control future events

wight: a person; a supernatural being;
a valiant man

wilsomely: wilfully, erringly

windowed: made full of holes

wist: knew

wold: an elevated tract of open coun-
try or moorland

won, wonit: dwell, live

won: earned; gained by labour

wont: to be accustomed to

woo: wool

wraith: a fantastic image or apparition

wreathed: contorted, twisted, coiled,
intertwined; covering, burying

wysit: wished

ycleped: called, named

yeaning: bringing forth a lamb

yernit: yearned

yird, yirde: earth

yirlisch: unearthly, uncanny

yirlischly: unearthly, uncannily

yollerit: yelled, bawled

youlit: howled

youtit, yowting: howling, roaring, yelling

yudith: youth

zephyr: a mild, soft breeze; the west
wind